ST ANTONY'S/MACMILLAN SERIES

General editors: Archie Brown (1978–85) and Rosemary Thorp (1985–), both Fellows of St Antony's College, Oxford

Britain and the Arab–Israeli Conflict, 1948–51

Ilan Pappé

Lecturer in Middle Eastern Studies, Haifa University, and
Fellow Researcher, Dayan Center, Tel Aviv University

in association with
ST ANTONY'S COLLEGE
OXFORD

First published 1988

Published by
THE MACMILLAN PRESS LTD
Houndmills, Basingstoke, Hampshire RG21 2XS
and London
Companies and representatives
throughout the world

Typeset by Wessex Typesetters
(Division of The Eastern Press Ltd)
Frome, Somerset

Printed in Hong Kong

British Library Cataloguing in Publication Data
Pappé, Ilan
Britain and the Arab–Israeli conflict
1948–51. — Basingstoke; Macmillan, 1888.
1. Israel–Arab War, 1948–1949   2. Israel–
Arab Border Conflicts, 1949–   3. Great
Britain—Foreign relations—1945–
4. Great Britain—Foreign relations—
Middle East   5. Middle East—Foreign
relations—Great Britain
I. Title   II. St Antony's College
956'.042   DS126.5
ISBN 0–333–40888–8

273 p.; maps

Contents

Acknowledgements

I wish first to make a respectful and grateful acknowledgement of my debt to Dr Roger Owen and Professor Albert Hourani, without whose assistance, guidance, observations and perceptions I would have found it difficult to complete this work.

The generosity of the Dayan Center enabled me to spend my post-doctoral year as a research fellow in the Center. The result of that stay is this book. I wish therefore to express my special debt to the staff and Fellows of this Center for their attention and assistance during that year.

Without financial assistance one would be at loss in trying to complete research in three different countries. Therefore with great pleasure I would like to record my deep gratitude to the Middle East Centre in St Antony's College, Oxford, for its assistance. The Bryce and Read, as well as the Arnold, Funds were most helpful during the first and second years of the research in Oxford. I am also thankful to the Board of Management of the Cyril Foster Fund, which took a keen interest in my work and contributed towards its completion.

I should also like to express my thanks to the staff of the Public Record Office, the Chatham House Press Archives, the assistant researchers in the National Archives in Washington and the archivists of the ISA, the Central Zionist Archives and the BGA. I will always recall my pleasant stay in the Truman Library in Missouri, whose staff went out of their way to make my brief time there as productive as possible. I wish to express my thanks to Lord Bullock, Dr Avi Shlaim and Professor Gabi Cohen for sharing with me their material and documents, as well as their thoughts. Professor Louis has kindly allowed me to see the manuscript of his book *The British Empire in the Middle East, 1945–1951*, and although the book is not quoted in this work it has assisted me considerably in understanding British and American policy in the area.

St Antony's College, its warden, staff, teachers and librarians all made Oxford an ideal place for writing a study on the Arab–Israeli conflict. In the calm atmosphere that the College provided it was easier to deal with such a complex subject.

Finally, I would like to thank Ms Marion Lupu for her invaluable help in editing and improving the style of this work.

ILAN PAPPÉ

List of Abbreviations

ADS	Arab Development Society
AHC	Arab Higher Committee
ALA	Arab Liberation Army
ASoS	Acting Secretary of State
BGA	Ben-Gurion Archives
BMEO	British Middle East Office
CIA	Central Intelligence Agency
CiC	Commander in Chief
CO	Colonial Office
CoS	Chiefs of Staff
ESM	Economic Survey Mission
GA	General Assembly
GHQ MELF	General Headquarters Middle East Land Forces
HC (Jerusalem)	High Commissioner in Palestine
IDF	Israeli Defence Forces
IFO	Israeli Foreign Office
IPC	Iraqi Petroleum Company
IRO	International Refugee Organisation
ISA	Israeli State Archives
MAC	Mixed Armistice Committee
MEJ	Middle East Journal
MoD	Ministry of Defence
NEA	Near Eastern Affairs Division in the State Department
NER	Near East Radio
PCC	Palestine Conciliation Commission
PGI	Provisional Government of Israel
PUSC	Permanent Under-Secretary of State Committee
SoS	Secretary of State
UNPC	United Nations Palestine Committee
UNRPR	United Nations Relief for Palestinian Refugees
UN UK NY	United Kingdom delegation to the UN, New York
UNRWA	United Nations Relief and Work Agency for Palestine Refugees

Introduction

This is an analysis of events which not only shaped the political history of the area after 1948 but are also still described and chronicled in two very different fashions. To this day, the Israelis regard the period under review as a miraculous time and as an important, if not decisive, step in the fulfilment of the Zionist ideal, whereas the Palestinians and the Arabs talk about the 'trauma of 1948' and claim that these were years of injustice which still require rectification. Arab and Jewish scholars alike find it difficult to treat and analyse the period objectively. In order to overcome some of the difficulties encountered by those researching the conflict, it seemed that a third viewpoint was needed. It had to be the point of view of a party which was sufficiently involved in the conflict at the time, and yet one that in reviewing the events today does not take the side of either adversary. Britain was such a party. We assumed that viewing the history of the conflict through the eyes of British policy-makers would provide us with a more accurate and less ambiguous picture than the one emerging from the Arab and Israeli accounts. It seems that the various British officials and diplomats who had dealt with and were in the Middle East had been deeply involved in the events under review in this work and that they had generally adopted an impartial position *vis-à-vis* the two parties of the Palestine conflict. Thus, their assessment in the past and their memoirs and recollections at the present are most helpful for the student and researcher of the Arab–Israeli conflict up to the late 1950s. For the British this was not a period of miracles or disasters but rather an unfortunate chapter in the history of the disintegration of the British Empire and a stage in the decline of Britain's global position. The Britons who took part in those dramatic events view their government's policy mostly with regret and a considerable measure of criticism. Their frankness is admittedly not tantamount to objectivity, but it makes the British view the best vantage point for describing and analysing the formative years of the Arab–Israeli conflict.[1]

British policy towards the Arab–Israeli conflict in the years under review was the outcome of two intrinsic factors: Britain's alliance with Transjordan, and Britain's pursuit of an *ad hoc* policy. The introduction will deal with these two elements. British policy towards the Palestine question was based on the strong Anglo–Transjordanian alliance which dated back to 1921, when the Cairo conference of the

Colonial Office decided to offer the rulership of Transjordan to the Amir Abdullah.[2] The reaffirmation of British commitment to the Amir in 1948 is in many ways the point of departure for our analysis. However, it seems that policy towards the Arab–Israeli conflict was not the only area affected by the Transjordanian orientation of the Foreign Office; Britain's general Arab policy was as well. The second important feature of British policy was the pragmatism of the Foreign Office and Ernest Bevin. Their *ad hoc* policy enabled the British government both to accept the existence of a Jewish state in the Middle East and to play a decisive role in the negotiations following the Palestinian war of 1948.

Britain's military and political alliance with Transjordan had turned it into an important party to the Jewish–Transjordanian understanding over the future of post-Mandatory Palestine. The Jews and the Transjordanians agreed to divide Palestine between themselves. The British support for the partitioning of Palestine between Transjordan and the Jewish state was consistent with the policies of both these states. The three parties (Britain, the Transjordan and Israel) advocated the division of Palestine according to the UN GA's partition resolution of November 1947. However, whereas the UN proposed the partitioning of Palestine between an Arab and a Jewish state, the three parties divided Palestine between the Jews and the Hashemites. The idea of a 'Greater Transjordan', that is, that the UN Arab state in Palestine be annexed to Transjordan, became the basis of British policy towards the Arab–Israeli conflict in 1948–51.

The withdrawal from Palestine in May 1948 left Britain with the need to review its Middle East policy in general and its policy towards the question of Palestine in particular. Both the Foreign Office and the British Army believed that the future of Britain's position in post-Mandatory Palestine depended on the loyalty and strength of the Hashemite kingdom.

The Middle East was still regarded as of vital interest to Britain in spite of the dissolution of the British Empire and the loss of Palestine and India. There are historians who claim that this was the consequence of Imperial thinking, a case of old habits dying hard, which led the British to ignore the dramatic shift in their global position without reappraising the new situation. This would certainly explain the unbroken link with its former colonies in the framework of the Commonwealth. However, it seems that even those British officials who viewed their government's interests in the light of the new international situation had reached a conclusion similar to that of their 'imperialist' colleagues: namely that the Middle East was still a vital interest for Britain. Hence the importance of the Middle East stemmed not only from traditional interests such as keeping the way to India in British hands but also from the new geopolitical constellation which emerged at the end of the Second World War. In fact, the importance of the Middle East grew in direct proportion to the increase of Western fears of another global war. In the late 1940s such a possibility was regarded as both realistic and imminent. The British leadership assumed, as did their American counterparts, that in such a war the Middle East would become a secondary arena, as in the previous wars. American and British intelligence predicted that Palestine and Transjordan would be the last line of defence in the path of a possible enemy invasion of the area which, according to British and American estimates, would be aimed at the Suez Canal and the oilfields in Arabia.[3]

The concept of Palestine as a defence line between Egypt and a possible enemy who might attack from the north was a deeply-rooted one. It was precisely for this reason that Britain had desired a foothold in the Holy Land before the outbreak of the First World War. However, in the years preceding the Great War this interest had been implemented by direct occupation or by the imposition of indirect rule in the form of a mandate from the League of Nations. In the period under review, the British depended on the goodwill of the Palestinians, Jews and Arabs alike.

The outcome of the 1948 war sharpened and clarified the problem for Britain. It was a question of gaining the support and cooperation of either the Jewish state in Palestine or of Transjordan, or of both. However, due to their close relations with the Eastern bloc the Jews were not considered allies and it was thought they could not be trusted as the guardians of British interests in Palestine. The Foreign Office felt that at best the new Jewish state was neutral in its attitude towards the East–West conflict, and at worst pro-Communist. Thus it was felt that Israel could not be trusted to serve British and American interests, and Britain was left with Transjordan as its main ally in Palestine. This conclusion was further strengthened by Abdullah's success in convincing the British that his and their interests coincided with regard to Palestine. The British Legation in Amman shared the King's views and conveyed the message to London that the stability and strength of Transjordan depended on its ability to maintain control over Palestine and its readiness to resist Jewish and non-Hashemite Arab dominance there.

At the same time, there was little doubt in London that in times of war Egypt was far more important than Transjordan as a strategic asset. However, the King and the pro-Hashemite school in the Foreign Office succeeded in communicating the message that in times of peace, and for the sake of British interests in the Arab world, Transjordan was probably more valuable than Egypt. The pro-Hashemite school was so successful that during the period of 1948–51 every Transjordanian problem, whether external or internal, became a British problem.

It seems that Transjordan became as important as it did because it was loyal in an area which had become, at best, neutral with regard to the bipolar conflict and, at worst, increasingly hostile to British interests. As the British minister in Amman described it, Britain was putting all its eggs in one basket because 'all the other baskets are unwilling to accommodate our eggs'.[4]

Since the 1930s Abdullah had been attempting to prove his usefulness and importance to Britain, first by participating in the Allied war effort in the Middle East and then by promising to protect British interests in Palestine.

Paradoxically this Hashemite allegiance to Britain had weakened Transjordan's position in the Arab world. It was therefore in the interest of both countries to refute allegations that Abdullah was Britain's protégé. Abdullah hoped to strengthen his position by expanding his kingdom, a tactic which, in the eyes of the British, had only further alienated him from the Arab world. The King sought to further his ambition by trying to implement the Greater Syria plan. The final attempt in this direction was made in July 1947, before the Syrian national elections, when the King contemplated the annexation of the Jebel Druze through the help of the Atrash family, the ruling Druze family in that area. The scheme failed owing to Glubb Pasha's opposition and refusal to use the Arab Legion (Glubb Pasha was its British Commander).[5] Abdullah came to realise that it was only in Palestine that his ambitions and British interests coincided.

However, Britain did not deem it necessary to enlarge Transjordan's territory into Syria in order to strengthen the latter's position in the Arab world. On the contrary, such territorial ambitions were believed to have a destabilising effect on the area, creating conditions conducive to Communist penetration as well as increasing the prestige of radical national movements. The Foreign Office suggested another means of strengthening the Hashemites' position in the area: the end of the British Mandate in Transjordan and a solid defence alliance between Britain and Transjordan. Britain hoped that the conclusion of the 1946 Anglo-Transjordanian treaty, followed by the kingdom's declaration of independence, would refute the accusation of British dominance in Transjordan. However, the cool reception accorded the treaty by the Arab world indicated that it did not improve Abdullah's image in the region. The main target of criticism was the clause which allowed Britain to station troops on Transjordanian soil.[6]

Britain's utilisation of treaties as a means of reinforcing its allies in a hostile Arab world must have stemmed from a strong conviction in London of its ability to deter other Arab states from interfering with its allies' domestic and external affairs. Furthermore, the British policy-makers had presumably perceived these means of deterrence as a factor of power in the political game of the Arab region. However, this policy failed since, apart from Transjordan, all the other Arab countries refused to conclude treaties with Britain. This convinced the Foreign Office to listen more attentively to Abdullah's theories and conception of the power game in the Middle East.

Abdullah decided to exploit the hostile reaction in the Arab world as a pretext for negotiating a revision of the treaty. However, contrary to what Monroe and Wright seem to imply, it appears that the King cared less about Arab reaction than about the situation in Palestine; he sent his premier to London with the proposal that the British and the Hashemites coordinate their policies towards the Palestinian question.[7] Thus it was Abdullah's territorial ambitions, together with the continued importance of post-Mandatory Palestine for Britain, which brought the two governments to concur on their respective policies towards Palestine and to attempt to coordinate their future political moves in the area.

The strategy was suggested by Abdullah, the tactics by Ernest Bevin and Foreign Office officials. The King proposed the division of Palestine between the future Jewish state and Transjordan. The British Foreign Office introduced the means for implementing this division: Transjordan would annex those areas in Palestine allotted to the Arabs in the UN partition resolution of November 1947. This British suggestion became the guideline for British policy-makers in their treatment of the Arab–Israeli conflict. The formula was first suggested by King Abdullah in order to strengthen his position; it was later approved by the British as a means of safeguarding their interests in parts of Palestine; and it was finally accepted by the Israelis as the best solution for the long Arab–Jewish conflict in Palestine.

The situation in Palestine was the main topic in the Anglo-Transjordanian meeting in London at the beginning of 1948; however, it is noteworthy that the revision of the Anglo-Transjordanian treaty was also discussed at this time. The revised treaty served to strengthen British control and influence in Transjordan. Whereas the negotiations with Egypt and Iraq on defence treaties had proved to be an ordeal for the Foreign Office and the CoS, the talks with Transjordan were a comparatively easy task. Owing to Britain's dominant role in Transjordan, the CoS had few problems in agreeing to revision of the 1946 treaty. In fact, the CoS recommmended to the Foreign Secretary that he agree to revise the treaty and comply with the Transjordanians' request, since they realised that the treaty's substance and spirit would not be altered.[8]

The main amendment in the revised 1948 treaty concerned the relationship of the CoS with the Legion; direct British control over the Legion was replaced by a joint board of defence. The British hoped to reduce the impression of complete British control by excluding Glubb Pasha from this body. However, the fact that its chairman was a British officer meant that in practice nothing had changed. Moreover, after the treaty had been concluded, the CoS sent two directives to the joint board. One was sent to the board itself, and it emphasised the relevant article in the treaty which called for cooperation; the second one was sent only to the British members of the Board. This latter directive stated that the board was incorporated into the British military organisation in the Middle East, and that as such it had become subordinate to the CiC of the Middle East Forces.[9]

As could have been anticipated, the treaty was widely condemned throughout the Arab world. It was, after all, almost the same draft that the Iraqis had rejected.[10] Regarding the latter, the Foreign Office was convinced that the cause of such strong opposition in Iraq to the revised treaty was the unpopularity of the Iraqi government, and not the treaty itself. This was a manifestation of the general British tendency to play down the importance of Arab opposition to the revised treaty. Thus the Office believed that the opposition was initiated by the Syrians because of their animosity towards King Abdullah and their fear of his ambitions towards Greater Syria.[11]

British dominance in Transjordan was not merely military; their political influence was no less important. Due to Sir Alec Kirkbride's immense influence on King Abdullah, Britain could rely on Transjordan's unhesitating cooperation and loyalty. As Elizabeth Monroe has summarised it: since Jordan was an absolute monarchy, an agreement with Abdullah was an agreement with Jordan.[12] This was certainly the case until 1949, when the King's position was undermined considerably with the emergence of Palestinian public opinion in the country.

Kirkbride enjoyed a position similar to that of a Colonial High Commissioner and, together with Glubb, occupied the most important position in the country after the King and his premier. In a letter to the head of the Eastern Department, Bernard Burrows, Kirkbride admitted that he was so well informed about the King's state of mind, and influenced his decisions to such an extent, that it caused him embarrassment. As he explained: 'As a result of our long association (27 years) King Abdullah had got into the habit of informing me of what he had in mind, in both official and private matters with such a frankness which is sometimes startling'.[13] The Minister in Amman was embarrassed since he conveyed Abdullah's thoughts to London, and this information was sometimes used to rebuke the King.

Both in London and in Amman it was realised that a British representative with similar standing should be found to succeed Kirkbride. Furthermore, every effort was made so that Abdullah's heir-apparent, Prince Talal, would be as much under British influence as his father. In October 1948, Kirkbride reported that Talal, who in the early years of the Second World War had displayed an anti-British attitude and was therefore excluded from succession to the throne, had considerably mended his ways and could be trusted to be pro-British. Kirkbride advised that a Foreign Office official who spoke Arabic be sent to win the confidence of Talal since he (Kirkbride) would 'not last for ever'.[14] According to Kirkbride, his personal influence over Talal would be the principal safeguard against the decline of British control in Transjordan.

Kirkbride was right for as long as he himself remained in Transjordan and personally secured British interests there. With his departure, however, Britain ceased to play an important role in Transjordanian politics.

THE FOREIGN OFFICE ORGANISATION IN THE MIDDLE EAST

Hitherto we have tried to answer the question of why Palestine was still important for Britain after its evacuation in May 1948. However,

Britain's motives for continued interest in Palestine are insufficient for explaining British policy in the ensuing years. Not all British actions and decisions in the immediate years after the end of the Mandate can be attributed to its traditional interests or the new geopolitical constellation which emerged at the end of the Second World War, for the history of the formative years of the Arab–Israeli conflict is *inter alia* an analysis of human behaviour. Thus, in order to understand British policy, one must attempt to fathom the minds and inclinations of those persons who dealt with the conflict in the Foreign Office. This is a most unenviable task for the researcher. Still, at least one feature of the officials' and politicians' mentality can be discerned, and this is their tendency to pragmatism and their preference for an *ad hoc* policy, rather than one based on a general design or strategy.

There were two principal reasons for Britain's pragmatism (sometimes tantamount to opportunism), in its Middle East policy. The first was the nature of the area itself; the second was the complex, somewhat anachronistic Foreign Office organisation in the Middle East.

The Middle East was an area of uncertainy, an impossible arena for the practice of traditional Western diplomacy based on certain known and acknowledged rules of the game. Grand or small, designs based on European political thought were bound to fail. For years, the rapidly changing conditions in the Middle East had forced British policy-makers to bow to every passing wind or to accept every *fait accompli* without having much chance of opposing it if it happened to be anti-British. Thus British policy changed in reaction to every new development in the area.

Adaptation and adjustment had characterised British policy towards the Arab world in general and the Arab–Jewish conflict in particular since 1917. An excellent example of British adjustment to developments which were sometimes contrary to her interests can be seen in its policy towards the creation of the Arab League in 1945, as illustrated in the works of Porath and Gomaa. At first Britain opposed the formation of the League; later she accepted it and tried to win it over to the Western block.

Was this mode of behaviour a virtue or a weakness? That this was a debatable issue even amongst British officials can be seen in their own discussions on the subject. In most cases, diplomats displayed a considerable measure of frustration over their government's policy. In their memoranda from past years and in their present memoirs and interviews, many expressed regret over the absence of British initiative in the area after 1948 as well as criticism for Britain's passive stance during that time.[15]

In the early 1950s diplomats belonging to a conservative school of thought suggested an alternative: a clear-cut British policy based on a division of the Middle East into friends and foes. It began with Sir Thomas Rapp, head of the BMEO, who complained in 1951 that:

> There is little that I can find in the immediate past which confirms the idea that our *ad hoc* basis for policy decisions has proved adequate, even admitting the difficulties occasioned by the rapidly changing conditions in the Middle East and the external threat to peace. In some respects the multiplicity of diverse passions, prejudices and interests involved has seemed to overawe us and we have hesitated to take a line until a crisis has arisen where an empirical solution has had to be sought in an atmosphere fraught with emotions.[16]

However, even before such sharp and clear conclusions were reached and pronounced, frustrated officials in the Office could not conceal their disappointment over the absence of British initiative. Indeed, the Greater Transjordan concept, revision of treaties with the Arab world, British policy towards Israel and her attitude towards the Arab–Jewish conflict in general were parts of a policy which followed events and did not shape them. The criticism regarding the shaping of events could not be levelled at Bevin, who initiated new policies from time to time, as will be illustrated later in this work.

In time of crisis, or when British interests were directly threatened, decisions were made by the Defence Committee. This body formulated British policy in reaction to the Anglo–Iranian crisis, the Anglo–Egyptian negotiations and the Israeli advance to the Gulf of Aqaba and Israeli penetration of the Sinai peninsula. But in matters such as Israeli–Jordanian negotiations, which were closely followed by the Eastern Department of the Office, decisions were taken at the level of the Superintending Under-Secretary of State. Some cases were even left in the hands of the ambassadors and the representatives in the various British legations.

The process of decision-making would usually begin with a survey carried out by all the British diplomatic posts in the area. The Office's attitudes towards the Arab League, Israel, and treaties with the Arab countries were formed in this way. In other cases the representatives would be recalled home for a conference. The first conference after the

Second World War was in 1945; four years later another was convened. Bevin explained that the conference was a medium for coordination so that 'HMG representatives would be able to speak in one voice'.[17]

It is not only the researcher who is bewildered by the tangled structure created to preserve British interests in the Middle East. One of Bevin's first actions as Foreign Secretary was to establish a coordinating body consisting of three main constituents. In London there were two committees: a ministerial one (the Middle East Defence Committee) chaired by Bevin, and an official one chaired by the Minister of State. In the Middle East the task was placed in the hands of the BMEO.[18] Its political function was to coordinate policy and liaise with the Arab League as well as to give advice to British army authorities in the area. BMEO was in communication with the Middle East Secretariat, a body left over from the War, which soon ceased to play any significant part in policy-making.[19]

The local military authorities and the head of BMEO were members of a joint committee which was subordinate to the Army organisation in the Middle East and to the CoS Committee. The area under the responsibility of the British Defence Co-ordination Committee of the Middle East included Greece and Turkey, North Africa, Ethiopia and the Persian Gulf. However, the Committee never functioned properly. It could only have done so if there had been a general British strategy for the Middle East, but there was not. As those who were members of this committee complained: 'There existed on paper machinery for co-ordinating all aspects of British policy in the Middle East', but 'Policy and strategy in practice were formulated separately.'[20] Thus in the Middle East itself the coordinating body malfunctioned or did not function at all.

The situation was similar in London. The coordinating ministerial committee never met. The official committee held eight sessions; however, its effect on British policy was only marginal. It was supposed to coordinate army and Foreign Office policy but could never find its way through the complex structure which stretched from the Defence Committee through the CoS Committee down to the CiC Middle East Committee. And, if all these were not enough to confuse the members of the committee, they also had to take into account the various intelligence committees and joint defence boards.[21] It was probably just as well that these three coordinating bodies hardly ever functioned: if they had, it might have complicated things even further. Thus when one looks at the chart of the Middle East organisation (see

Appendix 1), one has to ignore the coordinating machinery and presume that most of the activity was either between embassies and the Eastern Department or between local commanders and the CoS. In the cases where there were both military and political implications, it was transferred to the Defence Committee.

The main result of this complex structure was the Foreign Office's inability to initiate policy so that it became a receiving centre rather than an active participant in the area.

ILAN PAPPÉ

MAP 1 UN Partition Plan (November 1947)

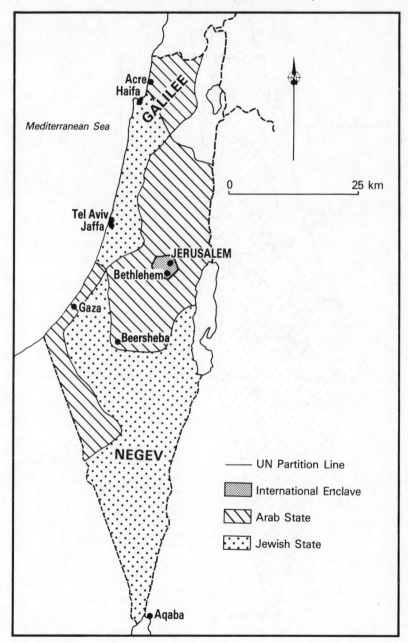

MAP 2   Bernadotte's Second Plan (September 1948)

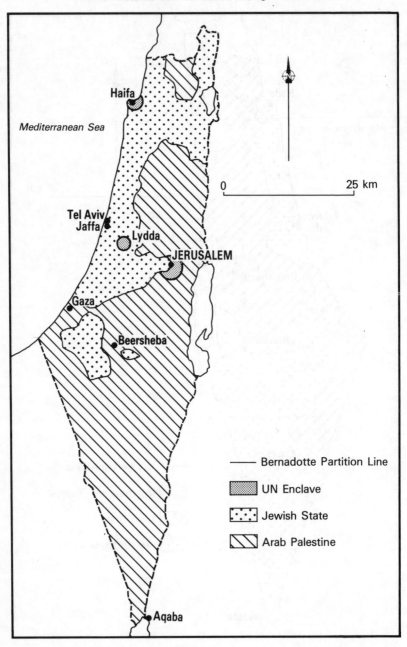

MAP 3 Final Armistice Lines (July 1949)

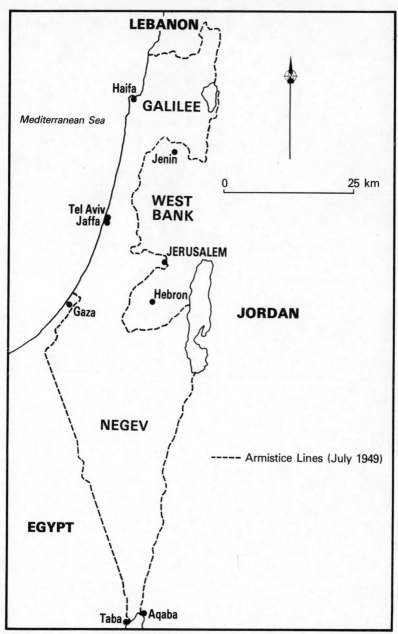

1 The Emergence of the Transjordan Option

PALESTINE IN THE LAST DAYS OF THE MANDATE

When the UN GA recommended the partition of Palestine, Britain could have pursued one of two distinct policies. As the Mandatory power, the government could have (and some would argue, should have) cooperated in enforcing the resolution on behalf of the UN, or at least could have facilitated the transition of Mandatory Palestine to its two successors, the Jewish and the Arab communities. Alternatively, the British government could have chosen to do 'nothing', ignoring the UN resolution. That is, Britain could have resisted the implementation of the resolution for as long as it was the sole authority in Palestine. The first option would have meant doing what the Jews wanted at the expense of the Arabs, whereas the second, doing nothing, would have favoured the Arabs and antagonised the Zionists. It seems, however, that what the British chose to do was done not in order to satisfy either side, but rather in accordance with purely British interests.

In many respects Britain's decision to refer the Palestinian problem to the UN was meant to extricate the government from a position in which it would have had to make a decision. As Bevin pointed out in the House of Commons in February 1947, while announcing the decision to withdraw from Palestine, Britain was unable to find a solution acceptable to both parties. The Foreign Secretary explained to the House in simple terms the root of the problem: 'For the Jews, the essential point in principle is the creation of a sovereign Jewish state. For the Arabs, the essential point in principle is to resist to the last the establishment of Jewish sovereignty in any part of Palestine.[1] This was still the situation after the UN resolution on partition, and Britain was still faced with the same danger of losing the sympathy of all the parties involved in the Palestinian conflict. According to Elizabeth Monroe they chose to do 'nothing'.[2] This 'nothing' meant that taking care to safeguard the British evacuation from Palestine was the sole objective of the government's policy in Palestine in the remaining days of the Mandate. This theory certainly explains British behaviour in Palestine between January and May 1948. However, doing nothing meant giving up Palestine altogether.

1

Thus both the Foreign Office and the War Office were preoccupied with the possible consequences of the government's decision to adopt a neutral posture towards the Arab–Jewish conflict in Palestine. How important and vital was post-Mandatory Palestine to British interests in the Middle East was the main question being asked in London in December 1947.

The CoS could not envisage the exclusion of Palestine from the British sphere of influence. Their committee ruled in January 1948 that one of the basic and essential British defence requirements was the maintenance of strategic rights in Palestine.[3] Most of the British diplomats in the Middle East shared this view. In fact, there was hardly any part of the Middle East which was not considered strategically important to Britain; hence the British efforts to obtain military alliances with most of the member states of the Arab League. Palestine was not a different case, and giving it up altogether was as unthinkable as the idea of leaving the Middle East itself. The British government was thus 'very far from thinking of moving out of the Middle East generally'.[4] Bevin himself made it perfectly plain that Britain's interest in Palestine was not lost. He told the American Secretary of State, Marshall, that the British government would not oppose the implementation of the UN resolution. However, he stressed that the British government would 'do their utmost to preserve their position and influence in that area'.[5]

Thus unless Britain could ensure it would have some impact, and indeed a decisive impact on the course of events in Palestine, after the termination of the Mandate it could not be confident of its ability to preserve its strategic rights in that country. The British policy-makers therefore had to concern themselves with questions such as the outcome of the Palestinian war, its implications for British interests in the area, and finally with the dilemma of the most desirable solution for the Arab–Jewish conflict from the British point of view.

This chapter will concentrate on the emergence of a British policy designed to solve the Arab–Jewish conflict while at the same time preserving the British government's interests in the area. This policy was formulated during the Anglo-Transjordanian negotiations in London in February 1948. The gist of this solution was a Transjordanian–Jewish understanding on the implementation of the UN partition plan. However, whereas the UN recommended the partition of Palestine into a Jewish state and an independent Arab state, this solution advocated dividing Palestine between Transjordan and a future Jewish state. It was first suggested by the Transjordanians to the Jews, in the earlier contacts between Abdullah and the Jewish Agency.

The factor which united the three parties concerned (the Jewish Agency, Britain and Transjordan) in their support for this concept was their opposition to the establishment of an independent Arab Palestinian state as provided for by the UN partition resolution. The Foreign Office, like the two other advocates of this concept, believed that such a state would be ruled by the Mufti of Jerusalem and the chairman of the AHC, Haj Amin Al-Husseini. The reasons for the Israeli, British and Jordanian opposition to a 'Mufti State' will be dealt with in the following chapters. In general one could say that its creation would have prevented both Abdullah and the Jews from implementing their territorial and national ambitions in Palestine. The Jewish Agency felt that the creation of a Palestinian state next to the Jewish state would have perpetuated the Arab–Jewish conflict in Palestine, whereas an agreement with Abdullah seemed more feasible and workable. As for Britain, it would have had to reconcile itself to the division of Palestine between two entities, Jewish and Arab Palestinians, believed by the British government at the time to be strongly opposed to British influence in the area.

The British Foreign Secretary was, more than anyone else, responsible for the shaping of this policy. He was motivated by a genuine desire (usually dismissed by Israeli writers) to find a solution acceptable to both sides. From the moment that a Jewish–Transjordanian (and later an Israeli–Jordanian) agreement seemed possible and practical, Bevin became their main protagonist.

This approach ignored two important factors in the Palestinian conflict. In the first instance, it disregarded the demands and aspirations of the Arab Palestinians. However, this was hardly a new phenomenon; since the active involvement of the Arab countries in Palestine's affairs (from 1936 onwards) this seems to have been the attitude of everyone concerned. Thus satisfying Arab demands did not necessarily mean satisfying those of the Arab Palestinians.

The concept was also unacceptable to the Arab League; in particular it antagonised Egypt and Syria. It caused a serious deterioration in Anglo-Arab relations, already considerably affected by the emergence of a new trend of anti-British Arab nationalism.

Notwithstanding these problems, the Foreign Office regarded this solution as the lesser evil. It seems that the UN and the Americans, as this chapter will try to illustrate, viewed the situation in very similar terms. Nevertheless it took some British persuasion before this concept of Greater Transjordan was accepted by the UN as the best solution for the Palestine problem.

Thus one has to differentiate between two main currents in Britain's Palestine policy during the Arab–Israeli war of 1948. There was on the one hand, a concern to safeguard the withdrawal of the British accompanied by a policy of non-interference in the developing Arab–Jewish confrontation. On the other hand, there were the British plans and ideas about post-Mandatory Palestine. This last effort was based primarily on the Great Transjordan concept, that is, enlarging Transjordanian territory at the expense of the UN's Arab Palestine. We are more concerned with the latter policy. The former (British behaviour in Palestine during the last days of the Mandate) is a subject which has been thoroughly dealt with by past and present studies. Still it cannot be dismissed without some analysis. It is always a relevant topic since Britain was subsequently blamed by Arab historians for its actions against Arab incursions and its role in the creation of a Jewish state, and by Israeli commentators for its response to the UN decision, which even today is seen as part of a British scheme to prevent the creation of a Jewish state.

Arab Incursions

In theory, Britain was still responsible for law and order in Palestine in the first half of 1948. In practice, however, the British took responsibility only for narrow zones in Palestine, where British forces were stationed.[6] Britain's main security concern was to prevent Arab countries from intervening in the conflict in Palestine itself, prior to the termination of the Mandate (15 May 1948). Furthermore, the Palestinian government did its utmost to prevent Jews and Arabs from taking up any positions which would obstruct the evacuation. The British government took further precautions to ensure its safe withdrawal by refusing to allow the entrance into Palestine of the officials of the UNPC who were appointed by the Security Council to assist in implementing the partition resolution.

Whereas in London the Foreign Office was mainly concerned with the policy of the Arab governments and their intentions prior to 15 May, the main worry of the Palestine government and the High Commissioner was the incursions of Arab irregulars from Syria and Transjordan.[7] These groups attacked Jewish settlements, and their presence in Palestine could have led to large-scale clashes with the British troops. There was a tendency within the Foreign Office to ignore the requests of the High Commissioner in Palestine that it exert pressure on Arab governments to stop the incursions into Palestine and to withdraw those bands which had already succeeded in infiltrating the country.[8]

The incursions were initiated by the Arab League. In October 1947, the Arab League Council met in Aley and decided to allow volunteers to enter Palestine after they had been trained in Syrian camps by Syrian and Iraqi officers. These irregulars were to form the nucleus of the ALA, to be commanded by Ismail Safwat, a senior Iraqi officer. Furthermore, it was decided that the Arab armies would be concentrated near the Palestine borders and put on the alert.[9] The Foreign Office had no desire to endanger its relations with the Arab world; it therefore failed to act against those incursions. The Foreign Office claimed that this Arab League policy implied that it was still of the opinion that the fighting in Palestine should be carried out by the Palestinians themselves. Thus London tended to ignore Sir Alan Cunningham's warnings that this concern with the precarious maintenance of good day-to-day relations with the Arab governments instead of preventing the Arab incursions would have grave consequences for Anglo-Arab relations.[10]

The Foreign Office advocated a policy of non-interference with the incursions unless they had aggressive intentions. The main reason for this was the British government's wish not to endanger British troops and to secure the evacuation. Monroe remarked that the news of the worsening situation in Berlin had an immense influence on the decision not to confront the Arabs and that the British had orders to avoid loss of life and equipment, since all would be needed for a future confrontation in Europe.[11]

From the Foreign Office's viewpoint there was an even more important, or at least equally important, reason. These incursions reduced the power of the much hated (in British eyes) former Mufti, Haj Amin Al-Husseini. The forces crossing the Jordan consisted of the Mufti's opponents. Moreover, the League's decision to form an independent Palestinian force subordinate only to the League's military committee indicated the League's determination to exclude the Mufti from the main Arab thrust in the future war in Palestine. Owing to the Iraqi and Transjordanian opposition, the League Council did not accept the former Mufti's proposals for a Palestinian government.[12]

Jewish Accusations of British Partiality

Britain refused to cooperate with the UNPC, a body appointed by the UN to facilitate the transition of Palestine from the Mandatory phase to independence. This was the most serious accusation brought by the Israelis.[13]

The British Cabinet refused to allow the UNPC to arrive in Palestine in February 1948, as was scheduled by the UN. As the Foreign Secretary explained in a minute he wrote to the Cabinet, the arrival of the Commission would have so gravely affected the security situation as to render impossible the task of maintaining civil administration over the whole of the country for more than a limited period.[14] This, of course, could not have been the only reason. The Cabinet could not appear in Arab eyes to be cooperating with the enforcement of the UN resolution. All it agreed to do was to consult the Commission in London and permit a nucleus of its staff to proceed to Palestine before 15 May. The UN declared that this behaviour was 'bordering on obstruction' and the president of the UNPC asked for a month to 'overlap' with the British administration, but was refused.[15]

This was not the only item in the UN resolution that the British failed to comply with. The UN plan stipulated that the Mandatory power should ensure that an area situated in the Jewish state, including a sea port and a hinterland capable of providing facilities for substantial immigration, should be evacuated no later than 1 February 1948. The British did exactly the opposite. They doubled the population of the detainee camps in Cyprus in January 1948, and the surveillance of Jewish ships continued until 4 April 1948.[16] The coastal blockade was maintained by a new decree issued in February 1948, which was intended to stop Jewish immigration and arms smuggling. The British effort to stop Jewish arms deliveries was extended at one point to the US, where many British agents were engaged in the search for arms suppliers. Thus there was certainly a difference in the way Arab incursions were dealt with and the way the flow of Jewish immigration was blocked.[17]

The British government explained that Tel Aviv had not been evacuated since it would cause unrest and 'render it impossible for the Arab states to maintain their existing policy of restraint'.[18] Again this was not the whole explanation. The Cabinet suspected rightly that the port would be used for importing arms to the Jewish Hagana and Irgun movements.

Ben-Gurion's biographer stated that the British were acting intentionally and maliciously towards the Jews. Apart from letting the ALA enter Palestine, Bar-Zohar pointed to various clashes between the Arabs and the Jews where the British were always on the Arab side. One tends to accept the assertion made by Michael Cohen that on the local level there were British officers who intended to settle old scores with the Jews, but this was a local interpretation of London's directive to evacuate Palestine without causing loss of British life and equipment.[19]

Christopher Sykes has suggested that a future researcher should look into the Foreign Office and the CO documents of the time to determine whether there was a planned anti-Jewish British policy. It seems that there was hardly any sign of planning in British policy towards the Middle East after 1946. This quite probably applied to British policy towards Palestine. Vague guidelines from London to protect British interests in Palestine (namely, a clean and smooth evacuation with a bias towards Abdullah's interests in Palestine) was the only coherent element in British policy. The rest was left to the local commanders' initiative.[20]

The British position became somewhat clearer in a decision taken by the Cabinet on 22 March 1948, a decision that reduced all the High Commissioner's efforts to maintain law and order to nothing. It was decided *neither* to oppose the entrance of Transjordanian and irregular forces into those parts of Palestine allocated to the Arabs in the partition resolution; and *not* to oppose any Jewish attempt to establish a state of their own prior to 15 May.[21] Thus the guideline coming from London could not be regarded as biased towards one side only. There were also the anti-Jewish decisions that were not made in Palestine, as Elizabeth Monroe has pointed out. The British refusal to let Jews of military age who were in the camps in Cyprus enter Palestine was a Cabinet decision which provoked Jewish resentment. In fact, the British decision not to comply with the UN resolution requirements, although not intended as such, was anti-Zionist in its implications. The motives, however, were purely pro-British.[22]

Before we approach the main theme of this work, a final word about British behaviour in Palestine during the last days of the Mandate. The British actions and conduct in Palestine were not part of a policy aimed at protecting British interests after the withdrawal from that country as was the Greater Transjordan policy. Nevertheless, it seems useful briefly to appraise its implications for Britain's position in the area and for Palestine's future. It seems that it cost Britain prestige and probably loss of influence, but Palestine paid an even greater price: chaos.

The British Cabinet decided to maintain administrative control until 15 May, thus not allowing any period of transition. This British policy, which was not accompanied by an effort to maintain law and order, was a formula for future chaos. The UNPC decided on gradual evacuation of the civil administration, but this was not achieved because there was no transitional period. The British Cabinet itself realised what its policy would mean in the final analysis. A Cabinet minute accurately described the collapse of civil, legislative and security systems in Palestine.[23]

The Jewish Agency offered an alternative which was accepted by the UNPC: an international force would impose partition on behalf of the UN. The Cabinet feared that this would open the door to Russian intervention, therefore it was decided to abstain in the GA or Security Council if the issue were brought to vote. In addition the British government, through its delegation in the UN, made an enormous effort to put across the idea that the security situation in Palestine rendered any use of international force impossible.[24] American documents indicate that the British effort to communicate the dangers which would be incurred by implementing partition, using a non-Palestinian force, affected to a large extent the American decision to introduce the idea of a trusteeship instead of partition. The Americans concurred with a gloomy British assessment that such an action would result in severe Arab measures leading to the stoppage of the flow of oil to Europe which was so necessary to the Marshall Plan. However, trusteeship was unacceptable to the Jews and was not endorsed by President Truman. Thus partition remained the most likely option.[25]

At the time, the consequences of the policy of impartiality and neutrality were not fully grasped. A decade later one of Britain's senior diplomats in the area, Sir Alec Kirkbride, would describe his government's refusal to hand over authority to the UN as a crime and 'inexcusable' act.

The need to appease the Arab governments, the desire to protect British lives and, above all, the lack of a thorough evaluation of the implications of their policy, led to the stigma attached to the British role in the days before the Mandate ended. Indeed, some of the British measures were taken as a result of a process of 'gut reaction', such as the decision to expel Palestine without warning from the Sterling Area, and to freeze over a million pounds' worth of Palestinian accounts in London, thus harming both the Jewish and the Arab communities. Rees Williams, the Under-Secretary of State for the Colonies, followed Kirkbride's line of self-accusation and declared in the House: 'On the 14th of May, 1948, the withdrawal of the British administration took place without handing over to a responsible authority any of the assets, property, or liabilities of the Mandatory government. The manner in which the withdrawal took place is unprecedented in the history of our Empire.'[26]

THE EMERGENCE OF THE GREATER TRANSJORDAN CONCEPT

At the end of 1947, Abdullah expressed his wish to revise the Anglo-Transjordanian treaty. Abdullah's request came as a surprise to the Foreign Office since only two years had elapsed since the last treaty had been signed. Before sending a delegation to London to discuss the revision, Abdullah explained that his main motive was to refute Arab allegations of his being a British puppet.[27]

As indicated in the introduction, Abdullah needed the treaty as a pretext for something else. The Eastern Department and Kirkbride suspected that the King was anxious to discuss the future of Palestine. Very few in the Transjordan delegation knew the real motives for the negotiations. In order to discuss Palestine, the Transjordan premier asked for a separate meeting without the knowledge of his minister for foreign affairs, who was considered to be more militant, a pan-Arabist, and one who would have probably refused to accept any deal over the future of Palestine. Already in Amman, Tawfiq Abu Al-Huda implied that he wanted to discuss a 'very delicate relationship' which would develop after the termination of the Mandate.[28] He was referring to the King's contacts with the Jewish Agency and his attitude towards the future Jewish state. It was not the first time that the British had heard about these negotiations; it was the first time, however, that the Transjordanian government had asked for British advice on the issue.

Abdullah warned Kirkbride that chaos in Palestine could harm his position. He urged the British to prevent hostilities between Jews and Arabs there. He offered a way: the annexation of the whole of Palestine or of the Arab parts in the country to Transjordan. Abdullah had talked publicly about this possibility already in 1946. For that purpose he commenced negotiations with all the parties concerned, namely the Arab Palestinians, the Jews and the British. He deemed it

necessary to have an outlet to the Mediterranean and could not accept
the idea of either an independent Palestine or a chaotic Palestine. Yet
before sending his premier to London the King had told Kirkbride that
he would occupy Palestine only if he were welcomed as a liberator by
the Arab world and if the British guaranteed to assist him in the
Security Council to the extent of using their veto. The Amman
Legation doubted Abdullah's chances of success in obtaining the
blessings of the Arab world and were confident that the British
government would never agree to use their veto for such purposes.[29]

One might surmise that Abdullah anticipated that the British would
not be enthusiastic about his plans. This presumably explains his
decision to give priority to contacts and agreements with the Jewish
Agency; otherwise it is difficult to understand why his contacts with the
Jews preceded the arrangements with the British. After all, the British
had the ability to grant Abdullah the Arab parts of Palestine with or
without Jewish approval.

In November 1947, King Abdullah met the head of the Political
Department of the Jewish Agency, Golda Meyerson (Meir), and offered
the Jews an independent Jewish republic as part of a Hashemite
monarchy covering Transjordan and ex-Mandatory Palestine. When
this was rejected, he asked for the Jewish Agency's consent to his
annexing the territories allotted to the Arabs in the UN partition plan.
The Jewish Agency representative gave her consent in return for the
King's promise not to attack the future Jewish state.[30]

In December these contacts continued and were conducted by Elias
Sasson and the King's private physician, Dr Shawkat As-Sati. In the
meeting in December the King reiterated his support for the partition
of Palestine between Transjordan and the future Jewish state.

In January 1948, the King communicated to the Jewish Agency that
he would formulate his final attitude after consulting the British. It
seems that in December 1947 the British were already informed about
these meetings and about Abdullah's intentions to annex the Arab
parts.[31]

At that stage only a few officials in the Foreign Office tended to
support Abdullah's scheme. Harold Beeley, the Office's expert on
Palestinian affairs, was the main opponent of such a possibility (the
annexation of Arab Palestine to Transjordan). It would have meant,
asserted Beeley, the enforcement of the UN partition by the
Transjordanians. He warned that this course of action would lead to
the destruction of the League and would deal a severe blow to the
British position in the Arab world. Beeley argued that supporting

Abdullah in this scheme would mean taking a position against the majority of the Arab League.[32]

Bevin expressed similar apprehensions in a conversation with Marshall. However, there was a significant difference between Bevin's and Beeley's outlook for the future. Beeley predicted that the local Arab Palestinians would launch guerrilla warfare against the Jews and would succeed in creating an independent state in Arab Palestine. Bevin, however, still hoped that in the end partition would prove a failure and the parties would go back to his own plan: the creation of provincial autonomy in Palestine. Bevin had already suggested in 1947 the setting-up of autonomous Jewish and Arab provinces controlled by the High Commissioner's advisory council in which the Jews and the Arabs would be represented, and with the proviso that after four years of restricted Jewish immigration the country could be granted independence. Beeley had already observed during the London conference (September 1946) that the Arab leaders believed that any scheme of provincial autonomy would lead to partition.

The British Support for the Transjordan Concept

Notwithstanding those divergences of opinion, the idea brought forward by the Transjordanians which had been hitherto rejected was now accepted by the Foreign Office. It should be noted that the idea itself was not alien to the British; they had already suggested it in 1936 in the Peel Royal Commission's report. At that time the programme failed owing to strong opposition from the Arab world to the recommendations of the commission *in toto*. Tawfiq Abu Al-Huda found a very sympathetic and receptive Foreign Office. Thus the whole British position had changed in less than a month.

What caused this shift in British policy and thinking? The most apparent feature that emerges from Bevin's behaviour on this issue was his pragmatism. As indicated earlier in this chapter, the Foreign Secretary looked for ways of maintaining a dominant British strategic position in the area despite the termination of the Mandate. Abdullah was the first to offer one. Thus although it initially seemed a risky option, the direct meeting with Abu Al-Huda and further thinking about it convinced the Office and Bevin that this was a credible policy. The British must have realised their inability to prevent Abdullah's participation in the general Arab war effort in Palestine. A Transjordanian abstinence from the general Arab commitment would have meant the exclusion of the kingdom from the Arab League and world. The new plan seemed to be a possible outlet for Abdullah. The annexation of Arab Palestine could have been easily accepted as a feasible development in case of war in Palestine. Thus, since the British found it hard to object or to force their own ideas on the King, they eventually responded favourably to the latter's suggestions. Now all that remained to be done was exploring the benefits and advantages for Britain in Abdullah's scheme.

After the Jewish successes in Palestine in April 1948, any remaining doubts about the desirability of this policy disappeared. It was also seen as the only way of leaving Palestine in an orderly manner. The Foreign Office adapted itself to Bevin's pragmatism with little difficulty. Under the Coalition government it had already shown its ability to adjust itself to new developments, even those which were initially regarded as anti-British, such as the Arab League. As Gomaa and Porath have illustrated in their books, the formation of the League was an Arab initiative viewed unfavourably by the Foreign Office. However, in a relatively short period the Office supported the new organisation and tried to direct it towards a pro-British policy.[33]

The failure of the Foreign Office to effect a reorientation of the League's policies along pro-British lines serves as an additional explanation for the formulation of a new British policy towards Palestine. One of the gravest consequences of Abdullah's action could have been, as the British perceived it, the deterioration of Transjordan's relations with the League. However, even before Tawfiq Abu Al-Huda's visit to London, the Foreign Office and Bevin had made up their minds about the future of Anglo-League relations. For them, the League was an unimportant political factor, merely a tool for Egyptian anti-British policies. Arab unity was regarded as mere Utopia and the Office advised the government to treat Arab countries individually.[34] The implication of this attitude was that Abdullah could win British support even if he acted in defiance of the League's decisions.

The High Commissioner in Palestine had supported Abdullah's plan even before it received the blessing of London. The Secretary of State for the Colonies, Creech-Jones, submitted to the Cabinet a memorandum based on information and opinions expressed by Cunningham in which he had objected to Bevin's provincial autonomy plan and advocated support for partition.[35]

The CO position, and in particular Cunningham's views, had immense importance for the Foreign Office. The reports from Palestine, as well as Creech-Jones' views, provided in the final analysis the evidence the Office needed to prove to the British Cabinet that the 'Transjordan option' was the right one. On the basis of these reports, the Eastern Department was convinced that the Arabs in Palestine showed no sign of attempting to work out any kind of civil administration for their part of Palestine. This information was reinforced by reports about the disunity and ineptitude of the local Arab forces in Palestine. It became evident that the local Arab Palestinian forces by themselves could not confront the Jews. Following this information, the Eastern Department concluded that such Arab inaction would result in a state of anarchy unless the UN administered the Arab areas, which was unlikely, or unless the Arab Legion did so.[36]

Once Bevin had decided to back the Transjordan option, it was quite easy for the Foreign Office to explore its advantages for Britain. Annexation of this territory to Transjordan meant the extension of the British rights contained in the Treaty to Arab Palestine, thus compensating the British for the loss of Palestine.[37]

After the discussion in London between Tawfiq Abu Al-Huda and Bevin, the Foreign Office took some practical decisions in preparation for the coming conflict. The officials in London thought that British officers serving in the Arab Legion should *not* be ordered out and that Britain should continue its subsidy of the Arab Legion. When the day of battle approached, Kirkbride suggested that until open warfare developed, British combatant officers should accompany their units even if they moved into Palestine proper. The Foreign Office approved his recommendation, thus probably leading to some involvement in the war by British officers. In an interview Kirkbride gave in the 1960s he admitted that even after the fighting had commenced, he ignored consecutive telegrams ordering the withdrawal of British officers because he believed that the Legion could not have done without them.[38]

It was decided in the Foreign Office that the Legion would be allowed into the Arab areas without hindrance. Sir Alec Kirkbride did not expect that the Transjordanians would be welcomed in those areas. However, he could not see any other way of preventing the chaotic situation that might prevail in Palestine.[39]

The possible hostile reaction in Arab Palestine was not the only problem facing the implementation of such a plan. The Foreign Office and Amman agreed that there was no need to declare that Transjordan was going to defy the League's decision. This was achieved with some success, and despite the rumours that accompanied the talks in

London and the long-standing knowledge of Abdullah's ambitions for a greater Transjordan, the Arab world had difficulty in discovering Abdullah's real intentions.

In Amman, as in any other Arab capital, the public and the press talked about the occupation of the whole of Palestine. As Kirkbride tells us in his memoirs, Azzam had frequently visited Abdullah to make sure that 'the Jordanian authorities did not fail to play the part assigned to them in the plan drawn [up] by the Arab League'.[40] For this purpose Azzam offered Glubb the League appointment of the post of CiC of the Arab forces in Palestine. Kirkbride and Glubb were convinced that the offer was made 'in bad faith' and in order to find a scapegoat for any future failure. Thus Azzam might have guessed Abdullah's real motives in entering Palestine, but for the sake of saving Palestine from the Jews he was prepared to support him; or indeed, as Kirkbride suggested, Azzam was looking for someone to blame in the future: who better than King Abdullah?[41]

The head of the Eastern Department was aware of Abdullah's need to toe the general Arab line. Thus he favoured a close Iraqi–Transjordan cooperation in Arab Palestine. Burrows argued that the Iraqi cooperation was needed first as a façade for the Arab world (to indicate that Abdullah was not acting alone). Moreover, it was believed in London that such a united force would be more welcome in Arab Palestine and would have a better chance of maintaining order in the Arab areas.[42]

For the Foreign Office the need to prevent the creation of what is called 'a Mufti state' was no less important than installing Transjordanian control in these areas.[43] The Legation in Amman warned the Office that the Syrians, in conjunction with the former Mufti, would work against Abdullah in Arab Palestine. Therefore Kirkbride advocated close cooperation with Al-Qawqji, who was an Iraqi protégé and one of the Mufti's main rivals. This attitude accounts for the ease with which Al-Qawqji entered Arab Palestine before 15 May, in spite of the protests of Sir Alan Cunningham in Jerusalem.[44]

However, there were voices against the Iraqi–Transjordan joint operation. Glubb and Ambassador Trott in Jedda were the two main opponents. Glubb was apprehensive of clashes with the Iraqis over the control of Arab Palestine. Both he and the High Commisioner asserted that there was no need for Iraqi participation, as the educated and wealthy classes in Arab Palestine were supporters of the King and it was only the 'uneducated and lower classes' who followed the Mufti.[45] The representative in Jedda and the experts on Saudi Arabia feared the reaction of the Saudis to a strong Hashemite contingent acting in Palestine. In fact, Ibn Saud warned that in a case of a separate Iraqi–Transjordan invasion he might go as far as declaring war on Transjordan. In order to reinforce this threat, Ibn Saud encouraged volunteers from the Najd to leave for Palestine and assist the Arabs there.[46]

This clash of interests with the Saudis demonstrated to the British officials that unless Abdullah at least pretended to follow the general Arab line, new complications would emerge from unexpected sources. Since 1940 Ibn Saud had demanded adjustments to the northern borders of the Hejaz (annexation of Ma'an and Aqaba to Saudia). Furthermore, he wanted the renunciation of Abdullah's 'rights' as a Sharif of Mecca, which Abdullah was unlikely to make publicly. Quite probably Abdullah had never relinquished his desire to return to the Hejaz. In order to lessen Ibn Saud's suspicions, the Foreign Office gave vague promises to the Saudi ruler that it would work towards rectifications of the Saudi–Transjordanian border in return for Saudi consent to Iraqi–Transjordan control of Palestine. However, it was only in May 1948, when it became clear to Ibn Saud that most of the League members wished Abdullah to be the supreme commander of the operation in Palestine, that the Saudi King altered his attitude. Ibn Saud wrote to Abdullah: 'All my armies are at your disposal for the fight in Palestine.'[47]

The assessment of the prospect of Abdullah's policy had to include the reactions of the UN, the Americans and the Jews. It seemed in London that there was no danger of UN opposition since it was the easiest way to enforce its decision of November 1947. It seems that whereas some of the members of the UNPC believed that Abdullah was 'playing his own game' and would enforce partition to his advantage, others asserted that this was the best solution for the problem.[48]

Bevin told Foreign Office officials that he was confident of American support for the Transjordan scheme, as it promised the creation of a Jewish state. He hoped his plan might even bring the Americans to pressure the Jews into the future state to give up a reasonable amount of their customs revenues to support the Transjordan economy.[49]

In fact, the Americans were informed at an early stage about the Transjordan government's wishes. However, the Anglo-American agreement concerning Abdullah's plan was not fully disclosed. In any case, the US supported the partition resolution and, like the UNPC, was pleased to see its implementation without the need to involve American forces or efforts: 'We should take no further initiative in implementing or aiding partition', recommended the Policy Planning Staff. The Americans were nevertheless clear on one major issue. They would not tolerate Transjordanian intervention before the end of the Mandate. They warned the British that the American reaction could amount to the despatch of forces. Bevin and Attlee assured Marshall that the Transjordanians would not enter Palestine prior to the end of the Mandate.[50]

THE UNWRITTEN AGREEMENT

Given the British outlook, it is understandable that the Foreign Office viewed the Transjordanian contacts with the Jewish leadership favourably. Bevin was satisfied with Abu Al-Huda's assurances that the Legion would not enter Jewish areas unless Jews invaded Arab areas. Michael Wright, the senior official dealing with the Middle East, reported that the King was about to come to a *de facto* agreement with the Jewish Agency that they would not encroach on each other's territory.[51] Hector McNeil, the minister of state in the Foreign Office in charge of contacts with the Jews, confirmed that the latter would welcome the annexation of Arab Palestine to Transjordan. In fact, according to the Ben-Gurion diaries, upon learning that the Jewish Agency knew about the secret meeting between Abu Al-Huda and Bevin, the minister of state conveyed to Ben-Gurion quite explicitly the idea that Britain would acquiesce with partition.[52]

Sharett told the State Department that he would prefer an agreement with Transjordan to a cease-fire. Marshall was the only person in the State Department who believed that the Jews would lose the war; the others were confident that a prior Transjordan–Jewish agreement would determine its outcome.[53]

There was, however, a significant deterioration in the King's relations with the Jewish Agency during March–May 1948. In March 1948 some of the main Jewish protagonists of the Hashemite–Jewish Agency understanding were dissatisfied with the lack of clear commitment on the past of Abdullah to reach an agreement with the Agency. They suggested delaying the Mandate termination for a year and looking for a new agreement.[54]

Abdullah himself felt that after the successive Jewish achievements in the March–April civil war, he would have to reconsider his position, and when at the end of April the Jewish Agency proposed continuing negotiations, he refused because of the publicity given to previous contacts. Abdullah had continued to publicly insist on a solution that offered only autonomy to the Jews.[55]

Whereas before April 1948 it seemed that the negotiations were progressing towards a non-aggression agreement, at the beginning of April the two sides found themselves in deadlock owing to the King's insistence, publicly and privately, on his 'Autonomy Plan'. Furthermore Abdullah declared that he would desist from sending messages of negotiation until 'both sides were in a more reasonable mood'.[56]

Notwithstanding this deadlock, at the beginning of May a meeting took place between two senior Hagana and British Legion officers (Colonel Goldie and Major Crocker). The two sides expressed their desire to prevent a war between the two armies. The main outcome of this meeting was the Hagana realisation that the Legion had no plans to go beyond occupying the Arab areas, even though it would have to participate in the Arab war effort. It was further understood that the Legion as well as the Jewish forces, would first try to decide the future of Jerusalem on the battlefield.[57]

Kirkbride summed up the opinions of officials in the field about the significance of that meeting. After the meeting he reported that whatever other voices could be heard from Amman and Tel Aviv, the Office should pay attention only to the fact that: 'It is understood that the objective of these secret negotiations is to define the areas of Palestine to be occupied by the two forces.'[58] Bevin, upon learning of such an agreement, remarked that a good reason for retaining the British combatant officers in the battlefield was to ensure that the Hagana–Legion understanding would be maintained. He further wrote that, 'I am reluctant to do anything which might prejudice the success of these negotiations, which appear to aim at avoiding hostilities between the Arabs and the Jews.'[59] Kirkbride's remarks were of great importance, given the growing tension between the Transjordanians and the Hagana, as well as the appointment of the King as the supreme commander of the Arab forces intent on entering Palestine.

The British officers indicated that the few incidents of fighting which had already occurred between the Legion and the Hagana were the result of misunderstanding and, furthermore, that Abdullah's public declaration about his intention to go to war 'against the Zionists' was made only for Arab consumption.[60]

Was this a correct assessment of the political and military intentions of both sides? The absence of any written agreement renders this question insoluble. However, from the outcome of the war, the behaviour of the two armies during the battles, and the reaffirmation of that agreement both in the armistice agreement (April 1949) and the draft of the non-aggression pact of February 1950 (both written agreements), one finds support for the British assessment.

Whereas the British archives supply ample information and documents about both Britain's and Transjordan's reliance on the unwritten agreement to divide Palestine between a Jewish and Transjordanian state, the Israeli sources are less clear about that point. However, an important indication of the Jewish Agency's serious regard for the *modus vivendi* with Abdullah as an essential factor in successfully bringing about the creation of the Jewish state was Ben-Gurion's warning to the leaders of the Jewish Agency that the newly-formed state would have immense difficulties in occupying the areas allotted to the Jews if the Legion were to go beyond the Arab areas. This was one of the few occasions in which Ben-Gurion had invested efforts to ensure that Abdullah stuck to his original scheme. In this context it is understandable why Ben-Gurion decided to send a letter to Abdullah denouncing the Jewish Agency's part in the massacre of Dir Yasin.[61]

The inability to determine whether or not the Jewish–Hashemite understanding was intact during the war of 1948 stems mainly from the nature of the last political meeting between the Jewish Agency and the King, which took place on 11 May 1948. The Jewish Agency asked for the meeting in order to obtain the King's blessing for and commitment to the military arrangement, and Abdullah sought to clarify his intentions towards the Jews. Golda Meyerson, the Jewish envoy, met the King and was highly disappointed when Abdullah announced that the only way to prevent war was by obtaining the Jews' agreement to stop immigration and not to declare a state of their own. In that case Transjordan would annex all of Palestine and the Jewish population would be represented in the Transjordan parliament. Abdullah explained that he had taken this step since he was 'one out of five' Arab armies entering Palestine, and therefore his hands were tied.[62]

Meyerson rejected these proposals and urged the King to remain loyal to the first promise he had made to her in November 1947. The King, according to various versions, replied that he could not break a promise he had made to a woman.[63]

It seems that the two parties had no intention of departing from the original understanding. Weizmann recalled that both sides had left the last meeting before the war with the impression, in spite of the divergence of opinions, that they had avoided a major clash between the two armies. The Israelis who participated in the meeting reported that their impression was that Abdullah would look for ways of improving his position by extending his territory somewhat beyond the 29 November resolution but would not attempt to occupy the Jewish state. American intelligence had reached the same conclusion at that time.[64]

However, notwithstanding these interpretations of the last meeting, one has to explain another incident that on the face of it meant deviation from the original agreement. This incident, the Gush Etzion affair, was so crucial that when it occurred two days before the war broke out, it could easily have provoked full-scale Jewish–Legion clashes. Gush Etzion was a Jewish settlement south of Jerusalem on the border of the UN Jewish state. The local Arab bands in the area put it under siege and threatened to capture and kill the inhabitants. Shortly after the siege had begun, Arab Legion units joined the besiegers in an attack on the settlement. Israeli sources claim that this was an unprovoked attack by the Legion. However, according to American documents, the Israelis had ambushed the Legion convoy on its way from Gaza to Amman, while the Legion was moving from Gaza to Amman as part of the British withdrawal plan.[65] The battle over Gush Etzion was not part of the struggle over Arab Palestine; it had more to do with the battle over Jerusalem on whose future the two sides had failed to reach an agreement. Thus answering the question of whether there was or was not an agreement, it is best to point out that there was an agreement, but that it was neither written nor binding.

In later years some of the participants of the war denied the existence of such an agreement. General Yadin, who had been the active Chief of the General Staff of the Israeli army, claimed that Ben-Gurion's actions were not guided by any such understanding.[66] He was right in arguing that there was no binding agreement. This explains Ben-Gurion's ambitions and plans towards the annexation of Arab Palestine (the West Bank) to Israel after the war and the need to reaffirm the agreement, as was eventually requested by the Jordanians and consented to by the Israelis. However, Ben-Gurion's plans and ambitions did not materialise, owing mainly to the Jewish–Hashemite understanding. The important point was, and still is, that the territorial map at the end of the war of 1948 was shaped according to this understanding.

The uncertainty about the agreement had bothered the Foreign Office as well. Sir Alec Kirkbride was pressed by the Foreign Office to find out in the last week before the war if any changes had occurred in Abdullah's plans. Kirkbride reported that Abdullah would not attack the Jewish state and that the British legation still hoped that Jerusalem would be excluded by a truce. The British Legion officers informed Kirkbride that a similar tendency to avoid clashes was implied in their meeting with the Hagana officers. Like Bevin, the British minister in Amman was relying on the British officers to restrain the King.[67]

The outcome of the first week of fighting indicated that whether intentionally or out of necessity, in the final analysis the Legion operation did not constitute a breach of the promise given to Meyerson in December 1947 and April 1948.

2 Britain and the War of 1948 (May–June)

BRITISH ASSUMPTIONS ABOUT THE ARAB WAR EFFORT

Most officials in the Eastern Department shared the view that although the Arab leaders were meeting ostensibly to prepare for intervention in Palestine, they would not ultimately enter into war. The inability to understand precisely what was going on at the Arab summits contributed to the doubts concerning the seriousness of the Arab leaders' intentions to invade Palestine. Only on 8 May was the Foreign Office confident that an Arab offensive would take place. Military intelligence in Jerusalem reported growing pressure on Abdullah throughout April, but did not deduce that invasion was inevitable. However, on 12 May it was clear that the Legion was already involved in fighting. It attacked Jewish settlements on that day and was moving towards Jerusalem in preparation for a large-scale attack on the city's Jewish sectors.[1]

The precise course of the attack was agreed upon in the Arab leaders' meeting on 30 April 1948. At that meeting, in Damascus, Abdullah agreed to enter Palestine, with the Iraqis occupying eastern Palestine and uniting with the forces coming from Lebanon and Syria.[2]

The information could have implied a serious Hashemite deviation from the Anglo-Transjordanian and Hashemite–Jewish understandings. Following this news, the Foreign Office was anxious to know whether the King, in spite of the Arab League plan, had altered his original plan and course of advance: a course he had worked out with his British Chief of General Staff, Glubb Pasha, in March 1948 immediately after the end of the negotiations in London. Glubb had stated at that time that the Legion objectives were Beersheba, Hebron, Ramallah, Nablus, Jenin and Tul Karem.[3]

Kirkbride turned out to be non-committal on this issue. He knew the King would not alter his original plan but was less confident about how Abdullah would proceed once he arrived at the Hebron–Ramallah line. He could only agree with Glubb that the extraordinary British position in Transjordan would enable it to know in advance the plans of the King, knowing that Glubb in particular was able to inform the British about Abdullah's military plans. Glubb was explicitly asked by the Foreign Office to continue serving his 'two masters', namely the British and the Legion. Glubb agreed, as he thought that by 'back stairs' methods he could continue to provide a large amount of help and information.[4]

The British ability to follow the Legion's preparation for the war allowed London to predict its outcome quite accurately. This was possible owing to the important role played by the Legion. In order to evaluate the significance of this role, it is important to consider the estimated strength of the parties involved in terms of manpower, equipment and ammunition. What we shall try to prove is the assumption that an agreement between two major factors in the conflict could have decisively affected the outcome of the war of 1948; that is, the creation of a greater Transjordan. An examination of the role of the Legion is essential since it was done by the CoS in the beginning of 1948 and it elucidated some of the differences of opinion that existed between the Foreign Office and the Army. The divergence of opinion between the soldiers and the politicians stemmed from the difference between political and military estimations. Therefore we have to remember that the CoS did not take into account the understanding between Bevin and Tawfiq Abu Al-Huda, or the various contacts between the Jewish Agency and Abdullah.

There were other differences as well. Unlike the Eastern Department and the government in Jerusalem, the CoS Committee had more confidence in the ability of the Arabs in Palestine to organise their forces and set up their own administration in the predominantly Arab areas.[5] The Eastern Department, on the other hand, doubted the success of local Arabs in confronting the Jews without significant external Arab assistance.

As the end of the Mandate approached it became clear that it would be important for both Arabs and Jews to win the battle over the mixed towns of Palestine: Jaffa, Haifa, Tiberias and Sefat. The British Army had addressed itself to this problem at the beginning of April, a few weeks before the battle over the urban areas began. In fact, the CoS did not anticipate a serious battle over the mixed towns or over Palestine itself before the end of the Mandate; not so much owing to the respect held by warring factions for Mandatory law and order, but rather because of the army's lack of belief in the local Arab military force's ability to initiate battle and the CoS' estimation (or rather underestimation) of the Jewish ability to launch an attack on their own. Neither did they anticipate a Jewish initiative before the end of the Mandate.

In the event of a major battle in Palestine before or after the end of the Mandate, the British Army believed the ALA and the Legion to be potent enough to determine the outcome, which they thought would be the occupation of the Arab areas by those two armies and the creation of a Jewish state on the coastal plain.[6]

At the end of April the CoS had to admit their miscalculations. The battle over the mixed towns did take place and in spite of massive support by the ALA, the local Arabs lost the struggle over Palestine at that stage.

The new constellation which emerged at the end of April 1948 necessitated a reassessment of estimations of the Arab and Jewish forces which might become involved in the fighting. It seems that the Eastern Department was more accurate in its predictions, owing to a correct appreciation of the political motives and aspirations of the Arab armies. Now that an external Arab invasion seemed imminent, there were no significant discrepancies between the presumptions of the Army and those of the diplomats or experts, apart from evaluation of the Legion's ability. In May 1948 both sections recognized the superiority of the Jewish forces in Palestine and predicted that the Jewish forces would be even stronger and better equipped in the future.[7] Less professional experts such as journalists are occasionally better forecasters, even when they base their predictions on intuition rather than on detailed political and military intelligence. *The Times*, as early as March 1948, reported that the Jews were on their way to a highly organised state which would succeed in establishing firm central control over the Jewish community, compulsory military service, and a ban on foreign travel.[8] Indeed, the Jewish success was, in the final analysis, not due to a better army, but to the creation of an embryo state in the mandatory period, while the Arab Palestinians' initiatives and efforts to establish an infrastructure for a future state had come too late. Incidentally, this was not exactly how things were viewed from the Jewish side. Ben-Gurion, although never doubting that a Jewish state would come into being, nevertheless feared its existence would be endangered by lack of food and fuel and demoralisation in Jerusalem.[9]

The British estimated that the Egyptians and the Legion would be the most important factors, from a strictly military point of view. The army reversed its earlier opinion of the Arab 'salvation army' (ALA); it became evident that although this force consisted of about 13 000 volunteers, it was in quite a miserable position and suffered from lack of food, medical supplies, and administration. This was a correct assessment, as only half of the force eventually took part in the fighting, sustaining activity for two months and achieving virtually nothing.[10]

It was most important then, as it is now, to remember that the Arab armies did not intend to (and actually did not) use most of their military force in the battle. This intention, although not made public, was apparent even then from the lack of intensity and amount of preparation for the war. This Arab reluctance to use all the forces at their disposal was fully realised by the CoS. From their legation in Baghdad, the British gathered that the Iraqis were unable to contribute any substantial manpower to the campaign. Internal security problems, mainly unrest in Kurdistan, allowed the Iraqis to send only two battalions. Logistically, the Iraqis could maintain only one battalion in the field, but even this was dependent on resources from either Syria or Transjordan. Owing to their proximity to the battlefield, the Syrians could maintain larger forces in the field for some weeks. However, they suffered from a lack of ammunition and lamentable maintenance. One would have anticipated better performance from the Syrians, but this was not forthcoming, probably due to a lack of motivation and the small number of troops.[11]

An excellent example of the fault of purely military predication was the CoS' assessment of the Legion's capability. The CoS predicted that the 7400 Legioneers would be able to stay in the field for eight months. Militarily speaking, it was reasonable to expect the well-organised and equipped Legion with its mechanised regiments to fulfil these expectations and probably change the outcome of the war.[12] However, its ammunition supply depended on the British who, as we shall see later, stopped supplying arms and ammunition in the early stages of the war. Second, the Legion had a purely limited military task and was mainly destined for the struggle in Jerusalem and its outskirts; otherwise it was employed to control the cities of eastern Palestine.[13]

The Saudis had no regular army and its irregular Bedouins had hardly any ammunition to exhaust. They were denied entrance to Transjordan and joined the Egyptian forces.[14]

The CoS had little confidence in the ability of the Egyptian army. Although it could deploy a large number of troops, it had no experience of maintenance in the field. The military experts expected that the soldiers' morale outside Egypt would be very low; a situation confirmed by Nasser's memoirs. Furthermore, like the other armies, the Egyptian army suffered from a shortage of reserves of ammunition. The military adviser in the British Embassy in Cairo stated that the forces trained in Egypt 'hardly warrant consideration as a serious invading force'.[15]

It is worth noting that it was rather problematical to ascertain the impact Egyptian participation would have on the Palestine campaign. In fact it was impossible to establish whether the Egyptians would participate at all. As late as April 1948, the Eastern Department did not expect Egyptian involvement. According to the British embassy in Cairo, the Egyptians did not actually object to the existence of a Jewish state if partition were imposed by an international force or, as Chapman-Andrews called it, 'an international force majeure'.[16] The embassy's reports were indicating Egyptian doubts about the success of the campaign. Yet the pressure from other Arab countries was mounting and, if Egypt were to maintain its leading role in the Arab world, it had no other choice. Sir Ronald Campbell, the British ambassador in Cairo wished the British would prevent Egyptian participation, but admitted that this hope was in vain. Arab historiographers of the war disagree and claim that the Egyptian army wanted to participate, and in April it had sent Egyptian units to the Palestinian border.[17]

In May, the Egyptian intentions and preparations were less obscure. The news of the Legion's entrance into Arab Palestine was probably what triggered King Farouk's decision to participate in the fighting. It seems that the palace was at odds with the Egyptian government. The monarch, who belonged to a non-Egyptian dynasty, needed to prove his Arab patriotism and loyalty. The government felt that the army was indispensable as an internal security force in a country where more and more political groups were resorting to violence and acts of terror. The Palace was supported by the Rector of Al-Azhar university and religious clergymen who declared the war in Palestine a 'Jihad' (a holy war), which led the British embassy to warn the monarch that unless the army participated in the war, the government would fall. The government was finally convinced after the Arab leaders had cleverly chosen to convene in Cairo the decisive meeting of the Arab League to determine the military operation in Palestine, thereby arousing the already excited Egyptian mob. In a meeting at the Zafran Palace, the Arab League Council decided to accelerate equipment of the Arab armies and grant the Legion, the main Arab force, 1.5 million Egyptian pounds. Three days before the invasion, the Egyptian Senate approved the intervention of the army. The army demanded this Parliamentary approval so as not to be the sole body responsible in the event of a defeat.[18]

One can only agree with Sir Ronald Campbell's assertion that Egyptian involvement would have more effect on the internal situation in Egypt than on the war in Palestine. On 13 May the Egyptian Senate declared an *état de siège* to secure the Egyptian army's means of communication, supplies, and so on. The embassy was concerned that this law would be abused in the future. After martial law had been imposed Mahmud Nokrashi, the premier, was nominated military Governor-General. He ordered general censorship and nominated military governors to certain areas.[19]

This was the situation on the Arab side. In terms of troops, the Jewish Agency could potentially mobilize the same number of soldiers as the Arab governments engaged in the fighting. However, as Ben-Gurion himself understood, the number of troops was not itself an important factor. He told the Jewish Agency that the Jews had enough personnel: the problem was equipment. The Arab armies benefited from the absence of a proper Jewish navy and air force and, more important, the Hagana's lack of artillery. This situation changed during the first truce.[20] Thus until the first truce, the Arabs enjoyed some superiority owing to their air force's ability to inflict considerable damage, but this superiority became useless once their ground forces could no longer advance.

In many ways the British were backing the right horse. They were not assisting in enforcing partition, yet they were assisting in implementing it by approving Abdullah's programme. The British involvement in Abdullah's plans enabled CoS to estimate accurately the outcome of the war, allowed the Foreign Office to control (to some extent) the development of the fighting, and granted the British Cabinet the opportunity to plan carefully the next stages of its policy towards the area. It is tempting to leave the analysis of British policy at this point and conclude that it was sheer pragmatism and perhaps opportunism which facilitated this British success. However, it would be an overstatement. The agreement with Abdullah should be considered in light of broader British interests in the Middle East. It was highly important for Bevin to signal to the Arab world that the evacuation of Palestine was not the beginning of British withdrawal from the Middle East. Bevin conceived the treaties with Iraq and Transjordan as substitutes for the loss of Palestine. However, if Palestine were to be shaped politically, it was necessary for Britain to devise ways of including the successors of Palestine in a general defence system covering the entire area.[21]

The main requirement of such a system, according to Bevin and the

CoS, was a network of bases which could be manned at short notice in case of a war in the Middle East. In February 1948 it was hard to envisage how a future Jewish state could be fitted into it. While the officials in the Eastern Department and Bevin accepted the state of Israel as a *fait accompli*, they showed little faith in the Jewish state. Israel was envisaged as a base for Communist infiltration into the Middle East. Thus if any territory was important strategically, as the Negev was for Britain, it was preferable to see it in Transjordanian hands before the frontiers were shaped. Furthermore, the Office and the Foreign Secretary realised that the borders as defined in the UN resolution were to be altered according to the intentions and ability of the 'actors' involved. The Negev was not included in the Arab state.[22] The head of the Eastern Department toyed with the idea that the borders would be reshaped.

> It is tempting to think that Transjordan might transgress the boundaries of the UN Jewish state to the extent of establishing a corridor across the Southern Negev, joining the existing Transjordan territory to the Mediterranean at Gaza. This would have immense strategic advantages for us both in cutting the Jewish state, and therefore communist influence, off [from] the Red Sea.[23]

Four main conclusions emerge from this study. Bevin's arrangements with Abdullah prior to the war in Palestine were the basis on which British policy towards the Arab–Israeli conflict was formulated. These arrangements guided the Eastern Department in its attitude towards the Bernadotte proposals and the Israeli–Jordanian negotiations. Second, the realistic British presumptions about the course of the war in Palestine enabled the Foreign Office to adjust itself with considerable ease to the new situation created by the establishment of the Jewish state. Third, those British assumptions before the end of the Mandate facilitated the inclusion of Israel in strategic British planning. Finally, this policy prevented British recognition of the existence of a Palestinian problem apart from the human aspect – that is, the refugees – in the years between 1948 and 1967. However, this attitude was shared by all the countries and powers involved in the Arab–Israeli conflict.

One might add another conclusion about Egypt's role in the Arab–Israeli conflict. The lack of enthusiasm on the Egyptian side for participating in the struggle to 'liberate Palestine', and the shelving of the Palestinian problem until the dispute with Britain was solved, explains the British tendency to see the Israeli–Egyptian dispute as one of minor importance. Indeed, until Nasser came to power it was impossible to regard it in any other way. Some writers, such as the very experienced Jacques Berque, tended to see the struggle against Zionism in 1948 as a fight against the ultimate imperialism. This assumption seems to be out of place;[24] the war in Palestine did not take the place of the struggle against the British presence in Egypt. Moreover, the pressure to enter Palestine came from Syria and Iraq, and not from Egypt. As Jon Marlow correctly remarked, the defeat in Palestine enabled the Egyptians to concentrate on issues which were more important with regard to their national aspirations.[25] The only person in Egypt to support the campaign whole-heartedly was King Farouk, who hoped to appear loyal to the Arab and Egyptian cause by taking a militant stand. His ministers, unlike the King, were not of foreign origin and therefore not suspected of lack of patriotism; thus they were less enthusiastic about the whole issue.

FROM THE BEGINNING OF THE WAR TO THE FIRST TRUCE

When the Arab operations in Palestine began and the last British soldiers were leaving the country, His Majesty's representatives in the various Arab capitals assured the Arab leaders of British diplomatic and political assistance. However, at an early stage the Foreign Office stipulated its conditions for such cooperation; the Arab governments would inform the Office of their intentions in Palestine in such a way as would enable 'the friends of the Arab countries to defend them'.[26]

Only the Lebanon informed the British of their intentions in answer to Bevin's inquiries. Riad Al-Sulh assured the British representative in Beirut that the Lebanese army was merely playing a defensive and token role in the war. He expected a British initiative in favour of the Arabs at an early stage.[27] However, the other Arab governments were interested more in military assistance. Diplomatic support had little importance in Arab eyes, since it became clear that the UN or Security Council resolutions were not enforceable unless imposed by the Great Powers or accepted by both sides. The flow of arms to the three Arab countries which had treaties with Britain continued until the first truce was announced by the Security Council. Arab refusal to renew this truce brought an abrupt end to this supply until the end of hostilities in Palestine.[28]

Thus British involvement did not, and was not, intended to tip the balance in the war. The British wanted to preserve the new status quo that had emerged after the first ten days of fighting. The shape of the political map at the end of June 1948 was satisfactory as far as the foreign office was concerned. Any further Arab or Jewish attempts to change this map, by continuing to fight, seemed to London to threaten British interests in the area.

During the fighting, British intervention was guided by the same principles as the evacuation process. That is, only when British installations or interests were under direct threat did Britain act firmly against the attacking side. The clash between the RAF and Israeli Air Force in the last days of the war was an exceptional event and its significance will be examined in a different context in this work. British intervention intensified when the truce negotiations began and when UN mediation was attempted from July 1948 onwards.

A week after the war between the Jews and the regular Arab armies had broken out, the situation was as follows: the Syrians and the Iraqis were withdrawing from the UN Jewish areas. The Lebanese were on the defensive and would not enter Palestine. The Legion tightened its siege on Jerusalem, and the Egyptian army moved mainly in the UN Arab state. This situation was viewed favourably in London. The Legion had most of Arab Palestine, and the UN resolution was implemented almost in its entirety; that is, except for a small part of the Negev, there were no regular forces in the territory recommended for the Jewish state.[29] Furthermore, since the Jews were in Arab areas (notably in Western Galilee), officials in the Eastern Department envisaged a possible solution: Western Galilee could be Jewish, while the Negev could be restored to the Arabs. Thus reasoned the officials in London, 'the two states would then be geographically cohesive'.[30] Hence, with these alterations in the map of the partition of Palestine, the Foreign Office accepted the UN resolution of November 1947.

British involvement intensified when the Arabs found themselves facing a Jewish offensive. By then it was clear that the joint Arab effort to save Palestine had failed. With this bitter realisation came, for the first time, an Arab appeal for more substantial British involvement. The Iraqi Regent told the British ambassador in Baghdad that if the war were to be stopped by a great power or by the UN, Arab honour would be satisfied. The Foreign Office suggested that the Arabs should agree to a truce. However, the trend in the Arab world was to continue the fighting. In Dara'a, the Arab leaders pressured Abdullah to deepen the involvement of the Arab Legion and to have it move against the Jewish state, an action regarded by Abdullah as insane.[31]

The Transjordanian King was thinking along different lines. After a week of fighting, the Legion had achieved most of its objectives. In order to preserve these objectives it was important to exert pressure on the Arabs to agree to a cease-fire. The continuation of the war by the Arab side depended on the supply of arms and ammunition; the only power which could supply them was Great Britain. It was then that the Arab leaders, and especially the General Secretary of the Arab League, Azzam Pasha, realised the decisive role Britain was playing. Encouraged by Britain's reluctance to follow the American example in recognising the state of Israel, Azzam wrote to Bevin that now was the appropriate time to reach a comprehensive Anglo–Arab agreement. Although Azzam did not mention the *quid pro quo*, namely British assistance in the war, it was clear that this was what was meant by that deal. The Syrians were even more desperate. The Syrian President asked for equipment and ammunition through Abdullah.[32] The British adamantly refused to comply with the Syrian request for arms, owing ostensibly to the organised opposition by the latter to the British treaties with Iraq and Transjordan. However, what mattered more was Britain's satisfaction with the course of the war. It was willing to support only the Legion and, like Abdullah, waited anxiously for the UN to impose a general truce. However, the Legion's plans for a swift implementation of Abdullah's ambitions were obstructed by the prolonged campaign over Jerusalem.

THE WAR IN JERUSALEM

The British did not consult Abdullah over the future of Jerusalem, mainly because the UN resolution granting the city a *corpus separatum* was supported by the Foreign Office. However, the UN committee of experts which was supposed to draft a paper on the issue failed to do so.[33] The High Commissioner in Palestine then urged the CO to find some solution since, 'It is unthinkable that Jerusalem should be left to become a cockpit of internecine strife and that the holy city should lapse into a pitched battlefield.'[34] However, the Foreign Office did not envisage the Israelis and the Transjordanians fighting around the holy places, and it seemed at the time (February 1948) that the status quo would remain; that is, the Jewish neighbourhoods would fall within the Jewish state while the Arab ones would come under a Legion occupation. Kirkbride supported this view and was convinced that both sides would exclude Jerusalem from the fighting.[35]

These British assumptions did not coincide with Abdullah's line of thought. The King was confident that by assuming the ancient role of his family, that is, of protecting the holy places of Islam, he would be granted Arab recognition for the annexation of the Arab areas of Palestine. Moreover, he hoped to emerge as the guardian of the holy places of all the religions in the eyes of the world. This aspiration, expressed in front of Kirkbride in February 1948, did not impress the British, and neither did Abdullah's letter to Bevin in which the King declared that owing to his religious and national duties to the whole of Arab Palestine and Jerusalem he was doubtful whether he could 'do nothing' in the war. Kirkbride thought the Legion was 'quite inadequate for such a task'.[36]

At the end of the first week the Legion was still engaged in fighting over Jerusalem, a state of affairs which in British eyes could have changed the hitherto successful implementation of the Greater Transjordan plan. Indeed Bevin, unimpressed by Abdullah's sentiments over Jerusalem, had warned the King at a very early stage of the war that such a situation would mean a departure from the original scheme and warned him that he would consider discontinuing military and financial supplies to the Legion.[37]

How then could Abdullah successfully continue the battle over Jerusalem? Fortunately for the King, Kirkbride had changed his mind somewhat about the chances of achieving political goals in Jerusalem through military means. He supported the King's arguments that he was forced to enter the battle over Jerusalem because of Jewish occupation of the Arab quarters of the city. Moreover, Kirkbride agreed with Abdullah that he could not simply reach the boundaries of the Jewish state and then remain inactive.[38] Thus Abdullah could have felt that he had Kirkbride's understanding, if not support, for his action in Jerusalem.

This is not to say that Kirkbride overlooked the strength of the Jewish position in Jerusalem (owing to the large Jewish population in the city) and of the depth of the Jewish sentiment towards the city. He and Foreign Office experts understood Ben-Gurion's refusal to consent to an agreement which would not include Jewish control over the Jewish quarters. That is, Ben-Gurion was unable to give up any part of Jerusalem due to its national importance and religious significance to the Jewish people. One British official even envisaged a *coup d'état* by the Irgun or Lehi in that case.[39]

One question therefore still remains unanswered. Why were Abdullah and the Jewish Agency not able to at least reach an understanding over partitioning of Jerusalem similar to the one they had reached over eastern Palestine? It could not have been out of negligence; it seems unlikely that such an important issue escaped the mind of either Ben-Gurion or Abdullah. A more plausible explanation (or, rather, speculation) is that both parties understood that the difference in opinion on this issue was too great and left it to be decided on the battlefield.

Like anywhere else in Palestine, the preservation of Jerusalem's special status depended on law and order. In April 1948, the clashes between Jews and Arabs were mainly on the roads into the city; within a short time they had escalated into a fierce battle in which each side aimed to capture the areas evacuated by the British. By 15 May the Jews had established themselves in their own neighbourhoods and in some Arab quarters. The outbreak of fighting ended a short cease-fire achieved by the efforts of the High Commissioner and agreed to by the AHC and the Jewish Agency. However, from 15 May onwards, the Arab partner was the Arab Legion.[40]

Military intelligence in Jerusalem asserted that the Jewish forces could seize Jerusalem with no great difficulty if they chose to do so. However, the Hagana knew about Abdullah's intentions to capture the city and preferred to consolidate their positions in the first days of the battle. Thus Abdullah was not stopped by the British and, contrary to their gloomy intelligence estimations, the King was able to carry out his operation since he directed the bulk of the Legion force to the city. Furthermore, he was assisted by an Egyptian contingent which captured the southern approaches to Jerusalem. Nevertheless, as was pointed out to Abdullah and his government by Legion officers, he was taking a great risk. Legion Headquarters held that if most of the Legion forces were directed towards the battle over Jerusalem, the rural areas between Hebron and Nablus would be exposed to possible Jewish offensives. Moreover the Legion was worried about leaving these areas in the hands of the Iraqi and Egyptian forces on the scene.[41]

Abdullah was nevertheless determined to carry on with his plans. The Hashemite–Jewish agreement seemed to be in real danger when Abdullah decided to launch his attack immediately after the British evacuated the city. By then both sides had thrown the bulk of their forces into the battle for Jerusalem. At that stage Abdullah informed the British of the course he was about to pursue. His main argument was that the situation in Jerusalem was obstructing him from carrying out his original plan. At the outset of its offensive, the Legion succeeded in keeping the old city and small parts of the new city. Thus, a week after the fighting had begun, the city was *de facto* divided.[42]

After the Legion's successes in Jerusalem, culminating in the capture of the Jewish quarter in the old city, the position of the Legion became more and more problematic. The fighting in Jerusalem had left the Legion spread over 6000 sq. km. of the country, leaving it to deal with policing operations while conducting a war against Jewish forces in the city. It was also a liability to Britain, owing to the participation of British officers in fighting within the old city, a development which had considerably embarrassed the Foreign Office. Bevin realised that the best thing to do was to preserve the *status quo*. He suggested to the King that he put the holy places under neutral administration in order to win over world public opinion, and that he agree to a cease-fire. It was indeed priceless advice. The Jewish forces improved their positions, and the lines on both sides seemed to be fortified and able to resist further attack.[43]

At this juncture it was highly important for the British to exert pressure on the Arabs to end the war in Palestine. In a letter to the Arab leaders, Bevin advocated that the Arabs accept a permanent truce in Jerusalem. The Transjordanians accepted the truce only too willingly, not only because of the strong Israeli position on the battlefield, but also due to their achievements which might have been endangered by further fighting: the Legion controlled the main supply routes into the city as well as the source of the Jerusalem water supply (Ras Al-E'in) and the city pumping station (Latrun). This was an advantageous political position, as the Jews were completely 'cut off' apart from a rough new road, the 'Burma road', which had been opened as a by-pass by the Jewish forces. Thus the Legion achieved some of its objectives in the war of Jerusalem. The cease-fire was, in fact, obtained after the Transjordanians were convinced by the Foreign Office to open the road between Tel-Aviv and Jerusalem, the principal Jewish precondition for accepting the truce.[44]

During the first truce it became apparent that Abdullah was satisfied with the results and agreed to the creation of the 'no-man's land' areas between the two parties. The new Jewish state desperately needed this agreement since it included the renewal of supplies to Jerusalem. However, the water supply was never resumed, in spite of the Security Council order to that effect.

THE FIRST TRUCE

Whereas the Legion's main effort had been directed towards Jerusalem, the other Arab armies operated in south and north Palestine. The latter operations were ineffective and hardly changed the situation. The Iraqi, Syrian and Lebanese forces had scarcely succeeded in crossing the Palestine frontiers. Although the Egyptian army had caused serious trouble to the Hagana at the beginning of the fighting, by the end of May it had decided to take up a static position north of Majdal, on the coast, with no intention of advancing any further.[45]

The Egyptian army seemed to have entered into a tacit non-interference pact with the Jewish settlements. The only settlement the Egyptians had occupied was astride the main road, thus giving them no choice. In the main it was a case of live and let live.[46]

It is worth noting that the British had opposed an American proposal in the Security Council for an immediate cease-fire on 17 May, partly because the Americans included a threat of sanctions under Article 39 of the UN charter, but mainly since Abdullah had not yet completed his occupation of the Arab areas of Palestine. The British claimed in the Security Council that they had 'grave doubts about the wisdom and expediency of involving Article 39 of the charter', since it was impossible to indicate who was the aggressor.[47] This seems to have been a British tactic to gain time for the Arabs. Thus, with British support, the Security Council agreed to comply with an Arab request to delay the resolution.[48]

Bevin explained to the Americans that it was Middle Eastern susceptibility to Soviet influence which caused him to oppose any measures taken against the Arab states.[49] Israeli writers claim that Britain advised the Arabs not to accept the Security Council call for a cease-fire; however, there is no evidence for this in the British documents surveyed for this work.[50] Nevertheless it is possible that some local British officials were encouraged by the initial Egyptian success and hoped that the Negev would eventually fall into Arab hands.

After a week of fighting the British not only sought to persuade the Arab side to accept a truce in Palestine; they even initiated a resolution of their own in the Security Council. This resolution called for a truce of four weeks. Furthermore, the resolution banned the introduction of fighting personnel or men of military age into the area and placed an embargo on the supply of arms for the duration of the truce. However, the Foreign Office had to consent to two amendments proposed by the Americans. The first was that the prohibition of the movement of fighting personnel and material should include all countries involved in the war (not only the local Arabs and Jews). Second, Israel could admit new immigrants of fighting age but could not train them.[51]

Thus on 29 May the Security Council adopted a resolution calling for a truce.[52] It should be emphasised that the Israelis had immediately accepted both the resolution initiated by the Americans and that initiated by the British, while the Arabs' acceptance was slow in coming.

The British attitude towards the Arab governments became somewhat harsher during the last week of May 1948. Whereas the British government opposed the imposition of sanctions by the UN, it was not deterred from threatening the Arabs with the very same sanctions. Bevin gave the Arab leaders a clear ultimatum: if they did not agree to a cease-fire, Britain would stop sending war material and withdraw British officers from the Legion.[53]

The Transjordanians in particular could not but accept this British ultimatum. By the end of May, the ammunition of the Legion was running out. The Legion had only enough ammunition for the first and second fronts. Furthermore, the Egyptian authorities had seized a ship loaded with ammunition belonging to Transjordan while it was on its way from Suez to Aqaba. This was an Egyptian sign of dismay at the British refusal to supply arms to them. The British army eventually agreed to replace the shipment, but the UN embargo was imposed before this could be done. Towards the end of the first truce, the Foreign Office made it clear that as long as the fighting continued in Palestine, His Majesty's government was unwilling to provide any war material for Arab armies engaged in the war in that country.[54]

The main reason for this British determination to stop the fighting was the Foreign Office's prognosis for the course of the war. According to the Eastern Department's assessment, Abdullah could eventually capture the whole of Jerusalem, but no other Arab successes were anticipated. On the contrary, gloomier prospects were predicted for the other Arab armies. The Syrian, Lebanese and Iraqi forces were considered out of the game. It seemed that any Egyptian advance would cause the destruction of their army. Thus the only thing the Egyptian commanders could do was to order their units to dig in, causing a stalemate.[55]

One should not, however, forget the role played by the Americans. As Bevin pointed out: 'At the same time we have been in constant

consultation with the US government with a view of trying to
harmonise our policies and prevent any further sudden developments,
like US recognition of the Jewish state.'[56] The coordination of policy
with the Americans was essential on the eve of the Berlin crisis; His
Majesty's Government could not allow a serious clash of interests to
arise. There was a need to follow the American suit.

There were additional reasons for British support for the cease-fire.
From the British viewpoint, Jerusalem was the most pressing problem,
and the Foreign Office hoped that during the truce the UN would set
up an international enclave there. Apart from Jerusalem, the British
were satisfied with the way the frontiers had crystallised after almost a
month of fighting (Jaffa, Acre and Western Galilee under Jewish
control; the Negev or most of it under Arab control). The Foreign
Office asserted that if the Arabs had accepted the idea of a Jewish state
at an early stage, they might have been able to claim considerable
frontier changes.[57]

However, as long as the British could not convince the Arab states
that the war in Palestine was lost, or that there was a face-saving
solution for the situation, it was clear that the fighting would go on. In
order to overcome the Arabs' 'lack of understanding' the Information
and News Department in the Foreign Office issued a series of
comments and communiqués to the effect that 'we do not regard the
Arab war as victorious'.[58]

The British effort paid off, and one can assume that more than
anything else it was Bevin's ultimatum which played the decisive role
in bringing about Arab acceptance of the truce. During the discussions
of the political committee of the League, the Egyptians and
Transjordanians were the major proponents of acceptance of the
Security Council proposal, while the Syrians and the Iraqis were the
main opponents. After a week of fighting, the Syrians realised that
Abdullah had deceived them by not fulfilling his role as the supreme
commander of the Arab forces in Palestine. Ostensibly the Iraqis took
a similar viewpoint, namely that the lack of success in the first week
was due to the shortcomings of the supreme commander. However,
the Iraqis were not prepared to replace the Hashemite bond by a
coalition between Syria and Iraq (not withstanding the Iraqi
realisation that the war was lost, very much owing to Abdullah's
policy). No one could escape the unpleasant truth that ten days after
the fighting had begun the weakness of the supply system of the Arab
forces and their lack of sources of ammunition and stores made itself
felt in a way that rendered any new campaign impossible.[59]

It is notable that the BMEO did not concur with Bevin's decision to threaten the Arab governments with the cessation of arms supplies.[60] As in many other cases in the period under review, when the issue was the British attitude to the Arab governments, the BMEO found itself alone amongst the diplomats in its advocacy of the Arab case. Sir John Troutbeck was supported by the CoS, who failed to see the advantages of the embargo. The complications arising from it embarrassed the CoS, who found it hard to disagree with an Iraqi appeal to renew the arms supply. The embargo was critically hampering the Iraqi air force's ability to act in the event of internal unrest in that country and, in particular in Kurdistan. However, a week after the Air Ministry had complied with the Iraqi request, the order was cancelled due to the pressure of the Foreign Office.[61]

The British embargo should be assessed against the background of the situation on the Israeli side. During the first truce, the Israelis had had time to consolidate their position by receiving arms from the Eastern bloc and by making the evacuated areas an integral part of the Jewish state.[62]

The Israelis had utilised the time for purchasing necessary equipment; the first cannons arrived during this period. The general mobilisation was completed and supplies to Jerusalem were resumed during the truce. Nevertheless, one should not exaggerate the extent of the reinforcement received by the Israelis. As Count Bernadotte noted in his report to the Security Council, the import of the war material was being closely observed and, apart from the case of the 'Altalena', there was no evidence of any large-scale import of weapons or, for that matter, of fighting personnel. Moreover, the reinforcements for Israel were balanced by further reinforcements of troops on the Arab side as more regular and irregular forces entered Palestine.[63]

Could Arab acceptance of the first truce be regarded as another British success? (The first one had prevented the Arab armies from entering Palestine before 15 May.) Bevin certainly felt it was an important British achievement. The Eastern Department was more cautious about this conclusion and advised the Foreign Secretary to omit this observation from a memorandum he had prepared for the Cabinet. Bevin certainly influenced Arab views, but the cause of the stalemate was also to be found in the situation on the battlefield: namely, Transjordan's reluctance to advance into the Jewish state. Furthermore, the Egyptian difficulties on the Southern front, the inefficiency of the Syrian and Lebanese forces, and the apathy of the Iraqi contingent had also contributed greatly to the new situation.

3 Britain, Bernadotte and the Greater Transjordan

On 20 May 1948, the Security Council appointed Count Folke Bernadotte, President of the Swedish Red Cross, UN mediator for Palestine. The GA empowered the mediator to cooperate with the Truce Commission (appointed in April that year) in observing the truce and in endeavouring to achieve a solution to the conflict.[1]

One writer has claimed that the British offered the appointment of a mediator only when it was clear that the Arab armies were exhausted and this was in order to be able to save them. While it stands to reason that the British offered mediation as a means of solving the conflict and thus of saving the Arab armies, the British became involved with Bernadotte mainly due to their concern about the impact of his mission on the British position in the area. For this purpose they decided to appoint the British consul in Jerusalem, Sir Hugh Dow, to undertake special liaison with the Count's headquarters.[2]

Bevin asserted that there were three possible lines of approach to the Palestinian problem in June 1948. As he wrote to the Cabinet, Bernadotte's efforts could lead to a partition or they could facilitate the implementation of Bevin's plan (provincial autonomy). A third possibility was the annexation of central Palestine to Transjordan and the south to Egypt. The Foreign Secretary and the Foreign Office preferred the last solution: 'We shall see no objection to this [solution] provided it was the wish of the inhabitants there, and there might indeed be certain advantages from our point of view.'[3] In fact Britain and Transjordan would have reaped all the benefits from such a solution. But they did not take into account the wishes or opinions of the local inhabitants.

As has been argued by some writers, there seems little doubt that Bernadotte was under strong British influence.[4] A close comparison between British presumptions about the development of the war and Bernadotte's later proposal brings us to the conclusion that the mediator was striving for a *Pax Britannica* more than anything else. It is, however, important to note that British thinking had little impact on the Count's first proposals, which were mainly an outcome of his impression of the Arab demands, and neither did the British participate in the first round of the discussion.[5]

Ben-Gurion, for one, was convinced that Bernadotte was a British agent and consequently firmly rejected all the Count's proposals. In fact the PGI as a whole showed little confidence in Bernadotte and treated him as an enemy. The Israelis' first representative to the UN, Abba Eban, declared that Israel did not trust the mediator and reiterated Ben-Gurion's call for direct negotiations. When the Count inquired about these Israeli declarations he was told by the IFO that Israel had never asked for the services of the mediator.[6]

BERNADOTTE'S FIRST PROPOSALS

Bernadotte's first suggestions were made at the end of June 1948.[7] The Count proposed that Palestine, as defined in the original Mandate entrusted to the UK in 1922 (that is, including Transjordan), would form a union comprising two member states: one Arab, one Jewish. The mediator had in fact reversed the UN partition lines. Whereas the state offered to the Arabs had included Galilee, Bernadotte's proposals granted Galilee to the Jews and instead gave the Negev and central Palestine to the Arab state. This exchange of territories was proposed by the American representative in the UN, Philip Jessup, and is therefore referred to as the 'Jessup principle'. This principle would be reiterated by the Americans when they became involved in the conflict. Thus, within the boundaries of this union between Transjordan and Palestine, the mediator suggested that the Negev be given to the Arabs and western Galilee to the Jews. Jerusalem would be in the territory of the Arab state and the Jews living in it would have administrative autonomy. Haifa and Jaffa would be free ports, as would Lydda airport. The two states would form an economic, military and political union. The frontiers, according to this scheme, would be negotiated. Immigration would be under the control of each member of the proposed union, and 'after two years either member would be entitled to request the Social and Economic Council of the UN to review policy of the union [on this issue]'.[8] The mediator suggested the prolongation of the truce to give time for both sides to consider and implement his proposals.[9]

Bevin and Bernadotte concurred on the principle of mutual Arab and Jewish acceptance of any solution. Thus as Sir Alexander Cadogan, the British representative in the UN, explained to the GA, the mediator was not sent to implement a UN partition resolution which was unacceptable to the Arabs; on the contrary, it was an attempt to get away from the impossibility . . . of enforcing that resolution'.[10] However, the first proposals seemed to cause even more resentment than the November 1947 resolution. Both sides rejected it categorically. The mediator hastened to stress that 'these ideas were put forth with no intimation of finality'.[11]

The Foreign Office thought that the main fault with the first proposals was that they were too vague and unbinding and therefore disapproved of by the Arabs. Azzam Pasha, the General Secretary of the Arab League, told the Count that the League was misled into believing that his proposals would not be influenced by any previous UN decisions and would be based on the political reality as it existed after the truce was implemented. Azzam claimed that neither condition had been fulfilled. The first proposals were merely another version of the partition resolution.[12] Furthermore, according to the Political Committee of the League, the proposals were based on the 'false conception' that there was a link between Transjordan and Palestine.[13] Azzam argued that this was a Zionist conception and unacceptable even to the Transjordanians themselves. At least in public, Azzam enjoyed the support of Tawfiq Abu Al-Huda in the Political Committee for this denial of the link between Transjordan and Palestine.[14]

The British could not accept a proposal which the Arabs had rejected. As the Head of the BMEO put it, the mediator should be impressed with the importance of carrying out his duties effectively; that is, to try to satisfy the Arab demands.[15]

Moreover Britain had to be clearer about its own attitude towards the mediator's proposals. Despite the low probability of the mediator's proposals being accepted by the parties, Britain had to assess the proposals independently. The Foreign Office had to find out the best means of safeguarding Britain's strategic requirements in Palestine. It had first to realise how the plan would affect its strategic position and then to determine what might be the reaction of each party, in particular the Arab side. Here lies the main difference between the Count's attitude and the Foreign Office posture. Whereas Bernadotte had a mandate from the Security Council to bring an end to the Arab–Israeli conflict, the Foreign Office, although agreeing with this objective, regarded the securing of British strategic requirements as Britain's main interest in the mediator's mission. On the other hand, it is striking that both the mediator and the Foreign Office tended to overlook the main source of Arab resentment. The Arabs were not prepared to accept the principle of the inevitability of a Jewish state.

The Count himself was wrongly convinced in July that the Arabs, although unwilling, would accept a Jewish state. He based his optimism on a conversation he had had with Mahmud Nokrashi, the Egyptian premier.[16]

Bernadotte considered three possibilities with regard to Arab Palestine. A separate Arab state, annexation of the Arab parts to Transjordan, or division of the territory between the Arab countries. He found out that the Egyptians had no desire to keep the Gaza Strip or any other part, so the last possibility was ruled out. Since most of the Arab world opposed the second possibility, Bernadotte tended to favour the first: a separate Arab state in Palestine.[17] However, British opposition to such a solution did not escape the Count's attention. The Foreign Office's Palestine experts did not expect an Arab agreement on the disposal of the Arab areas. Incorporation into Transjordan seemed to the Foreign Office to be the most practical and favourable solution.[18]

Moreover, Bernadotte shared the Foreign Office's apprehension and hostility to the Mufti. When asked by Nokrashi in Cairo whether he would shake hands with the Mufti, who was sitting in the next room, the Count replied: 'As I have shaken hands with Himmler, I don't mind shaking hands with the Mufti.'[19] So the Foreign Office's first concern was to avoid the creation of an independent Palestinian state and also ensure the incorporation of the Arab areas in Transjordan.

This was, no doubt, the bone of contention between Bernadotte and the British in their respective attitudes to the Count's first proposals. As for the mediator's suggestion for the future of Jerusalem, the British agreed to see the city in Arab hands, although officially they declared their support for an international city. There were other points which satisfied the British, such as the mediator's insistence that Haifa become an international port. An international Haifa would have enabled the British to use the port and would have prevented the Iraqis from blocking the flow of oil from Kirkuk. This argument in favour of an international Haifa indicates that, at the time, Britain could not envisage an agreement with Israel on Haifa. Until Britain recognised Israel in January 1949, the latter was considered a hostile factor in the area. Only the War Office suggested that in due course this arrangement could be replaced by an agreement with Israel.[20]

Notwithstanding their contentment with the solution offered for Haifa, the British still hoped that the Transjordanians would be allowed to have their own port on the Mediterranean. After all, even if the Transjordanians were granted a corridor to Haifa it would always be under the threat of Jewish bisection and constitute a source of continued friction. Thus the British preferred to see Gaza as part of the Arab territories being incorporated into the Transjordanian state. This would not only have secured safe access to the sea, but would also have given the British the same privileges they enjoyed under the Anglo-Transjordan treaty. Thus the main feature of British thinking, after they learned of Bernadotte's first plan, was to persuade him to accept this solution.[21]

One clear conclusion can be drawn from this British attitude: in June 1948 the Foreign Office preferred partition to federation (as offered in the mediator's first proposals). The officials in London believed that partition would weaken the Jewish state and they also hoped that it would promise the incorporation of the Arab areas of Palestine into Transjordan. Still, Bevin considered the first proposals more favourable to the Arabs than the UN partition resolution. The Foreign Secretary asserted that although the annexation of western Galilee to the Jewish state was an economic gain for Israel, the Arab world would gain geographical integrity (from Damascus to Cairo through the West Bank and the Negev) from the Bernadotte plan.

Bevin shared Arab apprehension about Bernadotte's specific proposals regarding immigration policy. The clause enabled each party after two years to question the immigration policy of the other by referring the matter to the Social and Economic Council of the UN. Bevin wrote in a Foreign Office minute: 'After having over-crowded their own country', the Jews would claim 'a right of immigration into Arab territories'.[22] However, Bevin understood but did not sympathise with Arab fears of an Arab–Jewish union. On the contrary, he hoped that this Arab fear would lead them to accept partition. Partition of any kind meant the creation of a Jewish state in Palestine. Hence any British pressure on Bernadotte to feature partition as the main element of his plan was tantamount to a recognition of the state of Israel. Bevin had probably realised the difficult position his country found itself in when he declared that Britain possessed the ability to reduce Arab opposition to an independent Jewish state. How was it possible to convince the Arabs of the inevitability of a Jewish state, when Britain itself did not recognise it?

BERNADOTTE'S SECOND PROPOSALS

Both sides rejected the first proposals. The Arabs rejected any form of recognition of the Jewish state. They feared that after two years the Jews would appeal to the UN for permission to continue immigration. Moreover, the Arabs rejected the idea that the Jews should have any say in the affairs of the Arab state.[23]

According to Ben-Gurion's biographer, the Israeli premier's main objection was that he could not agree to a plan sponsored by the British. The Israelis obviously rejected the idea of an Arab Jerusalem and the loss of the Negev. A disappointed Bevin told the British Cabinet that the Arabs had missed a golden opportunity: namely, Arab acceptance of the plan, in the face of Israeli refusal, would have made world public opinion more favourable to the Arab cause.[24]

However, more than anything else, the Israelis refused to consent to any final demarcation of lines before the end of the war. The IFO was advised by Jon Kimchi that the armistice conditions would determine the peace conditions and not *vice versa*. Sharett agreed.[25]

Yet the Israelis realised that they could not, economically, maintain a large army under war conditions for a long time; thus they were eager to use Bernadotte as a mediator for an armistice, but not for a peace agreement and only at a time convenient for them.[26]

Notwithstanding this realisation, the Israeli refusal was adamant: 'The Provisional Government of Israel has noted with surprise that your suggestions appear to ignore the resolution of the General Assembly, November 29, 1947.'[27] Strangely enough, the League accused the mediator of basing his proposal on that resolution. Moreover, the PGI opposed the proposals since it found it difficult to accept the fact that the Count had not 'fully taken into account the outstanding facts of the situation in Palestine, namely, the effective establishment of the sovereign state of Israel within the area assigned to it in the Assembly resolution'. In general Israel opposed the idea of an imposed solution, as it fiercely resented restriction on immigration.[28]

The total rejection by both sides forced the mediator to look for another plan. This time he worked closely with British Middle East experts on the revised proposals. Contacts were made through the BMEO in Cairo and the Embassy there.[25]

Transjordan was the only Arab state whose policy towards the Palestinian problem corresponded with British strategic thinking. Thus by including Abdullah's scheme for the annexation of the Arab parts of Palestine to Transjordan in Bernadotte's second proposals, the British could guarantee the approval of at least one Arab state. Whereas the mediator, in his first proposals, talked about a greater Arab Palestine (enlargement of the independent Arab state), the British suggested the option of the creation of a Greater Transjordan (allotting more territory to Abdullah). In the new constellation there was no room for an independent Arab Palestinian state.

Given Bernadotte's failure in his first proposals and his intensive consultations with the British, it is not surprising that he (and the Americans) accepted this British formula for extricating the UN from the deadlock it faced. Thus Bernadotte's main alteration to his previous proposals was a clear suggestion of the annexation of the Arab parts of Palestine to Transjordan.[30]

It took some time before Bernadotte resumed his attempts at mediating, owing to the continuation of hostilities. He had to consider two new problems: the refugees and the demilitarisation of Jerusalem. The Count urged the UN Assembly to have these problems on its agenda in its next session which was due to convene on 21 September 1948. For this session Bernadotte prepared his second proposals.[31]

The Americans and the British had together worked out a plan and a timetable for conveying to the mediator the desirability of annexing Arab Palestine to Transjordan. The timetable included a week for persuading the Count to accept the Foreign Office ideas and, in fact, that was all that was required to convince the mediator. The experts on both sides estimated that another ten days would be needed to convince the Israelis and the Arab states, and then 20 days of lobbying to secure the approval of the Security Council.[32] Only the first stage was successfully carried out. A high American official was sent to Rhodes to convince the Count that the Greater Transjordan orientation was the only feasible alternative.[33] Sir John Troutbeck joined his American colleague a few days later in a concerted effort. The American envoy reported: 'Two days were devoted to discussion of the substance of what may eventually be called the "Bernadotte plan".'[34]

The following points were included in his second scheme. The Negev was defined as part of the Arab territory as it had been in the previous proposals. The Count recommended the annexation of Arab Palestine to Transjordan: moreover, he added Ramleh and Lydda to Transjordanian territory. Galilee was defined as Jewish territory as it had been in the first proposals. There was no substantial change in the proposed position of Haifa and Lydda. However, there was a radical shift in the Count's approach towards Jerusalem: he suggested the internationalisation of the city. Only the reference to Jerusalem was unacceptable to Abdullah, who otherwise endorsed the plan.[35]

Bernadotte paid only lip service to the other Arab countries' interests in Palestine by suggesting that the disposition of Arab territories should be left to the Arab states to determine. However, in the same breath, the mediator recommended: 'that in view of the historical connection and common interests of Transjordan and Palestine, there would be compelling reasons for merging the Arab territory of Palestine with the territory of Transjordan'.[36]

Bernadotte added a clause on the refugees. They should have the right to return to their homes or receive compensation if they chose not to return. In general, he suggested that a conciliation commission replace the mediator.[37]

The Foreign Secretary was convinced that the other stages would be as successfully carried out as were the first ones: namely, convincing not only the mediator but also the parties concerned. Bevin himself tried to assess the merits of the second proposal in a discussion in the British Cabinet. He told its members that this plan, unlike the first one, did not compromise Abdullah's position and did not require the use of force for its imposition, as the November 1947 UN partition plan had. He based this assumption on a hope that Israel and Transjordan would reach an agreement on the lines of the second proposals.[38]

This undue optimism affected all the other Cabinet members who strongly supported the second proposals. There was even talk then on the importance of the Bernadotte plan for the defence of the Commonwealth, as if the plan had already become an established fact. The same hopeful atmosphere prevailed in the corridors of the Foreign Office and affected the Foreign Office officials. In fact, the Superintending Under-Secretary of State did not even refer to the plan as Bernadotte's proposals but as the 'Greater Transjordan Solution'.[39] The only voices of dissent were heard from British government representatives in the area. Notwithstanding the important role he had played in convincing the mediator of the desire policy, the head of the BMEO urged his colleagues to oppose the Greater Transjordan concept. Troutbeck warned the Foreign Office that this option would mean larger British financial assistance and would lead Abdullah to reach an agreement with Israel behind the backs of the Arabs.[40]

The representative in Damascus asserted that a Greater Transjordan would not allay fears of Abdullah's future intentions. Syria would resent any increase in Abdullah's territory or prestige.[41]

It is notable that these two, Troutbeck and Broadmead, added that, reluctantly, they had to admit that the Arab world preferred the Transjordan solution to partition. In any event, even if the Arab states resented the idea, there was very little they could do, if only because of their endemic lack of unity. The Syrians disapproved completely and the Lebanese followed the Syrian lead. Iraq could not accept the solution publicly as it had to resist any form of partition, but did so privately. The Egyptians and the Saudis were less interested in the whole problem and eventually acquiesced with their Arab brethren.[42]

Incidentally, the Transjordanians, unlike the British, were more concerned about international reaction than Arab response. The Transjordanian premier, Tawfiq Abu Al-Huda, was confident he could reduce Egyptian and Syrian opposition by giving them parts of Palestine (part of the Negev to Egypt and part of the Hula to Syria). As for Ibn Saud, his tacit understanding with Abdullah prior to the war in Palestine reassured the Transjordanians that this old enemy would hardly play a role in the question.[43]

Britain and Transjordan agreed upon the tactics to be followed. The Greater Transjordan solution should not be declared or advocated by either side since it would not help to abate Arab fears; on the contrary, it might have raised resentment. Time was the most favourable factor on the Transjordan side.[44]

THE LEGACY OF BERNADOTTE

It is noteworthy that whatever Bevin thought about the plan before Bernadotte's assassination, he had not viewed the proposals as final.[45] After Bernadotte's death the British launched a campaign to put across the idea that the Count's proposals should become a testament. Bevin told the House of Commons: 'The best way for us to commemorate his death is to complete his work on the basis of the proposals he put forward just before his death.'[46] In this speech Bevin reversed his previous rejection, during the Mandatory period, of any proposal which was not accepted by the two parties (which was the basic British argument against partition). He added: 'We do not expect that either side will welcome these proposals in total, but the world cannot wait forever for the parties to agree.'[47]

This assumption was in complete contradiction to Bernadotte's self-image of a man whose role was limited to 'offering suggestions as the basis on which further discussion might take place', and whose suggestions were submitted 'with no intimation of preciseness or finality'. Moreover there had been 'no question of their imposition'.[48] In this context it is worth noting that Bernadotte's successor, Ralph Bunche, like the British, held the mediator's proposals to be his 'sacrosanct will' and in that supported the British attitude, notwithstanding the inconsistency of such an attitude with Bernadotte's original intentions.[49]

However, the question of Bernadotte's real intentions was not the source of Bevin's problem after the Count's assassination. His difficulties stemmed from a radical change in the American attitude to Bernadotte's proposals shortly after the latter's tragic death in September 1948. When the first proposals were introduced in June that year the Americans whole-heartedly supported Bevin in his perception of the plan as a stabilising factor in the Middle East, as they had backed him in July–August 1948 in his efforts to realise the plan. However, once the second Jewish refusal was received the scheme was abandoned by the White House. The Americans were more interested in the practical short-term objectives of Bernadotte's efforts; namely, the conclusion of a long-lived truce. Furthermore, the US objected to the imposition of the plan on the parties, whereas the principle of an imposed solution was becoming more and more popular with British policy-makers. This American posture was argued for a long time before the assassination of the Count.[50]

It seems that the main American opposition stemmed from strong Jewish pressure on the President.[51] Nevertheless, both Truman and Marshall declared publicly that they viewed the proposals as a basis for a settlement, thus confusing the Foreign Office, for a while, about the real American stand. It became evident later that these declarations were part of Truman's election campaign. Moreover, the American attitude indicated a shift in American policy altogether. The next step by the Americans was to withdraw their support in October 1948 from the Anglo-Chinese resolution, intended to withhold Israeli advances in the south of Palestine, proposing instead the consideration of the imposition of sanctions on Israel or Egypt if they did not comply with the cease-fire order.[52]

On 15 October, Bernadotte's proposals were put before the First Committee of the GA. The British delegation supported the proposals as a final UN peace plan without reservations. The Americans, however, described them as suggestions for a possible basis for peace negotiations.[53] Whereas the Americans left it to the parties themselves to determine future frontiers and future relationships, Britain did not wish such negotiations to take place, but rather wanted both sides to accept the second proposals as a UN plan replacing partition.

In hindsight, Bernadotte's plan seems to have been a futile diplomatic effort. After his death the mediation was in the hands of an American official, who was responsible to the State Department, notwithstanding his subordination to the Secretary-General of the UN. Thus the Americans took the lead in observing the conciliation process in the Middle East while the British influence was restricted to the Israeli–Transjordanian negotiations.

It seems that the main cause of British dismay with regard to the Bernadotte affair was the failure to place the Negev in Transjordanian hands, which was the principal British strategic objective in the Palestinian context. By September 1948, however, most of the officials in the Eastern Department had given up the idea anyway. The first voices of disbelief in Britain's prospects of retaining the Negev in Arab hands were heard from Cairo. Ambassador Campbell doubted the validity of the Foreign Office argument that the Negev should remain Arab, just because it was occupied by the Egyptians (this was the argument put forward by Sir Alexander Cadogan in the GA, during discussion of the Bernadotte plan). Campbell claimed that this 'could serve as a boomerang'.[54] At that time his superior, in London, Michael Wright, disagreed and thought that Egypt and Transjordan had justifiable claims to the Negev.[55] But a few weeks later, after Israel had occupied most of the Negev, British officialdom gave up the idea of an 'Arab' or a 'British' Negev and looked for ways of reaching some kind of strategic understanding with the Israelis over this area.

4 The Anglo–Israeli War over the Negev

THE TEN-DAY WAR (9 JULY 1948–19 JULY 1948): THE COLLAPSE OF THE ARAB FORCES

From the British point of view, the renewal of fighting after the end of the first truce was a disaster. The British had accurately predicted the outcome of this Arab initiative. When the fighting was resumed on 9 July, the Arabs were unsuccessful everywhere. In fact, in a matter of a few days (9–19 July) they had lost most of central and northern Palestine. A well-equipped Israeli army succeeded in capturing large Arab areas, mainly in western Galilee, including the town of Nazareth. This campaign was the last Syrian effort in the war; it resulted in a complete Syrian defeat. The other Arab forces which took part in the fighting, namely Al-Qawqji's forces and the Syrian and Lebanese armies, were driven out of Palestine.[1]

The Legion's position became precarious. Although it succeeded in repelling Israeli attempts to occupy the eastern and northern entrances to Jerusalem, the lack of ammunition and inability of the Arab armies to send any reinforcements made itself felt. Thus certain Arab areas in the centre of Palestine were exposed to Israeli attacks with no substantial Arab force to protect them; as a consequence Lydda and Ramleh fell into Israeli hands.

In Arab historiography the fall of these two Palestinian towns is undoubtedly the greatest crime committed by Glubb.[2] Abdulla At-Tal, the Legion commander in Jerusalem, accused him of sending only one company to defend these two towns, while Aref Al-Aref, the Palestinian chronicler, blamed him for a premature decision to quit the battlefield; this allegation is supported by the Court Historian of the Hashemite kingdom. At-Tal claims that there was a British plot to safeguard Tel Aviv, to damage the Egyptian army's chances of success and to prevent the Mufti from keeping his two strongholds in Arab territory.[3] Kirkbride explains in his memoirs that Glubb had decided that it was preferable to defend Latrun and Jerusalem rather than these two towns.[4] However, even Musa and Madi, the Hashemite Court Historians, affirm Glubb's statement made a month after the battle: 'From the very commencement of hostilities, I had told the

49

Transjordan government that it was impossible for the Arab Legion to defend this area with the number available. The Government had agreed.'[5] British documents show that already on 19 May, such a warning had been issued by Glubb and Kirkbride.[6] Glubb remarked cynically that the Arabs had accepted the second truce after ten days of fighting only because they had a 'scapegoat': the Legion and the loss of the two Palestinian towns of Lydda and Ramleh.[7] At the time no one realised that the main significance of the loss of Lydda and Ramleh was that a large number of refugees were added to those who had already left, fled or been evicted from the country.

The incident had an immense implication for Glubb's position. After the loss of Ramleh and Lydda, demonstrations against the Legion took place in Nablus and As-Salt. Glubb was sent to attend an unpleasant interview with the King and the Council of Ministers, during which it was made clear to him that his reports of shortage of ammunition were believed to be part of British propaganda. At least this is Glubb's version of the conversation. Furthermore, Glubb claimed that the King had even told him that there was no need for him to remain in office unless he wished to. After that meeting the demonstrations continued against Glubb personally and the British in general, on account of news of the withholding of the Legion's subsidy by the British government. Glubb visited the front, where he was received with contempt and hatred.[8]

THE SECOND TRUCE

Bernadotte was informed by the Arabs and the Israelis of their acceptance of a second truce on 15 July.[9] Unlike the Security Council resolution which had called for the first truce, this was an order and not an appeal. Both sides, therefore, risked sanctions.

The Transjordanians found it fairly easy to persuade the other members of the Arab League to comply with the Security Council order. The main Israeli successes during the Ten-Day War were in the North of Palestine. The total defeat of the Syrian and Iraqi contingents and the inability of the Legion to launch any counter-attack enabled the Israelis to prepare themselves with all their strength for the decisive battle over the Negev.[10] Nevertheless, Britain was blamed for forcing the Arabs, and particularly the Transjordanians, to surrender to the Israelis' successes.

The further streams of refugees had caused strong hostility towards

Britain in the Arab countries and especially among the Arab population in Palestine. Various telegrams from the Middle East legations during July reported a growing trend of anti-British feeling in the Arab countries.[11] The fact that Britain had not fulfilled its obligations under its treaties with the Arab states was seen as a betrayal. The Palestinians believed that Britain was behind Abdullah's decision not to attack the new part of Jerusalem. The main cause of Arab resentment was the British government's decision to comply with the UN embargo on arms to the belligerent parties in Palestine. This decision had meant that the Legion, the main fighting force, had no further ammunition to continue the war, and neither could it launch an offensive. The second truce (15 July 1948) had probably saved the Legion from total collapse on the central front. But the war was not over and the Legion, at the end of August 1948, found itself at close quarters with the Jewish army on a front of 40 miles. This situation should be compared with the improvement on the Jewish side as a result of new waves of immigration and streams of arms from the Eastern bloc.[12]

The British reports from the Arab capitals pointed out that in many places, and in particular in Arab Palestine, Britain was more disliked than the US. Bevin tended to ignore these reports as exaggerated. He genuinely believed that the main resentment after the defeat in Palestine was against the Americans.[13] It is difficult to judge whose evaluations were the right ones. However, it is noticeable that American financial and oil interests were hardly affected as a result of the bitterness. This probably stemmed from the fact that not much was expected from the Americans owing to the position they had taken in the past and the belief of the Arabs that the Jewish lobby had immense influence on American foreign policy. In the British case it was, however, a deep disappointment that characterised Arab reaction. Arab governments had had high hopes of Britain's ability to tip the balance. Moreover, according to Fadhil Jamali, the Iraqi Foreign Minister, Bevin had promised the Arab leaders that he would never agree to partition. Jamali told the Iraqi court in 1958, where he was the main defendant appearing before a revolutionary tribunal (trying him and others for crimes which included, *inter alia*, the 'misconduct' of the monarchist government during the Palestine war), that after the conclusion of the Portsmouth Treaty the problem of Palestine had been discussed and Bevin had been adamantly against partition and the establishment of a Jewish state. Furthermore, he had promised to arm 50 000 Palestinians and send more equipment to the Iraqi army, which would be allowed to enter those parts of Palestine evacuated by the British.

Incidentally, the same allegations had even been made by the otherwise pro-British politician Nuri As-Said, in August 1948. At that time he published a pamphlet called 'Facts Concerning Recent Affairs in Palestine' which appeared in the local Iraqi papers. As-Said claimed that he and Bevin had arrived at a working agreement on Palestine. The basis of the agreement was similar to the one argued by Jamali. The Foreign Office record of the conversation which took place in January 1948 in London did not imply any such agreement. In an interview for an Iraqi paper in 1948, Jamali himself denied the existence of such an agreement.[14]

Abdullah for one, believed that such an Anglo-Iraqi deal on Palestine had been concluded. In a conversation with the British minister in Amman, the King complained that the Iraqis had been given precedence over Transjordan in the consultation about Palestine. In any case, Bevin made no such promises to the Iraqis and had hardly discussed British policy towards Palestine with them.[15]

This affair has been covered in detail since it sheds light on the feeling of the Arabs that before the war Britain had promised to do its utmost to prevent the establishment of a Jewish state.

However, at the end of the summer of 1948, this did not seem an important issue. The most pressing issue was the possibility of an Israeli attack on the Legion, which lacked artillery and mortar ammunition. Kirkbride struggled to convince London that unless Britain intervened, it would mean the collapse of British policy: 'The anti-British outbreaks which followed the fall of Lydda and Ramleh . . . [are] an indication of what would happen following a major defeat of this force'.[16]

It is worth noting that the Legation in Amman shared the feelings of the Transjordanians about the ingratitude of the British. Kirkbride was disinclined to accept the Foreign Office argument that there was a need to check the Legion: 'The Transjordan government has complied with our wishes to the best of their ability, both as regards general conduct of the campaign and as regards the truce.'[17] Yet, complained the British representative, Britain had not restored the subsidy or renewed the supply of arms. This Transjordanian dismay was reflected in a letter from Abdullah to Bevin.[18]

In answer to these allegations, the Head of the Eastern Department reiterated the commitments under the treaty of alliance, namely to protect Transjordan from an Israeli attack. However, he stressed that

Britain, under its obligation to the UN, could not directly supply war material to the Legion.[19] Thus in order to soothe Transjordan indignation, Sir Orme Sargent, the Permanent Under-Secretary of State, came up with a new suggestion: that Britain send war material to Transjordan to be held there under British control until further orders. The Foreign Office was reluctant to comply with a similar Iraqi request, which indicates that Transjordan indeed had priority over Iraq; and this was despite a specific request by the RAF to apply the same methods to Iraq.[20]

Sir Orme Sargent realised that this action would call for a discussion with the Americans since it was in a way a violation of the embargo. The danger was of course that the American government might lift its ban on arms supplies to Israel. Sargent hoped that the signs of 'Jewish aggression' would justify this action in American eyes.[21] The State Department certainly regarded the Israeli attitude as intransigent in the months of July–August 1948. Its officials believed the rumours of an impending Israeli attack both in south and central Palestine, and so they were willing to support the British plea. In this context it is noteworthy that the CIA favoured a situation without any embargo at all, since in that case no side could achieve a decisive victory and the US and the UK could determine developments.[22] Thus the British, for the first time after a long period, could have expected a favourable response from the White House to their Palestinian policy. The success of the Israelis and their reluctance to comply with UN decisions had irritated even the usually pro-Zionist President of the US. Truman was annoyed in particular with the Israeli operation in Jerusalem during August 1948, which included the seizure of the Government House, a place regarded as UN territory.[23] Thus the Foreign Office could carry out its plan and soothe Transjordan's complaints.

In a further move to pacify Transjordan's resentment, the Foreign Office was willing to influence the War Office to let the Transjordanian debt of £5 million stand another year (this debt was caused by the Transjordanian government overdrawing on the British subsidy).[24]

However, there was nothing Britain could or would have done to refute allegations by other Arab states. Most of them maintained that the Transjordanians were obliged by their British connection to betray the Arab cause and that Glubb obeyed the Foreign Office rather than the Transjordanian Government. Thus the Arab governments sought means of diminishing British influence on the Legion. One of these means was to reduce the British element in the Legion. This policy was pursued particularly by the Iraqi army,[25] with the result that during the second truce (19 July–15 October 1948) the Iraquis worked towards the unification of the Iraqi and Transjordanian armies.

Abdullah had realised already in May 1948 that when it was discovered that he had implemented the Arab League's plans only as far as they corresponded with his own schemes, his credibility as the supreme commander would be questioned. After he had completed the occupation of most of the Arab parts of Palestine, he had no desire to continue the war. According to information given by the Turkish minister in Baghdad to the British embassy there on the first day of the second truce, Abdullah had asked King Farouk of Egypt and King Ibn Saud to take over the post of titular CiC of the Arab armies. They both refused to comply with this request. In fact, Abdullah was eager to end this phase of a united Arab effort. He was irritated by the continued friction with the other Arab armies in the area controlled by the Legion. The Egyptian commander in Hebron refused to obey Abdullah's orders and the Iraqi general, Nur Al-Din, did not fulfil the role of policing the area.[26]

Yet we find that the King was receptive towards the Iraqi approaches and tended to consider the idea of unification favourably. Hence it seems that, notwithstanding his dispute with the Iraqis, it was still better for Abdullah to cooperate with them than with any other Arab army. Moreover he looked for ways of showing his resentment of the British attitude. Finally, he feared an Israeli attack on the areas he held. For all these reasons, he entered into talks on unification with the Iraqi army. The news of a possible unification of the two armies caused considerable concern in London. It could have affected the position of Glubb and the British officers in the Legion, in particular since it had been decided by the two sides that an Iraqi commander would stand at the head of the unified army.[27]

In the Iraqi–Transjordanian talks, which took place in August 1948, it was agreed that both countries would act as independent units. This should have brought some relaxation to London. Nevertheless, the Legation in Amman was convinced that there was a serious threat to Britain's position in Transjordan. The Legation believed the rumours that the Iraqis and some Arab officers in the Legion were aiming to break British control over the Legion by replacing the British subsidy by an Iraqi one and by compelling all British officers to resign, thus enabling the Legion to act freely in Palestine and open a new offensive.[28] However, the whole affair was soon over and proved to be a passing unimportant exercise of public relations on the part of the

Iraqi government for domestic consumption; thus when the discussions reached the practical level, the Iraqi premier released a public statement to the effect that unfortunately his country could not support the unification financially and therefore was not demanding, for the time being, the withdrawal of British officers. It is possible that strong British opposition had also played an important role and had caused the Iraqis to reverse their position. However, it should be noted that the Iraqis found themselves in dire straits. On the one hand, they did not wish to enter an open confrontation with the British; on the other, they were reluctant to stop fighting and did not wish to appear in the Arab world as defeatists. It is quite possible that the Iraqis relied on British assistance for such a move. A high official in the Foreign Office who was annoyed by this Iraqi policy expressed the hope that the Iraqis would soon be out of Palestine: 'If only the Russians would stir up some trouble in Kurdistan we should have no difficulties at all [in getting the Iraqis out of Palestine].'[29]

In any event, although it was stated in Baghdad that the unification of the two armies was carried out under the command of an Iraqi general, it was no more than a coordinating move of two armies which had long ceased to fight, and thus it had no effect on the position of the British officers in the Legion. The Iraqi–Transjordanian talks left matters very much as they were. In a sense, the futility of the talks was a personal failure for Tawfiq Abu Al-Huda, Transjordan's premier, who had strongly supported them. From that moment on, the British Officers in the Legion lost any confidence they might have had in him.[30]

But the Iraqi behaviour continued to be a source of dismay for the British officials dealing with the Middle East. In September the Iraqis, to the great annoyance of British officialdom in London, tried to convince the other Arab governments to attempt to reoccupy Jerusalem. Having serious problems at home (such as the Kurds and the student riots), the Iraqis wished the fighting in Palestine to continue for a while. Such an initiative (which would have meant violation of the truce) was regarded by Bevin as a most dangerous one. He believed that it would have ended in the occupation of the whole of Palestine by the Israelis. Thus Bevin ordered his Ambassador to convey to the Iraqi Regent that 'it is shocking that the Iraqi government should be willing to jeopardise the whole Arab position in Palestine and in the UN and with world opinion because they are afraid to tell the truth to the Baghdad mob'.[31] It was both British pressure and Arab helplessness which caused the failure of the Iraqi initiative.

Thus the Iraqi premier returned home after his tour of the Arab capitals with no concrete agreement in his hands. This fiasco ended the Iraqi war effort in Palestine.[32]

It was not only the Iraqis who discontinued their participation in the war. By the end of September, the Transjordanian, Syrian and Lebanese armies refrained from any large-scale military operation in Palestine and conceded an Israeli victory. The Egyptians would have undoubtedly joined the other Arab states in admitting defeat had its army not been stretched over most of southern Palestine. The Egyptian army was immobile and, at the same time, as yet unbeaten by the Israelis. Despite the uncertainty over the situation in the south, outside observers (including the British government) regarded the war as having come to an end.

By September 1948, the Transjordanian forces were no longer engaged in fighting. Transjordan's Ministers of Communication and Defence were instructed to submit to the Political Committee conditions for the Legion's continued participation in the war. Kirkbride explained that the conditions were phrased in such a way that they would clearly be unacceptable to the League.[33] Transjordan was prepared to resume the fighting if all Arab states did so and if the League provided the Legion *beforehand* with all the equipment and ammunition it needed. Transjordan warned that it would withdraw unless its demands were fulfilled. Furthermore, Abdullah insisted that no change be introduced to the agreement according to which each occupying army would administer its own territory. In that context, it should be noted that the Transjordan representative asked that no ALA units be stationed in the Legion area. Finally, they argued for the division of the refugees between Arab countries.[34] In November, Glubb told a meeting of the Transjordanian Cabinet that no assistance from Egypt and Iraq could be expected, which led Kirkbride to declare the war was finished.[35]

Kirkbride's and Glubb's assumptions were shared by most British officials in London. Despite their realisation that the battle over the Negev was not yet settled, those officials deemed it necessary to supply their government with a memorandum in which they tried to reassess and re-evaluate the effect the Palestine war was having on the British position and the stability of the Arab governments.

The Eastern Department of the Foreign Office believed that most of the Arab leaders recognised the inevitability of a Jewish state, although they took no steps to prepare Arab public opinion for the final outcome of the war. The head of the Department asserted that since the population in the Arab countries had been misled and cheated about the real situation in Palestine, there was no doubt that the Arab governments would choose Britain as the main scapegoat. His Majesty's Government would be blamed for failing to supply arms when they were most needed.[36]

The Army was also asked to give its own appreciation of the situation in Palestine. The generals were less cautious and more courageous with their conclusions. On the whole, the military authorities in Britain were impressed by two facts: the inevitability of a Jewish state and the fighting ability of the Legion. With hindsight, these would be the two principal factors guiding the British government in its attitude towards a solution of the Arab–Israeli conflict. The Foreign Office did not contradict the army's assessment and expressed its own satisfaction with the stabilisation of the Israeli–Transjordanian front. By September 1948 the front lines were established and maps delineating them had been signed by the two sides.[37]

However, Britain was soon to learn that its involvement in the war, as marginal as it had been hitherto, was not yet over. Although the Hashemites and the Jews had concluded their rounds of fighting, the battle over the southern front was not yet settled. The British, like all the other participants, soon realised that they could expect an Israeli advance to the Gulf of Aqaba and the international border of the Sinai. It should be remembered that Aqaba was considered by the British army as a 'focal point in the strategic importance of Transjordan [sic]'.[38] It was abundantly clear that although the Israelis might have accepted a freeze of the territorial situation in the eastern front, they were unhappy with the military position in the south. Count Bernadotte found it impossible to establish front lines in the Negev: much of it was wasteland with fortified Jewish settlements in the northern part. Hence the mediator's inability to impose a solution in the Negev necessitated a deeper British involvement in the southern front.

THE SOUTHERN FRONT

The British found it difficult to predict the course of events on the southern front. From 1946 onwards, they ceased to play an important role in the making of Egypt's foreign and defence policy; so it is little wonder that the British representatives in Cairo could not assess whether Egypt was about to withdraw or to launch an offensive.

Chapman-Andrews, the British minister in the Cairo Embassy, wrote that he was on his guard against an Egyptian agreement with Israel by which Israel would gain the Negev.[39] However, it seems that even if the Egyptians had wished to reach an agreement with the Israelis it was too late, as the latter had already decided to launch a large-scale compaign aimed at opening the lines of communication and establishing a political *fait accompli* in the Negev. In fact an accurate analysis of this Israeli design had been sent to London by the Jerusalem consulate shortly before the offensive began.[40]

It is worth noting that it was only over the Negev that British and Israeli interests directly clashed. This dispute stemmed from the great importance the British army had attached to the Negev as a strategic asset. Thus we find that the CoS regarded Greater Transjordan as including the Negev, or at least the northern part of it.[41] Moreover the growing difficulty of safeguarding the British bases in Egypt and North Africa had increased the Negev's potential value. Therefore the British army toyed with the idea that instead of Cyrenaica, the Negev and Gaza would be 'the main British Middle East military installation outside Egypt'.[42] In general, the Negev was regarded in London as an important territorial corridor between Egypt and the rest of the Arab world. All the British territorial solutions for the Palestine problem during the Mandate, from the Peel Commission to the Morrison–Grady plan, had excluded the Jews from the Negev. UNSCOP had shown itself insensitive to British strategic need in the Negev by awarding the area to the Jewish state. This was 'amended' by Bernadotte's plans, the second of which suggested dividing the Negev between Egypt and Transjordan, thereby cutting off the Jews from the Negev. Thus, for the first time, the demand for an Arab Negev was supported by the UN. Furthermore the Bernadotte proposal also had America's blessing.

However, in September it was realised in London that the Negev would probably fall into Jewish hands. The only military force able to confront the Jews there, the Legion, had no intention of doing so. King Abdullah declined Arab appeals for deeper involvement in the fighting in the south and was disinclined to try to occupy the area for Britain's sake only. Moreover the British stand was, as always, ambiguous about the whole issue. As much as the army wished the Negev to be part of Transjordan, the Foreign Office preferred to attain this goal without involving the Legion. It should be clear that there was no pressure on Abdullah to join the battle over the Negev; on the contrary, Kirkbride made every possible effort to prevent such folly from occurring. The British could only hope that in the case of an Israeli advance into the Negev (an operation which seemed imminent in September) the UN would be able to restrain the Israelis. The Foreign Office felt that 'there is little we could do to discourage them'.[43] Beeley, the Foreign Office's expert on Palestine, advocated not publishing the information about the Israeli preparations, since it might induce the Arabs to start fighting; 'if there is to be fighting, it would be even worse for the Arabs than for the Jews to start it'.[44]

One of the direct reasons for the Israeli offensive in the Negev was Bevin's intention to implement the Bernadotte scheme. The Legation of the PGI in London read carefully Bevin's speech in the House of Commons after Bernadotte's assassination, and pointed out to Jerusalem the following sentence from the speech (emphasised by Dr Eliash): 'it is our hope that the United Nations *will lose no time* in throwing the full weight of their authority behind *Bernadotte's proposals*'.[45] Ben-Gurion shared the IFO's apprehension. He regarded the second truce as endangering Israel's political standing. He perceived the truce as a path to peace but also as approval for the 'invading Arab armies to stay in Palestine', while Jewish immigration was restricted. Furthermore it seems that Ben-Gurion was encouraged by intelligence reports on the worsening situation of the Egyptian army.[46] Finally, most of the Jewish settlements in the Negev were isolated, and unless the Israeli forces acted, they would have been starved into surrender or evacuation.

In fact the situation of the 21 Jewish settlements in the Negev was the Israeli explanation for the launching of their offensive in the Negev. The Egyptian location between Majdal and Faluja had cut off the 'Jewish Negev' from the rest of the Jewish land. The PGI wanted to open an offensive in that area as early as the end of May, but the acceptance of the first truce compelled it to postpone its plans. Another attempt was foiled by the declaration of the second truce.[47] Thus, on 15 October, the third and final attempt to occupy the Negev was carried out.

The Foreign Office was convinced that the quarrel over the Jewish supply convoys to those settlements served as a pretext for the campaign. In reality it was an operation to occupy the Negev. The State Department shared this opinion. Robert Lovett, the Acting Secretary of State, believed that the incident in which a Jewish food convoy was shot at was contrived.[48] There is little doubt that the development of the Israeli attack had proved that the operation went beyond safeguarding free passage for the convoys. Moreover, Ben-

Gurion decided that the whole of Western Palestine would be occupied if and when the partition scheme failed. He was convinced that the Jewish state would be able to maintain both the Negev and Galilee.[49]

The Director of Egyptian Military Intelligence told the British Military Attaché that it was impossible to stop the Israeli advance. Indeed, in a short while the Israelis succeeded in thrusting towards Beersheba, capturing it and thus isolating the Egyptian troops in the Hebron area from the main Egyptian force in the Negev. The British and the Egyptians believed that the next Israeli move after their success in occupying the Negev plateau would be an advance into the Gaza area. This presumption was reinforced by the Hagana radio announcement that the population of Gaza was leaving for Egypt, since the Israelis expected to enter Gaza. However, this was part of an Israeli decoy operation to divert attention away from their preparations to take over the eastern and south-western parts of the Negev.[50]

Thus the only way of stopping the Israelis, short of military intervention, was resorting to active diplomacy. The British took a very intense part in the UN discussion on the war in the Negev. This was not an easy task, given the drastic shift in the American attitude towards the question of the Negev. The rejection of the Bernadotte plan by both sides had caused a reversal in American policy. The State Department now veered towards encouraging a territorial settlement by negotiation, owing to the new situation created by the Israeli offensive. However, while the State Department thought in terms of territorial exchange (that is, the Negev going to the Arabs and Galilee to the Jews), the President intervened to include, in addition to Galilee, all the Negev areas already occupied by the Israelis.[51] Truman was in the midst of an election campaign in which the other candidate repudiated the Bernadotte programme; the President therefore had to make a similar declaration.[52] One tends to agree with Forrestal's observation that in those days American policy was determined by the President's advisers, usually Clifford and David Niles, who were moved mainly by domestic considerations (Forrestal was Defense Secretary at the time). Nevertheless, Truman continued the same line after his election; he wrote to President Weizmann: 'I remember well our conversation about the Negev, . . . I agree fully with your estimate of the importance of that area to Israel, and I deplore any attempt to take it away from Israel.'[53]

We can assume that the Foreign Office realised that whatever the

Israelis succeeded in capturing in the Negev would be accepted by the US as Israeli territory. Therefore the British concentrated their efforts on achieving a Security Council resolution forcing the Israelis to withdraw northwards by threat of sanctions. This was the Anglo-Chinese resolution ordering Israeli withdrawal to the lines of 14 October and calling on the opposing sides to begin negotiations on an armistice. Once again this move was foiled when the American support for it died.[54]

In the meantime, Jewish forces had succeeded in driving a wedge through the Egyptian lines, isolating two main groups within garrison posts. By the end of October those two forces were besieged by the Israelis. During the first week of November the Egyptians began to withdraw, leaving the besieged garrisons to their fate.[55]

For the Foreign Office the situation could not have been worse. Three weeks had passed since the UN Security Council resolution had been accepted and the Israelis were in the same positions as before. Furthermore, if the Israelis succeeded in capturing the Faluja area (where the Egyptian garrisons were entrenched), they would get hold of ammunition and equipment which could have endangered the remaining Arab armies.[56] Moreover, a Jewish thrust towards the Gulf of Aqaba began at the end of the month. As far as Britain was concerned, this advance was 'an awkward situation' owing to the proximity of the Israelis to Aqaba. However, there was little Britain could or would do.[57] The Egyptian Ministry of Defence requested Iraqi and Transjordanian assistance, but neither army could spare any soldiers. The British, for their part, emphasised that they would intervene only if Transjordanian or Egyptian territory proper were invaded.

In their despair the Egyptians, in particular the Palace, looked for ways of negotiating secretly with the Israelis. In November 1948 talks began with Elias Sasson, a representative of the IFO. The Egyptians offered Israel a permanent armistice if Israel would agree to withdraw from Arab parts of Palestine and consent to the annexation of the southern part of the Negev to Egypt. This proposal was rejected, but it served as an opening for armistice negotiations.[58]

However, the trouble was not over yet. The Israelis occupied the eastern part of the Jerusalem–Lydda area. For the Foreign Office it seemed that, as this was a clear-cut case of Israelis moving into purely Arab lands, it could be used to convince the UN to take forceful action against the Israelis. The main issue for the Foreign Office was to prove the 'falsity' of Israeli propaganda that the 'battle for the Negev was fought almost entirely in the Jewish area'.[59] The Legion's response to

the new Israeli offensive was to check by force any Israeli advances
into areas previously held by the Egyptians, a task which it successfully
carried out. The Israeli advance into the Hebron area in November
1948 was seen as indicating that the Israelis harboured some hopes of
capturing areas which had been understood in the pre-war
negotiations to be Abdullah's territory. This was the interpretation
adopted by the Legion. The Israeli advance alarmed the British for
other reasons as well, since it coincided with Israeli threats to the Iraqi
army in eastern Palestine; it was further believed that the Israelis might
even attack Jerusalem. However, by the end of November it became
evident that both sides desired a truce in Jerusalem.[60]

The Egyptians withdrew an earlier consent that they had given for
entering into negotiations on an armistice; fresh fighting erupted in the
Negev. The Israeli army threatened Gaza, captured the highway from
Beersheba to Bir Asluj, and thrust across the Sinai border in the
direction of El-Arish, thus threatening the Egyptian rear. The advance
into purely Egyptian territory brought about an open clash with
Britain.

ON THE BRINK OF AN ANGLO-ISRAELI WAR
(DECEMBER 1948–JANUARY 1949)

In November 1948, the Security Council tried to stop the Israeli
advance in southern and northern Palestine by threatening the
imposition of sanctions. However, the Israelis were not deterred and
in December of that year launched yet another attack on the Egyptian
forces in the Negev and the Gaza Strip and even penetrated into the
Sinai peninsula. The Israelis declared that they were free to act against
the Egyptians since the latter had rejected the Security Council's call
for armistice negotiations. The main aim of the operation was the
evacuation of the Egyptian contingent in the Negev and its liquidation.
They entered Sinai for that purpose as well.[61]

After the Israelis had launched their attack, the British succeeded in
moving a resolution in the Security Council calling for a cease-fire and
the withdrawal of all forces back to the positions they had occupied
before October 1948. The Americans and the Russians abstained on
this vote. The State Department saw no point in introducing a new
resolution which repeated the provisions entailed in the previous one.
Thus, owing to the American reluctance to be associated with any
measures unfavourable to Israel, the Security Council was unable to

execute a former decision to impose sanctions on Israel (a resolution of November 1948). Bevin in particular was annoyed with this American stand since, at that time, the Americans were supporting Israel's application to the UN.[62] The Americans explained that they were disinclined to jeopardise their newly-acquired position in the PCC. They were further worried by the warning of their representative in Tel Aviv that they would be regarded in the same light as Great Britain in Israeli eyes.[63]

On 29 December the British government was informed by the Egyptians that the Israelis had crossed into Egyptian territory. The Foreign Office regarded these reports as unreliable, and British intelligence could not establish whether or not this information was correct. Moreover, the Israelis did not allow the UN observers to visit the front.[64]

The Americans were notified that the British Cabinet had taken a decision that, in the event of Israeli forces being found on Egyptian territory, the UK would invoke the Anglo-Egyptian treaty and would work towards rescinding the Security Council arms embargo. Such an Israeli invasion would be regarded by the Foreign Office as endangering the stability of the Middle East. The Americans replied that in such an event they would have to lift the embargo as well and advised the Foreign Office to confirm the information about the Israeli penetration.[65]

Notwithstanding this unenthusiastic American response, the State Department, which was as worried as the British Office, agreed to convey a warning to the Israelis. The warning was sent through James McDonald, the American representative in Tel Aviv. The British threatened the Israelis that they would come to Egypt's assistance if they were asked to (as they were obliged to according to the Anglo-Egyptian treaty of 1936).[66] In fact, the Americans issued a strong warning of their own, warning the Israelis that they would reconsider their application to join the UN as well as reviewing Israeli–US relations altogether.[67]

The Israeli Foreign Minister assured the Americans on 3 January that no Israeli troops remained on Egyptian soil. However, on the very same day British intelligence had confirmed the existence of Israeli forces well inside (20 miles) Egyptian territory. At this, the Defence Committee decided to put into effect the Cabinet decision about meeting Britain's obligations under its treaty with Egypt. In practice it was decided to reinforce the British contingent in Aqaba. This action became another source of tension, since at the same time the Israelis

were advancing towards the Gulf of Aqaba. Two battalions were sent
from East Africa to the Canal Zone, and some naval units were put on
the alert.[68]

The Middle East Land Forces headquarters prepared a plan,
codenamed 'CLATTER', for army operations in the Sinai in support
of the Eygptian army. In fact the Israelis anticipated some British
action of this kind. In such a case, Ben-Gurion ordered his force to
withdraw immediately back into Israel. The Israeli military spokesman
claimed that Israel had learned about British manoeuvres in
Tripolitania made under conditions designed to reproduce those which
would be obtained in landing operations in Israel.[69]

It is quite probable that some Foreign Office officials had thought in
the most expedient terms, as has been suggested by some writers: that
is, the Foreign Office wanted to exploit the opportunity offered by the
Israeli invasion to invoke the 'long disputed Anglo-Egyptian treaty'.[70]
Harold Wilson argues that: 'To curb Israeli successes, Bevin tried to
invoke the Anglo-Egyptian treaty.'[71] This is one of many cases where
Foreign Office tendencies and thinking were attributed, quite
wrongly, to Ernest Bevin; as we shall see, this occurred over and over
again. The IFO shared this assumption at the time, issuing a statement
to that effect. In response, the British consul in Haifa conveyed to Tel
Aviv the message that Britain had no wish to go to war with Israel (the
only official representative of Britain in Israel up to January 1949 was
the consul in Haifa).[72]

Sir Ronald Campbell, the British ambassador in Cairo, was one of
those Foreign Office personalities who had probably hoped to
capitalise on the developments in the Negev. In a letter to Bevin, he
argued that furnishing arms to the Egyptians would not be enough to
compel the Israelis to withdraw to the October lines. He suggested that
Britain should take action on its own initiative to clear the Beersheba–
Hebron road. The ambassador in Cairo reckoned that although the
Americans would resent the British action they would realise at the
end of the day that the road would be an essential strategic asset in the
next world war.[73]

The head of the BMEO had also recommended the involvement of
'our forces in the fighting'.[74] Otherwise, they had argued Britain and
Egypt would have to live with a peace imposed by Israel. Troutbeck
asserted that if Britain acted swiftly and with no hesitation, American
and domestic criticism would be avoided. The minister in Lebanon had
also requested direct British intervention to stop the Israeli advance in
Lebanon, which coincided with Israeli penetration into the Sinai. The

head of the Eastern Department did not rule out the possibility of British intervention if the Israelis were consistent in their refusal to withdraw from the Sinai.[75]

Troutbeck's and Campbell's opportunistic inclinations are clearly shown by their admission that they did not believe that the Israelis were trying to capture any part of the Sinai. Thus, although Egypt proper was not in danger, they still demanded the invoking of the Anglo-Egyptian treaty in order to involve the British army in the fighting over the Negev. The Permanent Under-Secretary of State rejected their request for active participation precisely on the ground that Israel was not aiming at Egyptian territory. Indeed, according to the formal version of the Israeli army, the operation in the Gaza area and Sinai was a decoy action. The real objective was to capture the whole of the Negev.[76] In the final analysis it seems that, given the warning conveyed to Israel, the Foreign Office in general and Bevin in particular had no wish to intervene in any manner in the fighting provided the Israelis were not advancing towards the Suez Canal.

According to Ben-Gurion the British warning and activities were the main reason for the Israeli withdrawal from the Sinai. Ben-Gurion insisted on emphasising that it was British pressure, not American, which had persuaded him to order his forces to return to Israeli territory. The Israeli premier claimed that the American warning was dictated by the British Foreign Office.[77] As Lord Bullock rightly assumes, it was more expedient for Ben-Gurion to appear to be giving in to British military pressure than to American verbal threats.[78] It seems that in the final analysis it was the joint Anglo-American pressure which brought about the Israeli withdrawal.

The most ironic development of this Anglo-Israeli conflict was that the sole direct clash between British and Israeli forces occurred after the end of hostilities on the Israeli–Egyptian front and after the decision of both sides to enter armistice negotiations. On 7 January 1949 the Israelis shot down five RAF aircraft on a reconnaissance flight. The flight was one of those intended to find out whether or not the Israelis had left Egyptian territory.[79]

In hindsight, it is difficult to understand why the British deemed it necessary to ask for an additional reconnaisance flight when the fighting had ceased; more so since the Egyptians had not only not requested this flight, but were in fact strongly opposed to it. The Egyptians realised that joint flights, or British flights on behalf of the Egyptians, could have implied Egyptian acknowledgement of the validity of the Anglo-Egyptian treaty; that is, if the request had come from the Egyptians. Moreover the Egyptians did not want to admit that Israeli forces had entered Egyptian territory. It should be mentioned that the Egyptian position on this issue had not been consistent, and that, according to American sources, they had at one point in the fighting (29 December 1948) asked to use British Spitfires, with Egyptian pilots, in order to stop the Israeli advance.[80]

The explanation for this additional flight, made after the cessation of hostilities, lies in the MoD's determination to learn more about Israeli intentions. It should be remembered that UN observers were still not allowed into the area even after the cease-fire agreement between Israel and Egypt had been signed. Therefore the MoD exerted strong pressure on Clement Attlee to prepare the British forces in the Middle East for the possibility of war with Israel. The MoD, the Eastern Department and the CoS deemed it necessary to find out the strength and structure of the Israeli Air Force and the location of the Israeli airfields so that operation 'CLATTER' (the operation designed for British action against Israel) would be successful.[81]

Clement Attlee was annoyed when the Foreign Office referred to those flights in Parliament as 'reconnaissance flights'. Attlee feared that this approach would reveal the true nature of the flights to the Cabinet and the House of Commons; that is, their link with operation 'CLATTER' would be realised. Attlee also wanted to conceal the fact that the MoD had decided to send armed aircraft over Israeli territory to protect the reconnaissance flights. The need to protect those flights arose from a previous incident in which an RAF Mosquito had been shot down by the Israelis. The premier suggested calling them 'training flights'.[82]

On the whole Bevin did not object to the MoD's tactics. He regarded the invasion as part of the Israeli strategy to negotiate with Transjordan while attacking Egypt and vice versa.[83] Thus those writers who claim that Bevin did not have personal responsibility for the incident were correct in pointing out that, once again, one could not hold Bevin responsible for the ill-advised decisions of the British government.[84] On the other hand, it should be mentioned that he did not oppose the Minister of Defence or Attlee in their determination to carry out the flight. Furthermore, the decision was not taken by the Air Officer commanding the Canal Zone alone; he was carrying out orders from the MoD. It is noteworthy that in the Defence Committee Bevin opposed the continuation of the reconnaissance flights, fearing that Britain would be accused of violating the truce. Nevertheless, he agreed that political considerations would not override military operations.[85]

One of the British pilots was captured by the Israelis. He admitted that his plane had been shot down over 'Palestine'. The British Cabinet was told by the Foreign Office that it was difficult to refute or accept this point. In fact, four out of the five planes had been shot down over Egyptian territory. However, the Israeli forces had dragged the wrecks into Israeli territory.[86]

The initial British reaction was to put the Royal Navy on the highest alert, reinforce the RAF in the Middle East and advise British citizens in Israel to leave the country. However, direct confrontation was prevented mainly due to American intervention. In fact, American rebuke of these British actions led to a more moderate British reaction.[87]

By comparing American and British documents one reaches the conclusion that Bevin was not fully aware of the degree of American bitterness and dissatisfaction with his policy. He was informed by the British ambassador in Washington that Truman stressed the need for peace in the area and that the President had suggested not exaggerating the whole incident. Truman was not prepared to make the Negev a sore point in Anglo-American relations: 'It was a small area and not worth mentioning.'[88]

What Bevin was not informed of was a particularly strong criticism of British, and especially his own policy in Palestine. This criticism was conveyed to the British ambassador in Washington, Sir Oliver Franks. The main spokesman on the American side was the Acting Secretary of State, Robert Lovett. Lovett complained that the British Foreign Office failed to recognise the alteration in the situation in the Middle East as a result of the establishment of the state of Israel. Robert Lovett told the British ambassador: 'It was clear as indeed had been proved by recent events that the state of Israel would be the most dynamic, efficient, vigorous government in the Near East in the future.'[89] The American official argued that it was highly important for the West to keep Israel under its influence. He described British policy hitherto as 'one of containing the Israelis even at the risk of permanently estranging them'.[90] In his view such a policy was unrealistic.

It seems that the British ambassador accepted most of Lovett's arguments; in particular, those relating to British policy towards the developments in the southern front. Lovett described Bevin's reaction as highly dramatic and emotional, a reaction which led to unhelpful acts such as the RAF reconnaissance flights, the reinforcements in Aqaba and the naval alert. Lovett indicated that the American diplomatic approach had achieved more. The proof for this, according to him, was the Israeli withdrawal from the Sinai. As for Bevin's threat to end the embargo, the American official wrote to ambassador Douglas in the American embassy in London: 'In fact Bevin's heated admonition to this government to back up Security Council resolutions sounds queer in light of his simultaneous willingess to violate SC resolution 29.5.48. by renewing arms supply.'[91]

Two points should be mentioned in connection with these remarks. First, Attlee, Alexander and the Defence Committee as a whole were as responsible as Bevin for the 'dramatic reaction'. Second, withdrawal was the result of joint Anglo-American pressure and not of American effort only.

In the final analysis what was important was the impression Bevin had derived from the American reaction. The Foreign Minister, unaware of the resentment that his actions caused in Washington, was particularly pleased by the American pressure on Israel. The Americans had exerted pressure on Israel not to submit a formal complaint against the British in the UN. Bevin believed that the way was now open for a joint Anglo-American declaration of policy,[92] a declaration that in his eyes could have restored the Arab world's confidence in the West. In order to facilitate such a declaration and to improve Anglo-American relations, the British Cabinet abolished the measures it had taken in anticipation of Anglo-Israeli clashes. Although the Foreign Office explained to the Cabinet members that this had been done in order not to prejudice the Israeli–Egyptian armistice negotiations, there is little doubt that the moderate British reaction owed more to the American pressure than to a desire to help the conciliation process.

Nevertheless the Foreign Office was pleased with the beginning of the armistice negotiations, especially as it extricated Britain from a very embarrassing situation. We should remember that Anglo-Egyptian relations at the time were at a low ebb, so any action against Israel would have first appeared to be taken on purely British initiative and, second, could have led to the Egyptian accusation that Britain was trying to impose the treaty on them.

As for the Israelis and the Egyptians, both sides came under strong American pressure and agreed to enter armistice negotiations. Ben-Gurion wrote in his diary that he agreed to withdraw Israeli forces and enter into the negotiations since he was confident that an armistice agreement 'would disintegrate the Arab front and weaken British influence in the East . . . and [would] prevent Bevin's hatred to Israel having any influence in Washington'.[93] Very much like the British Foreign Office, the Israeli premier found it difficult to admit that his retreat was caused by foreign pressure and not his own judgement.

THE *DE FACTO* RECOGNITION

Some writers and senior Israeli officials are convinced with hindsight that, had it not been for the shooting incident, Britain would not have granted Israel a *de facto* recognition.[94]

However, it seems that the incident had only accelerated the decision-making process and probably to some extent the timing of the recognition, since the two countries were moving in any event towards normalisation of the relationship. In fact the months preceding the incident were particularly important in this context. Bevin was seriously discussing with the Foreign Office the possibility of recognising Israel *de jure*, provided the military operations came to a halt. In a Cabinet memorandum the Foreign Secretary wrote that it would have been convenient to establish direct communication with Israel and recognise the Jewish state.[95]

This trend was not unique to the Foreign Office. In December 1948, the military (the CoS Committee) had informed the Foreign Office that in their view Israel possessed the strongest indigenous army force in the Middle East. The implication of this assessment was that Israel was vital for the defence of the area in time of war. Immediately after the shooting-down incident the Middle East CiC advocated the cultivation of friendly relations with Israel on strategic grounds. They argued that the Western allies would need Israel's cooperation in case the area fell under Russian occupation.[96]

But there were other opinions as well. Officials such as Sir Orme Sargent, the Permanent Under-Secretary of State, were to say the least not impressed by the incident, and in some ways reversed their views about the need to recognise Israel. Sargent feared that Israel would play the Arab states off against one another unless the Arab world were united.[97]

The main effect was on British public opinion. It appeared in favour of recognition. Whereas *The Times* (7 January 1949) justified the British behaviour in the Sinai, most papers criticised it. 'All sense of clarity and restraint in British policy appeared to have vanished into the clouds', declared the *Economist* (15 January). Leaders of the Liberal and Conservative parties demanded recognition.[98]

This pressure had its main effect on the Cabinet meeting on 15 January 1949. Bevin told the meeting that the Foreign Office had not opposed a Jewish state in the past and that, by supporting the Bernadotte plan, Britain in fact recognised the existence of such a state. However, he wanted to delay the recognition until the final definition of Israel's frontiers. Bevin realised that this could take time and therefore suggested a British consulate be established in Tel Aviv in the meantime. A day later he learned of the Israelis' refusal of this offer unless accompanied by *de facto* recognition. This step probably pushed Bevin even further towards recognition without the stipulation that Israel's frontiers first be defined. It is worth noting that Bevin's suggestion was made against the advice of the Eastern Department. The Department claimed that it would appear to the Arabs that the British were abandoning their impartial attitude under American pressure.[99]

The Foreign Office hoped the Cabinet would delay its decision on recognition until after it had obtained the opinions of British representatives in the Arab world. However, the Cabinet was facing a crucial debate in the House of Commons on Palestine on 26 January. Hence it had decided in principle to grant *de facto* recognition to Israel on 24 January, and agreed to delay the formal announcement until after the debate. The decision was therefore made before the Office had made up its mind. Nevertheless it enabled the Foreign Secretary to face the Opposition in the House by promising recognition within a short while.[100]

Three main reasons were given for the decision to grant recognition, and these were recorded by Bevin in a Cabinet paper on 17 January. First, Bevin explained that recognition was essential for the peace process: 'Nothing should be done at this stage that should prejudice the continuation of the Israeli–Transjordan and Israeli–Egyptian talks.'[101] Moreover Britain hoped to exert more influence on the peace process by the recognition.[102]

Second, it was a way of solving the outstanding financial disputes between the ex-Mandatory government and the new state. Or, as it was put in Foreign Office language, His Majesty's Government was convinced of 'the importance of entering into direct relations with Israel in order to facilitate day to day transactions covering the area of

Palestine occupied by the Jews'.[103] Finally, the Foreign Secretary regarded this move as a means of persuading the Arab governments that Israel was a *fait accompli*.[104]

Apart from these three reasons for recognition, we could add that Bevin's support for this action was part of his efforts to improve Anglo-American relations. However, he supported this decision in spite of his failure to present the recognition as an integral part of a new Anglo-American understanding about unity of purpose in the Middle East. The Foreign Secretary could, nevertheless, still point to the considerable improvement in the American attitude towards Jordan in return for the shift in the British attitude towards Israel.[105]

Even before the recognition of Israel, the Office was constantly on the alert to ensure that Transjordan and Israel would be treated equally in the international arena. Thus Israel's admission to the UN, in the Foreign Office's view, depended on Transjordan's admission. Both states, for that matter, were regarded as the successors to the Mandatory Palestine government.[106]

Bevin had certainly wanted to maintain the Anglo-American alliance, and for that reason alone would have followed the American policy. However, it seems that his own pragmatism would also have led him to recognition. He preferred to choose his own timing. This can be shown by pointing to the fact that he did *not* change his attitude towards Israel's existence: that is, despite his recognition of the inevitability of the Jewish state, he did not regard Israel in a positive manner. Only in July 1949 would Bevin change his attitude and convey to the Israelis his positive appreciation of their state.[107]

The developments in Palestine were debated on 26 January in the House. The debate became an all-out confrontation between Churchill and Bevin about whose policy in Palestine was more damaging to British interests. Churchill demanded recognition on behalf of the Opposition. In the debate, the House was not told of a final decision to recognise Israel, but only of the government's intention to do so.[108]

Israel was recognised by Britain on 30 January 1949. This gesture was preceded by the release of the illegal immigrants still detained in Cyprus. Throughout the first half of 1949 Bevin would continue to be ambiguous about Israel and display an equivocal attitude towards the Jewish state. His speeches in the House were still anti-Israeli but gradually, as the second half of 1949 passed, the Foreign Secretary would show a new face to the Israelis.[109] He would talk about a new era

in Anglo-Israeli relations and tell Sir Knox Helm, the first British
representative in Tel Aviv, that he was being sent to Israel 'to forget
the past and handle the future'.[110]

BRITAIN AND THE PALESTINE WAR: CONCLUSIONS

One can draw four main conclusions about the British policy at that
time. First, it seems that British policy during the war was influenced
by its posture towards Abdullah's territorial ambitions. Britain had
adjusted itself to these ambitions in a pragmatic way which was typical
of the conduct of policy by Bevin and the Foreign Office during that
period. The Foreign Office preferred to adapt itself to the policies of its
most loyal ally in the area rather than to oppose him, especially since,
under the guidance of Bevin, it had discovered that Abdullah's policy
in the long run would best serve British strategic interests.

Second, at an early stage of the war, the Foreign Office recognised
the inevitability of a Jewish state in Palestine and accepted partition as
the only solution. However, the Foreign Office (and for that matter
the military and the War Office) were dissatisfied with the proposed
boundaries. Everything possible was done to wrest the Negev from
Israeli hands and to annex it either to Transjordan or Egypt. This led to
a deep British involvement in the discussions in the UN about the
situation in the Negev, whereas it showed little if any interest in what
was happening in the north of Palestine.[111]

Third, given Israel's new strength as a result of its victory in the war
and given the lack of any direct formal Anglo-Israeli contact at the
time, the only hope Britain had was that the Americans would exert
pressure on Israel to accept a solution favourable to the British. The
Americans were unwilling to do so, however, because of domestic
considerations. Despite British disappointment on this particular
score, the hitherto strained relations between the two powers and
allies improved as a result of the American approval of the main
feature of the new British Palestine policy, namely the Greater
Transjordan option. The concept was accepted in principle by the
Americans.

Finally, Britain was acting in cooperation with the strongest Arab
force engaged in the war and thus could direct and, to some extent,
determine the course of the war. However, Britain's ability to
determine and influence the course of war was limited owing to its
desire to maintain its good relations with the Arab world. Moreover,

given the pragmatic nature of British foreign policy and also its ability to overcome past prejudices and emotions, it did not escape the attention of the Foreign Office that another strong (if not superior) military element had emerged in the area: the Israeli army.

This British pragmatism was clearly seen in their attitude towards the developments in Palestine and the area after the Palestine war, as the following chapters will illustrate.

5 The Creation of the Greater Transjordan

THE BRITISH ATTITUDE TOWARDS THE PALESTINIAN QUESTION, 1949–51

There is little wonder that the decision-makers in London saw no reason for changing their policy towards the Arab–Israeli conflict after the end of the war in Palestine. On the contrary, the war's political and military consequences followed British predictions along the lines of the Greater Transjordan concept.

Thus there was no need for revising the policy. However, it was necessary to follow closely developments in post-Mandatory Palestine. As an interested party, Britain was still involved in the peace process that followed the war. The same motives that had shaped its deep concern for events in the war were still relevant afterwards. Hence it seems only natural to continue our study of the implications of the Greater Transjordan concept on the course and outcome of the first Arab–Israeli war with an examination of British policy towards the question of Palestine in the post-Mandatory era.

It is noteworthy that no one talked about the Palestinian problem at that time (1948–51). There was a clear distinction between the *question of Palestine's future*, namely, the territorial problem as well as the question of sovereignty, and the *question of the refugees' future*, that is, the humanitarian aspect of the problem. The main implication of such an approach was that the Palestinians were not regarded as a nation or as a people who could constitute a side in this dispute. The main reason for this approach was the attitude of the parties involved in the conflict towards the concept of an independent Palestinian state alongside a Jewish state. Such a state as offered by the UN resolution of November 1947 had been ruled out by all the parties prior to the war in Palestine. Most of the Arab states and the Arab Palestinians demanded a unitary state in Palestine, whereas Transjordan, with the consent of the British and the Jewish Agency, contemplated the annexation of the areas allotted to the Arab Palestinians in that resolution. During the bilateral and multilateral negotiations which followed the Palestine war, the Arab governments tended to accept the principle of partition without recognising the Jewish state. In fact, each Arab country

74

suspected the other of conspiring to annex the territories allotted to the Palestinians.

Owing to Israel's refusal to give up any territory it had occupied during the war, the only Arab countries left with control over Palestinian territory were Egypt and Transjordan. Hence it is important to make the distinction between two categories of Palestinians. On the one hand, there were the local inhabitants in the areas under Egyptian, Transjordanian and Israeli control and, on the other, the refugees. The question of sovereignty was determined by each of these countries, whereas the refugee problem was the subject of multilateral discussions under the auspices of the PCC. The Arabs and the Israelis were only too pleased to leave the problem of the refugees in the hands of the Western powers (mainly the British and the Americans).

The researcher of the period will thus have to make the same distinction and look first at British policy towards the question of the sovereignty of the Arab Palestinian areas under Transjordanian rule, and then examine the British concepts concerning the possible solution of the Palestinian refugee problem. Such an analysis is essential not only for the student of British policy towards the Arab–Israeli conflict, but also for the understanding of the emergence of the Palestinian problem in its modern form in 1967, when it became the source of another Arab–Israeli conflict. Two important facts should be mentioned in that context. First, most of the Palestinians, either refugees or local inhabitants, were under Transjordanian rule or sovereignty. Thus it is necessary to study carefully British and Transjordanian approaches to their future. Second, the Palestinians did not possess any political power or any proper means of representing their case. They enjoyed very little support in the Arab world. The Arab League members had opposed the Transjordan annexation programme owing to their own territorial and national ambitions, and they had little interest, if any, in the fate of the Palestinians or their land.

The link between the British conceptions regarding the solution of the Palestine problem and the question of sovereignty of the Arab Palestinian areas seems quite obvious. By advocating the annexation of central and eastern Palestine to Transjordan, namely most of the areas allotted to the Arab Palestinians in the UN resolution of November 1948, on the one hand, and by accepting the inevitability of the Jewish state on the other, Britain ruled out (as did the Israelis and the Transjordanians) the possibility of an independent Palestinian state. Thus with the exception of the Gaza Strip, the question of the sovereignty of UN Arab Palestine was decided by Transjordan and Britain. These two governments tried to solve the question through the annexation of Arab Palestine by Transjordan. After securing Israeli support for the annexation, Britain and Transjordan succeeded in obtaining Bernadotte's approval for the Greater Transjordan idea. His proposals gave a certain international legitimacy to the annexation.

This chapter is devoted to the way that annexation was carried out by the Transjordanians. Apparently it was planned and executed by King Abdullah with some British intervention, mainly from the Legation in Amman. The second part of the chapter is an attempt to explore the connection between the concept of 'Greater Transjordan' and the attitude to the refugee problem. The problem is somewhat more complicated than that related to the question of sovereignty, and therefore should be dealt with carefully. It would be best elucidated by suggesting that the connection lay in the genuine British fear of an independent Palestinian state, as well as in British perceptions regarding the role the Palestinians should play in the Greater Transjordan. One of the main consequences of annexation could have been the Palestinisation of Transjordan. The resident Palestinians constituted half of the population of the unified state. With the refugees added, they composed three-quarters of the population. Integration could have meant equal representation in the legislative system and even in the executive. Indeed this was demanded by local inhabitants of the West Bank at an early stage. These Palestinians, partly for economic motives and partly for political reasons, pushed for the completion of the unification as well as for a larger degree of representation, and some would argue that what they demanded was a larger degree of democratisation. For the Legation in Amman it was seen as a serious threat to the autocratic rule of the Hashemites and *ipso facto* a danger to the whole British strategic build-up in the Middle East. Hence the possibility of solving the refugee problem as a whole in the framework of Greater Transjordan was ruled out.

BRITAIN AND THE INCORPORATION OF ARAB PALESTINE

The methods and actions by which American, Jewish and UN consent for the 'Greater Transjordan' formula was acquired were dealt with at length in the previous chapters. The aim here is to look at the policies concerning the effect of the implementation of the Anglo-Transjordanian understanding and agreement on the future of the Arab areas of Palestine.

One has to differentiate between the British role and attitude towards the various stages of the integration process in 1948–50 (up to the declaration of the unification of the two banks of the river Jordan) and the British effort to confront Arab opposition to the annexation of eastern and central Palestine to Transjordan. The former issue, namely British policy towards Abdullah's measures in the West Bank[1] and his relations with the Palestinian leadership there, was treated mainly in Amman by Sir Alec Kirkbride and the British Legation. Kirkbride enjoyed the King's trust as well as the ministers' confidence and thus London hardly intervened in its minister's policies towards the process of incorporating the West Bank into Transjordan.

In London, however, Arab reaction to Abdullah's policies was perceived as constituting a threat to British interests in the area and to Britain's position in Transjordan in particular. The Foreign Office tended to regard Egyptian and Syrian attitudes on this question as part of their struggle against British influence in the Arab world. Furthermore, Arab positions on this issue were received by the Eastern Department in the context of inter-Arab rivalries. Thus Arab opposition to Abdullah's policies in Palestine was seen as part of the rivalry within the Arab world between the Hashemites and the Anti-Hashemite blocs, the latter becoming more and more anti-British, so it was an issue of paramount importance to the policy-makers in London. This British assumption seems to have been correct. This was in fact the first dispute of the League. However, the dispute was not so much about territory as about the right to represent the Palestinians: representing them in the world at large and in the council of the Arab League.[2] We shall therefore devote our attention first to this Arab dispute and the British share in it.

Prior to the war in Palestine and as a result of the coordination between Britain and Transjordan on the Palestine policy, Abdullah had prepared himself for the next stages of his scheme, regardless and without the knowledge of the other Arab states. His first inclination was to declare his non-recognition of the existing Palestinian bodies (such as the AHC). However, Kirkbride succeeded in preventing the King from taking such a step by convincing him to consult the Iraqis before acting. Nevertheless, unlike Kirkbride, Abdullah asserted that an essential precondition for the success of his scheme was the elimination of any independent Palestinian representation; hence his constant preoccupation with, and apprehension about, the AHC's moves and policies in the first half of 1948. Indeed, the AHC did decide to establish an administrative organisation which would represent the Arab population in Palestine. Its head would have been a president and would have included, *inter alia*, a council and an executive committee. Thus, in spite of Kirkbride's criticism, the King deemed it necessary to state openly that he had claims to certain economic and strategic areas in Palestine.[3]

However, the AHC and, in particular, the Mufti, lost the support of the Arab League during March–April 1948. Already in March differences of opinion had been apparent between the Mufti and the League concerning the establishment of a Palestine government in exile. The Mufti favoured the establishment of a shadow government on condition that the League would allow him to constitute it on the pattern of the AHC, implying that it would have consisted almost entirely of members of the Husseini Party.[4] The Arab League opposed the establishment of such a government owing to the Arab states' disinclination to appoint the Mufti as the single controlling head of the Arab war effort in Palestine.

Thus the establishment of the government in exile was a Palestinian initiative, despite the League's resentment, as well as the opposition of some members of the AHC, such as Dr Hussein Khalidi and Ahmad Hilmi Pasha. Jamal Al-Husseini, an eminent member of the AHC, believed that once this government was established, the Arab states would no longer reject it. However, this member of the AHC failed in his endeavours to enlist support in the Arab capitals. The League's decision to appoint the Mufti as commander of the Jerusalem area alone had shelved the question of a Palestinian government until September 1948.[5] Nevertheless, the AHC retained some of its authority through the network of local defence national committees which ran public and defence affairs in their respective localities. In the areas where Legion units were present, the members of these committees were pro-Hashemite and facilitated the takeover of eastern Palestine by Abdullah.[6]

Thus, without the League's support, with limited financial resources, and with Abdullah appointed as commander of the forces liberating Palestine, the Palestinians could not have hoped to run their own affairs in the country. Moreover the Legion was strengthening its control over the Arab areas during April–May 1948. Abdullah aimed at reducing the authority of the AHC and at convincing the local

Palestinians of the desirability of linking their future to the Transjordanians. Glubb himself toured the Palestinian towns for that purpose. By May 1948, Abdullah's popularity had undoubtedly risen in some areas of Palestine.[7]

Once the Legion had taken some of the Arab areas of Palestine, Abdullah's first step was to appoint military governors for them. This was done, obviously, as a means of maintaining law and order, but it also helped the King to counteract talk of annexation. A few days after the occupation, pressure was exerted on Palestinians in those areas to accept administrative appointments offered to them.[8]

After four days of fighting, the Legion entered Nablus, Kalkilia, Tul-Karem and Jenin, and expelled the ALA units which had been quartered there since the beginning of 1948. In Tul-Karem the ALA was forced to withdraw under the threat of the Legion's arms. Ostensibly the ALA was ordered to withdraw with the aim of reinforcing the Syrian forces engaged in fighting in the north, and because it was looting Arab property. However, it was done mainly in order to establish Legion rule in these towns.[9]

A former Transjordan premier, Ibrahim Hashim, was appointed military governor of all the parts of Palestine effectively occupied by the Arab Legion. The Legation in Amman reported that this was a natural sequence of events, since it represented the effect Palestinian public opinion was having on Transjordan activities. (Hashim was a Palestinian.) Indeed the first steps were carried out successfully and even the chairman of the AHC Executive Committee could but greet Abdullah's entry into Palestine and offer cooperation with the Legion in the battle over Jerusalem. However, these efforts on behalf of the AHC were in vain, as Abdullah was determined to abolish this body. Thus a week later the British Consul in Jerusalem reported that: 'All references to the Arab Higher Committee gave the impression that it is regarded as non-existent.'[10] The Transjordanians decided to keep the National Committee in Jerusalem subordinated to the appointed military governor of the city, Abdullah At-Tal. Under his military administration, efforts were made towards establishing a new pro-Hashemite cadre of civil administration. At-Tal's next task was to disband the remaining units of the ALA.[11]

While the Legion was carrying out the *de facto* annexation of the West Bank, the Arab world was debating the question of the sovereignty of Palestine. Owing to the presence of Egyptian forces in the vicinity of Jerusalem and in the Hebron area, the Egyptian government's policies carried important weight in the League's discussions on the issue. The Egyptian government suggested a unitary state over all of Palestine as the ultimate objective of the war effort in Palestine. The Transjordanian and Iraqi delegates in the League opposed this suggestion, but the League's Council accepted the Egyptian proposal and decided to impose military rule on the occupied territories until the inhabitants decided their future. In a sense this was a compromise between the two viewpoints. The Transjordanian premier, Abu Al-Huda, had little doubt that the inhabitants of the Transjordanian-controlled areas would be unanimous in asking for a union with Transjordan.[12]

Abu Al-Huda's confidence was due to steps taken by the Legion to ensure the cooperation of the locals. The Transjordanians did not even try to conceal these measures and ignored Bevin's warning about world public opinion and Arab reaction. Bevin, who favoured the annexation as much as Abdullah did, was nevertheless worried about the King's eagerness to accelerate the process of formal unification of the two banks of the river Jordan. Kirkbride, too, pleaded with Abdullah to slow down the process. The British representative deemed it necessary to obtain American and, if possible, worldwide *de jure* recognition of the annexation before completing the process. He had also looked for ways of securing the newly enlarged kingdom against Israeli or Arab counteractions. The premier and most of the ministers in Amman were as cautious as the British and tried to restrain the King in his eagerness to accelerate the process.[13]

However, there were few signs that world public opinion was at all troubled by events in Palestine, or that Abdullah was troubled by what the world in general or the Arab world in particular had to say about the annexation. On the contrary, Abdullah's determination to quicken the pace of the annexation was reinforced by the publication of Bernadotte's second proposals. The revised proposals claimed that there were compelling reasons for merging the Arab territory of Palestine with the territory of Transjordan. These new proposals helped to soothe Foreign Office apprehensions and gave Abdullah's action in Arab Palestine international legitimacy. Bernadotte and Abdullah concurred on the inevitability of a Jewish state, and the Transjordan premier promised the Count that 'Transjordan would never oppose a decision by the UN General Assembly, even if the other Arab countries would do so.' More important, from Abdullah's point of view, was Bernadotte's conclusion that the Arab solution for the Palestine problem, a unitary Arab state, had become unrealistic.[14] Nevertheless, the Foreign Office pointed out to Abdullah that

Bernadotte was merely making a proposal, not an unequivocal recommendation. Indeed, Bernadotte's proposals were not as categorical as the Foreign Office wished them to be. Therefore Kirkbride was instructed to tell Abdullah that 'everything should be done to prevent the proclamation of an Arab government of Palestine. The United Kingdom would help him to that purpose.'[15] Thus, we can see that Abdullah was advised to do his utmost to prevent the creation of a Palestinian state, but at the same time was warned against taking drastic measures in this direction. Abdullah, so it seems, ignored this confusing and contradictory British advice.

Abdullah himself realised that notwithstanding Bernadotte's position, much was left to be desired regarding the consolidation of his rule over Arab Palestine. Thus he sought further and stronger affirmation of British support for his policy. This was granted to him by a letter from Bevin in which British support for the Greater Transjordan option was reiterated: 'an extension of Transjordan to cover the Arab areas of Palestine and Jerusalem and . . . the integrity of the expanded Transjordan would be assured by the terms of the Anglo-Transjordan treaty'.[16]

The reiteration of British obligations under the alliance treaty was issued in July 1948, and was of immense importance to the King. It came at a time when the League had begun discussing the future of the Arab areas of Palestine.

THE ALL-PALESTINE GOVERNMENT

In July 1948, the Political Committee of the Arab League met in Cairo to discuss the prolongation of the first truce. The Arab members by then had become suspicious about Abdullah's intentions in Palestine. In a step aimed at curtailing the King's ambitions, the Political Committee decided to establish a temporary Civil Administration in Palestine directly responsible to the League. This administration was to concern itself with purely civic affairs. The jurisdiction of the Administration was extended to all areas of Palestine occupied by the Arab armies in the past, present and future. The League further suggested the establishment of a government which would be in charge of this Administration.[17]

The proposed government would be assisted by a council. Both bodies, the council and the government, would be guided by decisions and directives of the Arab League Council or the Political Committee.

The council attached to the Administration would deal with social, financial and agricultural affairs in Palestine.[18] Thus the League attempted to cover all aspects of life in the future Palestinian state.

It is noteworthy that the League Council had already decided in April 1948 to hand over Palestine to 'its owners so that they may rule it in the way they wish'.[19] That decision also warned that 'should any Arab state violate this decision, it shall be considered as having repudiated its obligations as well as the provisions of the Pact'.[20]

Tawfiq Abu Al-Huda, who represented his country at that meeting, approved the proposal without referring the question to Amman. Therefore he did not accurately represent the Transjordanian attitude and caused further deterioration in his own position in Transjordan and his relations with the King. Kirkbride complained that by this Abu Al-Huda had diminished the King's chances of obtaining the Arab areas of Palestine. It seems, in hindsight, that Abu Al-Huda supported the Greater Transjordan concept as much as the British and the King did. But for tactical reasons, the premier believed it was better to toe the general Arab line while quietly carrying out the annexation. After all, the sincerity of other members of the League could have been suspect when they supported the Civil Administration proposal; namely, their opposition to Transjordan's move was mainly for domestic consumption and not out of concern for the independence of the Palestinians. Thus it appears that Abu Al-Huda believed that Transjordan should be committed publicly to an independent Palestinian state and at the same time continue the process of annexation.[21]

Abdullah was forced to accept the decision. He could not come out publicly and openly against the League. However, he decided to try to confront the League's decision by sending two Palestinian representatives with Abu Al-Huda, implying by this move that he, and not the proposed Administration, represented the Arab Palestinians living under his rule. Furthermore, the King raised the issue of who the 'real representatives of Palestine in the League' were, claiming that the Palestinian case was now represented by the Transjordanian delegation in the Political Committee and that therefore there was no need for independent Palestinian representation.[22]

At that point, Abdullah's aims in the Palestine war were revealed to the Arab leaders, and from then on a festering suspicion developed between the Arab states – especially Egypt – and Transjordan. In September 1948 the Egyptians, determined to block Hashemite annexation, announced their plans for a separate government in exile, to be called the 'All-Palestine Government' with its seat in Gaza.[23]

Azzam Pasha, the Secretary-General of the League, explained to British Middle East officials that this government was the one that had been agreed upon by the League members in July 1948. It is worth noting that British reports from Cairo gave the impression that Azzam did not seriously believe that this move would prevent Abdullah from annexing the West Bank. Azzam supported the Egyptian initiative since it seemed to satisfy most of the members of the League. Moreover, he told the British officials that it was a necessary step to bring order in the areas of Palestine under Egyptian control. The Secretary-General claimed that such a decision would strengthen the League's position in the UN. Azzam realised that Britain's main fear concerned the role which the Mufti might have played in that government. The Mufti had been elected president of an Egyptian-sponsored 'National Palestine Council' attached to the government. Azzam promised the head of the BMEO that the Mufti would remain in Egypt and exercise his influence from there.[24] He explained to a senior British diplomat that if the Palestine problem could be solved within six months, he would join those who wished 'to cut the Mufti's throat', but since it would not be solved for ten years at least, the Mufti could still be useful.[25]

There is thus little doubt that Azzam wished to reduce the importance of the whole affair. Azzam anticipated Abdullah's reaction and therefore told American journalists that it was a temporary move; one writer claimed that Azzam even tried to stop the declaration. However, the foreign minister designate of the All-Palestinian government had already informed the press of its establishment. Within two weeks, the government was recognised by Syria, Lebanon, Iraq and even Afghanistan. The Arab League invited all the other Arab states to follow suit.[26]

Had the whole affair been confined to a mere declaration by the League, the British Foreign Office would have accepted its Cairo Embassy's tendency to belittle it. However, the wide recognition accorded to the government throughout the Arab world alarmed it. The new development necessitated a careful examination of the consequences for British interests as well as for Transjordan.

The Foreign Office tried to analyse the motives of the various Arab states for supporting the initiative, rather than study the League's policy itself. It should be remembered that the League carried very little political weight in the eyes of the British. The Foreign Office concluded that the support had come because those countries wanted to placate Arab public opinion and also because they wished to safeguard the Arab juridical position, that is, the claim for sovereignty over the whole of Palestine. Some officials also believed it had been done in order to prevent any Arab government from recognising Israel. What the Arab governments were thought to have had in mind was the same pattern of exile government as used by the Allies in the Second World War (for instance, that of the Poles and Czechs). Kirkbride, in his memoirs, stated that recognition had constituted a move against Abdullah on account of his British contacts and his success in the Palestinian war. He understood it more as an anti-Hashemite act, that is, as part of Egypt's rivalry with the Hashemites for leadership of the Arab world. Both he and Glubb understood the actions against Abdullah as an Egyptian–Syrian plot against the King. It seems that the Foreign Secretary's explanation for the Arab motives for supporting the government is the most acceptable one. He saw the All-Palestine government as a 'counter move' to the Bernadotte proposals.[27] Abidi, Plascov and General Badri, who studied this affair, share this view and accept it as the best explanation for the Arab motives.[28]

Abdullah no doubt regarded it as an attempt to discredit him and to undermine his position in Arab Palestine. He immediately declared: 'I shall fight against this measure with all my power.'[29] At-Tal claimed that the Transjordanian representative who participated in the Political Committee session had approved the decision, although this was denied later in Amman.[30] In his memoirs, King Abdullah argued that he did not object in principle to the government but rather found the timing and composition ill-advised. As he wrote to Riad Al-Sulh: 'This action meant the acceptance and execution of partition.'[31]

The British realised that the establishment of a Palestinian government increased the difficulties of Abdullah's position, as well as their own, in the Arab countries. It followed that, if many Arab countries had recognised the new government, Britain and Transjordan could either wait for its collapse or Abdullah could claim sovereignty over the whole of Palestine. The latter was a claim he could withdraw later (a similar course of action was taken by Soviet-controlled North Korea which in 1948 claimed sovereignty over the whole of Korea). Such a course was suggested by the British Legation in Beirut but was rejected by the Foreign Office on the grounds that it would make it impossible for the UN to guarantee the

Israeli–Transjordanian borders, as it reopened the issue of sovereignty. Furthermore, it would have prevented the American government from recognising Transjordan and would have caused complications regarding the validity of the Anglo-Transjordan treaty. Abdullah, as could have been anticipated, initially wanted to follow that course and, for instance, had asked the Coptic Bishop of Jerusalem to proclaim him king of the city. However, he was advised by the British that he would do best to ignore the government altogether.[32]

Nevertheless the Foreign Office could not remain unconcerned. It was alarmed by news from Amman that the declaration of the Gaza government had been followed by intensive anti-Hashemite action, instigated by the Egyptians, in Hebron and Bethlehem. In the main, this had amounted to the distribution of arms to Abdullah's opponents, organised in a group called the Holy War Army (Al-Jihad Al-Muqadas).[33]

The Eastern Department was particularly worried about the Iraqi stance. If the Iraqis had cooperated with the new government, the position of Transjordan would have been extremely difficult. The Iraqis supported the government initially, but heavy pressure was exerted by the British government to get them to reverse their decision. Two months elapsed before the Iraqi position became clearer. In the mean time Abdullah threatened that he would reconsider his membership in the League and his participation in the war if the Iraqis recognised the Palestinian government.[34] The latter threat was meaningless, however, since by that time (October 1948) Abdullah was already out of the war. As for the Iraqis, throughout the short life of the government, they had been supporting it publicly and then condemning it privately in conversations with the King.[35]

Thus the first official move by the Foreign Office was to deplore the establishment of the government. British representatives were instructed to take every possible action to discourage any Arab government from recognising the new government. They were to convey to the Arab governments that His Majesty's Government regarded the Gaza government as 'ill-timed and that any such proposal seems open to all objections', mainly owing to the Mufti's influence in Palestinian affairs which would precipitate a Jewish claim for the whole of Palestine and possibly Transjordan as well. The British representatives were to claim that Israel, in that case, would be forced to adopt the Revisionist plan. Furthermore, they were advised to take the following line: on the one hand, they should explain that a separate

Arab state would not be covered by existing British treaties and, on the other, they should argue that the state would not be economically viable, which would make its absorption into the Jewish state inevitable.[36] Whereas the last argument certainly could have had an effect, it is hard to see how the threat not to include the state in the British defence system could have won any support.

The Foreign Office decided to recruit the Americans for the task. It was conveyed to the Americans that Bernadotte's report advised against a separate Arab state. The Foreign Office had no need to convince the State Department that the League's claim for the whole of Palestine would have undesirable implications. The State Department was asked to make a specific approach to the Arab governments on this issue. The Department, though doubtful about supporting annexation, cooperated with the British, since it saw the action as part of its support for the Bernadotte scheme.[37] It was at this time that the Palestinian government ceased to play any important role. The All-Palestine government fell not so much because of this concentrated British effort but rather owing to the uneasy alliance between the Mufti and the Egyptians, as well as to the pressure exerted by Abdullah himself.

In this affair, the Mufti undoubtedly acted as an Egyptian protégé, although he and the Egyptian government did not see eye to eye. They shared a common objective in their attempt to prevent the annexation of Arab Palestine. Thus, although most of its designate members were Mufti supporters, the government had no power at all and depended entirely on the Egyptians for funds, supplies and protection. In December 1948, the government withdrew to Cairo, a move which was intended to consolidate Egyptian control over the Mufti. The Mufti himself claimed that he had acted independently of the Egyptian government on the Gaza government.[38] In any event, the two sides' inability to cooperate was one of the main reasons for the failure of the Gaza government.

Moreover, the defeat of the Egyptians in the Negev forced some members of the government to move out of Gaza to other Arab cities. Some returned to Jordan hoping to be forgiven by the King. Abdullah tried to convince and bribe the proposed head of the government, Hilmi Pasha, to take his former position in the Transjordan administration, but failed to do so. He was more successful with most of the other members, who resigned from the government and joined the Transjordanian administration in the West Bank.[39]

Thus the whole affair was soon over and proved to have been a farce;

Abdullah was now 'justified' in replacing the Mufti with a candidate of his own.[40] He prohibited the foreign minister designate of the government from coming to the West Bank and canvassing for support. Finally, at the beginning of October, he organised a Congress of Palestinians in Amman to oppose and repudiate the All-Palestine government.[41]

One has to differentiate between the implications and conclusions drawn by the various writers from this episode, benefiting from the perspective of time, and the immediate reaction and assessment of the British Foreign Office and the Transjordanians. Most researchers of the period agree that the creation of the government brought the division of opinion between the Arab governments on the Palestinian problem into the open. The Arab governments had been manipulating and exploiting the question of the Palestinian representation for their own purposes. For the Foreign Office, however, it was an indication of the strength of the Mufti, and for Abdullah it was proof that Transjordan had been outbid by the other Arab governments and that he had, therefore, to accelerate the process of annexation.[42]

As mentioned earlier, one could argue that at that time the Mufti was an Egyptian protégé. It is notable, however, that the Foreign Office did not view his position in that way. The Office's assumption regarding the growing power of the Mufti was based on information gathered by the British Embassy in Cairo about the discussions that had preceded the establishment of the All-Palestine government. To their astonishment, the officials of the Eastern Department learned that during the meeting of the Political Committee in Aley in July 1948, the Egyptian delegation had joined the Hashemites in their opposition to the Syrian–Lebanese proposal to appoint the Mufti head of the Palestinian government. Thus, in spite of the Mufti's contacts in Egypt, the Department believed that he held an important independent position. Moreover, the Foreign Office saw him as the major stumbling block in the way of Egyptian–Transjordanian rapprochement. It seemed to the Office that without the Mufti's interference, Farouk and Abdullah could have reached an agreement on the partition of Arab Palestine and in so doing implement the Bernadotte proposals (which left the issue of the Arab territories in the hands of the Arab states).[43]

The Foreign Office expected a positive attitude from Egypt, owing to what the Office thought was the Egyptian government's growing fear of the Mufti's increasing influence in Palestine. The Foreign Office, and Bevin in particular, could not comprehend, throughout the period in question, the lack of understanding between Transjordan and Egypt on this issue. They tended to attribute it to personal animosity between the two rulers. In fact, Michael Wright, the Superintending Under-Secretary of State, attempted to convince the Americans that the issue was the Mufti and not the Palestinian government. He implied the existence of a school of thought, within the Eastern Department, which was prepared to give some legitimacy to the All-Palestine government if it replaced the former AHC.[44] The crux of the matter was, however, that the British could not have agreed to any political body whose very existence would put the right of Transjordan to annex parts of Palestine in doubt.

At the beginning of October 1948, Abdullah was advised by the Foreign Office to approach the Egyptians to try to reach an agreement on Arab Palestine. Abdullah rejected this British suggestion for two reasons. First, the King was convinced that Egypt would use the *démarche* against him and accuse him of accepting partition. Second, Abdullah understood Egyptian sponsorship of the Mufti as a means of indirect rule in Palestine preferable to direct annexation. Thus the King's disinclination to cooperate with Farouk had upset the hopes of the Foreign Office of bringing about a thaw in Egyptian–Transjordanian relations, and by that of reducing the influence of the Mufti. The Office had to accept Abdullah's concept that the best way to confront any moves by the Mufti was to endorse the immediate implementation of the principles of annexation of Arab Palestine in the Bernadotte plan. Nevertheless, the Office continued its independent struggle against the Mufti and instructed its representatives in the area to 'take such actions as they may find possible to prevent the growth of the Mufti's influence in Palestine'.[45]

The success in inducing Bernadotte to include the annexation of Arab Palestine to Transjordan removed the last international obstacle to the implementation of Abdullah's scheme. The King was left with the problem of facing Arab reaction and countering possible opposition in Palestine. Glubb reported, at the end of September, that he found widespread feeling amongst the Palestinians in support of annexation.[46] However, Kirkbride thought that Glubb was overestimating the desire of the Palestinians for union with Transjordan and underestimating the influence of the Mufti. Kirkbride believed the Legion was capable of consolidating its control over UN Arab Palestine, if Israel were deterred from attacking the Transjordanians and if the Iraqis and the Egyptians were forced to withdraw as a result of an Israeli offensive in the Negev.[47]

The Foreign Office was confident that the Legion would effectively control the Arab areas. However, the British were concerned about the implications of Arab resentment of Abdullah's action concerning their position and interests in the Arab world. It should be noted that this episode coincided with Britain's attempts to conclude defence treaties with as many Arab states as possible. The atmosphere in the Arab capitals had not changed for the better; in fact, in many respects it had worsened. The Lebanese premier demanded that Abdullah telegraph the UN to say that Transjordan did not accept union with any part of Palestine.[48] The Egyptians and the Syrians had sent similar protests throughout September both publicly and privately to the King, which indicated that this was not merely for domestic consumption but out of genuine resentment. However, the developing Israeli offensive in the south had put the Egyptians in dire straits and Farouk and his premier, Mahmud Nokrashi, hoped to obtain some assistance from Abdullah. Consequently, the Political Committee of the League avoided the subject altogether in its session during November 1948.[49]

This new development led Kirkbride to the conclusion that there was no need to fear Arab reaction, since no other solution to the Palestine problem seemed to be emerging from the League or from any of the other Arab governments.[50] It is noteworthy that in December 1948 the parties involved in the conflict were still convinced that it was up to the UN to decide upon the future of Palestine. Whether the decisions made would be accepted as obligatory or as imposing a solution was another matter.

THE PALESTINIAN CONGRESSES

The Amman Congress was an immediate reaction to the proclamation of the Gaza government; Abdullah hoped to show the Arab world that he was able to convene more representatives of the refugee community that the Egyptians had in Gaza. He therefore invited only representatives of the refugees. According to one writer, those who attended the Congress had been forced to do so. Through this congress, Abdullah attempted to manifest the resentment of the refugees against the All-Palestine government and their inclination to grant him the right to represent them. It was part of a wholesale campaign of appeals and petitions by refugees, thanking the King for 'redeeming' Palestine and asking him to take responsibility for the

Palestinians. Even a critical writer such as Plascov conceded that: 'contrary to the widely held belief outside Jordan, these various representations did reflect the feeling of a large segment of the population'.[51] Thus the Congress called for the continuation of the fighting in Palestine, appealed to the UN for justice, and repudiated the validity of the Gaza government.[52]

The relative calm with which the Amman Congress had passed convinced Abdullah that he could proceed with the annexation.[53] Hence one should view the Congress not merely as a tactical reaction to the establishment of the All-Palestine government, but rather as a stage (one out of three main stages) on the way to unification. The Amman Congress was followed by another congress in Jericho, and the last stage was the declaration of the union of the two banks of the River Jordan.

Abidi tends to perceive the Congresss in a different light. According to his analysis, Abdullah convened the refugees in Amman out of fear that Israel might recognise the All-Palestine government.[54] Kirkbride, for one, was apprehensive of such a development. He believed that the Israelis preferred a small non-viable state in Palestine.[55] However, the Israeli line of thinking evolved differently. During September 1948, Ben-Gurion tried to persuade his colleagues in the Government that Israel should and could annex the West Bank. To his Cabinet members, the Premier explained that it would be a suitable Israeli reaction to the strangulation of Jerusalem by the Transjordanians (in spite of the truce, the Legion did not resume the water supply to the Jewish quarters). In his diary, Ben-Gurion developed the theory that without Bevin's 'emotional inhibitions' the West would have realised that Israel had the right to the whole of the Palestine Mandate territory.[56] However, PGI ruled against Ben-Gurion's suggestion (though it was feasible from a military point of view). The main core of opposition came from the IFO. Its experts on Arab affairs had already predicted in July that Abdullah would convene a meeting of representatives from Palestine, and had suggested that Israel would not object to this development. The Office recommended that 'We should concentrate our policy not on the Arab League but on Abdullah and Arab Palestine.'[57] Later, during 1949–51, Sharett played with the idea of supporting an independent Arab Palestine, even if the price was severing the links with the King.[58]

In the meanwhile Abdullah, who for the time being was more worried about the League's reaction, entertained the idea of setting up his own Palestinian government in Nablus, but eventually decided to continue gradual annexation.[59] The next step was to obtain recognition of the inhabitants of eastern Palestine themselves for the union (after having secured partial recognition from the refugees in the Amman Congress).

The King could not have chosen a more propitious time. The Egyptain débâcle in the South occupied both Egyptian and Israeli attention. The Bernadotte proposals granted tacit consent for his plans by the UN and the West. Moreover, the news from Gaza was encouraging. The Mufti had been forced to withdraw to Egypt, under the threat of arrest, and Nokrashi promised the British embassy in Cairo that by that act the Egyptian government had ensured that the Gaza government would not be provocative.[60]

Some writers claim that Abdullah, after the successful Amman Congress, demanded that the British extend the treaty rights to the newly-added territory.[61] However, there was no reason for the King to exert any kind of pressure on the British to that end since, as was mentioned before, the extension of the treaty rights was precisely the argument used by the Foreign Office in favour of annexation, as early as February 1948. Yet it seems that Kirkbride deemed it necessary to persuade the Foreign Office that Abdullah was pursuing the right policy. In his book, Kirkbride claimed that the outcome of the Palestine war was the last proof needed to convince the British that this was indeed the right direction. After the war, asserted Kirkbride, everyone was convinced that 'no amount of misleading propaganda could conceal the fact that the Arab success . . . was an illusion and that, at least for the time being, the creation of an independent Arab state of Palestine was not practical'.[62]

Plascov maintained that the next step in the King's scheme, the Jericho Congress, was intended to convince Britain and the US that Abdullah was not imposing his will on the Palestinians.[63] This assumption coincides with Abidi's explanation for the motives behind the Amman Congress.[64] However, as was the case with the Amman Congress, it appears that Abdullah had no reason to fear an unfavourable British reaction to his plans. British documents from January 1948 onwards indicate that the Foreign Office did not stipulate the will of the Palestinians to go along with Abdullah's scheme as a condition for the success of the annexation. Furthermore, British and American approval were granted long before December 1948.

The second Congress was convened both as a means of placating Arab opposition and in order to safeguard the continuation of the annexation process. Abdullah wanted public Palestinian approval for his next steps towards the union of the two banks of the Jordan. He suggested Jericho as the venue in order to create the impression of spontaneity on the part of the Palestinians. The Congress was called by the executive of the Amman Congress. This executive was told by the King that he would like the Jericho Congress to pass resolutions acclaiming him King of Palestine and to accept tacitly the existence of a Jewish state.[65]

Preparations for the Congress, aimed in the main at ensuring full attendance, were entrusted to the military governor of the region occupied by the Legion. He was allowed to use threats if necessary. For that purpose, the military governor organised and coordinated the activity and the communication between the various military commanders, Legion officers and agents of the Court. The broadcasts from Ramallah and Amman concentrated on creating the impression of spontaneous support for the Congress.[66] According to At-Tal, Glubb took an intensive part in the groundwork and preparations for the congress by touring the areas and talking to Legion officers.[67] Kirkbride's reports indicated that the Legation had known beforehand about these measures and indeed cooperated with the King. Abdullah and the chairman designate, Mohmad Al-Jabri, decided on the Congress resolutions in advance.[68]

Notwithstanding these careful preparations, there was considerable overt opposition to the Congress. The supporters of the Mufti organised a meeting in Bir Zeit and Ramallah expressing opposition, and they sent delegates to disrupt the Congress, but these were arrested.[69] It seems that Abdullah wanted some opposition delegates to come to the Congress to give it a democratic 'flavour'. At-Tal claimed that Abdullah's opponents had agreed to participate because they wanted to influence the resolutions and ease the pressure of the authorities on them.[70]

In terms of attendance, the Congress was a success (3000 people attended). As far as fair representation is concerned, the question is more complicated. Kirkbride believed that the Congress was fairly representative of Arab Palestine. However, the mayors of the important towns did not attend, apart from Jabri, the Mayor of Hebron and the chairman of the Congress.[71]

Abdullah quite probably regretted the permission he had given to some opponents to attend the Congress, since he rejected the resolutions passed by it and instructed that they be redrafted after they had already been broadcast on Radio Ramallah. The revised draft was broadcast on NER (Sharaq Al-Adna).[72] At the end of December, yet

another version was published. The first called for the union of
Mandatory Palestine with Transjordan and recognised Abdullah as the
constitutional King of Palestine, as a preliminary stage to an all-Arab
unification. The revised draft omitted references, made in the original
resolutions, to the right of the refugees to their homes, and did not
mention the call made to the Arab countries to complete the task of
liberating Palestine. Instead it laid the foundations for the new
constitutional and administrative organisations of the 'Arab
Hashemite kingdom of Jordan', and it repudiated the AHC and the
Gaza government. The war in Palestine was not mentioned, and
neither was there any implication that the incorporation of the Arab
parts of Palestine was a stage on the road to a pan-Arab union. The
first draft can be found in At-Tal's memoirs, in the formal Jordanian
version of Musa and Madi and in Abidi's book, whereas the full text of
the second draft (broadcast on NER) can be found in Nevo's book.[73]
The whole subject was widely dealt with by these and other sources.
For this study, it is important to emphasise that the Foreign Office,
even if it did realise the existence of different versions, did not consider
them to be important.[74] There are indications that Kirkbride knew
about the various drafts. His report on the Congress was a combination
of the two drafts, and his main conclusions were that Abdullah would
not be proclaimed King of Palestine (as the original resolutions had
stated), and that the Congress intended to remove the settlement of
the Palestinian problem from the hands of the League and to authorise
Abdullah to effect a settlement on behalf of the Arab Palestinians. The
last conclusion appeared in the revised draft.[75]

Supporting congresses were held in Beirut and Tripoli throughout
December 1948. In Jerusalem a group of eminent Palestinians held the
Jerusalem Arab Congress, declaring the right of the people of
Jerusalem to decide their own destiny. However, it called upon the
Legion to remain in the city until it was liberated.[76]

Whereas almost all the League states, apart from Yemen, had
condemned the Jericho Congress, the individual reactions of the states
varied in scope and purpose. The Egyptian reaction went as far as
sending some arms and ammunition to the pro-Mufti elements in the
Jerusalem area, accompanied by one of the Husseins, who was
captured a short while after his arrival in Palestine. The Iraqis, on the
other hand, sent three eminent Iraqi statesmen (in fact, they were all
former premiers of Iraq: Nuri As-Sa'id, Jamal Baban and Jamal
Madfai') to persuade the King not to bring the Jericho conclusions for
discussion and confirmation by the Transjordanian Parliament. As in

its reaction to the Gaza government, Iraq pursued a twofold policy. Publicly, it joined the other Arab governments in severely criticising Abdullah's reaction; privately, As-Sa'id, who went to Amman in an unofficial capacity, told the British he believed the Arab world should thank Abdullah instead of criticising him.[77]

The Egyptian government found itself in an extremely difficult position. On the one hand, they deemed it necessary to protest against independent Transjordanian policy on Palestine and, on the other, they could not envisage a way out of the débâcle of their army in the Negev without the help of the Arab Legion. Furthermore, the Egyptians were seriously considering the possibility of concluding an armistice with the Israelis; however, they had no desire to be the only Arab country embarking on such a path. Hence a united front with Abdullah was still desirable from their point of view. That is probably why eminent Egyptian personalities, such as Karim Thabet and Prince Muhammad Ali, criticised Farouk's condemnation of the annexation in private discussions with the British.[78] Notwithstanding these doubts, the only voices which were heard publicly from Cairo were those of criticism and condemnation. These attacks were intensified during December 1948. The Ulema of Jerusalem and Al-Azhar commenced a battle of 'Fatwas' between themselves regarding Abdullah's right to represent the Palestinians. Consequently, Abdullah utilised 'his anger' over the Egyptian action to repatriate the Egyptian forces from eastern Palestine as he had planned to do.[79]

In this context it is important to mention that throughout 1949 and 1950, refugee delegations from Gaza asked for the annexation of the Strip to Egypt and were refused. This Egyptian policy, far more than the Gaza government, helped to keep the Palestinian issue alive. It should be noted that at that time, Bevin felt that the existence of both the Gaza government and the Jericho Congress called for a comparison between the two bodies. He suggested that Kirkbride stress the point that the 'Jericho Congress, although attacked by the Arab states is without doubt just as representative and influential as the Gaza Government, if not more so'.[80] In fact, Bevin believed that the Gaza government was unrepresentative and not statesmanlike, whereas the Jericho Congress was realistic.[81]

Sir Alec Kirkbride claimed that the Arab reaction had had an adverse effect on Abdullah's actions in the Arab parts of Palestine. The Minister in Amman argued that the abuse released by Egypt following the Jericho Congress had had the effect of hardening public opinion in Transjordan in favour of union with Arab Palestine.

Moreover, the CoS assured the Foreign Office that the Arab states posed no threat whatsoever to Transjordan; their armies were neither fit nor occupied in Palestine and 'had healthy respect for the strength of the Arab Legion'.[82]

Notwithstanding these assurances, Kirkbride was alarmed by Abdullah's eagerness to bring about an early implementation of the Congress' decisions. The King wanted a short and immediate process of formal annexation. Abdullah told his premier that he had been advised by 'foreign quarters' to push ahead with the implementation. The King claimed that he had been advised by Wells Stabler, the American representative in Amman, and Dr Bunche, the Acting Mediator, to present the world with a *fait accompli* in Palestine. We have only Abdullah's testament for these declarations. Nevertheless, Kirkbride advised the King not to push ahead with the annexation, since it would take place in any event.[83] Whereas Plascov is right in asserting that Britain feared the League's reaction to the formal union, his explanation could not apply to Kirkbride.[84] Kirkbride was more worried about the Council of Ministers' refusal to go any further than about acceptance of the decisions of the Jericho meeting.[85]

Kirkbride attributed the postponement of the immediate implementation of the decisions to his own influence. However, he complained that this influence was 'showing signs of wear and tear after its excessive use during the last months'.[86] The reality was that a new situation was developing in Transjordan. The Council of Ministers was emerging as an independent force, sometimes cooperating with the King, and sometimes opposing him. The King's unsuccessful attempts to find a premier who was prepared to pursue his policy towards the Israeli–Jordanian agreement, regardless of the opinion of the Council, accentuated the growing importance of the Council of Ministers. This phenomenon became more apparent during the Israeli–Jordanian negotiations, where Kirkbride felt that he was fulfilling the role of mediator between the King and his ministers; he usually tended to support the ministers, rather than the King. The ministers, quite probably, showed more realism in their politics, and their views seemed to correspond with those of His Majesty's Government. Tawfiq Abu Al-Huda and Kirkbride did not oppose the annexation, but thought that Abdullah was accelerating the whole process unnecessarily. Abu Al-Huda threatened to resign, since he believed, as did some British officials in the Eastern Department, that Transjordan could reach an agreement with Egypt. Kirkbride himself advocated only a *de facto* annexation, as long as there was hope for an agreement with Egypt. Farouk's adviser claimed that Egypt resented the acclamation of Abdullah as King of Palestine and not the annexation.[87]

Bevin was highly alarmed by the news of disagreement between Abdullah and his ministers. He requested Kirkbride not to inform the State Department about this dispute, since it might have hindered American support for the idea of a united Jordan. The King, incidentally, was supported in his desire for a rapid and formal annexation by a handful of Palestinian leaders who wished to see the Cabinet and Parliament re-elected as a result of the union, thus hoping for a larger Palestinian representation in these bodies.[88]

It is difficult to ascertain whether Kirkbride was right in stating that Arab reaction to the Jericho Congress had increased the support for Abdullah in Arab Palestine; there is little doubt that the King wanted to create the impression that this indeed was the case. The Jericho Congress was followed by another staged in Ramallah, which supported the Jericho decisions. Another one was held in Nablus; here Abdullah was proclaimed monarch of Palestine.[89]

Abdullah was confident enough to proceed with the annexation owing, *inter alia*, to the Iraqi delegation's promises that Iraq would not only object to a proposal to expel Transjordan from the League, but would undertake to ensure that this issue would not be discussed. Neither would it agree to the Gaza government operating in territory under Iraqi occupation. It should be remembered that rumours were circulating of an Egyptian–Syrian initiative to oust Transjordan from the Arab League.[90]

The Egyptian objection to the annexation of Arab Palestine had its impact on the position held by the British representatives on this question. Thus a dispute over Britain's policy towards the Palestine problem developed throughout 1949 between Sir Hugh Dow in Jerusalem and the head of the BMEO, Sir John Troutbeck. Dow claimed that there was no alternative to the handing over of the major part of Palestine to Transjordan. It was indeed perceived that way by the Foreign Office. However, Dow deemed it necessary to stress this point in a letter to Wright, since he was angered by Troutbeck's allegations that Abdullah was a 'land grabber'.[91] Troutbeck warned that the consequence would be a Greater Israel rather than a Greater Transjordan. He was supported by Campbell, who argued that a Greater Transjordan was not more viable than a smaller one. Dow asserted that Britain would have been 'gravely embarrassed' if Abdullah had not wanted that area. An independent Arab state in

Palestine was not viable, in the eyes of the Consul-General of Jerusalem, since it would be dominated by the Mufti, 'an improbable enemy both to us and the Jews'. Thus, he concluded: 'We ought to be thankful that Abdullah is a land grabber.'[92] Most Eastern Department officials agreed to this approach which was adopted by Dow and became the main feature of British Palestinian policy at the beginning of the 1950s. The deterioration of Anglo-Egyptian relations had increased Transjordan's importance for Britain.[93]

Bevin was asked to throw his weight into this matter. Kirkbride pleaded with him to give renewed assurances and guidance to Abdullah. He maintained that British support was more essential than Arab acceptance of the annexation. It seems that Abdullah was indeed left alone in the Arab world, since he had not consulted or even informed the Iraqis, his natural allies. Bevin's consent to Abdullah's activities following the Jericho Congress was conditional on the Foreign Secretary's request that they not follow the lines of the original Jericho resolutions. In other words, Bevin warned the King that Britain would not support him if he were aiming at the union of all Palestine and Transjordan, instead of annexation of the areas allotted to the Arabs in the partition resolution.[94]

As for the Egyptian–Transjordanian dispute, Bevin failed to see any reason why the two parties could not reach a working agreement. Bevin's optimism was based on encouraging accounts coming in from Cairo, where Ahmad Khashaba Pasha, the Egyptian Foreign Minister, suggested division of the Negev between the two countries as a solution for the Palestinian problem, and obtained Lebanese blessing for such a formula.[95] Kirkbride dismissed Khashaba's proposal as a 'dictate', whereas Campbell warned Bevin that His Majesty's Government would be backing the wrong horse if it chose to support Abdullah over annexation. Furthermore, Khashaba suggested that Bevin should be the midwife for such a solution, a role Bevin gladly assumed.[96]

One doubts whether at the beginning of 1949 Egypt possessed any serious territorial ambitions regarding the Negev. Karim Thabet's explanation, given at the time to Campbell, is reasonable and sheds some light on Egypt's motives. Thabet argued that the Egyptians needed to stay in the Negev and Gaza as: 'A justification to the people of Egypt for their sacrifices in the fighting'.[97]

There was an additional pressing issue which compelled Bevin to intervene personally in this Transjordan–Egypt dispute. British officers of the Legion had taken over command of Hebron from the

Egyptians. In fact, the British officers had expelled the Egyptians by force of arms, and Campbell in Cairo remarked that it was most 'unfortunate' that British officers had been sent for such a task.[98]

However, as mentioned before, Abdullah showed no inclination to compromise with the Egyptians after he had accomplished most of his territorial ambitions in the West Bank. Furthermore, the British despatches from Cairo and the BMEO give the impression that the League was more concerned and exasperated by Abdullah's contacts with the Israelis than by the annexation.[99] The League members were willing to acquiesce in the existence of a Greater Transjordan, but they could not accept a separate Israeli–Jordanian peace. It seems that the threat to expel Transjordan from the League if it carried out the annexation was enough to deter the Transjordanian government from concluding a peace with Israel, but not sufficient to prevent annexation.

Thus Bevin was probably right in reminding the King and Kirkbride that the Israeli and American reactions to the annexation were as important as the Arab reaction. Abdullah no doubt regarded the situation in that way and thus intensified his efforts to reach an agreement with Israel; in the main, he aimed at achieving an armistice which would perpetuate Transjordanian rule over Arab Palestine.[100]

The American position was somewhat more complicated than the British Foreign Office had probably anticipated. The Americans (the President and the State Department) differentiated between recognition of Transjordan and recognition of the annexation of Arab Palestine. The Americans were prepared to give only *de facto* recognition to the annexation. In August 1948, the Americans declared their support for *de jure* recognition of Transjordan, provided Abdullah cooperated with Count Bernadotte and accepted the conditions of the second truce.[101] Later, throughout 1949, it was understood by both the Foreign Office and the State Department that *de jure* recognition depended on both powers similarly recognising Israel.

However, the Americans refused to acknowledge and give their formal blessing to annexation. They believed that the best solution to the Palestinian question was a settlement by which Israel would retain Galilee and the Arabs the Negev. They objected to unilateral actions, such as annexation, which changed the territorial situation without an agreement having been concluded between the parties. The State Department's Near East division, in particular, was apprehensive that Abdullah's action would be reciprocated by a unilateral Israeli annexation of the Arab parts of Palestine it had occupied during the 1948 war. The Americans had also expressed concern about Abdullah's position in the Arab world following an annexation.[102]

British pressure on the Americans to support and argue for the incorporation of Arab Palestine into Transjordan increased during December 1948. The State Department replied that it would only support territorial changes made by an agreement between the parties.[103] American reluctance at that point was, quite probably, the result of a desire to await an Israeli decision about their own attitude towards this issue. Although supporting the idea of Greater Transjordan, the Americans did not consent to give their formal blessing unless it was part of an agreement.

The serious conflict which developed between Britain and Israel in the Gulf of Aqaba and over Israeli penetration into the Sinai had prevented American recognition of Transjordan. However, by then the State Department was convinced that the best solution for the eastern parts of Palestine was indeed their incorporation into Transjordan. Informal Congressional support was obtained after Britain's *de facto* recognition of Israel. In June 1949, the Americans went even further; Dean Rusk told Michael Wright that the US agreed that Jordan proclaim the union, provided it would not hinder a final settlement; namely, that no action would be taken before the PCC had completed its work. Thus American and British views coincided once more. However, the Americans did not deem it necessary to grant the annexation *de jure* recognition, owing to the State Department's fear of alienating the other Arab governments. For that reason it refused to accede to Abdullah's desire to visit the US in August 1949. The final American communication on the issue was made during the Middle East conference of the State Department in Istanbul, at the end of 1949. One of the conclusions of that conference was that the US accepted the annexation of Arab Palestine on condition that Arab Palestinians had fair representation in the Jordanian Parliament and Legislature.[104]

The Foreign Office had little reason to be annoyed at the conduct of Abdullah's policy in the West Bank. The implementation of the Jericho decisions was carried out systematically from March 1949 onwards; according to Abdullah's version of the resolutions, not the original ones. An extraordinary decree laid down details of administrative procedures and made various heads of departments in Palestine responsible to the relevant ministry in Amman.[105] The fact that the formal annexation started only in March 1949 was due, first to

Kirkbride's success in postponing the execution of the Jericho decisions and, second, to the fact that most of the ministers and the premier disliked Abdullah's tendency to accelerate the process of unification.

FROM THE ARMISTICE WITH ISRAEL TO THE FORMAL UNION (MARCH 1949–MARCH 1950)

On 30 March 1949, Israel and Transjordan signed an armistice agreement. The gist of the agreement was Israeli consent to the annexation of the West Bank to Transjordan. In return, the Israelis took over an area known as the Little Triangle. The Triangle was a strip around Wadi Arara which connected the Jewish settlements of Afula and Hadera and included 15 Arab villages with 35 000 inhabitants. The agreement provided that the villagers were free to leave or stay as they wished. Those who left were to be compensated. Some of the villagers were separated from their lands by the new armistice line.[106]

The armistice with Israel was poorly received by the Palestinians. It was believed to be part of Abdullah's plan to give up more Palestinian territory to Israel. Later the Transjordanian government would claim that they had been deceived into this arrangement: they had been presented with a fake map during the final negotiations. Sir Alec Kirkbride refuted these allegations in his memoirs with a photocopy of the map signed by both sides which shows clearly that the Transjordanians knew that the Little Triangle included those villages.[107] The Iraqi rank and file stationed in Palestine had certainly held the view that the King had betrayed the Palestinians and attempted to communicate this. Consequently, a delegation from Samaria, the area controlled by the Iraqis, came to Amman to protest against the armistice.[108] At-Tal also helped to encourage feelings of resentment by stating that an adviser to the King had told him that the Israelis would not fulfil their part in the Armistice.[109]

In July 1949 the Little Triangle was transferred to Israel. Israeli behaviour towards the villagers had increased the resentment amongst the Palestinians towards the armistice agreement. In some cases villagers who had sought refuge during the war in areas adjacent to their villages were not allowed to return, although the MAC had instructed the Israelis to facilitate their repatriation, and in other cases the Mukhtars (heads) of the villages had been bribed and sent to their fellow-villagers to spread the word that they would be maltreated on the Israeli side and that they would do better to remain under Hashemite rule. These groups of refugees claimed that they should have been consulted and represented in the armistice negotiations. In April 1949 they set up a committee which urged the King to arrange free passage for the landowners and re-examine the armistice map.[110]

The armistice was condemned in the Arab world as well. It seems that the British took upon themselves most of the propaganda work needed to placate Arab mistrust of Abdullah. The Eastern Department suggested to the British representatives in the Arab capitals that they adopt a line which would release the British from responsibility for conducting or even influencing Transjordan's policy. It appeared to be quite an impossible line. Even if the Arab world were convinced of the independence of Abdullah's policy, which was very unlikely, it would still resent his policies for what they were. Britain, in a letter addressed to the various Arab governments, had already justified Transjordan in an attempt to persuade them to accept Bernadotte's second proposals. In one of the paragraphs of that letter, it was stated that His Majesty's Government did not view the union as a threat to any Arab country. The letter implied that the British would restrict Abdullah in his ambitions, that is, they would not move from union to the Greater Syria plan.[111]

During 1949 the King and his government were acting in two somewhat contradictory directions in their attitude towards the Palestinians. On the one hand, leading Palestinians were allowed to resume their activities in the fields of commerce, finance and politics. Palestinian papers were permitted to reappear and some political activity was taking place. On the other hand, further steps were taken to abolish the Palestinian identity of these areas. Two ordinances were passed by the government. The first provided for the appointment of civil administration officials and the second granted Transjordanian passports and nationality to all Arab Palestinians. Moreover, the Egyptians turned over the civil administration in Bethlehem and Hebron to Transjordanian officials.[112] By the former act, the Transjordanians had in fact terminated the military governorship over the area. The Governor-General assumed the responsibility of the former British High Commission of Palestine.

This process culminated in May 1949 when the Transjordanian Ministry of Foreign Affairs sent a note to all diplomatic representatives in Amman to correct the name of the country to the Hashemite Kingdom of Jordan. Furthermore, the premier resigned in order to form a new Council of Ministers that would include three West Bank ministers (the platform of the new government, as might have been anticipated, dealt mainly with the union of the two banks).[113]

The British Consul-General in Jerusalem was aware of the fact that the three appointed Palestinian ministers were not regarded by the population as representatives.[114] The Consul reported that these ministers were busier arguing about their diminutive salaries than dealing with the affairs of the Palestinian community. Nevertheless the Legation in Amman believed that the Transjordanians had gone as far as they could with regard to the representation of the Palestinians in the administration.

THE TROUBLESOME SUMMER OF 1949 AND NEW PERCEPTIONS ABOUT THE PALESTINIANS

By May 1949, the Legation had formulated their views about the role and importance of the Palestinian factor in the new Jordanian kingdom. It was not, to say the least, a favourable impression. It is worth noting that at the same time as the Foreign Office in London was formulating its own policy towards the problem of the refugees, most of them were situated in camps in Jordan. The Legation in Amman was mainly concerned with the question of how to integrate the local inhabitants of the West Bank (as distinct from the refugees) into the future state. Nevertheless, any thoughts and perceptions about the local West Bank population reflected to a large extent British views about the refugees. Thus when British officials discussed the desirability of incorporating the West Bank population into the administration and politics of the Hashemite kingdom, they had also to concern themselves with the future of the massive number of refugees living in that area. This is best demonstrated by examining the numbers concerned. The East Bank population was 450 000 local inhabitants (half of them Palestinians) and 400 000 resided in the West Bank.[115] According to British reports there were about 94 000 refugees in the East and about 394 000 in the West Bank. Democratisation and fair representation of such a population would have turned Jordan into a Palestinian state.

The Legation in Amman agreed with the Jordanian authorities that the population in Arab Palestine was becoming 'prone to subversive influence'.[116] These assumptions were accentuated by rumours of a pending *coup d'état* in Transjordan. Already, in March 1949, a plot to assassinate Abdullah was discovered. A mine had been planted where the royal car usually passed. The perpetrators were Palestinians sent by the former Mufti. However, a more serious development occurred in May 1949, when a British national, advising the Defence Ministry in Damascus, reported the possible participation of At-Tal and the Syrians in such a coup.[117]

It is noticeable that the British representative in Amman did not consider these rumours seriously. Dow in Jerusalem pointed out that At-Tal could not stage a coup since the forces loyal to the King were under British commanders. Nevertheless, the rumours persisted and were taken seriously by the French representatives in Jerusalem who warned their British colleagues. Notwithstanding the initial British scepticism, the Legation in Amman had little doubt that the Palestinians were potentially susceptible to being used by the Egyptians, the Syrians and even the Saudis to overthrow Abdullah. In the main, the British suspected it could have been done by installing the former Mufti as ruler of an independent Palestinian state. One piece of evidence brought by Kirkbride to prove the existence of such a possibility was a report of the alleged intentions of the Saudis to invite Haj Amin Al-Husseini as guest of honour to the World Muslim Congress in Mecca. However, it was never confirmed by the Embassy in Jedda.[118]

If not everyone in the Foreign Office was convinced of the credibility of these reports and rumours, King Abdullah certainly took them for granted. This is probably why he replaced Abdullah At-Tal as a Mutasarif (Governor) of Jerusalem. At-Tal's memoirs do create the impression that he was not on the best of terms with his British colleagues; it is therefore of little surprise that the British had a major part in his removal.[119]

The replacement of At-Tal was the beginning of a short period of economic and political unrest in the West Bank. On the whole, Kirkbride was dissatisfied with Abdullah's conduct during these months. He doubted whether the replacement of At-Tal would have helped to solve the problems of Arab Palestine, which he regarded as being mainly economic ones. Kirkbride put the blame on the short-sighted policy of the economic administration of the country. The Arab Palestine Chamber of Commerce had no facilities for obtaining import licences. This indicated that the economic administration was subordinate to the officials in Amman who enjoyed an export–import monopoly. The Jordanian government promised £2 million to cover imports for the year 1949. However, only part of it became available, a situation which caused widespread dissatisfaction. Consequently, the Palestinian merchants had to rely on re-exports from Jordan which, due to officials in Amman with vested interests, kept prices in Arab Palestine approximately 25 per cent higher than in Jordan. Thus the commercial circles in fact became a driving force behind the Jordanian government's action aimed at abolishing the customs and passport facilities between the two banks.[120]

The annexation of Arab Palestine had reduced its economic level to that prevailing in Transjordan proper. Consequently the standard of living in Arab Palestine was lower than the one that had prevailed under the Mandate. Kirkbride warned that unless some measure of economic prosperity could be restored, serious political unrest 'may be expected'.[121]

One should be aware that Transjordan still had a primitive rural economy and low standard of living (owing mainly to limited economic resources). Incorporation of Arab Palestine did not improve the level of economic activity in Transjordan, but rather reduced the level in the West Bank. Kirkbride believed that only a 'miracle' such as the discovery of oil could have saved the Transjordanians from an economic disaster which would have led to Abdullah's downfall.[122] The Middle East Official Committee had more practical solutions in mind. It advised the government to work for the inclusion of Transjordan in the investigations of the International Bank, and suggested that a British commissioner be appointed for development affairs in Transjordan in order to reaffirm British control and supervision over the Transjordan economy. The last proposal was accepted by Abdullah.[123]

The economic problem was mainly created by an unwise financial policy. The annual British subsidy was only for the Legion's maintenance and thus was not much assistance. Furthermore, the redemption against Sterling of Palestine Currency Board notes brought in by the refugees (which was equal to the annual British subsidy) was rapidly exhausted.[124] Cutting off Palestinian trade from the Mediterranean had also seriously affected the economic growth.

However, the political discontent had its own roots, not necessarily economic as Kirkbride saw it. First, as was mentioned earlier, there was the unrest caused by the loss of land to Israel (to such an extent that King Abdullah was advised not to tour Samaria, as he wished, during the months May–July 1949). In that atmosphere, it seems that the Legation in Amman tended to identify Palestinian opposition with

Communist instigations; both Communist and Mufti influences were reported to be thriving in Samaria. These cells of Communist activity were regarded as a potential network for the return of the former Mufti. The Legation in Amman suspected that Ahmad Khalil, the Governor of Samaria (and the leader of the Jordanian Liberal party) was associated with the former Mufti's 'Kifah' organisation which was said to be gaining power.[125]

It seems that the main cause of unrest and dissatisfaction was not so much the result of Communist or former Mufti influence or activity, but rather the fruit of local resentment and opposition to certain measures taken by the Jordanian government. Some discontent appeared when Felah Madaha handed over the governorship to Ragheb Nashashibi. Nashashibi's first action was to ban the Ba'ath party (a party advocating a union between two independent states), leaving the Liberal Party (supporting the union) as the only legal party in Arab Palestine. Nashashibi disappointed many Palestinians who believed that he might be granted a position similar to that of the leader of a quasi-autonomous state. It should be noted that the resentment did not constitute a real threat to the Transjordanians; its manifestation was mainly through the *Filastin* paper which was suspended whenever it appeared to the Jordanian authorities to be going too far in its criticism.[126]

Despite their relatively marginal effect on the position of the Hashemites, the economic problems and the signs of resentment shown by some segments of the Palestinian population had enormous implications for the perception of the future political role the Palestinians were to play in the Jordanian kingdom. As the date of the formal union approached, it became clear that proportional representation would have given the Palestinian members a majority of seats (two to one, in fact). This was avoided by the decision to create parity in both houses of Parliament.[127]

The date of the formal union was set for 1 May 1950. However, the Legation in Amman, in concurrence with the King, suggested forwarding the act of Union to April 1950. The main reason, according to Kirkbride, was to prevent a 'Palestinian plot'. The nature of this 'plot' was to try to subject the new Council of Ministers to the responsibility of the Parliament. This was a suggestion made by two Palestinian ministers in the government.[128] In order to prevent attempts of this kind it was decided to bring forward the date of the union and the opening of Parliament. This all happened a few months after the period we are discussing here, but was quite probably a result of that summer of discontent. The Palestinian delegates elected to the new Parliament were suspected of being prone to Saudi, Egyptian and Syrian influence, and therefore regarded as potential opponents of the Union.

In this context it might be worthwhile to bring in two quotations relating to the possible role the Palestinians might have in the Jordanian state. The first is from the period after the elections of April 1950 and before the declaration of union, and was given by Kirkbride as an explanation for moving forward the date of the formal union: 'The Palestinians love to deal in a form of political bargaining closely akin to blackmail and therefore warned Kirkbride that "although the indulging in this pastime has brought them nothing but trouble in the past", they will go on intriguing in the new Jordanian Parliament.'[129] The second was made by Glubb, a few months earlier, with regard to the possible role of the Palestinians. Glubb claimed that the Palestinians were maintaining 'intellectual snobbery' and a high degree of 'dislike of foreigners, particularly the West'. In politics they were 'corrupted' often using 'intrigues against one another', and most important of all, their educated elite was anti-British.[130]

THE ISRAELI REACTION

The tacit Israeli consent to the annexation of Arab Palestine to Transjordan, given in the armistice agreement, prevailed through the troublesome year of 1949. The British and the Israelis even went further. Bevin and Dr Eliash, the Israeli representative in London, agreed in their talk in July 1949 that what was left of Arab Palestine could not stand by itself. Nevertheless the Israelis were not prepared to go as far as denouncing the Biltmore programme, as suggested by Sir Knox Helm; that is, giving up the Jewish Agency's demand for the whole of Palestine – which had been made in 1942 at the Biltmore Hotel in New York. Israel was still suspected by the Foreign Office of harbouring ambitions towards Arab Palestine, and Israeli statements of the kind given by Dr Eliash were inadequate as far as the British were concerned. Thus the Foreign Office believed that the best guarantee against Israel was first incorporating Arab Palestine and only then reaching an understanding with the Israelis. It would thus avoid creating an open invitation for Israel to expand.[131]

The Israelis described quite clearly what they believed to be a threatening situation for them. This was the possible extension of the

Anglo-Transjordanian treaty to include Arab Palestine and to establish British bases there. The State Department believed that, in such a case, the Israelis might seize more territories and reach the River Jordan in a matter of days, before the British could or would act. Only then, predicted the State Department, would Britain launch a counter-attack in order to honour its treaty with Jordan. But even so, it would not be an effective operation since Britain had limited resources in the area. In any event it would divide British public opinion and bring sharp reaction from large segments of American public opinion. Therefore Dean Acheson, the American Secretary of State, was advised by the State Department to tell Bevin that 'he could not rely on American support for all consequences of such an act'. Past records had suggested that Israel had more influence on the US than vice versa, as one official in the State Department remarked.[132] Thus it seems that the Americans anticipated that a serious crisis would develop as a result of the extension of the treaty over Arab Palestine.

However, the situation was viewed less drastically by the British and the Israelis. Through the good offices of Sir Knox Helm in Tel Aviv, the Israelis and the British reached an understanding on this issue. Helm obtained Bevin's approval for promising the Israelis that no British military bases would be established on the West Bank. Nevertheless Helm stressed in a conversation with Sharett that the extension of the treaty was a purely British affair. He further explained that in the event of a war in the Middle East or immediate threat, Britain might reconsider its promise. The Israelis were satisfied and did not demand any further concessions. In fact, a British concession on this issue would have been a damaging precedent and a sign of weakness on the British side. Finally, it should be noted that at least in the Israeli Foreign Ministry the extension of the treaty was perceived as a deterrent against further expansion.[133]

Both clarification of the British position and correct appreciation of the Israeli stand and intentions were essential for Abdullah before continuing with the process of integration. Thus the King could now proceed with the annexation. In his visit to Jerusalem and Ramallah, the King decided to make use of Ragheb Nashashibi's services. It should be noted that the Nashashibis were the main rivals of the Husseinis in the Palestinian community, so when Abdullah asked Nashashibi to take on the office of minister for refugee affairs and join the government, he was probably hoping to reduce the former Mufti's position in Arab Palestine even further.[134]

Abdullah's main predicament was still how to persuade the Arab world that he was the legitimate ruler of Arab Palestine. For that purpose he had to continue the struggle in the Arab League over the question of the 'legitimate sovereign' of Palestine.

THE ARAB LEAGUE AND THE PROCESS OF ANNEXATION

Throughout 1949, Abdullah faced bitter criticism from the Arab League. With great reluctance he agreed that Transjordan would be represented in Arab League meetings discussing the future of Palestine. Abu Al-Huda, the Jordanian representative in those meetings, consented to the participation of an independent Palestinian representative, a move which brought the King's wrath upon him. Abdullah sent a message to the League stating that all the representatives in the Jordanian delegation were of Palestinian origin and so there was no need for an independent Palestinian delegation.[135]

In one of the sessions, the delegations of Syria and Iraq opposed a Saudi–Egyptian proposal for the creation of yet another All-Palestine government. The motion was defeated, but once again the King felt threatened. He wrote to Bevin that any delay in uniting Arab Palestine with Transjordan 'is dangerous';[136] hence if any other Arab government was to set up a Palestinian state, Transjordan would announce the formal union of the two banks immediately and hold elections covering the whole area after having dissolved the Transjordanian Parliament. The Eastern Department was very much against such a precipitate move by the King, that is, before the subject of Palestine could be discussed at the UN. However, Kirkbride appreciated that on this issue Britain should not and could not alter the Transjordanian stand; namely, he realised that the Arab League might decide on the creation of another All-Palestine government without waiting for the UN to give its own opinion on the matter.[137]

In any event, Abdullah preferred action to declarations for the time being. At the end of 1949, he received another letter from Bevin which encouraged him and which indicated that, without doubt, Britain was behind him. Bevin spoke about the annexation question as a long-term commitment by Britain to Transjordan: 'HMG have always viewed with disfavour the establishment of a separate government for Arab Palestine.'[138]

In December 1949, the posts of Governor-General and his deputy, as well as those of the local commissioners, were abolished and their authority invested in the Ministry of Interior. A director of the West Bank administration was appointed, Jamal Touqan, and he headed an administrative system identical to that which existed in the East (namely, heads of departments corresponded with their respective ministers in Amman). Musa and Madi, the official historians of the Hashemite court, asserted that this was done 'with the view of removing the differences between the inhabitants of both banks'.[139] However, it seems that this act was less significant than the passing of new legislation, in the same month, which confirmed the rumours that the anticipated political union was about to be declared. The new legislation dissolved the Jordanian Parliament and doubled the number of representatives in the lower house so that it included 20 new members from the West Bank and added ten West Bank senators to the upper house. Furthermore, it amended the nationality laws with the effect of making all Palestinians in Jordan into Jordanian nationals.[140]

After succeeding in obtaining American and Israeli consent to the Transjordanian policy in Arab Palestine, the Foreign Office strived to induce the UN institutions to accept the new *fait accompli*. It appears that the Transjordanians, at least, were confident that owing to the support of the US and the British they would succeed in obtaining the GA's approval for the annexation. However, the discussion in the UN was postponed time and again as the GA waited in vain for the PCC (a body which had replaced Bernadotte in mediating between the sides) to finish its work and present its conclusions. Thus with most obstacles removed, Abdullah could finally officially complete the creation of the Greater Transjordan.

THE FORMAL UNION: A FEAR OF A 'PALESTINISED JORDAN' (MARCH 1950–JULY 1951)

With this more favourable atmosphere, the Jordanian authorities' apprehensions and sense of uncertainty were reduced and it seemed that all the obstacles in the way of the King's ambitions had been removed. For the time being, the period of unrest in the West Bank was over, due in the main to some economic measures which were being taken and which were improving the position of some of the local inhabitants. One of these was to deny local merchants licences for imports from Syria and Lebanon in order to encourage small industries in the West Bank. This, of course, caused considerable opposition from Palestinian merchants who had to move to Amman, thereby increasing the city's importance as a trading centre. Nevertheless the general trend was positive economically, and even the merchants, despite their initial resentment, were pressing for the abolition of customs control on the river; this was granted in November 1949.[141]

The Eastern Department now recommended a unilateral unification of the two banks by Jordan, that is, without waiting for Arab consent for the move, or a GA decision on the issue. By that time, Israeli personalities such as Sasson, and American diplomats such as Hare, had expressed their support for the union in conversations with the British.[142]

The elections and the formal union were due in April 1950. In the first four months of that year, differences of administration were gradually disappearing and it was reported by the British Legation in Amman that Palestinians on both sides of the Jordan wished to be represented in the legislative system. However, the Jordanian authorities reported signs of agitation in the West Bank to boycott the elections. This forced Abdullah to promise, as a counter-measure, that the next government would be responsible to a constitution and not to him, as was demanded by two Palestinian ministers. Kirkbride himself was warning against Palestinians colonising the East Bank, that is, controlling the economic as well as the political life of the state. This would have left the Hashemites with control mainly over the army (and even this was doubtful according to a Legation report, which stated that in the entrance examination for the Legion there were 300 candidates from the West Bank and only 40 from the East).[143]

The British government recognised the new union and, in order to further improve its relations with Israel, followed its recognition of the new Jordan by a *de jure* recognition of Israel. The Foreign Office hoped that this gesture towards Israel would secure an American and French *de jure* recognition for the union. However, those two countries, although accepting the new situation, refused to give their official blessing to it. The State Department's Near Eastern Affairs division was less than pleased about the British recognition of the union. In a despatch to the British Embassy in Washington it stressed its known position that such an act entitled Israel to annex all the territories it had occupied and that it would lead to a freeze of the territorial status quo. Moreover, the Americans believed that this British recognition amounted to acknowledgement of the partition of Jerusalem and an admission of the failure of the PCC. These were all valid points; nonetheless, one month later, in May 1950, France, the

US and Britain had jointly recognised the territorial status quo of the Middle East (the Tripartite Declaration). For the Foreign Office this declaration was tantamount to American *de jure* recognition of the union. However, the European or American reaction mattered less than the Arab League's possible counteraction.[144]

The Arab League had been deliberating on the issue a few days before the formal union was announced. The Egyptians succeeded in persuading the League Council to invite Ahmad Hilmi, the former head of the Palestinian government and now head of a Palestine department in the League. The Palestinian delegate proposed, as he had a year earlier, to discuss what he called the violation by Jordan of the League's decision from April 1948 to hand over Palestine to its inhabitants. Abdullah had sent the Jordanian minister in Cairo to attend the meeting, implying by this that he saw the whole discussion as unimportant.[145]

Following the union, Egypt requested the adjourning of the Political Committee, raising the issue of the April 1948 resolution. The Jordanian representative claimed that this was now a question of Jordanian sovereignty and could not be forced on Jordan. However, the Committee decided almost unanimously (with the exception of Jordan) that the Jordanian action was a violation of the April 1948 resolution. The League Council was due to meet in June 1950 to decide what sanctions, if any, should be taken against Jordan.[146]

In the meanwhile, the Egyptian press attacked Abdullah by capitalising on the publication of At-Tal's memoirs. The former Legionnaire had reported the secret Israeli–Jordanian negotiations before and after the war in Palestine. At-Tal's brother and the former Jordanian minister in Saudi Arabia joined this campaign in some Egyptian newspapers.[147]

At that moment the Iraqis came to the assistance of their Hashemite kin. This action was coordinated with the British Minister of State, Kenneth Younger. The Iraqi premier succeeded in watering down the League's resistance, whereas the British restrained Abdullah from making any provocative announcements. Nuri As-Said, from an official position, supported the union in his newspaper and, when asked, the Iraqi government refused to give financial support to any attempt to re-establish an All-Palestine government.[148] More important, however, for the Jordanians was the Iraqi support in the League. The Iraqi delegation succeeded in preventing the expulsion of Jordan from the League by introducing a compromise. The Jordanian minister declared that Jordan would hold Arab Palestine in trust until a final settlement of the Palestine problem. This had, in fact, been proposed by Salh Jabr and Nrui As-Said to Abdullah and he had refused. It was quite probable that the Jordanian delegate's declaration was made without prior consultation with the King.[149]

It should be noted that in May 1950, Azzam had already promised the head of the BMEO that Jordan would not be expelled. All the League needed was a decision to save its face, and thus all Abdullah had to do was in fact give a declaration on the lines suggested by Nuri As-Said and Salh Jabr in order to satisfy public opinion, a declaration that would indicate that the status of the West Bank was similar to that of the Gaza Strip.[150]

Kirkbride assured the Foreign Office that the whole affair had helped to heal the breach between the King and his ministers which had emerged as a result of the negotiations with Israel, and that it had had hardly any effect on the attitudes of the Palestinians towards the union. However, he, and also Glubb in particular, were still convinced that most of the Palestinians were opposed to the union owing to their susceptibility to Communism. The Arab Legion Headquarters reported that the former Mufti's efforts to join forces with the Communists in Jordan had failed for the time being. The Communist party was declared illegal and most of its leaders were arrested. Kirkbride warned that its influence would rise once again if the country went through an economic crisis.[151]

However, as far as the Palestinians and the British Legation were concerned this was not the real problem, as Kirkbride came to admit at the end of 1950. The crux of the matter was that Kirkbride's influence was reduced as a result of the union. He wrote to the Head of the Eastern Department, 'You do realize that we are in the throes of revolution here.'[152] Kirkbride referred to the struggle between the Legislation, with its politically-minded Palestinians, and the executive (namely the King and his ministers). As Kirkbride saw it, the executive lost the preliminary encounters for two reasons: the impatience of the King, which led him to direct confrontation with the government; and the fact that Abu Al-Huda gave up the struggle because of his dispute with the King. Consequently, Kirkbride's own influence declined and he was unable to exercise much influence on either side, mainly owing to what he called the negative Palestinian attitude to all British suggestions. Moreover, Kirkbride complained that the Palestinians were 'people with whom I never worked before'.[153] Kirkbride's solution was to form a new government with a smaller number of Palestinian ministers; otherwise, warned Kirkbride, Jordan would collapse and the place would be abandoned, to be divided by its neighbours. Thus a British edifice which took the last 26 years to build would be lost, concluded Kirkbride. The head of, and most of the officials in, the Eastern Department believed it was only a matter of time before the Palestinians would see things the same way as the King did.[154]

In the final analysis, Kirkbride's predictions and apprehensions proved to be exaggerated. Nevertheless, from a Hashemite point of view there was certainly a danger of 'Palestinisation' of the unified state. Hence the Jordanians took some steps to ensure the Hashemite character of the state, the most important of which was not to carry out a promise made to Palestinian jurists prior to the elections by Abu Al-Huda to form a new and enlightened legislative system. Instead the Jordanian government created a new system which was a mixture of Mandatory laws and new Jordanian martial law regulations. In August 1950, Kirkbride took another precaution against Palestinisation and warned the King that the position of the chief administrator of the West Bank (Jamal Touqan) was granting the area quasi-autonomous status. Thus, the post was abolished and the various departments in the West Bank were made directly subordinate to Amman.[155]

In the conclusion of his annual report for 1950, Kirkbride noted that the agitation against the unification and the elections was fostered by followers of Haj Amin Al-Husseini, aided by some Arab states and Communism.[156]

However, in spite of these warnings and precautions, the Palestinians seemed to gain from the elections. In theory, the seats in both houses were divided equally between representatives from both halves of the kingdom but in practice people from the West Bank dominated the Houses, since several East Bank constituencies were represented by Palestinians.

In December 1950, Kirkbride came to the conclusion that the presence of representatives from the West Bank in Parliament 'was affecting this institution profoundly and that the king and his ministers could no longer depend on an obedient legislature as they had done in the past'.[157] The first ever anti-British statements were made at the Parliament. This was somewhat changed when the new premier, Said Al-Mufti took measures to reduce 'the House to a more subdued frame of mind'.[158]

To sum up, in spite of the problem caused by the Palestinisation of Jordan, the main aims of the British Palestine policy in the post-Mandatory period were achieved. Its loyal ally in the Middle East had fulfilled its territorial ambitions, which coincided with British strategic interests and with what was believed by the Foreign Office to be the beginning of a solution to the Arab–Israeli conflict. What had begun as an act to prevent a larger Jewish state turned into almost a crusade against an independent Palestinian state by the British, the Jordanians and the Israelis. The short-term fruits of this policy were evident; they included an Israeli–Jordanian *modus vivendi* with merely verbal protestation from the League, and implicit American approval.[159] Moreover they ensured the strengthening of Abdullah and justification for his rule and existence as protecting British interests in Palestine. They succeeded in preventing what seemed to be a state hostile to Britain and a Communist stronghold or, alternatively, the turning of Jordan into such a state: namely, a Palestinian state.[160] For the time being, Jordan was saved as a British bastion, and the West Bank re-emerged as a 'problem' only long after the British had left the area.

The successful implementation of the process of annexation had drastically changed the geopolitical map of the Middle East. At the same time, another process was taking place which deserves our attention: the efforts of the UN to bring a solution to the Arab–Israeli conflict. Britain's policy towards the latter process was influenced by a desire to obtain UN recognition for the Greater Transjordan, to find a humanitarian solution to the refugee problem which would not turn Jordan into a Palestinian state, and finally to prevent King Abdullah from going too far in his efforts to conclude a separate peace treaty with Israel.

6 British and United Nations Conciliation Efforts

THE PCC AND THE LAUSANNE CONFERENCE

The failure of the GA in Paris, in September 1948, to agree upon the Bernadotte plan owing to the refusal of both sides to comply with it and to American reservations about it, ended in a new initiative by the UN to replace the mediator by a mediating body. This body consisted of French, Turkish and American delegates. The PCC was charged by the GA, under its resolution of 11 December 1948, with facilitating final settlement of all issues outstanding between Israel and the Arab states. After a preliminary meeting in Geneva, the PCC was due to set itself up in Jerusalem. The initial effort was to be confined to an attempt to bring the parties to direct negotiations. In March 1949, the PCC published its first progress report, in which it declared its intention to establish its headquarters in Government House in Jerusalem, and deal mainly with the future of the city. The general aspects of the conflict were still being discussed in Rhodes, under the framework of the armistice negotiations, by the Acting Mediator, Dr Ralph Bunche. During its stay in the Middle East, the PCC held two important conferences. One was with members of the Israeli Cabinet in Jerusalem and the other in Beirut with representatives of the Arab countries.[1]

In the Conference in Beirut the PCC succeeded in obtaining Arab acceptance for multilateral negotiations with the Israelis, in a neutral place with separate adjournments and indirect talks. In Jerusalem, the Israelis agreed to this proposal and it was Ben-Gurion's suggestion that Lausanne should be the venue for the discussions.[2]

The talks in Lausanne were, in many ways, the natural consequence of the armistice talks in Rhodes. Before the conference was convened, the second progress report of the PCC was submitted to the UN. This report summarised the Arab and Israeli attitudes to the refugee problem.[3] The negotiations in Lausanne dragged on wearily, throughout the summer of 1949, neither side being prepared to make proposals acceptable to the other, even as a basis for negotiations.

115

The Arabs refused to discuss general settlement before Israel agreed to the return of the refugees. Hence the third progress report, submitted in June 1949, defined the Commission's main problem as linking negotiations on refugees togther with territorial questions. The Arab delegations were giving priority to the refugee problem and the Israelis to the territorial questions.[4]

In July 1949, the territorial question was abandoned and the PCC was left to deal with the Jerusalem question and the refugee problem. The Americans, at that point, felt it was useless to continue the negotiations before the stalement over the refugee problem had been solved. By August 1949, the only agreement to emerge from the PCC was an Arab–Israeli understanding on frozen funds, and Israeli consent to unify Palestinian refugee families already in Israel. A final attempt to make some progress was made in August. The Arabs demanded that the 1947 partition map be accepted by Israel, and agreed to the American principle that Israel retain Galilee, instead of the Negev, as granted in the original resolution, thus compensating the Arab countries for the loss of territory.[5]

The main American proposal to the PCC was the 'Jessup principle'; namely, the principle of exchange of territory by which Israel would retain Galilee and the Arabs the Negev. It was first suggested by the Ambassor-at-Large and member of the US delegation to the UN, Philip Jessup. The government of Israel refused to heed any such ideas and preferred the status quo even at the price of losing any chance of a territorial settlement. Incidentally, the Arab states preferred an impasse to a peace in which Israel was not forced to withdraw. Notwithstanding the similarity between the Arab propositions and the State Department's principles of a settlement (the 'Jessup principle'), it should be remembered that American ideas of territorial compensation were always tentative and were never insisted upon. The Turkish representative on the PCC (after a conversation with the British Foreign Office) tried to suggest the handing over of the Negev to the Arabs, again on the line of the Jessup principle, and the French suggested trusteeship over the Galilee as the best solution. However, by venturing their own proposals, the three members of the Commission departed from the task of conciliation which had been entrusted to them by the GA and, furthermore, were about to confront the same problems and difficulties which the late mediator had had to confront while trying to impose a solution on the two parties. In fact, in order to overcome these difficulties, the State Department recommended that the PCC be replaced by an individual, such as an agent-general, but withdrew the suggestion in the face of British opposition.[6]

Thus at the end of August 1949, the Americans felt that the PCC had failed and that there was no use in continuing its work, whereas M. de Boisanger, the French representative (who was a candidate for the directorship of the Near Eastern Department in the French Foreign Ministry), saw the PCC as his own personal project and strove to prolong its life as much as possible. The Americans desired, as did King Abdullah, to transfer the debate to the UN GA, where they hoped to impose some kind of vague solution on the parties, and the King sought final approval for the annexation of the West Bank.[7]

The Lausanne Conference ended in September 1949 without any progress, and the PCC resumed its negotiations at Lake Success, New York, the following month. Under American guidance it hoped to move from conciliation to mediation; that is, to submit its own proposals. Hence it sought to prove its credibility by introducing its own peace plan. The Commission's members believed that they should first tackle the problem of Jerusalem and thus presented their scheme for the internationalisation of the city. However, by the time the PCC adjourned to Lake Success, the Israeli government informed the Commission (28 October 1949) that it saw no use in continuing an indirect dialogue through the PCC, and to spite the GA approval of the PCC's plan for the internationalisation of Jerusalem, Israel retaliated by moving its governmental offices from Tel Aviv to Jerusalem, declaring the latter to be the capital of Israel. Despite these steps, Israel professed its readiness to negotiate with any Arab government prepared to do the same.[8]

The PCC survived until the latter part of the 1950s; however, it seems safe to conclude that by August 1949 it was a failure. Its discussions throughout 1950–1, some of which will be referred to later in this work, were impractical and were aimed mainly at achieving an agreement over Jerusalem. By that time, priority was being given to bilateral negotiations, in particular the Israeli–Jordanian ones.

In January 1950 the PCC resumed its discussions in Geneva. However, the deadlock continued. Throughout 1950 a common basis for negotiations was sought and not found. In July 1950, the Commission moved to Jerusalem, and in September that year it admitted failure in its report to the UN. The activity then moved to the GA. In July 1951, the Commission resumed its efforts and tried to convene a conference in Paris. The conference was officially opened in September 1951. The Commission presented a comprehensive peace

plan, but by then the Arab world was in no mood to consider any
agreement with Israel. The conference failed, but the UN maintained
the Commission until the late 1950s, concentrating its efforts on
specific issues relating to the Arab refugees.[9]

THE FAILURE OF THE PCC

In more than one way the Lausanne conference was a rare opportunity
in the history of the Arab–Israeli conflict. The mere readiness of the
parties to go beyond the *de facto* arrangements achieved in the
armistice negotiations was a hopeful sign in itself. The conference was
opened in a productive manner. The Arab and Israeli delegations
agreed upon the 1947 partition map as the basis for territorial talks.[10]
Thus both delegations signed a protocol with the 1947 map attached to
it. Eighteen months later the Israelis claimed they had agreed to sign
the May 1949 protocol as a gesture to help break the deadlock but, they
had no intention of yielding territory.[11] Despite this reversal in Israel's
policy, it was the only time that the partition plan was accepted as a
basis for negotiations by both sides. It is noteworthy that the Arab
delegates, apart from Iraq, had consented in Beirut (March 1949) to
enter *peace* negotiations, after Israeli agreement to deal with the
refugee question as the first item.[12]

In their decision to let the conference fail the Israelis missed an
opportunity. The positive reports by the Israeli delegate about private
bilateral negotiations turned out to be unduly optimistic. The Arab
delegates were unable to turn their private promises into public
declarations, and the Jordanians prevented any Israeli–Palestinian
dialogue in Lausanne.[13] Furthermore, the Arab governments did not
reap the fruits of the American pressure on Israel. Before advocating
their ill-advised economic solution to the refugee problem, the
Americans succeeded in obtaining political concessions from Israel
which were never taken seriously by the Arab side (this particular issue
will be elaborated in the next chapter).

From the outset, the Israelis had resented the idea of the PCC as
much as they had objected to Bernadotte. Their attitude was bitterly
criticised at the time by Sasson, who wrote to the General Director of
the IFO: 'I understand that in our attitude towards the Conciliation
Commission, we are not displaying too much interest in it and are not
taking any initiative as far as it is concerned.' Sasson asserted that this
was 'a risky attitude and Israel should support such an initiative'.[14] The

British Foreign office believed that Israel showed readiness to negotiate even under the auspices of the PCC; however, it was advised by its Legation in Tel Aviv that, in practice, Israel was willing to participate in multilateral negotiations only in order not to ruin the chances for an Israeli–Jordanian peace. Ben-Gurion's memoirs confirm this British appreciation.[15] There is no direct evidence for this claim, but there is little doubt that the British Foreign Office agreed with Ben-Gurion's assumption that 'the key for peace with the Arab world [is] our consent for the annexation of the Arab part of Western Palestine to Abdullah'.[16] Moreover, the Israelis rendered it useless to continue the PCC work owing to the Arab refusal to negotiate directly.

Yet Israel cooperated to some extent with the PCC, partly because it preferred discussions in Lausanne to a general debate in the UN (very similar to the British point of view) but also because it hoped to facilitate its admission to the UN through participation in the PCC (the vote of France was particularly important in that sense).[17]

The Arabs insisted, overtly, on negotiating *en bloc* with the Israelis. While most of the heads of the Arab delegations met the Israelis privately out of court and reached various agreements, neither side could later adhere publicly to these unofficial agreements.[18] In general, Ben-Gurion preferred bilateral negotiations outside the framework of the PCC, and indeed Israeli–Syrian negotiations on peace were conducted without UN knowledge and to some extent were obscure to the IFO.

Furthermore, it is quite probable that Ben-Gurion consented to Eban's assertion that 'is no need to "run after" the peace . . . Armistice is enough, if we "run after" the peace – the Arabs will demand a price – the borders or the refugees (concessions on . . .), or both of them'.[19] Eban suggested waiting a few years. Nevertheless Israel made an effort at bilateral negotiations outside the framework of the UN. Peace, however, was not a priority, as was manifested both in the case of the Israeli–Syrian negotiations in 1949 and the Israeli– Egyptian talks in 1949 and 1954.[20] More regrettable was the Israeli and Arab concurrence (Jordan, Egypt and Syria) not to raise the question of the refugees in those bilateral negotiations, and the Israeli refusal to deal with it in an indirect manner.

Elias Sasson, who headed the Israeli delegation with Reuben Shiloah, saw the lack of joint meetings of the delegations, as the main reason for the conference's failure. He also assumed that the representatives of France, US and Turkey were attempting to utilise their participation in the conference in order to strengthen their countries' position in the Arab world.[21] This latter explanation seems weak, since those countries had better means and opportunities for improving relations with the Arab world. It is more likely that those representatives sought the furthering of their own careers in these talks.

BRITAIN'S POLICY TOWARDS THE PCC

Ernest Bevin told the British Cabinet in January 1949 that the creation of the PCC did not require any British initiative, unless it was to try to bring Egypt and Transjordan together on the question of the Negev.[22] In that sense, Bevin saw the PCC in very much the same way as he saw Bernadotte's endeavours; that is, as a means of protecting British strategic interests in the area. Yet there was no comparison between the energy and efforts invested by the Foreign Office in the Bernadotte affair and the low profile it maintained regarding the PCC discussions. This was due, first of all, to the PCC's concentration on the refugee problem, leaving aside the territorial questions. Second, as 1949 passed, Israel was considered less and less an enemy, even by Bevin, and thus its retention of the Negev was no longer regarded as a serious threat to British positions in the area. Finally, the tacit understanding between Israel and Jordan, reached by the first half of 1949, was perceived as the best guarantee for British interests in Palestine. This British theory was even acceptable in some circles in Israel and Jordan, as a means of ending the conflict or at least of bringing it into low profile.

Bevin added another argument against British participation in the PCC. When Marshall suggested, in October 1948, that Britain should be a member of the PCC, the Foreign Secretary rejected the idea. He explained to the Secretary of State that whereas American membership was derived from its participation in the Truce Commission, Britain had no *locus standi* to serve on the Commission. Furthermore, if Britain had participated, at home it would have seemed like coming back to Palestine. Dow, the British consul in Jerusalem, suggested that he or Troutbeck should be sent to Geneva to act as advisers to the Commission. Dow attached immense importance to the PCC's coming to Jerusalem as a means of preventing an Israeli takeover of the city. The Foreign Office, however, was disinclined to enter into direct confrontation with the PCC.[23]

However, the Foreign Office had ensured that the Turkish delegate would faithfully represent the Office's views. Indeed, the Turkish government promised not to commit itself to anything before consulting the Foreign Office. It is possible that this was due to British readiness to show more sympathy towards Turkey's aspiration to be part of NATO, although Lord Bullock tells us that both the Americans and the British were disinclined to include the Turks in NATO at that stage.[24]

The Foreign Office kept a watchful eye on the possible American candidate for the PCC. The Office was appalled by the State Department's intention to appoint 'one Mr. Kennan' known to the Office from his service in Japan as a 'drunkard and quarrelsome'. Truman was convinced by the British protestations and appointed Mark Ethridge, who was regarded as 'pro-British'.[25]

In fact, British newspapers such as *The Times* predicted very little success for the PCC and advised that the Americans and the British should rather impose their own settlement on the parties. Despite these views, the Office never pressed for abolition of the body, even in 1950 when its futility had become apparent. Michael Wright believed there was always a need for conciliatory machinery, especially for one controlled by the Americans. Wright and other officials in the Foreign Office believed that the creation of the PCC enabled Britain and the US to serve as mediators, even if they did not overtly declare their role as such (the French and Turkish roles in the Commission were conceived as marginal). Contrary to Jordanian wishes, the British did not want to transfer the debate to the GA before American–British proposals for peace had been accepted by the parties, or even imposed on them.[26]

However, the most important British effort towards the PCC was the introduction of a comprehensive British peace plan. This Eight-Point Plan, from the point of view of this analysis, is essential in understanding British policy towards the Arab–Israeli conflict. Thus the gist of the plan will be presented here, and referred to again in each of the following chapters, since it is related to all the themes under review in this work. (It can also found in Appendix 2.) From the Foreign Office's point of view, the most important points in the plan were connected with the Greater Transjordan concept. Thus the introduction of a British peace plan should be best regarded as part and parcel of the British effort to obtain UN approval for the annexation of the West Bank to Transjordan.[27]

In the final analysis, the PCC dealt chiefly with the refugee question and the Jerusalem problem. When this body was established, however, it was charged by the GA with facilitating a comprehensive peace settlement.[28] Although it was unclear whether or not the PCC would introduce its own peace plan, once the members of the Commission had submitted tentative proposals to the two sides it was felt in London that Britain should do the same. It was the first coherent British peace plan presented to the UN and the area since Bevin's Provincial Autonomy Plan of 1947.

The plan called for acceptance of the refugees by both sides in proportions to be determined by them. In its second and third points, the Foreign Office accepted the Gaza proposal, of which more will be said in the next chapter. The proposal suggested the annexation of the Gaza Strip to Israel with its refugee population in return for Israeli territorial compensation elsewhere in Palestine.

The fourth point suggested that their territorial compensation would be the transfer of the Negev to Egypt and Jordan. The Israelis were offered free passage through the Negev to the Red Sea.

The fifth point proposed a free port in Haifa, and the sixth the administrative division of Jerusalem between Israel and Jordan in an arrangement which would put the holy places under international supervision. The final point raised the issue of a joint Arab–Israeli project to exploit the waters of the Yarmuk and Jordan rivers.

The seventh point of this plan was the most important one and it read as follows: 'Central Arab Palestine should be formally incorporated into Jordan.' This plan was presented to the three member-states of the PCC and was brought into discussion with the Commission's other proposals, where it suffered the same fate: namely, it was never made into a formal peace proposal by the PCC. It is possible that when the Commission finally introduced its peace plan at the end of 1951, these British points had some bearing on it.[29]

Thus neither the PCC nor the parties involved had ever properly discussed this British plan (it is doubtful whether the Arabs or the Israelis even knew about it). The PCC felt unable to produce any territorial settlement and thus followed, in September 1949, the American lead in suggesting that political issues should be shelved for the time being in favour of an economic and technical approach to the refugee problem.[30] That is, the Americans suggested that the territorial status quo should remain and be altered only according to solutions proposed for the refugee problem.

This state of affairs naturally suited the Foreign Office. Consequently, the Office prepared an outline of its Palestine policy, based on the Eight-Point Plan. The principal point in this outline was the realisation, at the earliest possible moment, of the formal union between Central Arab Palestine and Jordan.[31] Moreover by utilising and somewhat exaggerating the troubled situation in Arab Palestine, the British succeeded in persuading the Americans that the uncertainty and disquiet there might have affected the stability of the whole area; and that only annexation would bring stability and help to solve the refugee problem.

Hence, as far as the British, the Americans and the Israelis were concerned, the claims for an independent Palestinian entity were all over and done with for at least the next 15 years.

7 British Policy towards the Refugee Problem

If one could venture to describe British policy towards the Arab–Israeli conflict in the post-1948 era as affected by what could be called the 'Palestine Syndrome', the best manifestation for this behaviour would be found in the British attitude towards the refugees and their political future. By the 'Syndrome' is meant the effect the Mandatory years had on the British readiness to be involved directly in the Arab–Jewish conflict in Palestine, which had cost so many British lives and so much effort in the Mandatory period.

The British, like all other parties involved in this conflict, were reluctant to reap this bitter harvest. There was a strong British inclination not to be entangled in the attempts to solve the refugee problem. The Foreign Office felt that whatever Britain had done in the past in terms of offering solutions, it was always portrayed in the final analysis as taking a biased line against one party or the other in the conflict.

However, there were contradictory British interests at stake which did not allow the same sort of British complacency towards the refugee problem. Owing to the large number of refugees in Greater Transjordan, the refugee problem was an internal Jordanian dilemma. As has been pointed out before in this work, any Jordanian problem became a British problem because of British involvement in that country.

Hence, while Britain was disinclined to be involved in the deliberations and negotiations on the question, and declined an offer to take part in the Conciliation Commission, it had to maintain some level of involvement in order to safeguard its own interests and position in Jordan, as well as in the Middle East as a whole.

The absence of any clear policy in London had left the scene to the inexperienced Americans. The State Department (in particular its adviser on refugee problems, Robert McGhee) believed in an 'economic' approach to the problem. McGhee's vision was based on the hope of introducing a 'Marshall Plan' to the Middle East; that is, he advocated Western assistance to the countries affected by the war in Palestine as a means of achieving a high standard of living and stability in the area, and thus protecting it from the infiltration of Communism and Russian intervention. The resettlement of the refugees (partly in Israel, mostly in the Arab world) was to be an integral part of that scheme.

Once the idea of an independent Palestinian state was abandoned, a combination of resettlement and repatriation was the most sensible compromise. However, this was true only if those terms were understood in the purely political sense, as indeed they were regarded by the Arabs and the Israelis; but for the Americans these terms were part of the economic terminology they introduced to the area. An economic solution was something the British, owing to their limited resources, could not offer; it was a concept they resented, due to their political expertise and knowledge of the Arab world.

The Americans introduced the new plan at the Lausanne conference. The Arabs and the Israelis, who had discussed territorial questions and military arrangements between themselves, willingly left the problem in the hands of the Americans and the British. It was not left to obligatory arbitration, but rather the hope was that these two powers and the PCC would accept the views of one side or the other. In short, the powers and the PCC could have sought a political solution based on either repatriation or resettlement, or a compromise which combined both. Indeed at one stage it looked as if things were going in that direction. It is likely that against the better judgement of the more experienced British experts in the Foreign Office, however, the Americans lost their patience and tended to take the lead in solving the problem.

Thus Britain, which could not offer an alternative policy, followed somewhat reluctantly the American 'business-like' approach to the problem: namely, it was not perceived as a purely humanitarian question, but also as one which could be solved by a group of professional experts. Consequently the Americans initiated the establishment of a technical team of experts (mainly American and British), aided by promises to provide Western financial assistance to all the countries which would share this attempt to find an 'economic solution' to the problem.

An attempt will be made here to understand the British and American motives for this somewhat curious move: curious, since it is rather hard to explain how an economic solution could have been introduced to try to solve a political problem. The results as we shall try to show here, were catastrophic for the Palestinians and, in the long run, disastrous for the area as a whole.

It is not intended to play down Arab and Israeli responsibility for the problem. However, it is noticeable that a political solution was sought by the parties in Lausanne, with British blessing, probably the first (and to date the last) attempt of that kind. The failure to bridge the gap between the Israeli and Arab delegates resulted in British acquiescence to the American viewpoint, so that eventually the ESM, composed of American and British experts, was set up to find a solution. Hence the political hurdle was never overcome, let alone approached, for a long time. ESM's report allowed the perpetuation of the status quo, in which relief was never properly replaced by a long-term resettlement programme or repatriation. Such a situation, it appears, was convenient to everybody concerned as, in the back of their minds, they probably hoped that the problem would somehow wither away.

The British role was thus reduced to ensuring that two possible solutions would not be introduced: either the concept of a separate Palestinian state or the resettlement of most of the refugees in Jordan. However, in practice, Britain's involvement became deeper and deeper, in particular from 1949 onwards. British pragmatism and its *ad hoc* policy resulted in the British first following the American lead and then, for a while, playing an even more important role than the Americans. The American need to consult the British had brought the appointment of British officials to all the important roles connected with the refugee problem. One might even say that the temptation to play an active role was immense.

THE RESPONSIBILITY FOR THE CREATION OF THE PROBLEM

The British attitude towards the solution of the refugee question was no doubt influenced by their view about the responsibility and causes of the Palestinian flight. Bevin publicly blamed it all on the Jewish side without being able to refer to any specific case, but just tackled the problem in general terms.[1] Was this the common British reaction? It is somewhat difficult to answer this question owing to the ambiguous attitude shown by the Foreign Office towards the problem.

Two years after the exodus, the Foreign Office thought that the Arab flight was caused by the 'not unnatural belief' that they would be 'exterminated' if they remained where they were. On the other hand, the British-backed NER directed the blame on the AHC for encouraging the exodus in the cases of Haifa, Jaffa and Jerusalem.[2]

The crux of the matter is that the Foreign Office paid little attention to specific cases and tended to blame the Arabs as well as the Jews for causing the problem. For the pragmatic British diplomats this was a necessary approach, since only by such means could the problem be treated. For that purpose, the Office even admitted British responsibility for the creation of the problem. As the formal historian of Chatham House at the time explained, the British tended to regard the question as one of the many refugee problems which emerged after the Second World War. He pointed out that once the Korean War was over the refugee problem there overshadowed that of the Palestinians.[3]

Finally, it is interesting to note what *The Times* had to say on the issue at the time. The paper stated that His Majesty's Government shared the responsibility for the problem in the eyes of the world, owing to 'its part in bringing about the plight of the refugees and for not seeking with all speed to help them'.[4]

PERCEPTIONS ABOUT THE REFUGEES' ROLE IN JORDAN

Movement of refugees to Transjordan started in January 1948 when, anticipating trouble, families moved to Amman. This first wave brought with it considerable funds to the Transjordanian capital, but Kirkbride remarked that these funds also caused an increase in rents and the cost of foodstuffs. By February, panic continued to spread throughout the Arab middle class in Palestine, and the High Commissioner reported a steady exodus of those who could afford to leave. Kirkbride considered this group to be an anti-British element which 'did not fail to affect the political atmosphere of Transjordan for the worse'.[5] He especially noted Communist instigation amongst the refugees. In April 1948, following the Dir Yasin massacre, a further influx of refugees entered Transjordan and the West Bank in 'an ever more bitter frame of mind'.[6]

The flow of refugees reached its peak after the fall of Lydda and Ramleh. The population of Amman doubled in a few weeks, and by August 1948 the refugees outnumbered the native inhabitants of the city. Glubb shared Kirkbride's apprehensions. He reported that this refugee element 'is seething with discontent and contains many Communist, Jewish and other spies and agents provocateurs'; an inaccurate description, to say the least, but nevertheless representative of Glubb's feelings and conceptions about the refugees.[7] Part of this impression was created owing to the fact that by the end of the British Mandate in Palestine, only the poorer refugees got as far as Arab Palestine and Transjordan, while the richer left for Lebanon, Syria and Iraq, where they found both employment and accommodation. On the other hand, it should be remembered that in October 1948 about 85 per cent of the refugees were estimated to be children under 15, pregnant and nursing mothers, people over 60, and the infirm. Thus Glubb and Kirkbride could have been thinking only in terms of the potential danger (in 1949, this estimate was reduced to about 60 per cent).[8]

It is noteworthy that Michael Wright on the whole shared Kirkbride's and Glubb's apprehensions and regarded the refugees as having an 'unsettling effect' wherever they were located. Other officials in the Eastern Department believed that the refugees were used by the Egyptians and Syrians as *agents provocateurs*.[9] In any case, the perceptions were not different from those about the local Palestinian population already mentioned before. One could only add that Transjordan regarded refugees in the same manner. A mixture of contempt for the uprooted Palestinians and displeasure with the general Palestinian attitude to Abdullah characterised Transjordan's policy towards the Palestinians.[10] Furthermore, this approach was not unique to Transjordan. The Iraqis and the Syrians also treated the refugees as a security risk; the Syrian security services established a special division to deal with the refugees, as did the Iraqi MoD.[11]

Some of the fears connected with the Palestinians were moderated towards the end of 1949. In his annual report that year, Kirkbride remarked that although in the earlier part of the year the presence in Jordan of a large number of Palestinians (refugees and locals) 'had a disturbing effect on the life and economy of the country', in the latter part of the year there was, 'a marked tendency of Palestinian refugees and others to establish themselves and their businesses at Amman and elsewhere to settle down, bringing new and often better methods of agriculture, business and handicrafts'.[12] Notwithstanding, the refugees in the camps in Jordan, who by conservative estimate made up a total of 150 000, were generally regarded as a breeding ground for Communism, and a serious threat to Jordan's survival.[13]

BRITAIN'S EFFORTS TOWARDS REPATRIATION

Since most of the refugees had fled while Britain was still responsible for law and order, there were attempts by Arab governments to facilitate their return through Britain. The Foreign Office and the British Army were asked by the Syrian Minister of Interior to safeguard the return of the refugees from Tiberias and Haifa. Michael Wright answered that Palestine would no longer be under British control after 15 May, but that if it were possible to repatriate them before that date, Britain would assist. However, no further approach on this issue was made before 15 May.[14]

Throughout 1948, the British position on the refugee question was similar to the American and UN point of view. The British and the Americans influenced, and some would even say dictated to, the UN mediator on the questions of territorial arrangement and sovereignty, owing to the importance they had attached to that aspect of the question. The gravity of the refugee problem, however, was not yet fully realised and was overshadowed by other problems. Furthermore, it was basically regarded as a humanitarian question. This was probably why the powers allowed Bernadotte to take the lead on this aspect of the Palestine question. It was precisely the humanitarian aspects of the question which convinced Bernadotte to adopt the Arab viewpoint that those refugees who wished to do so should be repatriated to their former homes and the others compensated.[15] This approach was adopted by his successor, Dr Bunche, and by the Americans and the British. The result was the eleventh paragraph in the UN GA resolution (of December 1948) which called for peace negotiations between the Arab states and Israel. This paragraph stipulated that 'the refugees wishing to return to their homes and live at peace with their neighbours should be permitted to do so at the earliest practicable date'.[16] Incidentally, Bernadotte's successor asserted that most of the refugees did not wish to return, owing to the destruction of the villages by Israel and the lack of employment possibilities for the middle class; he was thus thinking mainly of a gesture by Israel of taking back a certain number. This view was shared by Bernard Burrows.[17] However, in the early encounters with Bernadotte the Israelis had already made it clear that Israel would not allow the return of the refugees, not only for security reasons (as was repeatedly claimed by Israeli representatives in the various forums of the UN), but also in order to retain the favourable demographic situation created by the war in Palestine.[18]

From 1949 onwards, no one in the Foreign Office considered total repatriation a feasible solution. The formula was now based on a combination of resettlement and repatriation as a long-term solution on the one hand, and providing relief and employment as a short-term solution on the other. It is noteworthy that the Arab states unanimously voted against the UN GA resolution, and it was only in the spring of 1949 that they began to invoke paragraph 11.

At first, the PCC notified Israel that at least 650 000 refugees should be repatriated to Arab Palestine and Israel. However, neither the PCC, nor the Foreign Office could provide evidence concerning how many refugees wished to return.[19] For instance, the PCC estimated that the skilled workers and small landowners would not wish to return, fearing that only a small compensation awaited them in Israel, and that those in the urban sector would wish to do so (most of the refugees were agricultural workers).

The simplest way, of course, would have been to conduct a census. McGhee suggested the idea in April 1949, asserting that most of the refugees wished to return.[20] The State Department believed it was a feasible task. However, the PCC secretariat informed the Israeli government that: 'It is doubtless impossible at the present to ask the refugees which of them wish and which do not wish to return home.'[21] The PCC regarded this as 'superfluous' with regard to those coming from the parts of Palestine which were to remain Arab. The absence of such a census left the question unanswered and resulted in contradictory assessments of the issue.

BRITISH AND AMERICAN EFFORTS AT SOLVING THE PROBLEM

From 1949 onwards, British policy with regard to the PCC consisted mainly of conveying to the Americans their ideas about the best settlement for the conflict, including their suggestions for solving the refugee problem. From the start of the PCC efforts, the British favoured an arrangement which combined resettlement and repatriation. This was the gist of the first point in the Eight-Point Plan mentioned in the previous chapter.[22]

The main British interest centred on the question of where the refugees would be resettled. Throughout 1949, and during the Anglo-American negotiations on this question, it became apparent that the Foreign Office favoured the resettlement of most of the refugees in Iraq and Syria. At the same time the British urged the Americans to exert pressure on Israel to repatriate the remainder.[23] The American pressure produced, in the final analysis, some effect on the Israelis. However, it was altogether too inconsistent a pressure and, furthermore, it was not reciprocated by British pressure on the Iraqis and Syrians to accept the principle of resettlement. The only country Britain could have pressed to resettle the refugees was Jordan. However, as was pointed out earlier, this was the last thing the Foreign Office wished to do since it feared – as much as did Abdullah – the Palestinisation of Greater Transjordan.

As had often been the case, the only criticism of this policy was heard from the BMEO in Cairo. Troutbeck had reservations, not so much on the principle of combined resettlement and repatriation as on the Foreign Office's failure, in his opinion, to appreciate the priority given by the Arab world to the refugee question. He predicted that without a solution to this problem, an Arab–Israeli agreement would be impossible.[24] History would judge whether Troutbeck's assessment was correct in the long run. However, during the period under review, Arab–Israeli arrangements (not peace agreements) were achieved only through bilateral negotiations. Two subjects were dealt with in a multilateral fashion, the refugee problem and the internationalisation of Jerusalem, with no results whatsoever. Had the refugee problem been one of the topics in the Israeli–Jordanian negotiations, the responsibility for solving the problem would have lain, in the final analysis, in the hands of both countries and, to some extent, in Britain's. However, all these parties preferred to exclude that problem from their negotiations.

The outcome was an ambiguous attitude towards the Israeli position on this matter. *The Times* disclosed some of this ambivalence by condemning Israel for inhumane action, while also admitting that there were compelling and logical motives behind Israel's behaviour.[25] Ostensibly, Israel was blamed for its policy. However, privately, the Foreign Office even informed the Israelis that it regarded resettlement (in particular in Syria and Iraq) as the only solution, provided Israel would accept some refugees as a token of goodwill.[26]

One could say that British policy was aimed at maintaining the PCC as the main forum for negotiations on the refugee problem. The Foreign Office hoped that the PCC would serve as a mediating body through which the Americans and the British would transfer their ideas and solutions to the parties. Britain had no wish to make the topic into an issue in the bilateral negotations (in particular the Israeli–Jordanian ones), and neither was there any desire to bring it back to the GA before any Anglo-American understanding was achieved.

Before leaving the problem in the hands of the UN, the British had anxiously awaited the outcome of the American pressure on Israel. The Foreign Office realised that this American effort should be reciprocated by a British attempt to convince the Arab countries to resettle most of the refugees. The Americans – both the State Department and the President – felt that Israel particularly had to be persuaded to take a more flexible position, but nevertheless expected the British to use their influence in the Arab world so that it would be prepared to absorb part of the refugees. It seems that whereas the American pressure on Israel was intensive and carried some positive result, the British contacts with the Arab world were marginal and did not produce any change in the Arab position.

Hence in 1949 the British and the Americans made a final attempt to solve the refugee problem by imposing a political solution on the Arabs and the Israelis. The failure of this approach led the Americans to introduce an economic solution which depended on the powers' ability to finance resettlement projects instead of dealing first with the political responsibility of both Israel and the Arabs for the creation of the refugee problem. Thus it would be best to appreciate both the British and the American efforts to deal with the problem in political terms before analysing the failure of the economic approach. The Foreign Office had prepared specific resettlement programmes before it approached the Arab world.

The Anglo-Arab Discussions on Resettlement

In 1949, the Foreign Office tended to accept resettlement as the main solution to the problem. It had reached this conclusion after the Permanent Under-Secretary of State, Sir William Strang, visited the Middle East in June–July 1949 in order to assess the changes in the area. He was finally convinced that Israel would not allow the return of those refugees who wished to do so.[27] In July 1949 Bevin convened a special conference on the Middle East in the Foreign Office, in which he told the conference that the refugees should be settled in Syria and Iraq.[28] He instructed his officials to prepare resettlement programmes. These programmes pointed out the potential capability of each of the Arab countries to absorb and reintegrate the refugees. However, they were never passed to the Arab countries, the UN, the Americans or the Israelis. In October 1949, Chatham House published them as an academic review, but they were not regarded as any kind of guideline for a new British policy towards the refugee problem.

Under the programmes, Iraq and Syria (and to a lesser extent

Jordan) were found to be the most suitable countries, both economically and socially, for resettlement. Consequently Bevin asked the British representatives in the area to urge these Arab countries to agree to resettlement, although not to specific plans unless the initiative came from the Arab governments. Michael Wright translated Bevin's tentative ideas into more practical terms and told the Middle East Official Committee that the main targets of resettlement were Syria and Iraq.[29]

The only Arab country which showed any willingness to initiate talks with the British about resettlement was Syria. Colonel Husni Zaim, who took over the Syrian regime in 1949, declared his willingness to settle at least 120 000 refugees in Syria if outside financial assistance was given. The British experts estimated that about 150 000 refugees could be resettled there.[30] The American ambassador in Damascus was convinced of Zaim's sincerity and reported to his government that what the Syrian ruler wanted most was American military supplies in return for his readiness to absorb 250 000 refugees.[31]

The British government offered financial aid if the Syrian ruler made a public declaration about his resettlement programmes. The Foreign Office believed that most funds should come from the French, owing to their past and present interest in the Levant.[32] Needless to say the French did not share this point of view, although they were convinced that Zaim's offer was genuine. Zaim's fall at the end of 1949 ended the Anglo-Syrian discussions on resettlement.

Ever since 1911, British reports and surveys had noted that 'Iraq possessed perhaps the best long-range prospects for the development of agriculture of any of the Middle Eastern countries.'[33] Given the large percentage of agricultural workers amongst the refugees, it is no wonder that the British were so attracted to the idea of resettling most of them in Iraq.

The Eastern Department thought that Bevin himself should pull his weight in order to persuade the Iraqis to absorb at least 100 000 refugees, though they believed that the country could actually resettle 200 000. Bevin had to be brought in since the Iraqis refused to discuss such a possibility. The Iraqis told the Foreign Secretary that any land which became available under the irrigation schemes was required for the Iraqi and Bedouin peasants.[34] The Department found this an unconvincing argument since there were vast areas to be developed which would suffice for both categories. Moreover, the Department asserted that Iraq was badly in need of agricultural workers. The Department pointed out that the main source of finance should be the revenues from oil royalties. Ironically, at the time when resettlement schemes were being discussed, royalties depended on the negotiations between IPC and the Iraqi government, which were in deadlock throughout 1949. Nevertheless the Eastern Department indicated an alternative source: the sterling accounts which were released to the Iraqis at that time.[35]

The Americans urged the British to exert pressure on the Iraqis, as they themselves had reached the same conclusion about Iraq being the most adequate country for resettlement. Following this request the Iraqis were told by Bevin that the: 'Iraqi government would be failing in their responsibility as Arabs and as a Middle East government if they try to wash their hands of this grave human problem.[36] The Americans were more practical; they threatened to make an International Bank loan to Iraq conditional upon the willingness of this government to discuss the matter with Britain or the UN.[37]

The Iraqis refused to discuss the resettlement of refugees until September 1949. In that month, the Iraqi premier, Nuri As-Said, had raised the possibility of exchanging Iraqi Jews for the refugees. There were 180 000 Jews in Iraq, 120 000 of whom were in Baghdad. Many of them were men of wealth and position and included MPs. The British Embassy in Baghdad doubted Nuri's sincerity on this point and thought it was beyond Iraq's administrative capability to carry it out.[38] BMEO believed that Iraq had everything to lose by it, since it would be like 'exchanging the managing directors of I.C.I. for small shopkeepers from Peckham'.[39] It had also rightly predicted that what Nuri As-Said had in mind was the expulsion of Iraq's Jews, as indeed happened in 1950.

The Chatham House experts envisaged that 50 000 refugees could be resettled in Jordan.[40] Kirkbride accepted this number and advocated the resettlement of the remaining 300 000 refugees in Iraq, Syria and Israel. The ESM of the UN recommended the resettlement of 100 000 refugees. The Foreign Office estimated that with British finance 120 000 refugees could be resettled,[41] and the British treasury was willing to allocate £9 million for that purpose. However, it seems that this sum could not have represented a serious financial contribution; the amounts needed were in tens, if not hundreds, of millions. This should be compared with American estimates for a similar number of refugees, which amounted to $160 million.[42] King Abdullah, by the way, thought he could absorb about 100 000 refugees and did not believe the Iraqis would ever agree to accept any number of refugees; moreover, he doubted whether the refugees would be willing to go that far.[43]

Thus the British failed to impress the Arab countries with the need to resettle most of the refugees on their soil. The British pressure was not intensive and did not last for long. This was partly because of the American inability to pressure Israel into pursuing a more flexible policy, but mainly due to the American decision to introduce an 'economic solution' to the problem, ignoring the political aspects of the refugee problem.

The American Pressure on Israel and its Outcome

In order correctly to appreciate to what extent the American pressure on Israel was productive, it is important to recollect the initial Israeli stand on this issue. The Israelis saw the exodus as part of a possible exchange of population (as was, incidentally, offered by the Peel Commission, and the Labour Party Congress in 1945). After the war, the Israelis regarded repatriated refugees as a potential fifth column and an additional economic burden which might have restricted the ability of Israel to absorb Jewish refugees. The Israelis were not content with words alone and took some measures to prevent mass repatriation. Apart from deterring the refugees from returning, the Israeli Cabinet decided to turn the Arab villages under their control, which had been abandoned or from where the inhabitants had been evicted, into cultivated areas or no man's land in order to prevent repatriation.[44]

Given this Israeli viewpoint and action, it is, even today, surprising that it eventually agreed to take back 100 000 refugees. Moreover, the Israelis were happy to enlarge their territory, even if the price was the responsibility for 250 000 refugees, as was the case with the Gaza proposal.

The Gaza proposal, by which Israel would take over the Gaza area, and with it the responsibility for the existing population and the Arab refugees (estimated to be 230 000 by the Foreign Office), was first introduced by the Israelis during a discussion with Mark Ethridge, the American representative on the PCC.[45] In fact, the Egyptians had never concealed their willingness to relinquish the area. However, American documents give the impression that Ethridge was the first to raise the proposals in a talk with the Director-General of the IFO. Nevertheless, British and Israeli documents provide sufficient evidence for the fact that the Israelis were the authors of the proposal.

It is important to establish the source of this proposal correctly since it indicated that, notwithstanding the Israelis' adamant refusal to allow repatriation and the preparations it made to avoid such a possibility, there were circumstances in which Israel was prepared to accept the responsibility for a large number of refugees.[46]

The State Department did not initially insist on the Gaza proposal. However, after it had received an assessment from its embassy in Cairo that the Egyptians might accept the offer if they were given territorial compensation, the Americans regarded the proposal as the key to solving the refugee problem, all the more so since the State Department was still loyal to the idea of exchange of territory as the basis for a solution. The Americans hoped that Britain would participate in concerted pressure on both sides to agree to the proposal.[47]

The Foreign Office had to face some difficulties and divergence of opinion before formulating its policy on this matter. The Office learned about the offer from Sir Knox Helm, the British Ambassador in Tel Aviv. The British embassy in Cairo felt that, contrary to the Emerican appreciation, the Egyptians would reject the principle of bargaining territory against refugees.[48]

Both assessments were incomplete. When the Egyptians were informed about the proposals, their first tendency was to show readiness to discuss the issue. However, after three days, probably owing to pressure from the Palace, the Egyptian government rejected the proposal. Sir John Troutbeck believed the Egyptians favoured the proposal and wished the Israelis to keep the area, but feared the implication of an open agreement with Israel. He reported that the Egyptians could not even resettle the thousands of refugees who had succeeded in reaching Egypt, and had moved them back to the Strip. In 1949, the Egyptians told the Jordanians in a League meeting that they were anxious to get rid of the Strip somehow, which had been regarded as a breeding ground for Communism even in 1948.[49]

At first the Eastern Department tended to accept the Israeli offer and warned the Egyptian government that if they did not agree, they themselves would have to be responsible for all the refugees living there. Ambassador Campbell still claimed that it was not a fair quid pro quo unless such a transaction were part of a general settlement.[50] The Foreign Office, on the other hand, had received optimistic reports from Tel Aviv that the Israelis would not rule out the exchange of territory in order to induce the Egyptians to agree to that arrangement. It is noteworthy that in the first half of 1949 Anglo-Israeli relations were still strained and the British hoped that in exchange for the Strip, Galilee, Ramleh, Lydda and the Jerusalem corridor, the Israelis would concede the strategically important Negev.[51]

Campbell argued that the Egyptians should not be forced to give up the only reward they had obtained from the war in Palestine, and was supported by the British Consul in Jerusalem, who predicted that the Gaza refugees would become slave labour in the service of the IDF.[52] Campbell won the day, not so much owing to the arguments that he put forward but rather due to Kirkbride's intervention. As mentioned earlier, Kirkbride served as a watchdog. The Minister in Amman objected to the principle of territorial compensation for Israel in return for repatriation, and thus stated that it was desirable that Gaza should be retained by the Egyptians in order to consolidate Transjordan's rights over the West Bank.[53]

The Foreign Office agreed that its ambassador in Egypt would mention the subject as part of the concerted Anglo-American effort, but at the same time declared its reluctance to exert pressure on the Egyptians. Owing to Kirkbride's and Campbell's objections, the Foreign Office conveyed a new formula: Egypt should keep the Gaza Strip, and Israel should repatriate 150 000 refugees.[54] The American Secretary of State was bewildered by the news. He wrote to the American Ambassador in London that he found it hard to believe that the Foreign Office *had* proposed that Egypt assume responsibility for the refugees in the Gaza Strip in the light of what the State Department knew about Egypt's absorption problems and its attitude to the Palestinian refugees in general. By now, however, the Egyptian reaction was cool and uncooperative.[55]

The Israeli acceptance of the Gaza proposal eventually put the Israelis in difficulties. The Israelis stated that unless the Egyptians approved the Gaza proposal, Israel was prepared to repatriate only a small number of refugees. The State Department and the Foreign Office found it an unconvincing argument. How could Israel claim its ability to absorb 250 000 refugees with the Gaza Strip and in the same breath declare it could hardly repatriate any at all without territorial compensation?[56] This Israeli attitude brought about the beginning of American pressure on Isreal to change its policy.

After the failure of the Gaza proposal President Truman sent a special envoy, General Hildring, to communicate to the Israelis the President's concern about their attitude. This was coupled with an unprecedentedly sharp telegram to Ben-Gurion, in which the premier was warned that the American government would reverse its attitude towards the Israelis if they did not alter their position on the refugee question.[57] The IFO believed the American pressure to be solely for purposes of placating world public opinion.[58] However, this pressure grew and so did alarm in Israel. The State Department was convinced by Ethridge that the Israeli position on the refugees was the main reason for the stalemate in Lausanne. These American protests had their effect, and the Israelis consented to allow reunion of families of refugees (in the broader definition of the term 'family', according to the Arab concept). The Israeli reports spoke of a total of 25 000 refugees who had come back legally and illegally. The Americans were still not satisfied. In order to underline their misgivings, they made a promised loan to Israel of $100 million from the Import–Export Bank conditional upon Israel's altering its stand. Another note was sent by Truman, this time to President Chaim Weizmann, in which the American President blamed the Israelis for taking an uncompromising stance while the Arabs had come to the PCC with the object of achieving peace.[59] When these last two actions were made public, they were viewed with growing concern by the Israeli press and the Knesset.[60]

The American position was that maximum repatriation was required of Israel in the areas allotted to the Arabs. The State Department reasoned with the Israelis that the Congress would not agree to finance the resettlement when it had already agreed to the Marshall Plan and NATO. Moreover, resettlement was not feasible without a large measure of repatriation.[61]

The intensive American pressure resulted in another Israeli gesture. At the end of August it was leaked through an American correspondent that the Israeli government had communicated to the State Department a definite figure of 100 000 refugees which they were prepared to accept as part of a general peace agreement. Israel kept the right to resettle those refugees wherever it deemed suitable. Publicly, the Israeli Foreign Minister announced in the Knesset that if the Arab delegations were prepared for peace negotiations with Israel the refugee problem would be the first to be discussed. Sharett won the support of the Knesset for his proposal.[62]

The PCC considered the Israeli offer unsatisfactory, as did the Arab delegates. They demanded repatriation of all refugees and compensation for those who did not wish to return. The Arabs claimed that the Israeli proposal contradicted the UN GA resolution of December 1948, a resolution which called for the return of all refugees who wished to come back. As a compromise, the Commission suggested a mixture of resettlement and repatriation as the principal basis for solution. The Jordanian and Syrian governments stated they would be able to receive those refugees who did not wish to be repatriated. Privately, the Foreign Office learned that those governments agreed to the inevitability of a general resettlement programme.[63] The Americans had similar information, and that was why they believed the Israeli offer to be inadequate. Robert McGhee, the American official dealing with refugee affairs, was confident that if Israel were to repatriate 250 000, the Syrians, Jordanians and Iraqis could come to the fore and commit themselves publicly to resettlement. The Israelis claimed that absorbing more than 100 000 would be demographically suicidal for the Jewish state, since with the additional 150 000 Arabs already living in Israel this would increase the Arab population to 250 000.[64]

Acheson believed that Israel had allowed domestic public opinion to develop in such a way that any concessions on refugees were impossible. On the other hand, the American consul in Jerusalem was surprised at the relatively moderate reaction of the Israeli press.[65]

When the Israeli offer was made, Anglo-Israeli relations were such as to convince the IFO that it could turn to the British Foreign Office for advice and support. The Israeli ambassador requested British mediation on the question of the 100 000 refugees; however, the Foreign Office was reluctant to exert any pressure on the Arabs on this issue. The British found the Israeli proposal inadequate and unreasonable in view of its previous consent to absorb the Gaza refugees. Despite this reservation, by then the British position was basically closer to the Israeli understanding of the problem, seeing resettlement as the main means of solution; but this was never fully conveyed to the Arab governments.[66]

Nevertheless, the Foreign Office was convinced that the American pressure was bearing fruit. In August 1949, the Office formed the impression that Israel's attitude towards the refugees had improved owing to American pressure. Both the Office and *The Times* believed Israel was preparing vast areas in eastern Galilee and the Negev as reception areas for the refugees. *The Times* correspondent in Israel interviewed the designated staff of these areas.[67]

However, this period of Israel's positive attitude towards the refugees was short-lived. With the flow of Jewish refugees from Arab countries in 1950–1, Israel claimed it could not increase the Arab population within its territory.

Internal criticism within Israel, and the Arab refusal to resettle some of the refugees, thus caused the Israeli government to prevaricate even on its limited offer to repatriate 100 000 refugees. At this time the American position on the refugee problem was that Israel should implement the UN resolution of 11 December 1948, whereas the Foreign Office had supported the idea of combining repatriation and resettlement from the outset. In any event, once the second Israeli offer had been rejected by the Arabs, the Americans were disinclined to exert further pressure on Israel. The Americans decided to introduce a new solution to the problem by treating the whole question as an economic one.

THE ECONOMIC APPROACH

By the end of August 1949, there was no source which would have financed the relief work for the refugees. With the onset of cold and rainy weather around the middle of October, feeding and accommodation, as well as health services, became serious problems. Hitherto, relief had been provided by a special UN Relief Project (UNRPR). This agency coordinated and directed the work of all the charity and voluntary groups which were willing to support the refugees.[68] However, by August 1949 the voluntary organisations had become restive and were talking about packing up before the end of the year rather than risk losing their prestige if funds ran out in the winter.[69]

It is most surprising that at that stage, or even earlier, the IRO did not step in to replace or aid the voluntary groups. In fact Bernadotte suggested as early as the summer of 1948 that the IRO take over responsibility for the refugees. The IRO replied that it had given priority to other refugee problems and that it had limited resources.[70] In 1949 the British representative in the IRO urged the Foreign Office to transfer responsibility for relief to the IRO. The representative argued that since Britain and the US contributed 80 per cent of the IRO budget, they would have direct control over operations. He pointed out that resettlement could only solve the problem of the agricultural refugees; the city and town dwellers needed seed money and relief if their reintegration into Arab societies were to be successful.[71] Two senior Foreign Office officials supported this argument and point of view. However, the Treasury was unwilling to increase Britain's contribution to the IRO budget and was prepared to allocate money only for re-settlement, not relief. The Treasury had the full support of Clement Attlee and the British representatives in the Middle East. Although Bevin was prepared to consider a British contribution towards relief, he did not press the point and the Foreign Office rejected this suggestion.[72]

The Americans at least had the ability to increase their contribution to the IRO budget if it were necessary; the British did not. Indeed this was both the main British handicap and, at the same time, advantage; any kind of economic solution would not involve them to a large extent, owing to their financial disabilities. The British had already exhausted their overseas expenditure, planned to be invested in the Nile Water schemes, the Iraqi irrigation plans and development in Persia.[73]

Nevertheless, the IRO had shown its ability to cope with refugee problems and was no doubt the organisation best qualified for the task. In 1950, the Foreign Office would once again consider the possibility of using the IRO for the Palestinian refugees, and once again the Treasury would reject the idea.

The stalemate in relief operations particularly alarmed the newly assigned US coordinator for refugee matters in the State Department, Robert McGhee. He warned the American Secretary of State, Dean Acheson, that such a situation would be exploited by the Communists, and that in his opinion the only way of avoiding this was by introducing general development schemes which would precede a political solution.[74] This view was accepted by the State Department which, long before August 1949, had held that the absence of a territorial settlement should not prevent the development and implementation of ways to resolve the refugee problem.

The Foreign Office regarded these ideas favourably; in general, they corresponded with London's views, and particularly Bevin's aspirations for raising the standard of living in the area as the best means of preventing Communist penetration. The idea of sending a survey mission to explore the possibility of combining resettlement with development was raised in the Anglo-American talks in August 1949. However, the Foreign Office did not fail to warn its American counterparts repeatedly that such an idea was impossible due to the political complications.[75]

McGhee presented the basis of his concept in a speech to the Young Democratic Club in November 1949. He viewed the refugee problem mainly as an economic one, caused by economic dislocations arising from the Palestine hostilities. The return of the refugees or their integration were, for McGhee, economic solutions. He favoured the idea of an economic survey mission, since he believed that an outstanding and experienced American could cope with the challenge and would find a formula for solving the technical part of the problem.[76]

Unlike the British, Robert McGhee (inexperienced in Middle Eastern affairs) had overlooked the political complications and anticipated trouble elsewhere. He told his listeners that there were three preconditions to the political success of the schemes. First, the Arab countries would have to relax restrictive legislation which inhibited foreign commercial operations and private investment. Second, those governments should initiate fiscal reforms. Finally, they should begin with agrarian reforms.[77]

It seems that Truman hesitated before approving the initiative. McGhee had to fight in order to convince the President that an ESM would not commit the US to any line of action. The survey itself was to help those countries which would be prepared to absorb refugees. Thus it was agreed that the American representative on the PCC would urge the Commission to appoint an ESM, to be chaired by an American with two deputies, British and French.[78] This decision had already been contemplated in July 1949.

On 23 August the PCC decided to implement the GA resolution of 11 December 1948, by establishing an economic mission as a subsidiary body under its authority. The mission was charged with studying the economic situation in the countries affected by the war in Palestine, and with looking for solutions to the problem of development programmes required to overcome the economic dislocations created by the war. Furthermore, the mission was given the authority to recommend ways of facilitating the repatriation, resettlement and economic and social rehabilitation of the refugees and payment of compensation pursuant to the provisions of the UN resolution from December 1948 (in fact, resettlement was not mentioned directly at first, but only as a result of repatriation). Finally, the ESM was asked to look for means of promoting economic conditions conducive to the maintenance of peace and stability in the area. The chairman was to be an American and his deputies British, Turkish and French.[79]

The Mission was rapidly constituted and went to the Middle East in September 1949, establishing its headquarters in Beirut. Gordon Clapp, chairman of the board of directors of the Tennessee Valley Authority, accepted the appointment as the Mission's chairman. The Foreign Office suggested that Clapp and his British deputy, Sir Desmond Morton, be responsible to their governments and not to the

UN.[80] However, the American government dreaded such direct responsibility, and the overall authority was given to the UN. The Foreign Office, on the other hand, warned the State Department that throwing the question of resettlement and financial assistance into the hands of the UN and allowing the organisation to administer the whole project would remove it 'from the practical sphere of technical and financial assistance' and throw it 'into UN politics with all that that would imply in delay, inefficiency and Soviet intrigues'.[81]

Even before the interim report of the Mission was submitted to the PCC, and long before the idea of such a survey task had been conceived, the Foreign Office had had its doubts about the economic approach. The Eastern Department had warned that the outcome of an economic approach would be a freezing of the territorial situation. Indeed, with hindsight, the Office's warning was correct. However, it was also the sole preoccupation with the refugee question which perpetuated the territorial status quo. The possibility of consolidating the territorial status quo was not a marginal issue as far as the Foreign Office was concerned; it meant weakening British aspirations for the Negev, which were not abandoned until the beginning of 1950.[82]

There were other problems as well. The Foreign Office was apprehensive that McGhee's ideas about new development schemes would hamper the work of the BMEO in promoting programmes already in existence; thus the Foreign Office demanded that these projects be completed at first, under the supervision of the BMEO.[83]

It is important to emphasise that Britain had nothing positive to suggest as an alternative to the American approach. The Foreign Office was convinced that there was no need for further territorial changes, although it had to admit that the political approach had got nowhere. At least the principle, and its seems – in hindsight – the main lines of a better approach were clearer to the Foreign Office: that is, that the solution could only be a combination of the two approaches, the political and the economic. However, the British were unwilling, and perhaps unable, to exert pressure on the Arab side to accept this formula, which was accepted in principle, for a while, by the Israelis. Moreover, by September 1949, the Foreign Office had come to realise that politically resettlement was more feasible than repatriation, because large-scale repatriation would require the Jordanians to resettle refugees in their own state. The Foreign Office therefore suggested to the State Department that it concentrate on resettlement.[84] However, this did not fit the 'pure' economic approach of McGhee. Both McGhee and Clapp believed that only after assessing the economic capabilities of each country (including Israel) could the ESM determine the number of refugees it would be able to absorb. This assessment was to be made by 'an authoritative technical study'.[85]

The Americans were not deterred and the ESM began its work. The State Department believed that in a matter of weeks both Israeli and Arab approval for such a scheme would be forthcoming. In fact, the Israeli media treated the ESM in very much the same way as did the Foreign Office. It was approved of, but with more than a modicum of scepticism.[86] The Arab states were willing, albeit reluctantly, to consult with and meet the Mission. The Mission had little difficulty in approaching the Jordanians, Egyptians and Syrians. Iraq agreed to receive the Mission only after British pressure, but it did not cooperate in any way. Although the Americans put pressure on the British to use their influence in Iraq, Morton and Clapp understood their weak position *vis-à-vis* Iraq, since that country did not participate in the PCC's efforts and was not inclined to cooperate. However, the Foreign Office saw the greatest resettlement possibilities as being in Iraq and in spite of Morton's reservations the Mission visited that country. As for the Syrians, they announced their willingness to participate in preparing relief programmes with the assistance of the ESM. Publicly, the Syrians refused to discuss resettlement, but privately they told Sir Desmond Morton that with the right finance, it could be accepted.[87]

The Foreign Office assessed that the Mission was in general suspected by the Arab governments, since its members were from countries which supported the partition resolution, and that it was therefore regarded as pro-Israeli.[88]

BRITISH INVOLVEMENT IN THE SURVEY MISSION

Owing to Morton's active role in the preparations for the ESM interim report, British involvement was greater than initially intended. One notes that the American Embassy in Cairo had little doubt about Morton's dominance. They reported that Morton had got Clapp 'under his thumb'.[89] Indeed British and American documents give this impression, as the following survey will attempt to show.

A few weeks after the Mission started its work, Morton reported that the mission had the cooperation of the Arab governments for schemes of employment and relief, pending a permanent agreement on resettlement or repatriation. Clapp and Morton suggested that finance, complete or partial, should come from external and local sources; they wanted the Foreign Office help to allay Arab fears about the ESM.[90] The Foreign Office warned that these preliminary conclusions indicated a tendency to evade the political issues completely and to concentrate on temporary relief works: an attitude that might defeat the purpose for which the Mission had been set up. Thus the Office hoped 'that the work of the Mission will bring the Arab states to admit that the refugee problem could only be finally solved by a large scale resettlement in addition to repatriation'. The Office warned that unless relief was linked to resettlement, it would be impossible to secure funds either from the British Treasury or other countries: 'the Arab states have therefore to be brought around to the idea of resettlement before the Mission report is made public and any glossing over this aspect in talks with them is likely to lead to charges of bad faith and even of rejection of the Mission's recommendations *in toto*'.[91]

The State Department saw Clapp's and Morton's suggestions as a tactical move and believed that their views were in accordance with the Foreign Office; they told the British ambassador in Washington that the US did not intend the Mission to dodge the issue of resettlement.[92]

Morton and Clapp heeded these warnings. At the outset they had intended to totally ignore the political aspects of the problem. In replying to the comments of the Foreign Office and the State Department, the two officials suggested the dissociation of the Mission's work from that of the PCC, since at birth the Mission had been tainted with some of the odium acquired by the PCC. Morton, in particular, believed that the terms of reference given to the Mission by the PCC had proved something of a handicap. He asserted that if emphasis was put on economic development and not on solving the refugee problem by resettlement, the ESM report would sound better to Arab ears. This meant revision of the ESM terms of reference; that is, what Clapp and Morton wanted was a public declaration that economic assistance to Arab countries did not depend on their willingness to resettle the refugees.[93]

Eventually, Clapp and Morton had their way. The State Department was convinced by their arguments since it was concerned about any delay in finding resources for relief. Any mention of general resettlement in the ESM report would have led to a long debate in the GA, whereas the State Department wished to accelerate the process. The Foreign Office went even further. It suggested that the ESM entrust responsibility for relief to the hands of a new organisation established solely to deal with Arab refugees, UNRWA.[94] This suggestion, once accepted, meant that the ESM produced a solution aimed solely at providing relief, and not resettlement, for the refugees.

In this way, the Foreign Office suddenly found itself not only following an economic approach but also taking the lead, despite their recognition of the fact that Jews and Arabs alike wanted a political solution. From their experience in India they knew it could not work; Lord Wavell had tried it there, with the net result that Britain had to abandon India in August 1947 instead of June 1948.[95]

Although resettlement was the ultimate object of the Mission it was not mentioned publicly and the talks with the Arab countries concentrated on relief works. Morton reported that the ESM had found means to introduce the question of resettlement both in Syria and Jordan. However, the Mission could not publish the fact, and neither could it come to any practical implementation.

In its negotiations with Israel, the Mission's main aim was to obtain Israeli acquiescence to paying compensation. The Israelis refused and rejected Morton's suggestion to use German property in Israel, which amounted to £20 million, for that purpose.[96]

Given all these problems, Morton suggested that the ESM not refer to any political aspects in its interim report and advocated a short-term organisation to deal with relief which would be divorced from the unpopular PCC and dissociated from the UN Secretariat.[97] Morton was no doubt the moving spirit behind the ESM interim and final report.

THE ESM REPORTS

In November 1949, after two months of work, the ESM submitted its report to the PCC. Although everyone had to await the final report, the initial and interim reports were sufficient to indicate that the economic approach was doomed to fail: the main feature was the proposal to substitute constructive work for philanthropic work.[98]

The Mission stated that as long as the political stalemate continued, there was little hope for repatriation or large-scale resettlement. It pointed out that, so far, relief had prevented catastrophe. But it also recommended that resources should be directed towards resettlement and that responsibility should be transferred to local governments. The Mission noted the need for a census in order to decrease the number of persons receiving relief; it was believed that a considerable number of fictitious refugees were on the rolls. The census was also needed to organise employment of refugees.[99]

The ESM reiterated the call for financial assistance for the Arab states in order to encourage development schemes. Finally, the report discussed the potential opportunities for useful and productive work to improve and reclaim the land, increase the supply and use of water, strengthen and extend road systems and improve sanitation and shelter. In short, it proposed public works by refugees in order to raise the standard of living, the usual formula for preventing Communist penetration. But nothing practical was mentioned in that direction. A date was stated for the Public Works programme to begin in April 1950. Relief would be supplied by the UN until the end of that year, after which the responsibility would fall on the Arab governments. The principal product of the report was its last recommendation: the establishment of an agency to direct the work-relief programme and replace the UNRPR (UN Relief Fund): this was UNRWA.[100]

The Foreign Office was pleased with the report. It anticipated trouble only from the clause which advocated reducing the number of relief rations from 940 000 to 660 000. For this reason it warned the Arab governments of its contents before publication. Furthermore, it considered that Israel had been let off lightly, mainly because repatriation was not mentioned.[101]

The Foreign Office believed that the next step should be an initiative to offer Anglo-American help in selecting development schemes and in obtaining finance. Through its *ad hoc* policy, the Foreign Office was again about to be dragged, by its own initiative, into deeper involvement in the Middle East, which was prevented only by lack of resources.[102]

Troutbeck alone spotted a staggering miscalculation. The report suggested relief work which would employ 80 000 refugees. What about the others, asked Troutbeck, or rather what about the majority of the refugees? He warned that Jordan would be faced with an insoluble problem and would not be able to survive. Troutbeck suggested that the IRO provide for all the refugees. From the official point of view in London, he had entered the discussion much too late.[103]

At the end of 1949, the Americans organised a meeting of their representatives in the Middle East and the State Department's experts on the area in the city of Istanbul. One of the many items on the agenda was the interim report. Almost everyone at the conference displayed great dissatisfaction with it. The agreed conclusion of the conference read as follows: the problem of the interim report would be its implementation, which in the conference's view was 'handicapped at [the] start in certain states because of Economic Survey Mission's connection with the Palestine Conciliation Commission and the Palestine problem'.[104] The Conference hoped that UNRWA would be dissociated from the PCC. This was possible, but it is strange that the American Middle East experts believed in practice that they could take the UNRWA project out of the context of the Palestine problem. In fact, the experts even recommended separating the pilot projects, at least in the public mind, from refugees and the PCC; thus they depicted UNRWA as purely a development project.[105] Needless to say, such a concept departed from the terms of reference of the ESM, but fitted in with the ideas of Clapp and McGhee.

Both the Americans and the British were most impressed by the possibilities of resettling refugees in Iraq. The Foreign Office (and the IFO) saw it as the only desirable solution in the final analysis. However, since London was not even prepared to discuss the issue with the Iraqis, it was never made public. The Foreign Office realised that the Iraqi government was adamant in its refusal 'to go along with the projects of integration'.[106]

The American interest in Iraq, and not in Jordan, coupled with McGhee's support for the incorporation of Arab Palestine into Transjordan (he saw it as an important step towards solving the problem of the refugees) allayed any apprehension the Office had been harbouring as a result of the establishment of the ESM. Despite its negative evaluation concerning the Mission's success, it was at least evident that it would not affect British interest, or undermine the concept of the Greater Transjordan, which was the basis of British policy towards the Arab–Israeli conflict.

Not everyone in the Office was that cynical about the refugee problem; there were quite a few who believed that the interim report was an indication that the final report would include a suggestion for transition from relief to resettlement.[107] In fact, the British approach to the problem was quite probably not the result of a cynical approach but rather the outcome of the absence of clear ideas or policy towards the refugee question. All the Office could do, therefore, was to provide its officials with a vague guideline that in general suggested a combination of repatriation and resettlement.

The final report, both in letter and in spirit, indicated the Mission's admitted failure to solve the refugee problem through purely economic methods. 'Economic development cannot of itself make peace', conceded the Mission, and it added that 'where the political will to peace is lacking' economic solution had little meaning.[108] As one writer put it, the Mission finally, after contemplating the past, 'saw politics as the scourge of the Middle East'.[109] The report discussed academically the long-range economic development prospects in the Middle East, and it noted in particular that Israel and Egypt should be left out of this effort since Israel had already begun to develop irrigation and to 'employ modern agriculture methods, while possessing the scientific infrastructure required for development'. The report also excluded Egypt because the 'knowledge and skill available in that country are already on a high level'.[110]

As regards other Arab countries, the Mission had hardly anything new to offer. It excluded the possibility of large short-term projects in Syria, Jordan and Iraq, owing to the lack of capital, skills and research facilities, as well as of governmental organisation and administrative infrastructure. Instead it suggested pilot projects for those countries and Lebanon aimed mainly at improvement of the exploitation of water resources. The Mission also adopted the British notion of advising the Arab governments to establish a National Development Board.[111]

The final report reiterated the recommendation of the interim report for the establishment of the UNRWA. The new organisation was to start its work on or after 1 April 1950, and it would direct the proposed programmes of relief and public works. The agency was granted full autonomy to decide whether or not to undertake long-term development projects. This activity was to continue until the end of June 1951, when it would be re-examined by the GA. The hope was that this might provide the opportunity to remove 400 000 refugees from the relief rolls. Needless to say neither the figure nor the timetable was ever adhered to.[112]

The report was widely condemned both in Israel and in the Arab countries. In Israel, even those newpapers which welcomed the establishment of the Mission bitterly criticised the report. The press argued that the report encouraged Arab intransigence and did not emphasise resettlement. The Arab Palestine Press expressed dissatisfaction with the projects, which it believed would prejudice a final settlement; furthermore it was annoyed that the report did not place responsibility on Israel.[113]

The Egyptian delegation to the UN attempted to amend the UN joint resolution based on the ESM's final report, with the view of preventing the reduction in rations and generally prolonging the duration of UN relief for refugees. The British and the American delegations opposed those amendments and stated that savings were aimed at assisting the refugees by providing work for them.[114]

As soon as the final report was published, the Foreign Office felt that UNRWA, very much its own creation, would endanger its position. It feared that UNRWA would have advisory functions of planning development and preparing applications for external assistance. The Foreign Office did not want the new organisation to deal with long-term development schemes. The British government had difficulties convincing the Americans about the importance of this point. The State Department feared that Congress would only support the recommendations of the Mission if they were to include long-term development schemes. The Foreign Office claimed that creation of a new agency dealing with long-term development would reduce the chance of cooperation with the Arab governments, which would suspect that development was being imposed on them, as well as increasing administrative expenses and manpower, resulting in a delay in the execution of works.[115]

This was no doubt a genuine British point of view, emerging from their experience and contacts withthe Arab governments opposing the American line. Nevertheless, the British also had other, more important reasons for their objections to UNRWA's assumption of the role of development organisation. If the UN were to step in, it would have severely affected the work and the position of the BMEO. Moreover, the British had exerted an important influence through the work of the national development boards in Iraq and Jordan, and naturally they had no desire to lose this position. The final report adopted the British suggestion of limiting UNRWA's work to relief projects, despite American opposition; this was due to the dominant role played by Sir Desmond Morton, both in the Mission and in the drafting of the two reports.

The British also had their way in convincing the Americans that only an American national would be a suitable director for the proposed agency. But they did not succeed in conveying to the Americans the importance of including representatives of the Middle East countries in the advisory Council attached to UNRWA.[116]

The only consideration weighing with the British was the American view that some reference to a long-term agency was necessary if the State Department were to obtain funds directly from Congress after UNRWA ceased to exist in June 1951. However, the Foreign Office believed that its intention of continuing the work of UNRWA should not be mentioned publicly, as it might remove the stimulus to Arab governments to take over responsibility themselves.[117] It might be noted that, more than 30 years later, UNRWA continues to exist, and the Arab countries (partly for political reasons) never assumed responsibility for the refugees.

BRITAIN, THE US AND UNRWA

Discussion on the resettlement possibilities was cut short when the US and Britain reached an understanding with regard to concentration on short-term programmes rather than on long-range development schemes. The two governments concurred on the Mission's main conclusion that 'the region is not ready for resettlement', and therefore any attempt to realise large development schemes would be pursuing 'folly and frustration and thereby delay sound economic growth'. Nevertheless it was understood that the relief work suggested could lead to development, as was affirmed in the interim report.[118]

Thus, in December 1949, Michael Wright left for New York to work out the details of establishing UNRWA. The two governments reached an understanding that the new agency would not be administered by the UN secretariat, would not include 'Slav' or other 'undesirable' membership and would comprise only British, American, French and Turkish members. It was agreed that the British contribution would be in non-convertible sterling. The Chancellor was willing to agree to a contribution of £1.25 million. The Treasury, in spite of Foreign Office protests, felt it could not ask the Chancellor for more. Bevin intervened and ruled that the £1.25 million was sufficient. This fell short of American expectations. The State Department realised that Congress would only cover 50 per cent of UNRWA's budget, which left governments other than the US or the UK to contribute $21 million; the Treasury was unmoved. One official there told the Foreign Office that 'any further contribution to the relief of the refugees would add to the main impediment to British economic recovery'. Attlee supported the Treasury and approved a contribution only towards resettlement, not relief.[119]

However, public opinion and Congressional pressure persisted, and by April 1950, it became apparent that even the French were willing to contribute more than the British.[120] Bevin intervened once more, this time by exerting pressure on the drained Treasury, and by May 1950, **Britain announced** its willingness to contribute $7 million. Now the

American President could proceed and sign into law the US contribution ($27.5 million).[121]

Furthermore, the two Foreign Offices agreed on the appointment of General Kennedy as director of UNRWA, in spite of initial US objections to the appointment of an American national (Kennedy was in fact of Canadian origin). Sir Henry Knight was chosen as the British representative on the advisory committee, playing a role similar to that of Morton in the Clapp Mission. The Agency's headquarters were to be in Beirut.

The British representative warned his government from the outset that UNRWA's main difficulty would be finance. Sir Henry Knight undoubtedly made a very valid point. However, the political complications, such as UNRWA's status in Arab eyes, were even more problematic. Indeed he had also warned the Foreign Office that apart from the financial difficulties, he anticipated trouble from the need to negotiate with uncooperative Arab governments 'who will try to divert us onto the political issues to obtain their own private advantages'. Knight was worried by the low opinion of the UN Secretary-General concerning Kennedy's political experience and ability to negotiate with the Arab governments.[122]

The Foreign Office thus had to work out a guideline for Knight in order to prepare him for negotiations with the Arab governments. It suggested that the Agency should publicly emphasise that it was not concerned with the political aspects of the refugee problem, or with Palestine settlement as a whole. It held, on the other hand, that the Arab governments should be privately advised that without a political settlement, the Agency could not succeed in the long run.[123]

It was unrealistic, according to the Middle East Secretariat, to imagine that a political settlement would include massive repatriation. Even if Israel had agreed, there was no living space for the refugees. Resettlement within the framework of long-term development undertaken by the Arab governments themselves was seen by the Foreign Office as the only solution. Moreover, it was suggested that those governments should be told that no funds would be available after June 1951 and that 'it is therefore essential that Arab statesmen should plan on the assumption that at the end of that period the refugees would be entirely in their charge'.[124]

The same line was pursued in September 1950, just before UNRWA submitted its first report to the UN GA for an overall debate. The Foreign Office had concluded that it was not in the best interests of the refugees to return to Israel and that the only solution was resettlement.

Nevertheless, it agreed with the State Department that a UN resolution should make only a general call for peace, that there would be no reference to the political aspects of the refugee problem, and that only fund-raising should be mentioned.[125]

The Arab reaction came in June 1950 in the form of a communiqué from the Arab League to the effect that its Political Committee agreed to cooperate with UNRWA without prejudicing the right of the refugees to return. This was conveyed both officially and unofficially.[126]

With this more conducive political atmosphere, the Office had to consider the financial aspect of the problem as well. There were two major possibilities for obtaining funds for UNRWA, apart from seed money provided by the American, British and French governments. One was the American Point Four scheme; the other was financial compensation from Israel.

As could have been expected, the Arab governments were more forthcoming towards the idea of receiving money for development *per se* than for relief and resettlement purposes. The latter involved too many political implications. For this reason the Americans made it clear throughout 1950 that Point Four money (Truman asked Congress to allocate $50 million for foreign aid) would not be used to solve the refugee problem. In any event, the money allocated in this programme to the Middle East was insignificant.[127]

Britain was mainly worried about the American intention to entrust the financial aid, under the framework of Point Four, to the Arab League. This probably explains the unenthusiastic approach of Britain to the introduction of Point Four to the Middle East. One senior British official declared that the 'American Point Four is tending to become rather a nuisance politically'; another official suggested conveying to the Americans that 'it is useless to negotiate with the Arab League', which did not like to be 'side-tracked from more amusing political activities'.[128]

It was about this time that the question of compensation seemed to some British and American officials to be an even more feasible solution than external funds. Britain had raised the question of compensation because of its difficulty in contributing its share to UNRWA's budget. The possibility of Israeli compensation had been mentioned by the Foreign Office as early as April 1949, when it suggested to the State Department that Israel should make a direct contribution to the PCC. In the course of conversation with the ESM, the Israeli government reaffirmed its position that compensation should be considered as part of a general peace settlement together with the question of reparations for war damages. The ESM was of the opinion that Israel should agree to separate a general peace settlement from the principle of payment of compensation for abandoned property. In other words, for the ESM it was essentially not merely a financial problem but a moral and political one as well. Early compensation would give the refugees an incentive to choose resettlement as the best solution. The ESM had in mind an Israeli contribution of 10 to 50 per cent of the total sum of compensation.[129]

Despite Israeli opposition, the Foreign Office was asked by its representative in the UN to obtain a working estimate of the value of Arab land held by Israel.[130] This was an act of optimism derived from information given by the PCC, now convened in Geneva, that Israel had accepted the principle of compensating refugees for land abandoned by them. It was coupled with a communiqué from the Commission that Israel was willing to accept within the territory under its jurisdiction an Arab population of 250 000, and that Jordan and Syria were willing to resettle the rest. In July 1950, the Israelis announced their willingness to pay compensation for immovable property only as part of a general settlement, and within the limits of their financial capacity. The Foreign Office believed that if the Israelis had been prepared to discuss this issue separately, a big obstacle would have been removed from the way to a general settlement.[131]

In fact what the Foreign Office had hoped to achieve was financial compensation for Jordan; therefore it suggested that only refugees living in Jordan should be entitled to liquidate their property in Israel. This was also done in order to temper criticism in Jordan over an agreement with Israel. Incidentally, owing to technical problems, the Foreign Office was in favour of compensating the large landowners first. The British Consul in Jerusalem warned his government that although he appreciated the difficulties of obtaining compensation for all the refugees, rich and poor, it would be folly to compensate those who had sold their land in the past to the Jews; namely, the rich refugees. However, the Foreign Office felt that rich refugees would have more influence with the Arab governments and could hasten a settlement; the State Department, on humanitarian grounds, preferred that compensation should go to the poorer refugees.[132]

In any case the Israeli position did not change in the course of 1950. The Foreign Office was angered by the Israeli attitude, since it believed it to be the main stumbling block to an agreement. It was now prepared to make an effort to convince the Arab states to give up the idea of repatriation altogether, if Israel were to consent to compensation. In fact, the Foreign Office preferred compensation to the ideas put forward by some UN officials involving the secession of territory from Israel to Jordan in order to resettle refugees there. Ostensibly, it was argued that compensation was the major bone of contention in the conflict. However, it can be suspected that Kirkbride's objections to enlarging the refugee population in Jordan played a decisive role in the Foreign Office's view. In February 1950, the Americans considered putting pressure on Israel for that purpose but gave up after assessing that it would not change the Arab point of view.[133]

The failure to find adequate internal or external sources of finance for UNRWA's work and the abandoning of the resettlement schemes produced a new solution for the problem. It was suggested that UNRWA, with its limited budget, should concentrate on assisting the refugees to help themselves by putting them to work on public projects which had already been depicted by the ESM as beneficial to the economies of the countries surrounding Palestine. However, most of the Arab countries refused to comply with UNRWA's suggestion that after the end of their contracts, skilled refugees would acquire the nationality of the countries in which they had been working. This applied to Egypt, the Persian Gulf states, Saudi Arabia and Lebanon, while the Iraqis were prepared to accept a small number. Meanwhile, the BMEO was making an effort to find employment for the refugees in the Middle East but meeting with little success.[134]

As for the relief works themselves, there was little progress owing to the refugees' feelings on the subject. In various camps strikes broke out in protest against the implementation of works projects, which were regarded as leading the refugees away from repatriation.[135] This attitude was reflected in the Palestine Arab press; the press expressed doubts over the ESM's temporary settlement projects, which they saw as prejudicing a final settlement favourable to the refugees.[136] Altogether, as one of the British officials working for UNRWA put it, the attitude of the refugees was 'cool and somewhat mistrusting'.[137] Instead of being made more self-supporting, the refugees were paradoxically being made more dependent, since the UN became their employer as well as their provider. As the UNRWA report concluded, the UN was held by the refugees as responsible for their past and present misfortune and for their future fate.[138]

NEW TERMINOLOGY, OLD SOLUTION, 1950–2

By November 1950, the time of the publication of the first UNRWA report, the Foreign Office was following the American lead reluctantly, although it was realised in London that economic inducements were becoming less and less important in the case of the Arab refugees. The Arab governments felt that the refugee question was their strongest political card. McGhee did not accept this theory, which was probably why the Americans were still seeking economic solutions throughout 1951 and 1952. Hence, contrary to British expectations, the report did ask the GA to grant UNRWA power to arrange resettlement.[139]

The Foreign Office believed that there was hope for a change of mood on the Arab side which could have facilitated resettlement. The Office, as well as the PCC, saw a way out by limiting compensation to resettlement. In other words, Israel's readiness to compensate would, or could, have led to Arab acceptance of resettlement. However, this link was not mentioned in the interim report, which dealt only with the hardships encountered by the Agency in providing employment for the refugees. The report recommended that relief would therefore continue until the end of 1951. The Agency stated that the main reasons for its failure to supply employment were, first, the increase in the number of relief recipients to 950 000 (in contrast with the PCC estimate of 750 000 refugees), and second, the lack of cooperation on the part of the Arab governments. The reports assessed this attitude as the result of a misunderstanding of UNRWA's purpose. Finally, UNRWA complained that the contribution to its budget was less than the amount recommended by the ESM and asked for further contributions. The report suggested a budget of $50 million for future activities. It was recommended that the money be put into a reintegration fund which would aim to rehabilitate refugees and remove them from the relief rolls. For the period of July 1951 to June 1952, the sum of $20 million was required for relief, and $30 million for reintegration of the refugees into the Arab countries.[140]

On the basis of this report, the *ad hoc* Political Committee of the UN began its deliberations on the refugee problem. In those discussions Britain defended the methods hitherto employed for financing the UNRWA projects voluntarily and rejected suggestions to go over to an assessment system which in its opinion might have opened the way to undesirable elements who could pay and then demand political compensation (namely the Soviet Union).[141] Thus, at the end of November 1951, the British, the French, the Americans and the Turks tabled a draft resolution instructing the establishment of a reintegration fund with a budget of $50 million, on a voluntary basis. The resolution was approved after a Pakistani amendment was added to the effect that the new resolution reaffirmed the 11 December 1948 resolution: it was without prejudice to the principle of repatriation.[142] As the *New York Times* remarked, reintegration was definitely a political term and was basically no different from resettlement.[143] Thus, reintegration meant resettlement and repatriation, and did not offer any new solution; it was just a change of name.

UNRWA's report no doubt departed from the terms of reference granted it by the ESM. It was mainly a compromise between the American and the British understanding about the best solution. As Lord Macdonald, the British representative in the *ad hoc* Committee, told them, Britain believed that as a result of psychological barriers and economic problems, it could not suggest the repatriation of the refugees unless it were part of a general peace settlement. The American position on the refugee question had not changed, but the willingness to exert pressure on Israel to accept repatriation had declined. The Americans had told the Israelis on many occasions that they supported the basic principle of repatriation and compensation for those who did not wish to return.[144] Thus one might say, almost ironically, that the Americans had accepted the Arab view, whereas the British supported the Israeli concept. Hence reintegration without prejudice to repatriation was the new magic formula, although it differed little from previous solutions, and each side could, and did, interpret it as it wished.

American pressure was applied only once more in 1950. In March that year the Knesset was about to pass legislation to allow the Alien Property Custodian in Israel to sell the property of Arab refugees. American pressure delayed the execution of such procedures until May 1951.[145]

At the beginning of 1951, the State Department and the Foreign Office once more discussed the possibility of resettlement. The Foreign Office suggested Syria as the country offering the most promising opening for permanent resettlement of large numbers of refugees. There was a belief in London that the US enjoyed considerable influence in Syria and could thus implement a large-scale programme there. The Americans were once again prepared to explore resettlement possibilities; once more they put the emphasis on providing Syria with experts and surveyors. The Foreign Office claimed that financial assistance would be more of an inducement. It argued that the Arab world had seen enough surveys and technical assistance without much capital flow. The Americans accepted this concept and energetically hastened to formulate a new solution. By that time, the voices in London advocating the withdrawal of Britain from UNRWA had become stronger and stronger, and thus Britain finally left the problem in the hands of the Americans and the UN.[146]

CONCLUSIONS: THE DECLINE OF BRITISH INTEREST

In the second half of 1951, the British quite probably lost interest in the problem, and it seems that the financial and political aspects of the problem were then dealt with by the Americans without much consideration either for their partners in the PCC or for Britain. Following their determination to provide financial assistance (in the form of capital), the Americans told the Israelis and the Arab governments that they would ask Congress to grant $50 million for the Arab refugees under a new Foreign Aid bill. The Americans refused a British request to see the bill before it was introduced to Congress. This finance was to be administered through the UN agencies. The new American concept was that the US government would negotiate bilaterally with the Middle East countries and would offer financial assistance for resettlement (half of the finance was intended for relief and the other half for resettlement). The Americans excluded everyone but themselves and the countries concerned from dealing with resettlement. This included the refugee office formed by the PCC under a UN resolution in May 1951.[147]

It is doubtful whether the British had a greater appreciation of the American 'business approach' than they had for the 'economic approach'. However, at least the Americans recognised the importance of encouraging resettlement. It should be remembered that UNRWA was about to become an integration agency and was supposed to transfer responsibility for feeding the refugees to the Arab governments. However, the new American initiative had precisely the opposite effect. UNRWA was turning into a permanent relief agency, while the Americans were taking the resettlement issue upon themselves. The Foreign Office would not allow the Americans to effect a bilateral agreement with Jordan, but otherwise welcomed the initiative, which was seen as part of a new American drive for greater involvement in Middle East affairs; this was apparent in June–July 1951.[148]

However, in order to overcome Congress's lack of enthusiasm towards an exclusive American role in financing, the State Department hoped that Britain would contribute more money to UNRWA. The Department claimed that Congress would not authorise the American government to grant the $50 million without a British contribution of one-third of this figure. This time the Treasury, as well as the Foreign Office, believed that it could go no further without knowing how funds granted so far had been used. The Treasury was horrified at the prospect of inflating the budget of this 'impractical' body (that is, UNRWA).[149] In any case Burrows, in the British Embassy in Washington, assured the Foreign Office that it was all for the sake of public opinion to show that the burden was shared by Britain, but otherwise the US would act independently. Furthermore, Britain was fully occupied with securing Jordan's economy. The year 1950 proved to be one of Jordan's worst years. The enormous burden of the refugee population and the loss of Palestine as a market had a damaging effect on the economy of the country. The Jordanians drew heavily on their sterling accounts in order to bridge the gap between income and expenditure.[150]

The Jordanians as well as the British must have derived satisfaction from UNRWA's annual report for 1951, which was published in September of that year. It concluded that refugees should be given work only in countries of greater economic possibilities (the report specifically noted that Jordan and Lebanon were not such countries). In general, the report indicated that not much progress had been made on resettlement and that the number of refugees in the camps had increased. There was a tendency to move from the villages and the towns into the camps.[151] One notes that by the second half of 1951, UNRWA had begun to build mud huts; these became a familiar characteristic of the camps and remain so to the present day.

In the years that followed, UNRWA tried to introduce several schemes for resettlement in Syria, Sinai and elsewhere to no avail.[152] In the years 1953–6, UNRWA concentrated on resettlement in the Yarmuk Valley in order to move the refugees away from the West Bank. In that period it was suggested by some Israeli Cabinet members that reparations from Germany could be linked to compensation, but the proposal was rejected.[153] The mood of the refugees was apparently becoming more and more bitter, as the Consul General of His Majesty's Government in Jerusalem had put it in November 1954: now the refugees did not want to resettle, work, or return to Israel. Ironically, the same large-scale development schemes that had been suggested since 1949 would be reintroduced in 1959 and, as anticipated, rejected by the Arab governments.[154] Therefore UNRWA's annual reports put the blame on the Arab governments.

Sir Desmond Morton told the Foreign Office that the refugee problem merely accentuated another profound problem. At the same meeting, Clapp said he was convinced that if 'no refugee problem existed, the Survey Mission, in considering economic development of the Middle East, would nevertheless have made the same approach and come to the same conclusions'.[155] The crux of the matter was that this might have been an important discovery had the refugee problem been an economic and not a political one. McGhee gave the other side of the coin of the same approach: 'existing tensions in the area cannot be relieved unless these countries can be assisted in their programmes of economic development'. The problem of the refugees therefore 'cannot be solved unless there are more opportunities for settlement and useful employment'.[156]

Indeed for Clapp, integration schemes were seen as a means of introducing American economic ideas; that is, the importance of economic stability lay in its guarantee against Communism. McGhee was the main protagonist of these ideas. His views originated in what he had seen in Europe. For him, solution of the refugee problem was an opportunity to introduce overall development schemes to the whole area based on the same principles as the European Recovery Programme: that is, economic and social development was the best guarantee for stability and therefore the best safeguard against Communist penetration.[157] However, these efforts were frustrated by the British through Morton's insistence on the necessity of concentrating first on relief, leaving development for future consideration between the two powers. Thus the British accepted the economic approach only as far as relief was concerned; they never saw it as a formula for solving the refugee problem.

Another qualification, probably even more important, made by the British to the American economic approach related to Jordan. As a direct consequence of the war in Palestine, the resident population of Transjordan had increased from 400 000 to 800 000, and there were also 400 000 refugees under Hashemite jurisdiction. Owing to Jordan's alliance with Britain and its strategic importance to the UK, the Foreign Office had to secure its viability; resettlement of the refugees in Jordan would have turned it into a Palestinian state. On the other hand, the continued presence of a refugee population was an impossible economic and financial burden for the kingdom. Hence by focusing the attention of the UN and the Americans on the need to fund the relief and maintenance of the refugees on the one hand, and advocating the resettlement of most of them in Syria and Iraq on the other, the Foreign Office hoped to save Jordan. In this, the British point of view was closer to the Israeli concept than to that of the Americans or the other members of the PCC. The British eventually despaired of the Americans' ability to pressure Israel into repatriation. By 1950 they were convinced that this was impractical, not only because of Israeli objections but also because of the lack of living space in Israel.

Relief prevented the refugees from starvation and from further deterioration of their situation. However, it also prevented a permanent solution. Some writers blame the UN for treating the problem only from the humanitarian aspect, and for trying to solve it by economic means.[158] The UN, however, had very little to do with it; it was mainly American ideas and British reluctant acquiescence that produced the economic solutions. Moreover, repeated reference to the UN resolution of 11 December 1948 and the reiteration, owing to American insistence, that any solution not prejudice the right of the refugees to return, intensified the refugees' hopes of return, if and when a political solution could be introduced.

The lesson of the first formative years in the history of the Arab–Israeli conflict had been learned. It became clear that economic development could not by itself bring peace and that the source of the conflict and the refugee problem was political, perhaps even ideological, and not only economic. If it were a political problem, then a possible solution for the conflict would have been the consolidation of the Israeli–Jordanian understanding over the future of post-Mandatory Palestine. This book will therefore end with an analysis of British policy towards this unique effort by Israel and Jordan to solve the Palestinian conflict in the years 1948–51.

8 British Policy towards the Israeli– Transjordanian Negotiations

The two main elements of British policy towards the Israeli– Transjordanian negotiations were the realisation of the need to ensure Israeli agreement to the annexation of the West Bank by Transjordan, and the recognition that a renewed Israeli–Hashemite understanding would help to solve the Palestine problem. The policy was also characterised by a constant effort to maintain a balance between retaining a dominant position in the Arab world on the one hand, and starting a new chapter in its relations with Israel on the other. With hindsight, it seems that the British position was not a unique one. Any other power that tried to maintain and cultivate good relations with Israel and its Arab neighbours, and at the same time attempted to solve the Arab–Israeli conflict, was faced with the same dilemma.

Kirkbride's problem was of a different nature altogether. The British minister's immense influence on Abdullah was one of the main reasons for Britain's unhesitating reliance on Transjordan's loyalty. Kirkbride enjoyed the King's confidence and, as was emphasised in the introduction to this work, was a party to all his domestic and external decisions and plans. However, despite Kirkbride's influence on Abdullah, the King had a major ambition, the full import of which he failed to disclose to the British minister. This was Abdullah's determination to conclude a formal peace treaty with Israel. Although Kirkbride approved of the need to reach a tacit agreement with the Jewish Agency prior to the war in Palestine, he disliked Abdullah's methods of dealing with the Agency; that is, he resented the direct contact with Jewish representatives, and preferred indirect negotiations.

Kirkbride's view on the desirability and nature of the negotiations changed several times during the talks. His dissatisfaction with the King's conduct was particularly strong whenever he felt he was being kept in the dark by the King with regard to the talks. However, there were, of course, other reasons for Kirkbride's oscillating attitude towards the negotiations; these will be touched on later in this chapter.

Pragmatism was the main feature of British policy towards the negotiations. In addition, two basic principles served as general guidelines for all the British departments and personalities dealing with the negotiations. The first was the need to protect the Greater Transjordan state from any external and internal enemies. The second was that attempts should be made to end the hostilities between Arabs and Israelis. The conflict was regarded mainly as an Israeli–Jordanian dispute over boundaries and territory. Solving the outstanding problems between these two countries seemed to most officials in the Foreign Office the best way to dissolve the deadlock. That is, the conflict was seen as a struggle not between two ideologies or national movements, but between two states which had many interests in common. This must have affected British beliefs about the gravity of the conflict and the chances of solving it.

We must remember that as the Cold War developed, Britain's desire to secure Israel's and Jordan's loyalty to NATO added a new element in British policy towards the Israeli–Jordanian negotiations. It was most important to ensure that regional or local disputes would not cause the defection of NATO's allies to the East. This recognition made itself felt in the beginning of the 1950s once Anglo-Israeli relations had been normalised.

In this part of the book we shall also distinguish positions adopted by Britain at various phases of the negotiations. This is a necessary methodological approach given the *ad hoc* nature of British policy. In general, and for the sake of analysis, we may divide the negotiations into three phases. During the first period, from July 1948 to March 1949, while Bernadotte's initiative was still alive, the British tried to check the King's tendency to seek a formal peace with Israel. The Foreign Office at the time favoured an imposed solution to the conflict. Only when this initiative failed did the Office give its blessing to the attempt to conclude an armistice between the two countries.

The second phase, from March 1949 to March 1950, was marked by the two states' attempt to conclude a proper peace treaty. Its main feature was Kirkbride's effort to maintain a balance between the King, who wanted to conclude a peace treaty with Israel, and his ministers, who were reluctant to defy the Arab League.

The last stage began in March 1950 and ended with the King's assassination in July 1951. Israel was by then regarded as a pro-Western state by Britain, and the Foreign Office no longer saw any urgency in concluding a formal peace treaty, but rather looked for ways of consolidating the 1947 *modus vivendi*, which was maintained until 1967.

Finally, one should not underestimate the genuine effort made by both Jordan and Israel to conclude a peace treaty. The years 1948–51 were unique in the history of the Arab–Israeli conflict. During this period Israeli officials were frequent visitors in Amman and helped to lay the foundation for a long-term understanding between the two countries which held until 1967.

BRITISH OPPOSITION TO THE PRELIMINARY CONTACTS, JUNE–DECEMBER 1948

Abdullah had already achieved most of his aims in Palestine by the end of the first week of fighting. Thus he had only reluctantly continued the military effort, out of the need to toe the general Arab line, and owing to his wish to decide the battle over Jerusalem. At a very early stage, the King therefore found a way of conveying to the Israelis his desire to renew the pre-war understanding in spite of the continuation of the war.[1]

Even prior to the first truce there was a genuine desire in Israel to end hostilities. For that purpose, the Israelis consulted the State Department about ways to negotiate peace with the Arab states. They stipulated one main precondition: that these talks would not involve British mediation. Thus information about the first moves can be gathered mostly from American and Israeli documents. It is difficult to find information about these contacts in British documents since Abdullah, for his part, did not inform the British of the initial contacts in June 1948.[2]

At this time, contacts took place in the American Consulate in Jerusalem. The two local commanders met there and American officials were convinced that a sincere desire for peace existed on both sides. In these talks, Abdullah delivered a promise not to allow large-scale operations against the Israelis.[3]

The low profile of the British Foreign Office during these contacts was due to the lack of any formal Anglo-Israeli relations. Nevertheless it seems, according to Israeli documents, that unofficially the Foreign Office conveyed to the Israelis its support for an Israeli–Hashemite rapprochement.[4]

Officially, however, the Foreign Office was backing the main diplomatic initiative in the area, namely the Bernadotte proposal, which aimed at imposing a solution on the sides, and did not place much hope on an understanding between them. It was still possible that even Bernadotte himself believed that a prior consent between Israel and Transjordan on certain outstanding problems would facilitate the success of his plan.[5]

It seems that the British minister in Amman had more at stake as a result of such a direct Israeli–Transjordanian approach. In July 1948, Abdullah notified Kirkbride about his intention to conclude a peace treaty with Israel in order to be able to withdraw from the fighting. Kirkbride reported that Abdullah intended to approach Bernadotte for that purpose, which in Kirkbride's mind was the attitude of a 'frightened and selfish man'.[6]

It is worth noting that, unlike Kirkbride, London found no fault with the King's conduct and, like Bernadotte, praised him for accepting the mediator's second set of proposals as well as for his readiness to prolong the truce as advised by Bevin. Kirkbride explained that he doubted Abdullah's ability to survive both external and internal opposition. As would become clear throughout 1949–50, Kirkbride was mainly worried about domestic opposition which might damage the integrity of the kingdom. He was less apprehensive of Arab opposition: after all, he advocated basing British policy in the Middle East on the Hashemites. Most important of all, it seems that Kirkbride was annoyed by the fact that for the first time in his long stay in Transjordan, he was not a party to a major feature of the King's foreign policy. One is more doubtful about Kirkbride's concern about the King's tendency not to inform his government. Kirkbride himself tried to convince the Foreign Office to base its Arab policy on absolute monarchs like Abdullah, since such rulers were able to impose their wills on their ministers.[7]

The outcome of this situation was that Kirkbride sided with Tawfiq Abu Al-Huda. The latter, who was more of a pan-Arabist than the King, had opposed any independent Transjordanian policy towards Israel. Thus Kirkbride had lost the complete confidence of one centre of power and was trying to win the allegiance of another. By the end of 1951, the British minister would regret this move.

However, Kirkbride still enjoyed some influence on the King and, together with the premier, forced the King to pursue a twofold policy towards Israel. The talks with Israel were conducted on two levels, official and unofficial. The official one was public and was conducted by emissaries of the government while the private, unofficial, negotations were between the King's private advisers and special Israeli envoys.

Abdullah depended for his survival on Britain and was thus reluctant openly to pursue a policy which he believed would be unacceptable to Britain. Britain agreed with Abdullah that in order to safeguard Arab Palestine some sort of agreement with Israel was required. However, the British differed from the King about the desirability of formal peace. The Foreign Office asserted that a *de facto* agreement was sufficient to consolidate the understanding between the two countries.

MEETINGS IN PARIS (AUGUST–NOVEMBER 1948)

These meetings were the outcome of Israel's rejection of the mediator's proposals and Abdullah's disappointment with Bernadotte's failure. The Israelis rejected the Bernadotte proposals and tried to initiate direct talks with Arab representatives during the GA session in Paris at the end of 1948. Abdullah was the only Arab leader to respond to this Israeli overture. He agreed to send his Ambassador in London, Prince Abdul Majid Haidar, to discuss with Eliahu (Elias) Sasson, the adviser on Arab affairs in the IFO, the possibilities of mutual understanding. The two men met in Paris in August 1948.[8]

Sasson suggested that the Israelis should use their good offices with the Americans and secure Washington's political and financial support of Transjordan in return for a joint Israeli–Transjordanian front against Bernadotte's proposals. These contacts did not end with any concrete decisions, but both sides took the opportunity to exchange views on their policies.[9]

The British legations in Amman and the Foreign Office learned about these talks only in November 1948. The British were sceptical about the value of a direct approach and doubted whether it could contribute at all to the settlement of the Palestinian problem. The Americans, on the other hand, were encouraged by the news coming from Paris and were optimistic about the outcome.[10] The main reason for the British scepticism concerning direct talks was their mistrust of Israel's aims in Palestine. The Foreign Office suspected the Israelis of contemplating the occupation of the whole of Mandatory Palestine, a suspicion that was reinforced by reports on the new build-up of the Israeli army and air force. Nevertheless, the British were careful not to induce the Arab countries to commence another round of fighting; for instance, notwithstanding these suspicions, the British government decided to maintain the embargo on the delivery of arms to the Arab states, sending arms stocks only to British bases in Transjordan. Thus, the British maintained a watchful eye over the King but did not prevent his initial encounters with the Israelis. The British involvement deepened as the danger of an Israeli attack on the West Bank increased during the last months of 1948.[11]

The presence of Iraqi forces in the Samaria area was the main Israeli concern at that time. Since August 1948, the Israelis had demanded the evacuation of these forces whose presence was welcomed by neither Abdullah nor Kirkbride, who regarded them as anti-British as much as anti-Abdullah.[12]

For the sake of removing the danger of an Israeli attack, Abdullah was prepared to conclude a separate peace treaty with Israel. The British believed that an attack could have been prevented by the full implementation of the Bernadotte plan. Bevin's main worry was, as he explained to the British government, that in the course of direct negotiations the territorial status quo would be changed in Israel's favour. Kirkbride, who shared these apprehensions, warned the Foreign Office that nothing should be done to encourage the King to enter direct negotiations with Israel since 'he is already flirting with the idea'.[13] The Minister in Amman stressed that on this question he had the full support of Abu Al-Huda.

The Foreign Office was aware, as was the King, that an Israeli attack on Arab Palestine could take place before the GA decided to impose Bernadotte's proposals on the two parties. The British Cabinet could thus have either prepared a direct intervention in the case of an Israeli attack or supported Abdullah's endeavours to reach an understanding with Israel.

One of the Foreign Office's main predicaments was how to assess Israeli intentions correctly. The lack of direct contact prevented the flow of accurate information about Israel's plans. Thus the Office failed to comprehend the degree of disagreement amongst Israeli policy-makers on the question of whether Israel should take over the whole of Palestine. Ben-Gurion's initial desires to enlarge Israel and expand to the west were restrained by his colleagues in the Israeli government and by his own rethinking on the issue. In October 1948 the Israeli premier regarded the Negev as the most vital element for the state's survival and thus abandoned, for the time being, any thoughts of occupying Arab Palestine. Moreover, the euphoric mood

which characterised Ben-Gurion's thinking in July 1948 was replaced
by a more realistic and sober approach. His main conclusion in
November 1948 was that Britain would oppose by force any Israeli
attack.[14]

Ben-Gurion was wrong in this last assumption. The British would
not have intervened directly to protect Arab Palestine, neither in May
1948, nor in November that year. This was despite their obligation to
do so under the first article of the annexe of the alliance treaty which
read as follows: 'In the event of either party becoming engaged in war,
or of a menace of hostility each . . . party will invite the other to bring
to his territory or *territory controlled by him* the necessary forces of
arms.'[15]

The Arab writer Muhafaza claimed that the Transjordanians were
notified by Bevin that this article would not apply to Arab Palestine.
Glubb had stressed the same point, remarking that 'that remarkable
document' was absurd since it referred to different enemies, the USSR
for Britain, and Israel for Transjordan.[16] In fact, Bevin recognised this
contradiction in a speech he made in the House of Commons.[17]

Bevin's disinclination to invoke the treaty was partly political, due to
his realisations that the Americans would object to such a British
action, and partly military, due to the CoS' estimation of the British
ability to intervene. The CoS doubted Britain's ability to sustain a
long war against Israel and suggested confining British intervention to
the supply of arms and ammunition.[18] As will be indicated later, it was
only when British installations proper were in danger that British
intervention was seriously considered.

However, even complying with the recommendations of the CoS to
send arms to the Legion depended on American consent to lift the
embargo. President Truman was reluctant to cause any shift in US
policy in an election year; his consent for this action was given only
after his re-election. It is noteworthy that in Washington, even the
State Department failed to see the reason for the British anxiety in
those months; the British reaction was regarded as 'unrealistic'.[19]

In the light of these developments, the Foreign Office felt it could do
one of two things: recommend that Transjordan leave Palestine, or
encourage it to reach an agreement with Israel. This dilemma was
accentuated in November 1948, when Abdullah felt too vulnerable to
pursue the talks with the Israelis without British protection and
appealed for a fresh British commitment to strengthen him so that he
would not enter the negotiations from an inferior position.[20]

Abdullah then apologised to Kirkbride for not having informed him about the negotiations. The Transjordanian ambassador in London – the main participant in the Paris negotiations – was instructed to inform the Foreign Office about the negotiations. However, it seems that the ambassador was reluctant to give out any significant details of what had occurred in Paris and did not fulfil a promise he had given to the Eastern Department to inform them in advance of any further meetings. When the Foreign Office learned from Kirkbride that the talks were continuing without its knowledge, it concluded that the Transjordanian ambassador was 'pretty disingenuous'.[21] It dawned upon the head of the Eastern Department that the 'Minister's talks had already gone some way before he came to us'.[22] The British were bewildered by Abdullah's failure to confide in them, although this did not affect the attitude of the Office towards the King.

In November 1948, Kirkbride assessed that the talks in Paris had become more substantial, since the King had sent his personal secretary, Abdel Ghani Karami, to the talks. The minister in Amman speculated that Karami would be presented with Israeli approval for Transjordanian rule over Arab Palestine in return for the Negev, Latrun and the whole of Jerusalem.[23]

The Americans, on the other hand, reported that the two sides had agreed to negotiate only over the fate of the Negev, Jaffa, Ramleh and Beisan. Moreover, this report stressed that the Israelis had tried to discover the degree of British involvement in the talks.[24]

However, Ben-Gurion's diary gives the impression that the two sides were only exploring possibilities for serious negotiations. In fact, Ben-Gurion felt that he had not much to discuss with Abdullah before he completed the occupation of the Negev, and he just wanted to maintain momentum in the negotiations. This is contradicted by some Arab writers who tended to assign considerable importance to the talks in Paris. They claimed that those talks resulted in Abdullah's decision to remain neutral in the case of an Israeli attack on the Negev.[25]

Although there is no evidence that the talks in Paris amounted to any such agreement, it is safe to agree with the Arab arguments that Abdullah had intentionally refrained from assisting the Egyptians in the Negev, thus eventually saving his forces from an Israeli attack.[26]

The reason for this approach by Abdullah was that the Negev was more of a British interest than a Transjordanian one. Britain was interested in securing the Negev as a land communication between Egypt and Transjordan, whereas Abdullah's desires were confined to a corridor to the Mediterranean, a request granted him by the Israelis (in principle) at the beginning of 1950. Abdullah was not suspected by the Israelis of harbouring any ambitions towards the Negev and therefore his minimal involvement in that area was perceived by the Israelis as part of a British design to wrest this part from Israel.[27]

THE SHIFT IN BRITISH POLICY (DECEMBER 1948): SUPPORT FOR THE ISRAELI–TRANSJORDANIAN NEGOTIATIONS

By November 1948 Kirkbride, who had scorned Abdullah earlier in the year for his 'cowardly' behaviour based on the King's desire to reach a separate agreement with Israel, was himself terrified by the prospect of an Israeli attack on Arab Palestine. The Minister in Amman envisaged an Israeli offensive that would lead to the fall of Gaza, the Negev and Jerusalem into Jewish hands. This gloomy scenario was shared by Glubb Pasha. Bevin and Wright in London had reached similar conclusions regarding Israel's ability and ambitions. Moreover the Foreign Office, in December 1948, had realised that the Americans were not fully behind Bernadotte's proposals, and that the Arab world resented them as much as the Israelis and the Hashemites did.[28]

Thus the Foreign Office instructed Kirkbride to convey to the King Britain's support for negotiations with Israel, but pleaded with him to consult His Majesty's Government about any further contacts. Notwithstanding Kirkbride's opposition in the past, he himself supported negotiations with Israel at the end of 1948. His main worry was that Israel would attack Transjordan if the latter did not enter peace negotiations. Kirkbride's apprehensions about an imminent Israeli attack grew after the talks had moved from Paris to Jerusalem in December 1948.[29]

The two main participants in those talks reported that the Israelis gave their consent and blessing to the Jericho resolution and suggested the *de facto* partition of Jerusalem and the conclusion of a permanent truce along the Legion front. The Israelis demanded the eviction of the Iraqi and Egyptian contingents. As for the King's demands for Ramleh, Lydda and Jaffa, they were rejected. The main practical outcome of the talks was the consolidation of the *de facto* partition of Jerusalem by the introduction of mutually agreed military arrangements.[30]

However, Sir Alec Kirkbride, like his American colleague, sent an altogether different account of the meetings. According to him, the Transjordanians were presented with an ultimatum: unless they were prepared to enter full peace negotiations, the Israelis would resume military operations against them. Kirkbride, somewhat confused, reported that the Israeli position was a mixture of a desire for peace and a readiness to resume the fighting. Thus, in the midst of the meeting in Jerusalem, the Minister in Amman felt that even negotiations with Israel would not necessarily prevent an armed clash in Arab Palestine, since the Israelis were prepared to resort to military pressure if their demands were not met. At-Tal and Dayan, the two principal negotiators from each side, never mentioned any ultimatum or threats made in the meeting. In fact, nothing concrete was agreed upon.[31] The Israeli documents indicate that the Israeli government took a decision to continue peace negotiations with Transjordan and to continue with military operations against the Egyptians.[32] It seems that both the American and the British accounts emerged from a somewhat misleading version given by the King himself. Kirkbride admitted that the King was hardly taking him or the premier into his confidence, and that when Abdullah did pass on information it was confused and misleading. In this case, contrary to the King's report, it seems that nothing concrete was agreed upon and the two sides consented to continue the talks towards armistice in 1949.[33]

There is little doubt that Abdullah wanted to create the impression when informing the Americans, the Brtitish and his premier, that the Israelis would not be satisfied with anything less than a formal peace. The King wanted to persaude them that unless they gave him their blessing, they would be responsible for the resumption of hostilities.

Whether the Israelis had or had not submitted an ultimatum, the fact remains that both Kirkbride and the American representative felt that Transjordan was in real danger. The consulates in Jerusalem reported Israeli movement of troops, adding support to the conviction of the State Department and the Foreign Office that an Israeli attack was imminent. President Truman warned Ben-Gurion that the American government might review its attitude towards Israel in the light of an aggressive Israeli policy. Ben-Gurion was surprised by the American warning and denied the allegations.[34]

On the other hand Abu Al-Huda did not believe the King. He appreciated correctly that the King would now look for governmental support and thus offered his resignation. Kirkbride persuaded Bevin to send a special message to the premier urging him to remain in office; this was done and Abu Al-Huda stayed.[35]

Kirkbride still believed the King and appealed to the Foreign Office for a lead as to the most desirable policy towards the Israelis. Kirkbride claimed that now the Bernadotte plan had proved a failure, a new guideline was necessary for him and the Transjordanian premier; otherwise the King would enter the negotiations from an inferior position and might lose Arab Palestine.[36]

Thus Kirkbride forced the Foreign Office to formulate a new guideline as a result of the failure of Bernadotte's initiative. Bevin's immediate reaction, characteristic of this pragmatic statesman, was to endorse the direct negotiations as an alternative to the mediation efforts. The Foreign Secretary justified the negotiations in a letter to Kirkbride as essential for safeguarding the annexation of the West Bank.[37] Bevin looked for ways of appeasing possible Arab reaction to the negotiations as well as seeking American cooperation, realising it contradicted their support for the PCC's role as the exclusive peace medium in the area.

The Foreign Secretary hoped that eventually all Arab states would consent to a settlement to divide central Palestine between Israel and Transjordan. He regarded Egypt's consent as the most important factor in facilitating such an Arab response.[38]

Bevin proposed granting Israel Galilee and dividing the Negev, south of Beersheba, between Egypt and Transjordan. He hoped to mitigate Israel's suspicions about this solution by promising most of the Negev to Transjordan and internationalising Lydda and Jerusalem; that is, he assumed that the Israelis would prefer the Transjordanians to the Egyptians on their southern border. Bevin was now looking for a solution that combined Bernadotte's second proposal with the 'Jessup principle' (giving Galilee to the Jews and the Negev to the Arabs).[39]

The Foreign Office found the Transjordanian premier eager to approach the Egyptians and reach an understanding on this basis. However, Abdullah succeeded in averting his intentions to go to Egypt to discuss the plan, The King would never have accepted such a guideline from the Foreign Office. Neither before the war in Palestine nor after it did he show any inclination to involve the Egyptians in his plans.[40]

The Egyptians wanted the British to serve as mediators between them and Abdullah as long as they needed the Legion's help to extricate their army from its débâcle in Palestine.[41] Once the Israeli–Egyptian negotiations in Rhodes commenced, the Egyptians saw no further use for a joint front.

The British ambassador in Cairo strongly supported a rapprochement since he believed that otherwise Transjordan would fall into an Israeli trap. Similar opinions were voiced by Sir John Troutbeck, who cautioned against a Palestinian settlement that did not involve Egypt. This was mainly because it would damage Anglo-Egyptian relations, which were already strained.[42]

However, Kirkbride was opposed to the idea of dividing the Negev as well as to His Majesty's Government serving as a mediator for that purpose. Kirkbride's apprehension was about Israel, not the Arab world. Most of the Eastern Department officials were also less enthusiastic about the idea, which was mainly Bevin's conception. They advocated that Britain should not interfere in the complex relations between Egypt and Transjordan, since Britain would lose in the end: the necessity of supporting one side would cause it to antagonise the other. In the Deparment's opinion, an Egyptian–Transjordanian rapprochement was desirable, but not preferable to Hashemite control in the Negev. Bevin found more support amongst his representatives in the Middle East such as Sir Hugh Dow, the consul in Jerusalem, who stressed the importance of obtaining Egyptian consent to the Greater Transjordanian concept.[43]

The main conclusion Bevin might have derived from this failure to convince Abdullah and Kirkbride to approach the Egyptians could have been that, by December 1948 the Negev was considered part of Israel by the Transjordanians. In fact, a statement to this effect was made by Abdullah in a conversation with an Israeli representative in the talks of January 1949. Sir Hugh Dow and Sir John Troutbeck pointed out this fact to the Foreign Office in their despatches.[44]

In December 1948, Bevin defined his position as follows: 'It would be strategically convenient for us, if Transjordan could get the whole of the Negev, or such part as may be allotted to the Arabs, but we wish to be careful not to antagonize Egypt.'[45] Antagonising Egypt seemed less important to the Eastern Department. However, they appreciated the strategic value for *Britain* in that area. The possibility of establishing bases there, as well as controlling an area situated between British installations in Transjordan and the British zone in Egypt, did not escape the attention of the officials.[46]

Moreover, the considerable improvement in Anglo-Israeli relations following the *de facto* recognition by Britain in January 1949 had turned Israel into a friendly country, not a hostile one. Thus the fact that the Negev was in Jewish hands no longer seemed a disadvantage from the British officials' point of view.

In March 1949 it was apparent that the Egyptians and other members of the Arab League would not give formal approval to the annexation of Arab Palestine to Transjordan. However, the Arab position was not the only factor the British had to consider; they also had to take the attitude of the Americans and the UN into account.

The Foreign Office saw no reason to check the negotiations on account of the creation of the PCC or its arrival in Jerusalem in order to assume the role of the late mediator. Bevin accepted this line, owing to the uncertainty about the precise role the PCC might play in safeguarding Britain's interests. Only Sir Ronald Campbell in Cairo resented this directive and asserted that direct negotiations at the time were 'untimed and unwise'.[47]

At that point the Americans were undecided with regard to the Commission's role and informed the British Foreign Office that they would not object to direct talks parallel to the Commission's efforts. The Office thus did not anticipate American opposition. Incidentally, the Americans suspected the British of restraining the Transjordanians from conducting direct talks with Israel.[48]

Thus after taking into account all these considerations, Bevin advised Abdullah to pursue a separate policy towards Israel and 'look for the best deal you can', regardless of the Arab reaction.[49] The Israelis, however, could not bring themselves to accept the change in British policy; until the end of negotiations in July 1951, some of the Israelis, still believed Britain had been acting against these contacts. In fact there are many Israelis who still take this view.[50]

BRITAIN AND THE ARMISTICE NEGOTIATIONS (JANUARY–APRIL 1949)

The round of talks in December 1948 ended with a decision to authorise official delegates on both sides to pursue the talks. The main agreement which stemmed from the January 1949 talks was to confine the discussions to the Legion front and to accept, in principle, the cease-fire line as the future border between the two states: namely, not to suggest any territorial changes as had been done by Bernadotte, or implied by the Jessup principle. However, the Transjordanians failed to obtain formal Israeli recognition for the annexation of Arab Palestine, and the Israelis failed to receive an explicit Transjordanian approval for Israeli control of the Negev.[51]

A few days after the first meeting in January 1949, Kirkbride learned about it. He reported a more conciliatory Israeli attitude which he attributed to American pressure. This time, Kirkbride's account coincided with Transjordanian and Israeli versions.[52] The Foreign Office attached little importance to the beginning of the negotiations between the two accredited delegations, owing to the growing tensions between British forces in the Middle East and the Israeli army.

The Israeli penetration into the Sinai almost resulted in hostilities breaking out between Israel and Britain in the beginning of 1949. In that atmosphere Ben-Gurion viewed Britain as Israel's worst enemy and expected the British and the Iraqis to launch an attack from Samaria. The direct cause of the Israeli concern was the detachment of British troops in Aqaba which had arrived there as a result of the Anglo-Israeli tension. The Israelis were assured by the King that the troops had been sent on Britain's own initiative. However, it seems that the King himself had requested this force, owing to the Israeli advance towards the Gulf of Aqaba, alongside Wadi Arava.[53]

Abdullah's main apprehension was that the Israeli thrust to the south would end in an Israeli penetration of Transjordan proper. Such a possibility was not ruled out by Britain. For the British, a simultaneous invasion of the territory of Egypt and Transjordan (two countries allied to them by a treaty) without proper British response could have meant, as a senior British official put it, the loss of the British position in the Middle East.[54] Nevertheless, the British acted mainly in a defensive manner; thus Abdullah was told that: 'these moves were *not* made with the idea that they will enable the Arab Legion to take the offensive in Palestine'.[55]

Despite these grave developments in Anglo-Israeli relations, they seemed to have had only marginal effects on the Israeli–Transjordanian talks. It was mainly owing to Abdullah's assurances to the Israelis that he was able to restrain both the Legion and the Iraqi forces (which had been stationed since the war in Samaria and were still there in January 1949) from any attack on Israel. In any case, the tension died out as quickly as it had arisen and ended with Britain's decision to grant *de facto* recognition to Israel and to the armistice negotiations between Israel and Egypt.[56]

However, the British position towards possible armistice negotiations was not yet clear. The Transjordanian delegates had warned the Israelis that Britain would object to them advancing further towards the Gulf of Aqaba; namely completing the occupation of the Negev by Israel. However, the two Israeli delegates, Elias Sasson and Moshe Dayan, returned from their meetings with the King (which took place in Abdullah's winter palace in Shuneh) with the impression that Abdullah wanted to free himself from British control.[57]

The Israelis expected the meetings in Shuneh to end with a mutual agreement to comply with the UN invitation to convene the two delegations in Rhodes and commence armistice negotiations. However, the King explained that, owing to considerable opposition from the ministers and the British, he was unable to embark on proper armistice negotiations.[58] The British reports and some other sources indicate that there was in fact no opposition in the Transjordanian government to these talks in Rhodes, since they were in accordance with the general Arab line; neither did Kirkbride object to them. It seems that the King was reluctant to negotiate an armistice when there were other Arab delegates in Rhodes. Furthermore, the King preferred the talks to continue in Shuneh where he could personally intervene whenever there was a deadlock.[59]

The Foreign Office was in favour of an armistice and it resented the idea of formal peace, which it suspected Abdullah had in mind. The Office claimed that a formal peace would have incurred the animosity of the rest of the Arab world. The Foreign Secretary suggested that all political matters should be left to the PCC. Bevin's confidence in the PCC's prospects of success differed somewhat from the sceptical attitude shown by Foreign Office officials towards this body. Bevin was mainly impressed by the effective American intervention in the Israeli–Egyptian negotiations, and believed American membership in the PCC could bring about similar results in the Israeli–Jordanian negotiations.[60]

It seems that the Foreign Secretary hoped to renew the Anglo-American understanding which had brought about the Bernadotte scheme. That is, he desired close Anglo-American cooperation to provide the parties in the Palestinian conflict with a guideline as to what would be a desirable territorial agreement. However, Bevin's main predicament was that the Americans saw no harm in keeping the Negev in Jewish hands if Israel were to make concessions elsewhere, whereas he considered the division of the Negev between Egypt and Transjordan an essential part of his guideline.[61]

The Foreign Secretary did not despair and urged the Americans to consent to at least joint declaration which would emphasise the degree of cooperation between the two powers on Middle Eastern affairs. As Bevin explained to the Americans, in January 1949 such a joint, or even a tripartite (with the French), declaration was necessary to refute the 'false impression' created by the failure of the Bernadotte proposal that the two powers did not see eye to eye on the Middle East.[62]

Initially the Americans were reluctant to join in such a move which, in their view, would irritate the Russians, who might see it as a move to create another NATO in the Middle East. Furthermore, the State Department feared the prospect of such an embarrassing issue being debated in the Congress; neither did the French show any inclination to join in such a declaration. The French Foreign Minister was apprehensive about the reaction of the North African population.[63]

However, the Foreign Office soon found out that the Americans would be willing to join this declaration in return for a British public gesture of goodwill towards Israel. This American appeal could not have come at a better time. When it was made, in the middle of January 1949, the Foreign Office was already considering granting Israel *de facto* recognition.[64]

Bevin's request was thus complied with on the other side of the Atlantic once it was apparent that Britain was to recognise the state of Israel. A White House press release read as follows: 'While at the time there may have been differences of opinion in London and in Washington as to how best to deal with the Palestine problem, there has been no difference whatever in our main objectives.'[65] Bevin made a similar declaration in the House: 'President Truman's aims and ours are the same.'[66] This was coupled with a *de jure* recognition of Israel and Transjordan by the US.

In the final analysis, notwithstanding the good relations between the two powers, the American participation in the PCC did not bring with it the desired Anglo-American formula for solving the Palestine question. American guidance to their representative in the PCC was to look for a comprehensive settlement, including the solution of the refugee problem and Jerusalem; it did not share the British view of the desirability of a piecemeal Israeli–Transjordanian agreement.[67]

THE SHUNEH NEGOTIATIONS

The Israelis were invited to Shuneh in February 1949 by the King, who had assured them that he had been given a free hand by the British to discuss an armistice with them. He hinted that although he had no interest in the Southern Negev, His Majesty's Government would never allow him to negotiate on this area.[68] British documents do not provide any indication of explicit guidelines to Abdullah to avoid discussion of that or of any other topics. The King probably mentioned that there was British pressure on him in order to obtain concessions from Israel or to prevent Israeli demands for concessions.[69]

The King was still reluctant to send a delegation to the official armistice negotiations in Rhodes and preferred direct negotiations in his Palace in Shuneh. He wanted to discuss with the Israelis two topics which he had realised could not come under the framework of an armistice agreement: an outlet to the sea and an agreement over the Negev and the West Bank.[70]

Bevin wrote personally to the King asking him to negotiate territorial questions in Rhodes. This letter played an important role in Abdullah's compliance with the UN invitation to conduct negotiations there.[71] In the meantime, however, in Shuneh the two sides agreed that they would participate in the PCC and Rhodes negotiations only to satisfy Anglo-American pressure, but that the real negotiations would take place in Shuneh. Dayan and Abdullah were the architects of this formula: namely, that the two sides would reach a prior agreement in Shuneh and then sign the armistice in Rhodes.[72]

Fortunately for both sides, the Arab League did not decide to negotiate *en bloc* in Rhodes: it was thus possible to conduct bilateral negotiations. The Egyptians themselves informed the Foreign Office that they were insistent that 'no other Arab state shall come to terms with the Jews until they have completed their negotiations'.[73] The Israelis announced that they would not negotiate with a joint Arab delegation.[74]

It was only at the end of February that the Transjordanian delegation proceeded to Rhodes. It was instructed by its government not to discuss political matters, a guideline approved by the King who knew he would continue to conduct political negotiations in Shuneh.[75] In Shuneh, it became clear that the two main obstacles remaining in the way of armistice were the Israeli determination to complete the occupation of the Negev and the presence of Iraqi forces in Samaria.

The Israeli delegation to Rhodes was instructed by Ben-Gurion to delay any agreement on final borders until the Israeli army had completed operation 'Uvda' aimed at capturing the Southern Negev down to the Gulf of Aqaba.[76] Arab writers had little doubt that British acquiescence to Israeli actions ensured the successful implementation of the operation. However, it seems that the British, more than anyone else, were threatened by the Israeli advance owing to their anxiety about the safety of the British contingent in Aqaba.[77]

The last stage of the operation began on 7 March and it was some time before the British realised the direction of the Israeli movement. The initial response of the British was to reinforce their contingent there, and then the entire British force in the area was put on the highest alert.[78]

As for the Foreign Office, its main reaction was to appeal to the Americans and ask them to do everything in their power to restrict the Israelis. In Washington, Sir Oliver Franks told Dean Acheson that the Israeli action 'touched his people on a very raw nerve'.[79] However, the State Department was reluctant to act before the UN observers established the extent of the Israeli advance. Even after it had been established that the Israelis were heading towards the Gulf, the State Department was reluctant to condemn the Israelis, apprehensive that it might obstruct the armistice negotiations. The only concern was to prevent an Israeli penetration into Transjordan proper. The Americans asked the British 'not to allow any minor incident to set off the balloon' and to behave with restraint.[80]

The Foreign Office was also assured by the Israelis that there was no intention of crossing the border; nevertheless, the Israelis justified their advance to the Gulf by claiming that they were advancing into an area that had been allotted to the Jews in the partition resolution.[81]

The British warned the Israelis that their forces in the area were instructed to fire on any Israeli unit which crossed the border between Palestine and Transjordan. The British were thus prepared once more to invoke the alliance treaty with Transjordan if the Israelis invaded.[82] On the other hand, the Legion units in the area in which the Israelis advanced were ordered by Glubb, the British Chief of the Legion General Staff to withdraw, which is another source of bitterness mentioned by some Arab writers.[83]

The Israelis reached the Gulf without crossing the border and without clashing with the British.[84] They could now negotiate with the Transjordanians over the future of the West Bank without linking it to the future of the Negev, which was not fully in their hands. Only one obstacle remained: the presence of Iraqi forces in the West Bank.

The Israelis had been demanding since July 1948 the evacuation of the Iraqi forces stationed in Samaria (the area is sometimes referred to as the Arab Triangle: the apex of the Triangle was Nablus and its base stretched from Jenin to Tul Karem). The Israelis contemplated occupying this area several times, but the plan was postponed owing to opposition within the Israeli government and Ben-Gurion's rethinking on Israel's priorities in the war in Palestine.[85]

The Foreign Office was annoyed by the Iraqi government's refusal to enter armistice negotiations. Considerable pressure was exerted by the British on the Iraqis to enter the talks. Alternatively, the British suggested a gradual Iraqi evacuation, which they thought should not be completed before the future of the area was settled: that is, the presence of the Iraqi forces, although a burden in many respects, was helpful as long as there was the danger of an Israeli attack on the area. The British pressure resulted in Iraqi consent to begin gradual evacuation of the Iraqi troops from the front into the heart of Samaria.[86]

However, by March 1949 the Israeli position had hardened. The Israelis were not satisfied with merely substituting the Legion for the Iraqi forces. Ben-Gurion was under pressure from the Israeli army to occupy the area; only counter-pressure from the IFO had prevented this. The Israeli premier was at first doubtful whether the Iraqis could keep their promise to evacuate their forces and thus was willing to consider a military operation.[87] However, there is no indication that a specific and detailed operation was on its way as is claimed by Jon and David Kimchi.[88] There were, however, Israeli manoeuvres near the area as part of a war of nerves conducted by the Israelis to accelerate the Iraqi withdrawal and to indicate strong Israeli interest in the area.[89]

THE SHUNEH AGREEMENT (THE ARMISTIC AGREEMENT, APRIL 1949)

By the time the two delegations began negotiations in Rhodes, the Israelis had accomplished their territorial ambitions in the Negev, whereas the King still feared Israeli designs and actions against his rule over the West Bank owing to the Israeli demands with regard to Samaria. Other issues, such as the formalisation of the partition line in Jerusalem, were agreed upon in Rhodes. The question of the Iraqi forces in Samaria was left to negotiations in Shuneh and in Jerusalem.[90]

In March 1949 the Israelis specified for the first time the quid pro quo they would demand in return for approval of Legion rule over the Iraqi front. This involved widening the Israeli coastal strip between the West Bank and the Mediterranean. They indicated the area around Wadi Arara (A'ra) and the road running through this valley as the territorial concession desired by Israel. This area included strategic high places overlooking the Wadi Arara road which connected the

Israeli settlement of Afula with the town of Hadera on the coast. This area was later named the Little Triangle.[91]

Abdullah gave his immediate consent to the Israeli demand. The main reason for Abdullah's favourable reaction was the Iraqi decision to repatriate its contingent in Palestine. The Foreign Office's pressure on Baghdad to maintain the Iraqi units until the future of Samaria was decided was ignored.[92] Abdullah was left alone facing the Israelis, and there was little Britain could suggest with regard to his next steps.

The Eastern Department and the British Legation in Amman viewed Abdullah's readiness to give in to the Israeli demands with gravity. They were concerned that the Israeli demand would leave the Israelis with control over important strategic points in the Samarian area.[93] The Foreign Office appealed to the Americans. The Americans, although in general sharing the Foreign Office's apprehensions of a possible Israeli attack on Samaria, were reluctant to intervene unless tangible evidence of Israeli preparations for an attack could be provided. As mentioned earlier, such an attack was not being prepared, and thus no evidence could have been produced by the British.[94]

The British Legation in Amman asked for practical British intervention: sending British forces to Samaria or, alternatively, allowing the Legion to reinforce its forces there and by entrusting the task of guarding the southern part of the kingdom to British hands. This last suggestion was ruled out, since the acting mediator strongly opposed it. As for sending British troops to the area, CoS were prepared to despatch British forces only in the case of an Israeli attack on Transjordan proper (an operation codenamed BARKER had been contemplated in case of an Israeli thrust into the Hashemite kingdom).[95]

Abdullah was not even informed about British readiness to protect Transjordan proper, so he must have felt growing insecurity. Moreover, whereas the Director-General of the IFO assured him that Israel was not interested in Samaria, Ben-Gurion's emissaries had informed the acting mediator that the Legion occupation of former Iraqi positions in Samaria was a violation of the truce. In an internal memorandum, the Director-General explained that Israel wanted the King to realise that their consent to his rule over Samaria was a concession for which Israel demanded the Little Triangle.[96] In any case, Abdullah must have felt both threatened and deceived, and therefore he and his government consented to the agreement offered by the Israelis.

However, only towards the end of March 1949 were the final details agreed upon. Kirkbride was responsible for this delay. He reported that at this meeting the Israelis had reiterated their demands with overtones of threats and duress. In order to convey to London the strength of his feelings, he described the meetings in Shuneh as taking place in circumstances 'strongly reminiscent of Hitler and the late Czech president'.[97] This impression was also shared by the American representative in Amman.[98] Thus, Kirkbride did his utmost in order to delay the ceremony of the signing of the armistice.

Kirkbride convinced the Transjordanian government to demand the postponement of the final signing of the agreement until after the return of Abu Al-Huda from Beirut, where he was attending the PCC's conference. This was done in order to gain time. Kirkbride hoped to achieve two things: first, to convince London of the gravity of the situation and, second, to urge Abdullah to appeal personally to President Truman to exert pressure on the Israelis to modify their position; that is, to give up their demand for the Little Triangle. In this last endeavour the British representative enjoyed the full cooperation of his American colleague in Amman, Wells Stabler.[99]

However, it seems that Kirkbride and his American colleague were more alarmed by the terms of the proposed armistice than the Transjordanians themselves or the Foreign Office in London. Bevin, in particular, was not impressed by Kirkbride's arguments. The Foreign Secretary was preoccupied in Europe and Asia with problems whose settlement involved large areas and sometimes entire countries; he could not be impressed by a dispute over a strip of 15 km (the Little Triangle).[100]

The British and American representatives in Amman were equally disappointed with the respective positions of their governments. The Eastern Department was willing to appeal to the Americans. The Foreign Office note to the State Department stated that the proposed deal would endanger Transjordan's 'internal security' as well as its position in the Arab world.[101] The Office pointed out that if it were to advise the Transjordanians to reject the Israeli demands, then 'we should no doubt be saddled with some, at least, of the responsibility for any consequences which might follow from the Transjordan refusal. The whole question of our own support for the Transjordan forces in Palestine would be reopened.'[102] The Permanent Under-Secretary of State, Sir William Strong, who drafted this note, concluded it by emphasising the mutual embarrassment which would be caused to the Americans and the British.[103]

The State Department replied by admitting that it had limited influence on the Israeli government, and would not go beyond verbal protestations. President Truman had in vague terms asked Moshe Sharett, the Israeli Foreign Minister who was visiting Washington at the time, to urge Ben-Gurion to display a more compromising attitude. Moreover, the President had sent a letter to the King advising him to proceed with the negotiations and not wait for American guarantees against Israel.[104] Many Arab writers believe that his letter convinced the King to finalise the armistice agreement with Israel.[105]

Kirkbride and Stabler, on their own initiative and without referring to their government, nevertheless advised the King not to conclude the agreement with Israel.[106] Unfortunately for the King, they did not offer any alternative course, and neither could they guarantee their governments' support for such an act by the King.

Meanwhile the Transjordanian premier had returned from Beirut to participate in the last meeting of the Transjordanian government before the final ceremony. At that meeting he suggested accepting the Israeli demands and ratifying the agreement, which had been finalised in joint meetings in Jerusalem and Shuneh. He also accused Britain of putting Transjordan in such a position that it had to surrender to Israeli pressure.[107]

On 30 March 1949, in the presence of the Israeli and Transjordanian delegations to Rhodes and the entire Hashemite Cabinet, but without any Israeli ministers, the formal armistice was signed. The gist of the agreement was the taking over of the Iraqi front (Samaria) by the Transjordanians in return for the Little Triangle (the strip around Wadi Arara). This area included 15 villages and a population of 35 000 inhabitants. The new armistice lines separated most of the villagers from their lands, and in some cases the villages were divided in two. The other main component of the agreement was the establishment of a special committee (article 8 of the agreement) which was to finalise the problem of access to Jerusalem and formalise the partition of the city.[108] In coming years this committee would become the main medium for Israeli–Jordanian negotiations, as will be elaborated in Chapter 9 of this book. The two delegations flew to Rhodes, where the official document was signed on 3 April 1949.

It is worth noting the different conclusions reached by the British CoS and the Foreign Office following the signature of the Israeli–Transjordanian armistice. The military asserted that the agreement increased Transjordan's vulnerability *vis-à-vis* Israel. The CoS warned the Foreign Office that if Israel did not succeed in obtaining territory

by negotiations in the future, 'she will probably resort to force to do
so'. The CoS therefore suggested the lifting of the embargo on arms
supplies to the Arab countries.[109]

The Foreign Office, on the other hand, asserted that strengthening
the Arab countries could lead to their intransigence and would hinder
the peace negotiations. Most of its officials shared the military
perception of Israel as an expansionist country but, unlike the army,
the Office wanted to open a new chapter in its relations with Israel.
The Foreign Office was mainly concerned with the Arab reaction to
the agreement. However, since the Arab League had in general
approved armistice negotiations, it did not act against the agreement
(despite the League's suspicions about a secret annexe to it). It would
act differently once Abdullah tried to go beyond the framework of the
armistice agreements.

9 The Elusive Peace: Britain and Abdullah's Quest for Peace

The armistice marked the end of major military operations for both sides. In many ways it also meant the re-establishment of the Jewish–Hashemite understanding over the partitioning of post-Mandatory Palestine. The armistice had provided the two sides with two possible forums for direct negotiations: the MAC, which was formed with the aim of supervising the implementation of the agreement, and the special Article 8 Committee intended to formalise plans agreed to in practice about the freedom of access to Jerusalem and its holy places.[1]

The King was eager to continue the dialogue with the Israelis, either in the committees or preferably in direct contact. His eagerness to conclude a peace treaty can be explained mainly by his wish to obtain official Israeli approval for the annexation of the West Bank. It is also quite possible that he was motivated by a desire to portray himself in the eyes of world public opinion as the statesman who had brought the Palestinian conflict to an end. As for the Arab world, Abdullah could present himself as an Arab ruler who had saved a large part of Palestine from Jewish occupation.

The Jordanian government had no intention of using the two committees for political negotiation and made every possible effort to curb King Abdullah. In fact, Abdullah could not use the committees for his purposes since the discussions there were public and were conducted by Jordanian officials and not by the King's personal envoys.[2]

The King was also warned by the Americans not to neglect the PCC as the main forum for political discussion. The State Department regarded any Israeli–Jordanian negotiations outside the PCC as damaging to the prospects of peace. The Foreign Office agreed with the Americans that the Israelis had wanted the Lausanne conference to fail in order to allow direct Israeli–Jordanian contact. However, the Foreign Office was convinced that there was no feasible way out from the deadlock in Lausanne and did not believe in the PCC's chances of success. Moreover the lack of progress in negotiations for the implementation of Article 8 – due to the Jordanian government's policy of non-cooperation in the committees – had also contributed to the stalemate in the peace process. The Foreign Office feared that this situation would lead to an Israeli offensive on the West Bank. During the summer of 1949, the Legation in Amman had sent reports of an imminent Israeli attack; this had been followed by the intensification of border clashes and incidents, culminating in the taking over by Israel of Government House in no man's land in Jerusalem.[3]

Thus the Foreign Office found itself in a dilemma. On the one hand, it could not advocate that the King submit to the Americans and the UN. On the other hand, its representative in Jordan and Glubb Pasha, the Chief of the General Staff of the Legion, warned that Israel's dissatisfaction with the lack of progress in the Article 8 Committee and in the political negotiations could lead to another round of fighting. Glubb, in fact, felt that the King would negotiate with the Israelis with or without British blessing. He therefore advocated the conclusion of a treaty with Israel as soon as possible: namely, before Israel became even stronger and was able to extract more concessions from the Jordanians in a peace deal.[4] The Legation in Amman was even more sceptical and believed it was too late in any case, and that Israel would obtain far-reaching concessions in case of a peace treaty.[5] The eyes of the British diplomats in Amman and elsewhere in the Middle East were turned to the Foreign Office Middle East conference in July 1949, with growing hopes that clearer guidelines were on their way from London.

THE LONDON MIDDLE EAST CONFERENCE AND THE ISRAELI–JORDANIAN NEGOTIATIONS

The conference devoted considerable time to the desirability of peace between Israel and its Arab neighbours. It was affected mainly by the shift in Bevin's attitude towards Israel. A few days before the session on the Arab–Israeli conflict, Bevin had met for the first time the Israeli representative in London, Dr Eliash, and left the meeting with the impression that Israel owed its allegiance to the West and could be relied upon. The Middle East conference had thus been told by the Foreign Secretary: 'The Israelis were now ready to look to us for practical advice.'[6]

Bevin impressed the participants at the conference with the urgency of solving the Palestine problem. This could only be achieved by direct negotiations, without neglecting the PCC's efforts. His reference to the Commission was due mainly to American pressure. The State Department deemed the maintaining of an exclusive role for the PCC vital for the success of the peace process in the area, particularly since the Americans did not want the Israelis to escape responsibility for solving the refugee problem which could be achieved only in multilateral discussions. Bevin therefore authorised the Office to participate in the Commission's efforts by introducing a British plan for peace.[7] This plan has already been discussed here, and as has been mentioned, the plan was never endorsed by the Commission; it served mainly as a guideline for the Office. The most important point in this plan was the Greater Transjordan concept.

It seems, therefore, that Bevin was not impressed by Kirkbride's gloomy analysis or by Glubb's warning. He advocated support for Israeli–Jordanian negotiations since he regarded this as a territorial settlement between two allies of the West. Moreover, he hoped that the agreement would bring a solution to the Palestine question that he had been trying to solve in the last years of the Mandate.[8]

The shift in Bevin's attitude towards Israel was typical of his pragmatism, but it was too sudden for his diplomats. They had generally regarded Israel as a force that might drag the Arab world out of the sphere of British influence. In their opinion, expressed in the conference, the only way to prevent this was by objecting to the separate Arab–Israeli agreements. The British representatives in the Middle East therefore advocated multilateral agreements under the UN or any other international body, so Britain could supervise the process.[9] These views were shared by most of the diplomats, apart from the Consul in Jerusalem and the British minister in Tel Aviv.[10]

However, Foreign Office officials shared Bevin's views to a large extent. With their support, the Foreign Office concentrated on the Israeli–Jordanian negotiations as the basis for the Palestinian settlement. It was hoped in London that the PCC would give its support to these negotiations, thereby placating Arab opposition. In fact, with the aid of this argument Bevin succeeded in convincing the Americans that they should moderate their opposition to the negotiations and allow them to continue parallel to the PCC's efforts. This new American stand enabled Abdullah to resume direct negotiations with the Israelis in the second half of 1949.[11]

THE RESUMPTION OF THE NEGOTIATIONS

In October 1949, Abdullah initiated another round of direct contacts with the Israelis. The King seemed obsessed with the need to obtain Israeli approval for the formal annexation of the West Bank. Sir Alec Kirkbride suggested postponing direct contacts until after the completion of the formal union. Kirkbride believed that the resumption of talks with Israel would be a political blunder which would complicate the process of unification, since it would arouse the indignation of the Palestinian population in the West Bank, a population which was about to be represented in considerable numbers in the Jordanian parliament and Cabinet.[12]

Kirkbride also foresaw correctly the possible reaction of Abu Al-Huda. Before entering the negotiations, the King decided to appoint Samir Ar-Rifai special Minister to the Palace, with status equal to that of the premier. Unlike Abu Al-Huda, Ar-Rifai was more inclined to execute the King's plans and wishes without pursuing his own policy. Abu Al-Huda left the kingdom for two months in protest, leaving the government in no position to oppose the King. It was clear that the holder of the posts of minister of the court and premier could not co-exist for long. Furthermore, for Kirkbride it was a clear indication that he would not be consulted about the next stages should the King have a loyal premier next to him.[13]

However, Abdullah's eagerness was not reciprocated by the Israelis. The priorities of the state of Israel had changed during 1949. The armistice agreements brought relative calm to the borders, and peace was no longer the first priority. The government was preoccupied with absorbing new immigrants and overcoming economic difficulties. It seems that the policy-makers were satisfied with the *modus vivendi* in relations with their Arab neighbours.

In December 1949, after two months of negotiations between Samir Ar-Rifai and Reuben Shiloah, the dispute was narrowed down to the question of Jordan's right to a corridor to the Mediterranean. Both sides agreed to sign a document entitled 'Political questions and territorial changes'.[14] Three major points were made in the document. First, Israel recognised the vital importance of a sea outlet to the Jordanians. Second, the Israelis stated that they consented to a corridor from Hebron, via Beersheba to Gaza, to come under Jordanian sovereignty. Finally, in return the Jordanians agreed to fix passage points in the corridor and to its demilitarisation, as well as promising that the Anglo-Transjordanian treaty would not apply to the corridor.[15] In this connection, it might be useful to mention Pollack and Sinai's reference to that document, in which the two writers state that the document in question was a draft peace treaty and that it was almost signed, but for Kirkbride's intervention.[16] However, the paper was by no means a draft peace treaty, and neither was it signed as such. In February 1950, a peace treaty was about to be concluded, and it could be that Pollack and Sinai confused the two documents, as did Abidi and Dayan in their respective versions.[17]

The British and American accounts of the meetings do not differ. The American accounts are referred to here since they were more detailed. There was, however, a considerable disparity in the two countries' assessments. Whereas the American representatives in Tel Aviv, and even in Amman, were optimistic about the outcome of the meetings, Kirkbride's accounts constantly reported lack of progress and absence of understanding.[18] It seems that Kirkbride was exaggerating when he described normal political negotiations as 'stormy meetings'; after all, it was not a meeting between two British diplomats.[19] On the other hand, there were sufficient grounds to be pessimistic, not so much because of the course of the negotiations but rather owing to the prospects of a separate peace between Israel and Jordan being accepted by the Arab world.

As for the paper agreed upon, Kirkbride thought that Israel had forced Jordan to make more concessions. The officials of the Eastern Department were disappointed that Israeli approval for the annexation of the West Bank was not mentioned; they feared that the absence of such approval would delay the process of incorporation of the West Bank into Transjordan. These fears were not conveyed to the Jordanians since the Foreign Office had decided to stay aloof and to interfere only if requested by the Jordanians.[20]

However, there was one point which concerned Britain directly and necessitated more active British involvement. This was the question of the extension of the Anglo-Jordanian treaty to the annexed West Bank. The Israelis opposed such a move while the Jordanian Cabinet insisted on the extension. The Israeli government believed that such an extension would lead to the establishment of British bases west of the river Jordan. 'It would be easier for Israel to recognise Greater Jordan if the British did not return to Palestine', explained Shiloah in a conversation with Ar-Rifai at the beginning of December 1949. Following Ben-Gurion's initiative it was decided to leave the matter for discussion between Israel and Britain without involving the Jordanians. The Foreign Office made it clear to the Israelis that this was a matter of principle between Britain and Jordan and none of Israel's concern. However, Sir Knox Helm was instructed to convey to the Israelis that Britain had no intention of establishing bases on the West Bank. In case of a war in the Middle East, however, the Foreign Office would regard Arab Palestine as a *British* area.[21]

THE ATTEMPT TO SIGN A PEACE TREATY: FEBRUARY 1950

The negotiations in 1949 ended with Ar-Rifai's attempt to persuade the Jordanian government to accept the paper of principles agreed upon in December 1949.[22] Both in London and in Amman British officials regarded the involvement of the Jordanian government in the negotiations as vital for their success and as essential to the stability of the state, first because Abdullah seemed too eager to reach an agreement and might, they feared, surrender too much to Israel, which was pressing for peace and needed, in particular, an agreement over Jerusalem. Second, it was feared that without his government behind him, the King would not be able to confront the Arab world.[23]

Indeed the King's main predicament was his relationship with the government. By the beginning of 1950, Abdullah had completely lost the confidence and cooperation of his ministers. The Cabinet was fully behind him on the question of the union but did not back him in his negotiations with Israel. The King had also ceased to enjoy the advice and assistance of one of his closest aides, At-Tal, who had left Jordan clandestinely in January 1950.[24]

Sir Alec Kirkbride found his loyalties divided between the two centres of power in the kingdom. He was driven into this position not only because of his diplomatic functions but also as a result of his own desire to hold the balance in the monarchy.

Kirkbride was in a most delicate situation. It created the impression amongst some writers that Kirkbride was bitterly opposed to direct negotiations and was the main cause for their failure. Whereas Kirkbride sided with the ministers in their attempt to check Abdullah's too eager tendency to conclude a peace treaty, he did not share their absolute opposition to such an agreement. Kirkbride advocated a cautious progress towards peace with Israel. The practical outcome of this approach was, nevertheless, that the King did not have Kirkbride's blessing for the pursuit of his own policy.[25]

Another problem with which the Foreign Office felt it had to deal was the vulnerability of the Jordanians to the Israeli pressure, a situation which had characterised the 1949 negotiations. According to the legal adviser of the Foreign Office this problem was already solved since – he asserted – the Anglo-Transjordanian treaty extended to the West Bank. The legal adviser of the Office was consulted on what the Office described as an important policy decision: namely, the obligation of His Majesty's Government to come to Jordan's assistance if attacked by Israel in the West Bank or Jordan proper. The same dilemma applied to an Israeli attack on Gaza, which could have led to the invocation of the Anglo-Egyptian treaty.[26] Thus, despite their promise to Israel, and before the formal union of the two banks, the British had already extended the treaty, the main reason being to protect Jordan from Israeli military pressure during direct negotiations.

In what seems today to have been a curious manner, the Foreign Office decided not to inform the Jordanian, the Egyptian or the Israeli government about their decision. In fact, the Jordanians had reached their own conclusions and asked the Office for its views. The Office chose to conceal its decision since 'our primary interest is that a settlement should be reached between Israel and Jordan', and that 'any notification of the above sense (public or private) to either Jordan or Egyptian governments would have the effect of stiffening their attitude in the negotiations with Israel'.[27] (In the 'above sense' the Office meant their new interpretation of the Anglo-Egyptian and Anglo-Transjordanian treaties as covering Gaza and the West Bank.)

Thus the Jordanians were told that 'we will formally indicate to them our views with regard to our treaty obligations when their frontiers with Israel have been settled'.[28] It seems that the Foreign Office did not trust the Jordanians and the Egyptians to the extent of informing them that the UK would protect their possessions in Palestine in the case of an Israeli attack. It was felt in Whitehall that Jordan was now protected against Israeli aggression or pressure in the future, although it is difficult to see how this could have benefited Jordan in its negotiations with Israel. The American position was less complicated by that time, and they gave their full-fledged support to the negotiations in a letter from Truman to Abdullah.[29]

There were sound reasons for the growing concern of British officials about the precarious position of the King both *vis-à-vis* his government and the Israelis. The Israelis began to display signs of impatience towards the end of January 1950. Reuben Shiloah, Ben-Gurion's main emissary to the talks, sent a letter to the King warning him that Israel would abandon the negotiations unless the Jordanian government considered the working paper agreed upon in December 1949.[30] The Israeli pressure was the result of their wish to reach a final agreement about the partition of Jerusalem before the UN completed its discussions on the future of the city. It may be worthwhile at this point examining the Foreign Office's attitude towards the question of Jerusalem, since the negotiations in 1950–1 were mainly concerned with the question of internationalisation and partition of the holy city.

At the beginning of 1949, the Israelis and the Jordanians found themselves confronted with world public opinion which desired to see the holy city under an international regime. In April 1949 the task of finding a solution for the problem of Jerusalem was entrusted to the PCC. The Foreign Office wished the Commission to formulate a scheme according to the sixth point in their peace programme (the Eight-Point Plan mentioned earlier in this work). That sixth point read as follows: 'There should be partition of Jerusalem for administrative purposes with international supervision, particularly of the holy places.'[31] This formula, incidentally, was accepted throughout 1949 by the IFO.

The PCC suggested in September 1949 that Jerusalem be internationalised and that the administrative and municipal responsibilities be left in the hands of the Jordanians and the Israelis. However, the sovereign of the city was to be an international body.[32] The Israelis reacted by declaring their part of the city the capital of Israel.[33] The British representatives in Jordan exerted pressure on the Foreign Office to reject the plan, since it was unacceptable to the Jordanians and the Israelis. The Foreign Office then notified the Americans that it regarded the plan as impractical and suggested joint support for partitioning the city.[34]

The Foreign Office's arguments convinced the Americans not to submit the PCC's plan to the UN. However, this was done by the Australians, who felt committed to the November 1947 partition resolution which they had supported at the time and which called for the establishment of a *corpus separatum* in the city.[35]

The UN *ad hoc* political committee decided to instruct the Trusteeship Council to prepare a detailed plan according to the Commission suggestions. This decision was endorsed by the GA on 9 December 1949 in a resolution which called for the internationalisation of the city. The Israelis, the British and the Americans voted against the resolution.[36]

The Trusteeship Council held its discussions in Geneva in 1950. The President of the Council, Roger Garreau, drafted a plan based on the PCC's suggestion and which proposed that the Jerusalem area be constituted as a *corpus separatum*. His plan was also supported by the UN *ad hoc* political committee.[37] However, the Garreau Plan, like those schemes suggested before it and the plans and resolutions that would follow it in the 1950s, were doomed to fail. This was owing to the UN inability to implement them as a result of Israeli, Jordanian and British opposition, and American reluctance to offer troops for such an act. In 1950 it was mainly the Israel–Jordanian efforts to conclude a peace treaty, including an agreement on Jerusalem, and not the UN initiatives which attracted the Foreign Office's attention.

THE DRAFT PEACE TREATY OF FEBRUARY 1950

The UN efforts to find a solution to the Jerusalem question convinced Abdullah and the Israelis of the urgency of reaching a final agreement before the UN did. The King suggested at the beginning of 1950 that Ben-Gurion and Samir Ar-Rifai should meet, hoping that the seniority of these two men would facilitate a rapid agreement.[38] However, Ben-Gurion left the negotiations with Abdullah to his aides, as he had been doing since 1947, which shows something of his priorities as well as his attitude towards the King.

The Israelis were the first to suggest a resumption of direct contacts with the King in his palace in Shuneh. Kirkbride and the Foreign Office urged the King to delay his answer to the Israeli suggestion until the situation in the UN had been clarified. The King ignored this advice, however, and invited the Israelis to Shuneh.[39]

At the meeting, the Israelis suggested forming a united front in the UN to block the organisation's schemes for the internationalisation of Jerusalem. The Jordanians rejected this proposal and proposed instead to concentrate on practical arrangements regarding the future of the city.[40]

The Foreign Office was highly impressed by the Jordanian ability to negotiate. Kirkbride was convinced, as indeed were the Israelis, that the armistice line would divide the city. He asserted that all that was needed was some 'simultaneous prods from the Americans and the British to Israel and Jordan and a settlement could be reached'.[41]

The Embassy in Tel Aviv was also showing signs of optimism. The Israeli representative reported that an understanding over the corridor question had been reached. Like his opposite number in Amman, Sir Knox Helm urged a joint Anglo-American intervention. British representatives in the area voiced similar appeals and appreciations.[42] Thus it seems that for the British representative in Amman an imposed solution was the only way of protecting Jordan. He warned the Office that stability in the Middle East would be endangered unless an Israeli–Jordanian settlement were reached. The main reason for the Foreign Office's disinclination to intervene was the improvement of Anglo–Israeli relations. At the beginning of 1950 the UK had granted *de jure* recognition to the state of Israel. This was followed by various commercial and financial agreements.[43] Moreover, the Foreign Office refrained from any action which might be perceived as pressure on the Jordanian Council of Ministers. At the end of 1950, the British government would totally reverse its attitude towards the ministers and become hostile towards them, but for the time being the Foreign Office was cautious in its attitude towards the internal conflict in the Hashemite kingdom. The significance of the British attitude was that the Jordanian Council of Ministers did not feel it was acting against British policy.

Kirkbride hoped that the joint pressure would help to convince the Israelis to moderate their positions in regard to two issues on which the Jordanian government insisted: redefinition of the demarcation line in Jerusalem and the establishment of a Jordanian corridor to the sea. Kirkbride suggested that Abdullah instruct Ar-Rifai to continue meeting the Israelis, despite these two problems, as he still hoped to persuade his government to exert pressure jointly on the two sides. The King tended to accept the Israeli suggestion for a Jordanian road via Israel to the Mediterranean, as well as their proposal for the implementation of Article 8 (leaving Mount Scopus and the Jewish quarter in the old city under Israeli rule). The ministers, however, were strongly opposed to the King's tendency to accept the Israeli proposals, as was Glubb, who maintained that they would leave Jordan in an inferior strategic position.[44] Ar-Rifai still supported the King, but his attitude would change once he took office as premier. The Jordanian Cabinet was convened after the first Israeli–Jordanian meeting in February 1950. A unanimous decision was passed regarding Jordan's refusal to give Israel any part of the old city. Thus the Jordanian government was prepared to give up Mount Scopus only in return for the Arab quarters of the new city. However, the King did succeed in preventing Abu Al-Huda's suggestion for Jordanian support for the Garreau plan to internationalise Jerusalem.[45]

The Israelis, aware of Abdullah's difficulties with his government, suggested resorting to the old way of negotiating: namely, directly with the King. This was gladly accepted by the King, and on 17 February Ar-Rifai and Shiloah met at Shuneh. The King presented the Israelis with a new approach. In a dramatic move, Abdullah was about to break the deadlock of the past three years by suggesting a bold move: leaving aside all problems connected with Jerusalem and the armistice and signing a non-aggression pact and a peace agreement for five years.[46]

The King's new initiative was an attempt to assert his authority *vis-à-vis* his ministers, as well as the expression of a genuine desire to accelerate the peace process. Abdullah submitted a seven-point draft agreement to the Israelis. The Israeli representatives were pleased with the agreement, and gave their approval in principle pending their government's consent. A jubilant Abdullah told Shiloah that he would replace his Cabinet if it were to oppose the agreement.[47] A week later, representatives of both sides met to initial a draft treaty. It was probably due to Ar-Rifai's influence that this draft treaty was accepted by the Jordanian government. The latter accepted it with one reservation: although it was privately willing to acknowledge that peace would include resumption of trade between the two countries, it demanded that this clause be omitted from the initial draft.[48]

Kirkbride reported the existence of two different drafts and suggested that the Israelis had altered the draft to their advantage. However, a look at the Israeli and Jordanian drafts indicates that the only revision was introduced by the Jordanians, and that it related to the resumption of trade.[49]

The gist of the agreement was a non-aggression commitment for five years. In addition, the sides agreed to abolish the no man's land, and to free both Israeli access to Mount Scopus and Jordanian movement on the Bethlehem–Jerusalem road. There was no explicit reference to the refugees. It was agreed that compensation should be paid to property owners in Jerusalem whose property remained under the control of the other party. In very vague terms it was agreed to initiate a process of liquidating Arab property in Israel and Jewish property in Jordan (the West Bank).[50]

In general, from the Foreign Office's point of view, the lines of the agreement seemed fairly sound and it made few reservations. One was that the period of five years was too short; London officials remarked correctly that the armistice clearly provided for an undertaking of non-aggression, and that there was need for a stronger affirmation.

Second, the Eastern Department received the abolition of no man's land as an Israeli wish to get rid of what the Israelis saw as a symbol of UN authority in Jerusalem; the Office therefore advocated a more careful approach on the part of the Jordanians.[51]

The Jordanian premier's initial reaction was hostile. He proposed putting the agreement to the government's vote, hoping to secure a negative response. He threatened to resign, which he was supposed to do in any event in view of the pending election of April 1950. However, Ar-Rifai refused to replace him, and Abu Al-Huda consented to stay in office until the election, on condition that the agreement be approved by the government elected after April. Kirkbride played an important role in convincing Abu Al-Huda to remain in office, by pointing out to him that the seven-point agreement was merely a draft proposal and not a final one.[52]

The British ambassador in Tel Aviv, Sir Knox Helm, reported that the Israeli government was under strong domestic pressure and would be disappointed at the suspension of the negotiations until after the elections in Jordan. Helm looked for means of assuring the Israelis that it would be worth their while to wait. He suggested to the Foreign Office that an official and public British communiqué would link the extension of the Anglo-Transjordanian treaty to the annexed territories with a public British promise not to establish bases in the West Bank. As mentioned earlier, such a secret obligation had been granted in 1949. However, the head of the Eastern Department objected to this proposal, since he thought it would stiffen the Israeli position in the negotiations.[53]

The Israelis were thus told about the suspension; they reluctantly agreed to wait until after the Jordanian elections. The Israeli government pleaded with the Americans for US political and economic assistance to Jordan, so that it could ratify the agreement. The State Department consulted the Eastern Department on this question. The head of the Department, Furlonge, assessed that the opposition to Abdullah's policy was such that any American encouragement would be useless. The American Assistant Secretary of State, Raymond Hare, accepted this assessment, and Truman approved of his decision to turn down the Israeli request. The Israelis were even prepared to make more territorial concessions to increase Abdullah's prestige. But these views were never conveyed to the King; moreover, it was too late for him to make any use of them.[54]

ARAB REACTION AND ITS EFFECT ON THE JORDANIAN GOVERNMENT

Rumours of this agreement circulated throughout the Arab world after the Israeli press had reported the existence of a direct Israeli–Jordanian contact.[55] Consequently, Abdullah was exposed to heavy pressure from the Arab leaders. The Syrians warned him that they would close the border if Jordan were to continue the negotiations with Israel.[56] Ibn Saud threatened that the Arab world 'would build an impenetrable wall around Jordan'.[57] The Arab League met in March 1950 (25 March–13 April), and the main issue on its agenda was the Israeli–Jordanian talks. In this conference Abdullah was bitterly attacked. Neither did Britain escape the wrath of the Arab delegates. The Egyptian press distributed a fabricated story that the February 1950 agreement had been concluded between Ben-Gurion and Abdullah aboard a British battleship. This coincided with the publication of At-Tal's version on the March 1949 agreement in the Egyptian press, in which he attributed an important part to British intervention in favour of an agreement.[58] Azzam's biographer, Ad-Daly, who based his version on the minutes of the League Council, claimed that Abu Al-Huda had notified both Azzam Pasha and Tawfiq As-Sweidi (the Iraqi premier) about the agreement, and that Azzam reported its content to the League Political Committee (Ad-Daly added that Azzam could not produce any documents when challenged by the Jordanian Foreign Minister, Muhamad As-Shariqi).[59]

The Egyptian delegation proposed to expel Jordan from the League if it concluded a treaty with Israel. Because of this Egyptian pressure, the Jordanians had to vote in favour of a Lebanese proposal that any member concluding an agreement with Israel should be expelled.[60]

The Arab pressure had an enormous effect on the newly-elected Jordanian government, under the premiership of Said Al-Mufti. The ministers decided not to ratify the February 1950 agreement.[61] Abdullah ignored the growing discontent among his ministers and continued to meet the Israelis, mainly Shiloah, without his ministers and, sometimes, without Kirkbride's knowledge. Eventually Kirkbride learned about the secret meetings and had to consider and reassess his stand. Kirkbride decided to continue to act as a mediator between the King and the ministers in order to preserve the integrity of the Kingdom.

The CoS did not exclude the possibility of an Israeli attack after the new Jordanian government had rejected the agreement. They pointed out that, in such a case, His Majesty's forces should engage the Israeli forces by land, sea and air. However, the absence of a corridor between the Suez and Jordan made this quite impossible. Therefore the CoS suggested to the Defence Committee that it concentrate on strengthening the Legion and raising its subsidy.[62]

THE FORMAL UNION AND THE NEGOTIATIONS

These apprehensions about a possible Israeli attack on the West Bank continued to prevail amongst Foreign Office officials owing to reports from Tel Aviv sent in by Helm. Reuben Shiloah, by now Ben-Gurion's main adviser on Arab affairs, gave Helm the impression that unless a final agreement were reached Israel might still strive to annex the West Bank, owing to pressure from extreme circles. The Foreign Office, however, confined itself to the *de jure* recognition of the formal union, and the extention of the Anglo-Transjordanian treaty to the West Bank. The Israelis were once more notified that Britain would not establish bases in the West Bank and were granted *de jure* recognition. The *de jure* recognition of Israel and of the new enlarged kingdom was granted in order to create conditions 'more favourable for Israeli–Jordanian relations'.[63] The Israelis were further informed that the British recognition of the union was to counteract the League's opposition to Abdullah, as was manifested by the 'League resolution which combined condemnation of Jordan with imposing an economic blockade on Israel'.[64]

The IFO, however, saw the British recognition of the formal union as an impediment to progress in the negotiations. They were annoyed by Bevin's declaration in the House of Commons in which he stated that he opposed separate peace settlements in the conflict, preferring collective and comprehensive peace agreements. This was done in order to placate Arab public opinion since, privately, the Foreign Secretary supported an Israeli–Jordanian agreement. Helm explained to the Israelis that Bevin's statement was not an official declaration but rather 'the personal spontaneous reaction of an old trade unionist', and suggested that they ignore it altogether.[65] In any case, this statement was later corrected by Bevin's Parliamentary Secretary, Ernest Davis, who implied British encouragement for the talks.[66]

The Foreign Office welcomed the Jordanian decision to postpone the talks until after the elections. They hoped that after the Jordanian elections the Israelis would take into account the strength of public opinion in the kingdom, and would be more compromising in their attitude. The King, on the other hand, was asked by the Foreign Office not to work towards a formal peace treaty before consulting the new government.[67]

However, neither the British entreaties to the King to consult his government nor the government's opposition deterred the Jordanian monarch. Abdullah suggested to the Israelis the resumption of the confidential negotiations with the view of turning them into formal negotiations. He wrote to Ben-Gurion that, if necessary, he would leave the League.[68]

Thus, loyal to his previous promises to the Israelis, the King resumed contact after the elections, meeting Shiloah in Amman and expressing his confidence in the government's support. However, all that the King could promise was a continued dialogue. The Jordanian Cabinet learned about the meeting a few days later and denounced the resumption of the talks.[69]

When Kirkbride learned about the resumption of the direct negotiations through Tel Aviv he warned the King that they would be futile, unless the Cabinet approved them. A similar warning was sent from London to the King. The King then asked Kirkbride to serve as a mediator between the Palace and the Cabinet. Kirkbride was reluctant to fulfil such a function formally, though he had been acting as such since 1948, for it would have been regarded by the Cabinet as siding with the King.[70]

The Foreign Office felt it could not offer any advice to its representative and left the Legation to decide on the best policy. In an internal memorandum the Department asserted that Abdullah had not asked for their advice and thus the Foreign Office could not interfere. The department was convinced of the genuine determination behind the Arab League threat to expel Abdullah. However, the Foreign Office experts were unable to determine whether this was a serious blow to the British position or not. After all, the Foreign Office had been ignoring the organisation as an important political factor since 1948.[71]

Kirkbride shared the views of the Foreign Office about the insignificance of the Arab League. Nevertheless, he deemed it unnecessary to enter into a new clash with the League after the successful annexations of the West Bank. As he himself put it: 'it would be a folly to provoke another storm immediately afterwards on a much more sensitive question'.[72]

Kirkbride's pleas had no impact on the King. From May 1950

onwards, he continued to meet the Israelis. Eventually he replaced
Said Al-Mufti with Samir Ar-Rifai. Once in office, however, the latter
felt no more able than his predecessor to go against strong domestic
and external pressure, and publicly he kept to the government line;
but privately he did his utmost to reach a *modus vivendi* with the
Israelis to prevent deterioration of the situation.[73]

Kirkbride asked the King not to extricate himself from the
difficulties with the Israelis by telling them that he had been curbed by
the British. However, this was precisely what Abdullah did. In a
meeting in May 1950, the Israeli delegate was told that the British had
advised Abdullah 'to go slow' with the negotiations. However, the
King stated that he was nevertheless determined to go ahead with them
without consulting the British further.[74]

The British did not conceal their position from the Israelis. Wright
informed the Israelis that, in spite of Britain's desire for peace, it
would not push the King towards a formal agreement.[75] However,
Sharett accused Britain of being responsible for the deadlock in the
talks although, as he wrote to the Israeli Embassy in London, he could
not understand the British motives.[76]

In May 1950 the Israelis made their last attempt to facilitate an
agreement by offering a territorial concession in Samaria (Jenin) in
return for Jordan dropping all claims to the Negev area.[77] However,
by then it seemed that both the Jordanian and Israeli governments
were satisfied with the territorial status quo, which was approved by
France, Britain and the US in the Tripartite Declaration.

THE IMPACT OF THE TRIPARTITE DECLARATION ON THE TALKS

The draft for the joint declaration was provided during the Anglo-
American discussions in London in May 1950. The declaration was
published on 25 May 1950. It promised the three powers' commitment
to arms control in the area by supplying arms only for self-defence and
internal security purposes. The three powers promised to prevent
change by force of frontiers within or outside the framework of the
UN. Finally, it asked the Middle Eastern countries to give assurances
that they would not undertake aggressive action against other states.
The reluctance of most of the countries in the area, apart from Jordan
and Israel, to give this last assurance implied that the declaration

remained an act aimed at coordinating the Western powers' activity in the area as well as excluding Russian intervention in the Middle East.[78]

The main impact of the Tripartite Declaration on the Israeli-Jordanian negotiations was the Western powers' recognition of the Israeli–Jordanian border. However, it had no impact on the course of the negotiations; neither did it prevent a serious escalation of hostilities on the Israeli–Jordanian border in the second half of 1950. The Declaration was mainly a manifestation of Anglo-American cooperation and coordination of policy in the face of what was seen as Russian intransigence. It also aimed to encourage resolving the Arab–Israeli and other conflicts in the area, as a means of bringing stability to the Middle East.[79]

The Foreign Office viewed the Declaration as a means of strengthening Jordan's border against Israeli or Syrian attack. In fact, the Foreign Office suggested timing the Tripartite Declaration so that it would coincide with the announcement of the formal union, in order to deter any internal or external opposition to the union. The British had in mind possible Israeli pressure, and hoped that the Declaration would allow them joint action with the Americans and the French in case of disruption of the Israeli–Jordanian frontier.[80] The Foreign Office asserted that the validity of the Declaration would be put to the test especially in frontier incidents on the Israeli–Jordanian border.[81] However, if this was the criterion for the Declaration's validity, then it was not applicable to the Israeli–Jordanian dispute, as was proved during the escalation of the border clashes in the summers of 1950 and 1951.

On the other hand, the Office had perceived the Declaration as a stimulus for peace. Michael Wright had suggested in the preliminary meeting preceding the Declaration that it be made only after an Israeli–Jordanian peace agreement had been signed. Unlike most of the officials in the Office, he was prepared to give Israel public assurance that Britain would not establish bases in the West Bank, and was generally more optimistic about the prospects of the February 1950 agreement being accepted by the Jordanian government. The Assistant Secretary of State in Washington, Raymond Hare, had similar ideas, but the Americans did not wish to delay publication of the Declaration.[82]

Incidentally, Kirkbride reported the King's dissatisfaction with the Declaration, supporting as it did the existing frontiers in the Middle East, as he still entertained the hope 'that one day he might induce HMG to let him march the Arab Legion into Syria'.[83] On the other hand, according to Kirkbride, the Council of Ministers were of the opinion that owing to the Declaration, there was no hurry to conclude an agreement with Israel.[84] Kirkbride might have been right, but the ministers were less impressed by international guarantees than by the dangers of an agreement with Israel due to the possibility of a hostile reaction and the subsequent isolation of Jordan.

THE SHILOAH–ABDULLAH EFFORT
(MAY 1950–JULY 1951)

The Israelis, who previously had been as eager as the King to conclude a formal treaty, seemed to be satisfied with the political situation in the Middle East after the publication of the Tripartite Declaration. The Declaration had frozen the territorial status quo in Israel's favour. Moreover the explicit Israeli support for the UN action in Korea had normalised Israel's relationship with the West. In the second half of 1950, the Israelis could not ask for more, and peace with Jordan was perceived as a 'bonus' but not as a necessity.

Yet the talks continued; this was due in part to Shiloah's personal ambition, which matched that of the King, to conclude a peace treaty of which he would be the architect. Shiloah risked his reputation on his efforts to bring about the peace settlement.[85] Whereas Abdullah's mistrust of Kirkbride was growing, Shiloah's confidence in Britain was increasing, and whatever was not reported from Amman was soon completed by information from Tel Aviv provided by Shiloah (the King had emphatically asked Shiloah not to inform the British). This reversal of Israeli and Jordanian attitudes towards Britain was the beginning of a military understanding between Britain and Israel culminating in the Anglo-Israeli joint operation in the Sinai in 1956.[86]

However, Shiloah's ambition was not the main factor that kept the contact alive. The continuation of the Israeli–Jordanian negotiations in 1951 should be analysed against the background of the political development in the Hashemite kingdom. In the first half of the year, the struggle between the old and new order in politics continued. Thus Abdullah saw the continuation of the negotiations as proof of his authority in the kingdom. This struggle culminated in the assassination of the King. Sir Alec Kirkbride had this to say about the process: 'The transformation of the tribal patriarchy of Transjordan into the pseudo-democracy of Jordan complete with the nationalistic ideologies of a modern Arab State which began with the union of

Transjordan and Arab Palestine in April 1950, was continued in 1951. The assassination of King Abdullah in July 1951 was the most outstanding event in this process.'[87]

Abdullah's main predicament was the difficulty of finding a government willing to incur public odium by making peace with Israel. Meetings between Abdullah, Ar-Rifai (who became premier in December 1950) and Shiloah continued intermittently until Abdullah's death, but efforts were limited to extension of cooperation under the Rhodes agreement.

The unwillingness of the Jordanian Cabinet to participate in any negotiations and the continued anti-British statements in the Jordanian Parliament had intensified during 1950. The Council of Ministers in Amman accused Britain of bias towards Israel to Jordan's disadvantage. The Eastern Department assessed that this anti-British attitude was the result of political and constitutional changes in Jordan: 'The West Bank deputies are inspired by a shortsighted, but unshakable resolve to have nothing to do with Israel.' They behaved that way, according to the officials, since they did not wish to disturb Arab unity. One Foreign Office official disagreed with his colleague and remarked that the anti-British feeling expressed 'has nothing to do with Israel and was bound to emerge with the growth of "democracy" in the country'.[88]

Yet the negotiations continued in spite of these difficulties. In the beginning of 1951 contact was through correspondence between Shiloah, the ailing Israeli President, Weizmann, and the King. In the main, it concentrated on solving the various border disputes, but it also dealt with the question of peace. Shiloah, by his own initiative, suggested the return of the Arab quarters in Jerusalem to Jordan as part of a peace settlement. In January 1951, Shiloah met Ar-Rifai to discuss these issues. Shiloah offered compromise over the disputed electricity plant in Naharim in return for the implementation of Article 8 of the armistice (which provided access to the holy places in Jerusalem).[89]

All that Samir Ar-Rifai could offer was his participation in a joint effort to explore ways of implementing the armistice agreement more fully. At the end of the January 1951 meeting, Ar-Rifai declared that that meeting was the last secret one and all ensuing contacts would be under the MAC.[90]

There was very little hope of turning the MAC into a forum for political talks. The Jordanian delegates to the Committee came from the Jordanian Foreign Ministry, whose leadership was almost all

Palestinian. These delegates were authorised to discuss military
matters alone. The West Bank ministers also prevented Samir
Ar-Rifai from going too far in his negotiations with Shiloah, or rather
from implementing the King's policy.[91]

It seems that only Kirkbride felt that the integrity of the Kingdom
was in great danger as a result of the negotiations. The Eastern
Department had generally professed its satisfaction at the amount of
agreement which still existed between the two parties.[92] The British
policy at that point was to allow its representative to act independently
for the improvement of Israeli–Jordanian relations. Thus the Foreign
Office had encouraged its ambassador in Tel Aviv to maintain his
support for the separate Israeli–Jordanian accord while at the same
time instructing Kirkbride to carry on with his endeavours to persuade
the Jordanian government to accept the PCC's mediation. The
Eastern Department deemed it necessary to point out to the Foreign
Secretary that 'the advice Helm and Kirkbride have given to their
respective governments are not necessarily incompatible'.[93] This may
have been the case but Helm believed that Kirkbride had been
instructed by the Foreign Office to prevent the King from entering
direct negotiations with the Israelis. Helm had supported direct
negotiations from the moment he became the British ambassador in
Tel Aviv. He regarded Kirkbride's support for the PCC as opposition
to direct talks. However, it seems that Kirkbride supported the PCC
because he believed that this was the only method acceptable to the
ministers.[94]

The new head of the BMEO, Sir Thomas Rapp, had his own views
on the situation. Rapp advocated a more pro-Israeli policy and
pleaded with the Office to strengthen King Abdullah in his conflict
with his ministers. Rapp warned of the diminution of British influence
in Jordan owing to the Arab Palestinian participation in the Parliament
and government. In general, Rapp suggested that the British should
pressure Jordanian politicians to take a more flexible stand.[95] Whereas
the Office accepted this analysis, it still regarded the Israelis as the
'tougher' party in the negotiations. The Eastern Department asserted
that Rapp's suggestion overlooked the importance that the Cabinet
and Parliament in Jordan attached to the Arab League's policy.
Furlonge, the head of the Department, revealed that already in the
summer of 1950 he had discussed with Michael Wright the desirability
of applying pressure on Jordanian politicians and concluded that such
pressure would merely weaken the British position in the Kingdom,
since 'Arabs may be led, but cannot be driven.' Furlonge believed

Britain was more respected for acts of a positive nature, such as participation in the Tripartite Declaration.[96]

JORDAN AFTER ABDULLAH'S DEATH

On 20 July 1951 a Palestinian serving with the former Mufti's paramilitary group, Al-Jihad Al-Muqadas, assassinated King Abdullah in Jerusalem. The assassin, Mustafa Shuqri Ashu, was allegedly instructed by an Arab Catholic priest, Father Ayat, and by Musa Husseini to carry out the assassination. The latter two were arrested shortly after the murder and accused of being Abdullah At-Tal's agents. Ayat was acquitted later, while At-Tal was sentenced to death *in absentia*; others who were allegedly connected to the former Mufti or to At-Tal were executed in September 1951.[97]

For Sir Alec Kirkbride, Jordan after Abdullah's assassination moved closer to the pattern of the other Arab countries. As the Legation in Amman put it, it was no longer in a 'fearlessly independent position within the Arab League'.[98] However, for Kirkbride it was even worse than that; it was a serious blow to his position within the Hashemite kingdom. The British representative in Amman, who had spent almost 30 years in the palace, felt that a new era was beginning in the Middle East in which Britain would have only a marginal role to play.

Sir Alec had little doubt about those who were to blame for the assassination and the consequent decline of his own position: 'This crime was a notable manifestation of the fact that the once peaceful and amiable [state of] Transjordan had largely been taken by the Palestinians.'[99] He reported that the parliamentary elections following the King's death were dominated by 'loud anti-British nationalists from the West Bank' who also won the elections there.[100]

Kirkbride was not the only one to pinpoint the Palestinians as being responsible for the King's death. The Jordanian authorities blamed the former Mufti's supporters and Abdullah At-Tal for instigating the murder. The Israelis shared this view but, like the Jordanian court, failed to produce any substantial evidence concerning the former Mufti's intervention.[101] It seems that both Kirkbride and Israel believed that one should not absolve the former Mufti from personal responsibility for the murder. In recent years, Jordanian writers have implied a strong American and British involvement in the plot to assassinate Abdullah, but there does not seem to be sufficient evidence to accept their theory.[102]

One might note that the Foreign Office in London was circumspect in its reaction and was in fact worried by Kirkbride's and the Jordanian government's tendency to put the blame on the Palestinians. Eastern Department officials warned that only the former Mufti would benefit from such a campaign against the Palestinians.[103]

Kirkbride's main point was the direct responsibility of the Palestinians for the King's death, and also their role in bringing about the changes within Jordan. He was strongly supported by the head of the BMEO on this issue. In fact, before Abdullah's death Sir Thomas Rapp had predicted that the movement of approximately 250 000 Palestinians to the East Bank would turn Jordan into a more nationalistic Arab state and would drag it away from Britain and the Western camp.[104]

Kirkbride shared the conclusion of this report, and after the King's death added that the Palestinians would push towards constitutional changes which would undermine Britain's position even further.[105]

The Foreign Office in London did not view the picture in such a gloomy light. The Office did not sense any change in the strength of the Anglo-Jordanian alliance (the only Anglo-Arab alliance left in the Middle East after the abrogation of the Anglo-Egyptian treaty). Nevertheless, the Eastern Department was aware of the growth of Arab nationalism in Jordan and advocated a more sensitive policy, avoiding any act which might cause resentment. The Office explained precisely what it meant by a more sensitive policy; although 'we pay the piper so we should call the tune', Britain should allow some degree of independence in Jordan's foreign and Arab policy.[106]

Fortunately for the Office there was considerable agreement between Britain and Jordan on the main foreign and Arab policy issue after the King's death. This issue was the Iraqi attempt to convince the Jordanians to enter into union. An idea suggested by Abdullah himself before his death, it stemmed from his apprehension concerning his two sons' inability to rule the country after his death.[107] Neither Talal, Abdullah's heir, nor the Jordanian government favoured the idea. The Americans and the Israelis had also opposed the proposed merger, the latter even viewing it as a *casus belli*.[108] The Foreign Office regarded the Iraqi campaign as having a destablising effect. Moreover, the Office, like the legation in Amman, considered the Legion to be a pro-British element in the Hashemite kingdom which should be protected from any external influence.[109]

CONCLUSIONS

The Israeli–Jordanian negotiations came to an end with Abdullah's death. In spite of a continued cycle of infiltrations and reprisals, the basic understanding reached in November 1947 was kept; in fact, one might say it was kept until 1967. Britain had a most important role in bringing about this understanding. One of Britain's last contributions towards consolidating it was allaying the Israelis' fears about the possibility of an Iraqi–Jordanian union. Britain promised the Israelis that such a union would fail to gain Britain's support.[110] Thus, immediately after the war, the Foreign Office accepted the King's argument that only a renewed understanding would safeguard the West Bank from an Israeli attack aimed at occupying it. Such Israeli plans did exist in 1948–9 and were not executed partly owing to Israel's preoccupation with the Southern Front, but also owing to the chances of reaching an agreement with Abdullah. Ben-Gurion also feared the British reaction to such an act.

The Jordanian government progressively altered the aim from peace agreement, to a non-aggression pact, to a full implementation of the 1949 armistice agreement. Abdullah, on the other hand, persisted in his efforts to conclude a formal agreement with Israel in spite of strong internal opposition and British advice. He did so mainly in order to protect the West Bank from Israeli occupation, and he regarded peace with Israel as the best solution for the Palestine question. It seems that both the external Arab and the domestic Palestinian opposition have utilized Abdullah's eagerness to conclude a separate peace treaty with Israel in order to hit the King in the struggle over the political hegemony in Transjordan and the leadership of the Arab world.

However, the Foreign Office in London and Sir Alec Kirkbride in Amman did not regard a formal peace between Israel and Jordan as a prerequisite for sustaining the 1947 understanding. From 1950 onwards, the Israeli government accepted this assumption in principle, with the exception of Reuben Shiloah who sought to further his own political career by achieving a formal peace agreement with King Abdullah. Whereas the Israeli government allowed Shiloah to continue the negotiations as long as he deemed it useful, the Jordanian government strongly resented the King's eagerness to conclude a formal peace treaty with Israel because of the opposition in the Arab world to such an agreement.

Kirkbride sided with the ministers, not out of opposition to an Israeli–Jordanian peace but owing to his fears that the continued resistance to Abdullah's efforts both in the government and the annexed West Bank would end in the disintegration of the kingdom. In fact, in many ways Kirkbride saw the assassination as the beginning of this process in Jordan.

The Foreign Office lost interest in the negotiations in the summer of 1949, when it seemed that both sides were pleased with the understanding they had reached over the partitioning of Mandatory Palestine between Israel and Jordan. At that point the Foreign Office's view towards Israel had already changed. This is probably why the Foreign Office did not throw its weight behind the negotiations, which could be one explanation for their failure. It also would have meant acting against the ministers and the parliament. What is quite clear is that Britain did not act perfidiously to sabotage the negotiations.

10 Conclusions

The Anglo-Transjordanian understanding of the best solution for the question of post-mandatory Palestine served as the main guideline for the British policy towards the Arab–Israeli conflict in the years 1948–51. The essence of this understanding was the partition of Palestine between the Jewish state and the Hashemite kingdom. The main feature of this partition was the creation of Greater Transjordan: the annexation to the Transjordan of the areas allotted to the Arab Palestinians by the UN November 1947 resolution. In many ways this understanding determined the outcome of the Arab–Israeli war of 1948. It also enabled the Foreign Office to predict the course of that war correctly.

The Anglo-Transjordanian understanding was reached because of Britain's desire to maintain its influence in Palestine. Palestine was an important buffer zone and a defence line against any power seeking possession of the Canal Zone and the oilfields of Arabia. In the period under review a Russian invasion of the Middle East seemed imminent, both to the Americans and the British. Giving up direct control over Palestine was acceptable to the British government, but leaving it to the influence of another power was unthinkable.

This British concept was the fruit of an *ad hoc* policy which had been pursued by the Foreign Office since the end of the First World War; this policy had enabled Britain to adjust itself to any new developments in the area and to confront any radical alteration of the political situation. Once it was clear that Israel was a *fait accompli* the Foreign Office advised the British government to consider the Jewish state as a new factor in the Middle East; it also suggested the formulation of a policy which would take the Jewish state into account.

The Foreign Office had thus found a scheme which would both ensure British interests in former Mandatory Palestine and serve as a solution for the Arab–Jewish conflict there: a conflict that had plagued that area throughout the Mandatory era. In the years following the war in Palestine, the efforts of the Foreign Office were directed towards consolidating the Greater Transjordan concept, first by keeping a close watch on the process of annexation of the West Bank and, second, by protecting the area from an Israeli or Arab offensive.

The task of watching the annexation was entrusted to Sir Alec Kirkbride, the British representative in Amman, who together with

209

the King had arrived in Palestine in 1921 to create a Transjordanian monarchy for the Sharif Hussein's sons. His long stay in Jordan and his subsequent strong influence on the King made him an ideal person for this mission. Kirkbride's main worry was that the large Palestinian majority would undermine Britain's position in Greater Transjordan. Kirkbride warned that the Palestinians' demands for a greater share in Jordan's political affairs would turn this absolute kingdom into a constitutional monarchy. Such a process according to Kirkbride, would have ended in the Palestinisation of Jordan. The British representative in Amman, like most of the Foreign Office's officials, had no doubt that a Palestinised Jordan (or an independent Palestine) would be an anti-British factor and a Communist stronghold. The British animosity towards the Palestinian leader, the Former Mufti of Jerusalem, Haj Amin Al-Husseini, had contributed much to this British fear.

The second way to ensure the success of the British and Jordanian scheme was by protecting the kingdom from an Israeli attack. The Israeli plans for the West Bank were a mixture of the territorial ambitions of Ben-Gurion and most of his army commanders and a genuine Israeli fear that the West Bank would serve as a launching-pad for a joint Anglo-Iraqi attack on Israel. Nevertheless, the Israeli threats to occupy the area should be seen as part of an Israeli tactic to force Abdullah to formalise the tacit Jewish–Hashemite understanding about the partition of Palestine, reached prior to the war of 1948. In fact, Abdullah was most eager to follow this policy, but the strong opposition from the ministers, particularly Premier Tawfiq Abu Al-Huda, to a formal peace treaty with Israel prevented the King from going very far in his relations with the Israelis.

The dispute between the King and his ministers put Kirkbride in a difficult position. After first agreeing to serve as a mediator between the King and his government, the British representative decided to side with the latter. Kirkbride believed that the King's policies might bring about the disintegration of the Hashemite rule in Transjordan and end in a *coup d'état* instigated by the former Mufti. There is little doubt that Abdullah's decision not to make Kirkbride a party to his secret negotiations with the Israelis had also contributed to his somewhat hostile attitude to the King's policies.

The immediate fruits of the Greater Transjordan concept were soon reaped by Britain. For the time being another round of fighting between the Arabs and the Israelis was prevented. The allegiance of Israel and Jordan to the West was secured as well. Moreover, the creation of the state of Israel did not seriously damage the Anglo-Arab relationship. This could be illustrated by pointing to the absence of any linkage and causality between the Arab–Israeli conflict and the Anglo-Egyptian crisis at the time, a crisis which had strongly undermined Britain's position in the area. The Foreign Office had assessed correctly that the conflict with Egypt had little to do with Britain's Palestinian policy. Egypt's grievance against the British was based on Britain's refusal to evacuate the Canal Zone. Furthermore, towards the end of 1951 the Egyptian reluctance to be part of the Western Alliance on the one hand, and Israel and Jordan's support for the UN action in Korea on the other, further proved the loyalty of these two countries to the West.

In the early 1950s the Arab–Israeli conflict was regarded by the Foreign Office as merely a territorial dispute between Israel and Jordan. The pro-Western orientation of these two countries contributed to the reduction in the importance attached to this conflict. The *modus vivendi* reached between Jordan and Israel before the war in Palestine seemed to hold after the end of hostilities there and London hoped that, like similar disputes in southern Europe, the hostilities in the early 1950s would be concluded by a peace treaty.

It should be noted that both the Americans and the UN backed the British in most of their decisions on the Arab–Israeli conflict, and that any divergences of opinion were tactical rather than strategic. Furthermore, neither the UN nor the Americans were able to offer a more feasible solution for the Arab–Israeli conflict.

In the ensuing years three new factors would affect the course of the conflict: Egypt's Arab nationalism under Nasser's regime, the Soviet Union, and the re-emergence of the Palestinian national movement. These factors would intensify the conflict and turn it into a regional dispute that has brought the two superpowers to the brink of confrontation. As for the Egyptians and the Russians, it appears that Britain could not have predicted their appearance before Nasser's coming to power in Egypt in 1954. The same cannot be said about the Palestinian question.

Between 1948 and 1967, the Palestinians were insignificant as a political force, at least as far as the Arab–Israeli conflict was concerned. This was probably why Britain chose to disregard the Palestinians as a factor to be considered in finding a solution for Palestine. This situation affected all the other parties concerned. The Palestinian leadership was disorganised as a result of the war, and the various bodies and organisations which came forward as representatives of the Palestinians were usually suspected of being exploited by the Arab governments for the latter's own political interests. Another reason for Britain's hostile attitude towards the Palestinians was that it feared the Palestinians might take over Jordan and, under the leadership of the Mufti, turn it into a state hostile to Britain and the West.

The lack of a strong political movement amongst the Palestinians had paradoxically complicated the efforts for finding a solution for the problem of the refugees. All parties in the conflict were prepared to discuss the humanitarian aspect of the refugee problem. In fact Israel and the Arab states had been willing to negotiate a solution to this problem at the Lausanne conference in the summer of 1949. That conference was in many ways a missed opportunity: it was the first and only time that an All-Arab delegation and Israel concurred on the principle of partition according to the UN resolution of November 1947. It was also the last time the Israelis were prepared to admit joint responsibility with the Arab countries for the refugee problem by making a gesture and offering to repatriate some of the refugees. The Israeli motives were practical and partly the result of American pressure, but nevertheless they had opened the way for a political solution to the problem.

It was only natural that such a solution would take some time to work out. However, the Americans, who underestimated the political significance of the question, believed they had in their hand a magic and rapid solution to the refugee problem. This was the 'economic solution', a formula which ignored the political sensitivities of both the Israelis and the Arabs with regard to the refugees. The British reluctantly supported this American initiative and even took the lead at one stage of the process. When this solution did not work out the UN, into whose hands the problem was entrusted, treated the problem as one which called for temporary relief rather than an overall solution. In the years to come, until 1969, all peace initiatives in the area would continue to ignore the political aspect of the question. During the period under review this situation was welcomed both by the Israelis, who hoped that the Arab states would resettle the refugees, and by the Arab states, who decided to exploit the conditions in the refugee camps as a political card against Israel.

The main British concern was to prevent Jordan from becoming a new home for the refugees, most of whom were located in Greater Transjordan. The Foreign Office could not come out openly against a proposal to resettle the refugees there, but owing to their desire to keep Transjordan under Hashemite rule, the Office suggested the resettlement of the refugees in Iraq and Syria.

Finally we should not forget that the critical assessment of Britain's policies, decisions and stances made in this work have the benefit of hindsight. We should bear in mind that the Arab–Israeli conflict was not the only problem facing the Eastern Department of the Foreign Office, which also had to deal with Iran and Egypt. Moreover, the history of the conflict hitherto has shown us that the other external powers who became involved in the conflict were faced with the very same problems. Those powers suffered from the very same misconceptions as did Britain in its attempts to solve the conflict and, at the same time, ensure their own interests in the area.

Appendix 1
Where Was Policy Made?

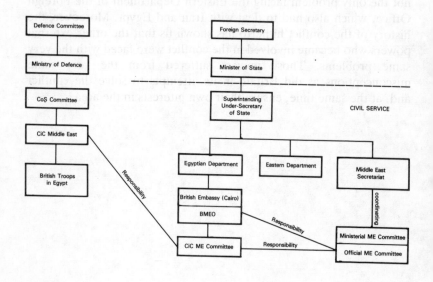

Appendix 2
Palestine: The 'Eight Points' Suggested as a Basis for a Settlement

(i) Acceptance of refugees by both sides in proportions to be determined.

(ii) Israel's proposal to incorporate the Gaza Strip with the refugees at present in it could form part of a general settlement subject to the following conditions:

    (a) It should be made clear that there is no question of a mere deal between territory and acceptance of responsibility for refugees. Territorial compensation for the Gaza Strip should be found elsewhere by Israel for the Arabs – see (iii) below – provided the Arabs demand such compensation;

    (b) Some safeguards should be devised in regard to the future treatment of the Gaza refugees in Israel; they should be permitted to return to any part of Israel where they had property or special interests and they should be able to earn a livelihood and presumably have full rights of citizenship.

(iii) Territorial compensation for the Gaza area (if ceded) and for other areas held by Israel but not allotted to her under the 1947 Plan should be provided if the Arabs demand it. The following areas appear politically and geographically suitable for this purpose i.e. contiguous to other Arab areas:

    (a) a land-bridge in the southern Negev between Egypt and Jordan;

    (b) an area in the Negev north of Beersheba connecting with Arab central Palestine;

    (c) an area along the Egyptian frontier south of El Auja;

    (d) the restoration of part or all of Western Galilee;

    (e) the Ramleh–Lydda area.

We see no reason to insist that any one of these areas should form the exclusive field for compensation. They could, if necessary, be combined in various proportions. This would certainly provide greater flexibility for the discussions. But the shape of the eventual territorial compensation should in any case be governed by the requirements of either side in regard to communications and outlets to the sea (see (iv) below).

(iv) Communications and outlets. If the territorial compensation to the Arabs were to be in the form of the awarding to Jordan, or to Jordan and Egypt, of part of the whole of the Southern Negev, thus providing a land bridge between Egypt and Jordan, Israel should have guaranteed freedom of access and communication to the Red Sea. Equally the Arab States should have guaranteed freedom of communication and access to the Mediterranean. If another solution were adopted for the Southern Negev

215

there should nonetheless be guaranteed freedom of communication and access across it between Egypt and Jordan and between Israel and the Red Sea. An alternative method of providing for freedom of communication and access might be by a neutral zone or zones.

(v) A free port (or at least a free zone for all Arab states) should be established at Haifa with an arrangement by which Iraqi crude oil could be freely exported in return for the provision by Iraq of normal supplies for the Haifa Refinery.

(vi) There should be a partition of Jerusalem for administrative purposes with international supervision, particularly of the holy places.

(vii) Central Arab Palestine should be formally incorporated into Jordan.

(viii) Israel and the Arab states concerned should agree to share for their mutual benefit the waters of the Jordan and Yarmuk.

Notes and References

Introduction

1. I have found two books which are particularly objective and reliable as a historical survey of the period under review: Taha Al-Hashimi, *Mudhakarat*, Vol. 2 (Beirut, 1978); Dan Kurzman, *Genesis 1948: The First Arab–Israeli War* (World Publishing House, New York 1970).
2. R. Bullard, *Britain and the Middle East* (London: Hutchinson, 1951), p. 113.
3. FO 371/75067, E13989, PUSC, 30 April 1949. See also A. Bullock, *Ernest Bevin, Foreign Secretary, 1945–1951* (London: Heinemann, 1983), p. 273; and P. Darby, *British Defence Policy East of the Suez, 1947–1968* (London, 1973), pp. 9–46.
4. FO 371/68864, E13843, Kirkbride to Burrows, 21 October 1948.
5. FO 371/68403, E300, Damascus to FO, 13 January 1948, and E2001, Amman to FO, 24 April 1948.
6. E. Wright, 'Abdullah's Jordan, 1947–1951', *MEJ*, 5 (1951), pp. 439–60; E. Monroe, *Britain's Moment in the Middle East 1914–71*, 2nd edn (London: Chatto & Windus, 1981), p. 156.
7. B. Shwadran, *Jordan: A State of Tension* (New York: Council for Middle East Press, 1959), p. 217; and see FO 816/110, Amman to FO, 18 May 1948.
8. FO 371/68818, brief of Bevin's meeting with Abu Al-Huda, 6 February 1948 in CoS (48) 24 (0), 29 January 1948.
9. Article 3a in the Annexe to the 1948 draft treaty in FO 371/68818, E1899, FO Minute, Pyman, 3 February 1948; and FO 816/118, Amman to FO, February 1948, see also FO 371/68818, JP (48), 24 February 1948.
10. For details on the Anglo–Iraqi negotiations of 1948 see E. B. Penrose, *Iraq: International Relations and National Development* (London: Benn, 1978), pp. 112–13.
11. FO 371/68385, E4371, FO Memo, 1 March 1948.
12. E. Monroe, 'Mr. Bevin's Arab Policy', *St Antony's Papers No. 11* (London, 1961), p. 113.
13. FO 371/68818, E2832, Kirkbride to Burrows, 16 February 1948.
14. FO 371/68864, E3843, Kirkbride to Burrows, 21 October 1948.
15. FO 371/75064, E4691, FO Minute, Beith, 29 March 1949.
16. FO 371/91182, E1022/7, FO Minute, Bowker, 12 June 1951.
17. FO 371/75072, E9043, Foreign Office Middle East Conference, 21 July 1949.
18. It was an offspring of the two war-time institutions in Cairo: the resident minister of state and the Middle East Supply Centre.
19. FO 371/81926, E1052/20, T. Rapp to FO 1 January 1950, commenting on directives sent to him and on those sent to Sir John Troutbeck in 1947.
20. FO 371/75072, E10304, FO Middle East Conference, 25 July 1949.
21. Like the Joint Intelligence Committee Middle East and Joint Planning Staff; FO 371/68819, JP (48) 17, FO Minute, Burrows, 2 March 1948.

1 The Emergence of the Transjordan Option

1. Bevin in the House of Commons in CO 537/2343, Beeley's history of the British Mandate in Palestine, 18 February 1947.
2. E. Monroe, *Britain's Moment in the Middle East, 1914–56* (London: Chatto & Windus, 1963), p. 167.
3. DEFE 4/10, CoS Committee (JPS), 13 January 1948.
4. Troutbeck to Cunningham, Cunningham Papers, Box 6, File 1, St Antony's Private Papers Collection.
5. FO 371/68365, Washington to Bevin, January 1948.
6. Monroe, *Britain's Moment*, p. 168.
7. FO 371/68635, E862, Amman to FO, 21 January 1948 and E941, Amman to FO, 21 January 1948.
8. FO 371/68635, E1256, HC (Jerusalem) to FO, 31 January 1948.
9. A. Al-Aref, *Al-Nakbah, 1947–1952* (The Catastrophe) (Sidon: Mashurat Al-Maktaba Al-Misriya, undated), p. 15.
10. FO 371/68366, E1785, HC (Jerusalem) to SoS for the Colonies, 5 February 1948.
11. Monroe, *Britain's Moment*, p. 169.
12. FO 371/68366, E1702, FO Minute Beeley, 6 February 1948, and Arab version of events: Salih Saib Al-Jaburi, *Mikhnat Filastin Wa-Asraruha As-Siyasiya Wa-Askariya* (The Palestine Ordeal) (Beirut, 1970), p. 123.
13. Among many others: H. Sacher, *Europe Leaves the Middle East, 1936–1954* (London: Allen Lane, 1972), p. 508: J. and D. Kimche, *Both Sides of the Hill: Britain and the Palestine War* (London, 1960), p. 36; M. Bar-Zohar, *Ben-Gurion* (Hebrew) Tel Aviv, 1977), p. 669; IDF, *Toldot Milchemet Ha-Kommemiut* (The Israeli War of Independence) (Tel Aviv), p. 66; and C. Sykes, *Crossroads to Israel, 1917–1948*, 2nd edn (London: Indiana University Press, 1973), p. 336.
14. Cab 128/12, CM (48) 12, Bevin, 5 February 1948.
15. FO 371/68531, E1388, NY to FO, 31 January 1948.
16. FO 371/68513, E85, Commissioner for the Jewish Camps to SoS for the Colonies, 8 January 1948.
17. ISA 65/4, HC (Jerusalem) to Bevin, 5 February 1948.
18. CAB 128/12, CM (48) 12, Bevin, 5 February 1948.
19. Bar-Zohar, *Ben-Gurion*, p. 669 and M. Cohen, 'The Birth of Israel – Diplomatic Failure, Military Success', *Jerusalem Quarterly*, 17 (Autumn 1980), p. 33.
20. C. Sykes, *Crossroads*, p. 333.
21. PREM 8/860, MoD to CO, 22 March 1948.
22. CAB 128/12, CM (48) 12, Bevin, 5 February 1948.
23. Ibid.
24. FO 371/68531, E1277, NY to FO, 28 January 1948.
25. *FRUS 48* (Foreign Relations of the US), Defence Department Files, Memo Joint CoS to Truman, March 1948, p. 798; the State Department initiated the Trusteeship proposal. It was proposed to the UN on 19 March 1948. But the President, immediately after the declaration in the UN, had announced his support for partition once more. M. Truman, *Harry S. Truman* (New York: Morrow, 1973), pp. 387–9; A. Bullock,

Ernest Bevin, Foreign Secretary, 1945–1957 (London: Hutchinson, 1951), pp. 560–1.

26. *Hansard*, House of Commons Debates, Vol. 461, p. 2050, 24 February 1948.
27. FO 371/68818, E1901, brief for Bevin's meeting with Tawfiq Abu Al-Huda, 6 February 1948.
28. Ibid.
29. FO 371/68365, E548, Amman to FO, 11 January 1948; ISA 163/4, Report by the Political Department of the Jewish Agency, 27 October 1947; FO 68364, meeting between Dajani (King's Representative) and Legation officials, 7 January 1948. For more details see Y. Nevo, *Abdullah ve-Arviyei Eretz Israel* (Abdullah and the Arab Palestinians) (Tel Aviv, 1975), pp. 61–8.
30. Ben-Gurion, *Yoman Hamilchama* (War Diary), ed. Rivlin and Orren (Israel Defence Ministry, 1983), p. 100; and H. Abidi, *Jordan: A Political Study, 1948–1957* (London, 1965), pp. 26–7.
31. GZA S25/9038, 26 January 1948; FO 371/68364, E101, FO Minute, Beeley, 31 December 1947 and Al-Aref, *Al-Nakbah*, p. 67.
32. FO 371/68364, E504, FO Minute, Beeley, 22 December 1948; FO 371/68364, E306, Amman to FO, 7 January 1948.
33. Abidi, *Jordan*, p. 24; CO 537/2343, Beeley's History of the Palestine Mandate, p. 38. For details on the British policy towards the foundation of the Arab League see W. Gomaa, *The Foundation of the League of Arab States* (London, 1977), pp. 195, 212, 229, and Y. Porath, *Bemivhan Ha-Ma'aseh Ha-Politi* (In Confrontation with Reality in Politics) (Jerusalem: Yad Ben Zvi, 1985), pp. 304–14.
34. FO 371/68381, 68382, 68443 and 75051. This was also partly owing to a personal animosity between Azzam and the British which dated back to the 1930s; see M. R. Coury, 'Who Invented Egyptian Nationalism?' Part I, *International Journal of ME Studies*, 14 (1982), pp. 249–81.
35. FO 371/68364, E101, FO Minute, Beeley, 31 December 1947; CAB 129/16, CP (47) 28, Annexe to Creech-Jones' Memo, 13 January 1947.
36. FO 371/68368, E229, FO Minute, Buss, 13 February 1948; FO 371/68367, E2406, Amman to FO, 11 February 1948.
37. FO 371/68818, E1899, FO Minute, Pyman, 3 February 1948.
38. FO 371/68852, E6008, FO Minute, Walker, 11 May 1948; Kirkbride's interview with Monroe in September 1959 in Monroe Papers, St Antony's Private Collection.
39. FO 371/68367, E2046, Amman to FO, 11 February, 1948.
40. A. Kirkbride, *From the Wings: Amman Memoirs 1947–1951* (London: Cass, 1976), p. 22.
41. The first possibility is explored by W. Ad-Daly, *Asrar Al-Jamiaa Al-Arabiya wa-Abd Al-Rahman Azzam* (The Secrets of the Arab League and Abd Al-Rahman Azzam) (Cairo: Ruz Al-Yusuf, 1982), pp. 233–5 and the second by J. B. Glubb, *A Soldier with the Arabs* (London, 1957), p. 23.
42. FO 371/68367, E2120, FO Minute, Burrows, 21 February 1948.
43. FO 371/68364, E504, FO Minute, Beeley, 22 December 1947.
44. FO 371/68367, E3371 memo by Glubb, March 1948; FO 371/68369,

E3729, Amman to FO, 20 March 1948; and FO 371/68369, HC (Jerusalem) to the SoS for the Colonies, 24 March 1948.

45. FO 371/68369, E3371, Memo by Glubb, March 1948.
46. FO 371/68369, E3366, Jedda to Amman, 11 March 1948; and FO 371/68368, E2299, FO Minute, Buss 13 February 1948.
47. FO 371/68368, E2564, Wright to Mack, 27 February 1948; and FO 371/68372, Jedda to FO, 6 May 1948.
48. J. G. Granados, *The Birth of Israel* (New York: Knopf, 1948), p. 190: Granados was a member of UNSCOP (UN Special Committee of Palestine).
49. FO 371/68368, E2969, FO Minute, Burrows, 9 February 1948.
50. *FRUS 48*, Vol. 5, Part 2, British Embassy in Washington to the SD (State Department), 5 January 1948, p. 535; memo by the PPS (Principal Private Secretary), January 1948, pp. 550, 553; and Douglas to SoS, 29 April 1948.
51. FO 371/68367, E1980, FO Minute, Wright, 1 February, 1948.
52. FO 371/68367, Goldman to Easterman, 4 February 1948; and BGA Diary, 12 and 19 January 1948.
53. Ibid.
54. CZA (Central Zionist Archives) S25/9383, Sasson Memo, March 1948. Sasson and Shimoni doubted whether Abdullah was generally aiming at dividing Palestine. Sasson even suspected a British plan to assist Abdullah to go as far as Haifa and Rafah in order to ensure access to the sea.
55. FO 816/123, Amman to FO, 9 June 1948.
56. FO 371/68852, E5163, Amman to FO, 24 April 1948; and CZA S25/1704, Sasson to Abdullah's Chamber, 23 April 1948.
57. Goldie, commander of the 1st Brigade, and Crocker, an operations officer; see in J. Lunt, *Glubb Pasha* (Harvill, London, 1984), p. 140; BGA, Diary, 25 May 1948 and FO 800/477, FS 48/7, May 1948.
58. FO 800/477, FS 48/7, 13 May 1948; and see a similar American impression in FO 371/68852, E6372, FO Minute, Bevin reporting a telegram from Marshall to the American Embassy in London.
59. Ibid.
60. Glubb, *A Soldier*, p. 107; and Ben-Gurion, *War Diary*, 2 May 1948, p. 383.
61. FO 371/68552, E5087, Kirkbride to Burrows, 15 April 1948.
62. Ginzach Hamedina (ISA Publication), *Minhelet Ha-A'm Protocolim* (The People's Assembly Protocols) (May 1978), Meyerson report to the Assembly, 13 May 1948.
63. Abidi, *Jordan*, p. 27; and FO 371/68821, E8053, Amman to FO, 12 June 1948.
64. FO 371/68821, E8052, FO to Amman, 13 June 1948, reporting Weizmann declaration in Paris on this issue; CZA, S25/5634, Arab Department meeting, 13 May 1948; and Truman Library, Clifford Papers, Box 13, Palestine ORE 7–48.
65. The Israeli version in ISA, *Minhelet Ha-A'm*, Yadin report; American version in SD867 n. 01/5–14 48, Jerusalem to SD, 14 May 1948; the defenders who surrendered were massacred by the local villagers.

66. Interview to *Al-Hamishmar*, 17 April 1983.
67. FO 371/68852, E6008, Amman to FO, 8 May 1948.

2 Britain and the War of 1948 (May–June)

1. FO 371/68370, E5298, FO Minute, Balfour, 26 April 1948; FO 371/68372, E5918, Amman to FO, 8 May 1948; FO 371/68504, E5464, M13 to MoD, 23 April 1948.
2. A. Al-Aref, *Al-Nakbah*, 1947–1952 (The Catastrophe) (Sidon: Manshurat Al-Maktaba Al-Misriya, n.d.), p. 288, fn. 1.
3. FO 371/68369, E3371, Glubb memo, March 1948.
4. FO 371/68852, E4681, Kirkbride to Burrows, 13 April 1948.
5. DEFE 4/12, CoS (48) 48, 1 April 1948.
6. Ibid.
7. FO 371/68371, E5603, FO memo, 2 May 1948.
8. *The Times*, 13 January 1948, 18 and 24 March 1948.
9. BGA, Meeting of the Jewish Agency Directive, 16 and 24 April 1948.
10. FO 371/68369, E3916, Damascus to FO, 27 March 1948 (this information was based on a report by a British national working in the Syrian Ministry of Defence); FO 371/68822, E11049, Glubb's report on the Transjordanian situation, 20 April 1948.
11. DEFE 4/12, CoS (48) 56, 23 April 1948.
12. FO 371/68822, E11049, Transjordan situation, 20 April 1948.
13. J. B. Glubb, *A Soldier with the Arabs* (London, 1957), p. 101.
14. DEFE 4/2, CoS (48) 56, 23 April 1948.
15. FO 371/68368, E2353, Cairo to FO, 12 February 1948.
16. FO 371/68531, E1290, Chapman-Andrews to FO, 28 January 1948.
17. FO 371/68370, E5109, Cairo to FO, 24 April 1948; S. S. Al-Jaburi, *Mikhnat Fil astin Wa-Asra ruha As-Siyasiya Wa-Askariya* (Beirut, 1970), p. 219.
18. FO 371/68371, E5528, Campbell to FO, 29 April 1948; SD 867 n.01/5–13–48, Cairo to SD, 13 May 1948; Al-Aref, *Al-Nakbah*, pp. 282–3; and *Journal d'Egypte*, 12 May 1948.
19. FO 371/68370, E5109, Cairo to FO, 24 April 1948; FO 371/68372, E6251, Cairo to FO, 13 March 1948; FO 371/68372, E6307, Cairo to FO, 15 May 1948.
20. According to the Defence Ministry estimation the Jews could deploy 50 000 armed men. This is roughly the number of Arabs deployed. According to the official Israeli version Israel had 26 000 men and an equal number of reserves (DEFE 4/12, CoS (48) 56, 23 April 1948; IDF *Toldot Milchemet Ma-Kommemiut* (The Israeli War of Independence) (Tel Aviv), pp. 27, 71–3; BGA, The Jewish Agency Directive meetings, 1 February 1948.
21. These ideas were expressed by Bevin in FO 371/68367, E1980, FO Minute, Bevin, 11 February 1948.
22. C. Sykes, *Crossroads to Israel, 1917–1948* (London: Indiana University Press, 1973), pp. 323–4.
23. FO 371/68368, E2696, FO Minute, Burrows, 9 February 1948.

24. J. Berque, *Egypt: Imperialism and Resolution* (trans. J. Stewart) (London: Faber & Faber, 1978), p. 656.
25. J. Marlow, *Anglo-Egyptian Relations, 1800–1953* (London: Cresset, 1954), p. 330.
26. FO 371/68373, E6636, FO to Damascus, 9 May 1948.
27. Apart from Transjordan which gave some information before the war; FO 371/68373, E6692, Beirut to FO, 20 May 1948.
28. The British stopped supplying arms and ammunition at the beginning of June: see CAB 21/1922, CoS (48), June 1948.
29. FO 371/68373, E6694, Amman to FO, 21 May 1948.
30. Ibid.
31. FO 371/68373, E6722, Baghdad to FO, 22 May 1948; and E6770, Amman to FO, 22 May 1948.
32. FO 371/68373, E6769, Amman to FO, 22 May 1948.
33. FO 371/68531, E1302, J. Martin (CO) to Wright, 27 January 1948.
34. Ibid., Cunningham to J. Martin.
35. FO 371/68852, E6008, Amman to FO, 8 May 1948.
36. FO 371/68852, E4667, Kirkbride to FO, 13 April 1948; and FO 816/120, Amman to FO, 16 March 1948.
37. FO 816/120, Bevin to Abdullah, 17 May 1948.
38. Ibid., Bevin to Abdullah, 15 May 1948.
39. FO 816/120, Kirkbride to Bevin, 22 May 1948; two-thirds of the population of Jerusalem was Jewish (Count Bernadotte report to the SC/UN A/648, p. 8).
40. Cunningham Private Papers, Box 6, File 1, a letter to Lloyd, 15 January 1948; and FO 371/68371, Pearson (CO) to McAlpine (Bevin's private secretary), 1 May 1948.
41. FO 371/68504, E5464, M13 to MoD, 23 April 1948; *Salomon Private Archive*, Intelligence report to the Jewish Agency Executive, 14 April 1948; see also FO 371/68822, E11049, the Transjordanian situation by Glubb, 12 August 1948. Incidentally, Kirkbride warned Abdullah that he was exposing Ramleh and Lydda. See FO 371/68506, E6564, Amman to FO, 19 May 1948.
42. FO 371/68372, E6304, Amman to FO, 17 May 1948.
43. FO 371/68822, E11049, The Transjordanian situation by Glubb, 12 August 1948.
44. FO 371/68373, E6841, Amman to FO, 22 May 1948; Bevin to Middle Eastern posts, 26 May 1948.
45. See note 43 above.
46. FO 371/68510, E7639, Amman to FO, 7 June 1968.
47. J. Zasloff, *Great Britain and Palestine* (Munich, 1952), p. 134; UN Security Council, Official Records 3rd Year, no. 67, pp. 2–4, draft resolution S/749.
48. G. Kirk, *Survey of International Affairs: The Middle East, 1945–50* (London: RIIA, The Royal Institute for International Affairs, 1954), p. 272.
49. *FRUS 48*, Douglas to Marshall, 25 May 1948, p. 1047.
50. Ben-Gurion, *War Diary*, editorial note, p. 422.

51. F. Bernadotte, *To Jerusalem* (London: Hodder & Stoughton, 1951), p. 21; SC OR 3rd Year, Supplement S/801.
52. Ibid.
53. CAB 24/1922, CoS (48) 125, 4 June 1948; FO 371/68373, E6841, Kirkbride to FO, 22 May 1948; and see G. Goldstein, 'A Talk with Mr. Bevin', *Zionist Review*, 9 February 1951, p. 10.
54. FO 371/68373, E6800, Amman to FO 23 May 1948; FO 371/68222, E11049, the Transjordan situation by Glubb, 12 August 1948; and FO 371/68510, E7851, Sir O. Sargent to Sir Leslie Hollis (MoD), 11 June 1948.
55. FO 371/68373, E6897, Amman to FO, 22 May 1948.
56. FO 371/68509, E7220, Bevin's draft note to the Cabinet, 27 May 1948.
57. FO 371/68374, E7887, Amman to FO, 9 June 1948.
58. FO 371/68374, E8322, FO Minute, Balfour, 14 June 1948.
59. FO 371/68222, E11049, The Transjordan Situation by Glubb, 12 August 1948.
60. FO 371/68374, E9072, BMEO to FO, 5 July 1948.
61. CAB 21/1922, CoS (C) 125 (0), 4 June 1948; Al-Jaburi, *Mikhnat*, p. 148.
62. Sykes, *Crossroads*, pp. 354–5; BGA, Diary, 5 June 1948.
63. IDF, *Toldot*, pp. 231–2, 239; *UN Papers*, Count Bernadotte report in ISA 2425/2.

3 Britain, Bernadotte and the Greater Transjordan

1. G. Lenczowski, *The Middle East in World Affairs* (Ithaca, New York: Cornell, 1980), p. 408.
2. FO 371/68509, E7220, Bevin's draft note to the Cabinet, 27 May 1948.
3. Ibid.
4. Note in particular S. Persson, *Mediation and Assassination: Count Bernadotte's Mission to Palestine, 1948* (London: Ithaca Press, 1979), pp. 193, 297–313; H. Sacher, *Europe Leaves the Middle East, 1936–1954* (London: Allen Lane, 1972), p. 524; J. and D. Kimche, *Both Sides of the Hill: Britain and the Palestine War* (London, 1960), p. 198; and J. G. McDonald, *My Mission to Israel: 1948–57* (London: Victor Gollancz, 1951), p. 20.
5. ISA 2424/20, Shiloah to Sharett, 25 June 1948.
6. ISA 2424/21, Sharett memo, 22 July 1948; ISA 2426/5, Sharett–Bernadotte conversation, 26 July 1948.
7. Persson, *Bernadotte*, p. 143.
8. FO 371/68374, E8962, UN UK to FO, 1 July 1948; F. Bernadotte, *To Jerusalem* (London: Hodder & Stoughton, 1951), p. 128; ISA 2424/20, Bernadotte's proposals.
9. FO 371/68374, E8962, UN UK to FO, 1 July 1948.
10. FO 371/68374, E8564, FO Minute, Wright, 24 June 1948; Bernadotte, *To Jerusalem*, p. 171.
11. Bernadotte, *To Jerusalem*, p. 154; ISA 2424/20.
12. A. Darawza, *Al-Qadiya Al-Filastiniya* (The Palestine Problem) (Beirut, n.d.), app. 1, p. 41 as quoted in Mahdi Abd Al-Hadi, *Al-Masala*

Al-Filastiniya wa-Mashari' Al-Hulul Al-Siyasiya, 1934–74 (The Palestine Question and its Political Solution) (Beirut, 1975), p. 126.
13. Ibid.
14. Ibid.
15. FO 371/68375, E9216, BMEO to FO, 8 July 1948.
16. Bernadotte, *To Jerusalem*, p. 186.
17. ISA 2426/5, Bernadotte–Sharett conversation, 10 August 1948.
18. FO 371/68861, EII675, Beeley to Kirkbride, 3 September 1948.
19. ISA 2426/5, Sharett–Bernadotte conversation, 10 August 1948.
20. FO 371/68374, E8564, FO Minute, Wright, 24 June 1948. American support for this position was also sought. See *FRUS 48*, Vol. 5, Part 2, Douglas to Marshall, 18 June 1948, p. 1123.
21. Ibid.
22. FO 371/68375, E9168, FO Minute, Bevin, 5 July 1948.
23. FO 371/68374, E9005, BMEO to FO, 4 July 1948.
24. FO 371/68374, E9061, Cabinet Conclusions, 1 July 1948.
25. ISA 2424/21, L. Kohn to Sharett, 22 July 1948.
26. ISA 2424/21, Eytan to Sharett, 28 July 1948.
27. ISA 2424/21, Sharett to Bernadotte, 5 July 1948.
28. ISA 2424/21, Sharett to Bernadotte, 5 July 1948.
29. FO 371/68374, E9005, BMEO to FO, 4 July 1948.
30. FO 371/68375, E9453, Cairo to FO, 12 July 1948.
31. Zasloff, 'Great Britain and Palestine: A Study of the Problem before the UN', thesis submitted to L'Université de Genève (1952), pp. 149–50.
32. *FRUS 48*, Vol. 5, Part 2, Douglas to SoS, 1 September 1948.
33. *FRUS 48*, SoS to McClintock, 10 September 1948, p. 1387.
34. *FRUS 48*, Griffith to SoS, 15 September 1948, p. 1398.
35. Zasloff, 'Great Britain', p. 151, and Persson, *Bernadotte*, pp. 193, 273, 297–313.
36. Ibid.
37. UN Papers, A/638, 18 September 1948.
38. CAB 128/13, CM (48), Bevin, 8 July 1948.
39. FO 371/68861, E12205, Wright to Amman, 17 September 1948.
40. FO 371/68861, E11717, BMEO to FO, 6 September 1948.
41. FO 371/68861, E11760, Damascus to FO, 7 September 1948.
42. FO 371/68861 (the whole file).
43. At least according to British documents, FO 371/68861, E11809, Kirkbride to FO, 8 September 1948.
44. Ibid.
45. FO 371/68371, E9168, FO Minute, Bevin, 5 July 1948.
46. *Hansard*, House of Commons Debates, Vol. 456, Col. 899–900, 22 September 1948.
47. Ibid.
48. Introductory statement to the first proposals in ISA, 2424/20, Bernadotte to IFO, 27 June 1948.
49. BGA, Ben-Gurion's diary, conversation between Bunche and Horowitz, 7 October 1948.
50. *FRUS 48*, Vol. 5, Part 2, Jessup to SoS, 30 June 1948, p. 1161.
51. *FRUS 48*, Clifford to Lovett, 29 September 1948, p. 1161.

52. The circumstances of the American change of mind are discussed later.
53. UN GA, Official Records, 3rd Session, Supplement no. 11, A/648, p. 18.
54. FO 371/68641, E10241, Cairo to FO, 31 July 1948.
55. FO 371/68641, E9552, FO to Cairo, 22 July 1948.

4 The Anglo-Israeli War over the Negev

1. FO 371/68375, E9715, Amman to FO, 18 July 1948; FO 371/68828, E11409, Glubb's 'Transjordan Situation', 12 August 1948; IDF, *Toldot Milchemet Ha-Kommemiut* (The Israeli War of Independence) (Tel Aviv), pp. 240, 246, 283.
2. A. At-Tal, *Karithat Filastin* (The Palestine Disaster) (Cairo, 1959), p. 245; A. Al-Aref, *Al-Nakbah, 1947–1952* (The Catastrophe) (Sidon: Manshurat Al-Maktaba Al-Misriya, n.d.), part 3, pp. 216–18; S. Musa and Munib Al-Madi *Tarikh Al-Urdun Fi Al-Qarn Al-Ishinn* (The History of Jordan in the Twentieth Century) (Amman, 1959), p. 509.
3. At-Tal, *Karithat*, pp. 247–9.
4. Sir Alec Kirkbride, *From the Wings: Amman Memoirs 1947–1957* (London: Cass, 1976), p. 44.
5. FO 371/68822, E11409, Glubb's 'Transjordan Situation', 12 August 1948; Musa and Madi, *Urdun*, p. 509.
6. FO 371/68506, E6564, Amman to FO, 19 May 1948.
7. At-Tal, *Karithat*, p. 245; Kirkbride, *From the Wings*, p. 47. According to Glubb's biographer, Tawfiq Abu Al-Huda and Glubb were agreed on the impossibility of defending Ramleh and Lydda. This was mainly due to the strength of the Jewish force. See J. Lunt, *Glubb Pasha* (Harwell Press, 1984), p. 150.
8. FO 371/68822, E10325, Pirie-Gordon to Burrows, 25 July 1948; J. B. Glubb, *A Soldier with the Arabs* (London, 1957), p. 166.
9. UN Papers, A/648, Report of Count Bernadotte (see also in ISA 2425/2).
10. IDF, *Toldot*, pp. 242–82, 284.
11. FO 371/68375, E10252, BMEO to FO, 24 July 1948; and 10078, Jerusalem to FO, 18 July 1948.
12. Musa and Madi, *Urdun*, p. 521; FO 371/68822, E10325, Pirie-Gordon to Burrows, 25 July 1948; and FO 371/68822, E11409, Glubb's 'Transjordan Situation', 12 August 1948.
13. CAB 128/13, CM (48) 53, Bevin, 22 July 1948; Jamali's Defence Speech, 23 September 1958, *MachKamat S As-Shaa'b* (People's Court, 26th Session), p. 1093.
14. FO 371/68451, E11378, Richmond to Bevin, 25 August 1948; Jamali's interview in *As-Shaa'b*, 20 August 1948. See also in C. Hollingworth, *The Arabs and the West* (London: Methuen, 1952), p. 15.
15. FO 371/68635, E1211, FO Minute, Beeley, 22 January 1948.
16. FO 371/68822, E11049, Kirkbride to Bevin, 12 August 1948.
17. Ibid.
18. FO 371/68822, Abdullah to Bevin, 12 August 1948.
19. FO 371/68822, FO Minute, Burrows, 17 August 1948.
20. CAB 21/1922, CoS (48) 125 (0), 4 June 1948; FO 371/68860, Burrows to MoD, 8 September 1948.

21. FO 371/68822, E11409, FO Minute, Sir Orme Sargent, 18 August 1948.
22. *FRUS 48*, Vol. 5, Part 2, Jessup to SoS, 9 August 1948, p. 1298; McDonald to Truman, 24 August 1948, p. 1337, and CIA Report, 5 August 1948, p. 1280.
23. *FRUS 48*, Jessup to SoS, 9 August 1948, p. 1298.
24. FO 371/68822, E11409, FO Minute, Burrows, 17 August 1948.
25. At-Tal, *Karithat*, pp. 255–8; W. Ad-Daly, *Asrar Al-Jamiaa Al-Arabiya Wa-Abd Al-Rahman Azzam* (The Secrets of the Arab League and Abd Al-Rahman Azzam) (Cairo: Ruz Al-Yusuf, 1982), p. 240; Glubb, *A Soldier*, p. 191; and S. S. Al-Jaburi, *Mikhnat Filastin Wa-Asraruha As-Siyasiya Wa-Askariya* (The Truth about the Catastrophe in Palestine) (Beirut, 1970), p. 274–5.
26. FO 371/68375, E9732, Baghdad to FO, 18 July 1948.
27. FO 371/68376, E11020, FO Minute, Walker, 24 August 1948.
28. FO 371/68376, E11518, Kirkbride to Bevin, 24 August 1948.
29. Ibid.
30. The general designate was the former Iraqi Chief of General Staff, Salibi Saib Al-Jaburi: FO 371/68376, E11284, Baghdad to FO, 26 August 1948; and E11194, Amman to FO, 25 August 1948.
31. FO 371/68376, E11462, Bevin to Baghdad, 2 September 1948.
32. FO 371/68376, E11590, Amman to FO, 4 September 1948; E11622, Baghdad to FO, 5 September 1948.
33. FO 371/68822, E11836, Kirkbride to Burrows, 6 September 1948.
34. Ibid.
35. FO 371/68822, E14188, Amman to FO, 13 November 1948, and E14189, Kirkbride to FO, 3 November 1948.
36. FO 371/68379, E12211, FO memo, Burrows, 'Effects of the Palestine situation on internal affairs throughout the Middle East', 8 September 1948.
37. FO 371/68822, E11049, FO Minute, Burrows, 17 August 1948; UN Papers, Bernadotte report to the Security Council, A/648, p. 15.
38. FO 371/68860, E11665, FO Minute, 2 September 1948; JP (47) 136, 24 October 1947.
39. FO 371/69273, J5641, Chapman-Andrews to Wright, September 1948.
40. FO 371/68698, E13424, Jerusalem to FO, 16 October 1948.
41. FO 371/68860, E12387, Burrows to Price (MoD), 25 September 1948.
42. Ibid.
43. FO 371/68689, E11605, FO Minute, Beeley, 2 September 1948; *Haaretz*, 29 August 1948; *Davar*, 29 August 1948.
44. Ibid.
45. BGA, Ben-Gurion's diary, 8 September 1948; Bevin in the House of Commons, 22 September 1948.
46. BGA, Ben-Gurion's diary, 12 August 1948.
47. IDF, *Toldot*, pp. 229, 279.
48. FO 371/68696, E14041, FO to UN UK Paris, 3 November 1948. Lovett based this information on American intelligence reports, ISA 73/4, Lovett–Epstein conversation, 10 November 1948.
49. BGA, Directorship meetings of the Jewish Agency, 1 February 1948, and Ben-Gurion diary, 8 September, 31 October 1948.

50. FO 371/68689, E13489, Cairo to FO, 18 October 1948; E13440, Amman to FO, 18 October 1948; and IDF, *Toldot*, p. 349.
51. ISA 173/4, Luria to Epstein, 3 November 1948 (Dr Ginsburg's conversation with Lovett, 11 November 1948, reported also in ISA 64/15); *FRUS 48*, Vol. 5, Part 2, Acting SoS to US UN Paris, 23 October 1948, p. 1508.
52. *FRUS 48*, Vol. 5, Part 2, Acting SoS to SoS, 23 October 1948, p. 1507.
53. W. Millis, *The Forrestal Diaries* (London, 1952), p. 327; and see H. Truman, *Memoirs*, Vol. 2 (New York, 1956), pp. 162–4.
54. *FRUS 48*, Vol. 5, Part 2, Acting SoS to SoS (Marshall was at the time in London), 30 October 1948, p. 1533; British policy towards Israel (November 1947–May 1949) in ISA 2412/26.
55. One was Suweidan Menshiye which was captured by 9 November 1948, and the other was Faluja where about 400 soldiers were stationed: FO 371/68690, E14089, Amman to FO, 30 October 1948.
56. FO 371/68690, E15378, Amman to FO, 29 November 1948. In order to prevent the Israelis from capturing the ammunition and equipment a Legion expert was sent to demolish them in case the place should fall into the hands of the Israelis. See also FO 371/68690, E14977, Amman to FO, 22 November 1948.
57. FO 371/68690, E15378, Amman to FO, 29 November 1948.
58. ISA 2425/7, Sharett report to the PGI, 4 November 1948.
59. FO 371/68390, E14041, FO Minute, Balfour, 2 November 1948.
60. FO 371/68390, E13440, Amman to FO, 18 October 1948; E15089, Burrows to UK UN NY, 25 November 1948; E15294, Jerusalem to FO, 29 November 1948.
61. CAB 129/31, Part I, CP (49), 15 January 1949, Historical memo; the Israelis had also launched a further attack on Southern Lebanon, reaching the Litani river. See also in IDF, *Toldot*, pp. 345–7.
62. A. Bullock, *Ernest Bevin, Foreign Secretary, 1945–1951* (London: Heinemann, 1983), p. 649; *FRUS 48*, ASoS to US/UN (Paris), 26 December 1948, p. 1691.
63. *FRUS 49*, McDonald to SoS, 5 January 1949, p. 614.
64. FO 371/75045, E167, FO Minute, Burrows, January 1949; CAB 128/15, CAB 3 (49), 17 January 1949.
65. FO 371/75045, E167, FO Minute, Burrows, January 1949; CAB 128/15, CAB 3 (49), 17 January 1949; *FRUS 48*, Lovett–Sir Oliver Franks conversation, 30 December 1948, pp. 1701–2.
66. ISA 36/12, McDonald's note, 31 December 1948.
67. *FRUS 48*, ASoS to McDonald, 31 December 1948, p. 1690.
68. ISA 36/12, Ministry of Foreign Affairs to US Government, 3 January 1949; FO 371/75045, E367, brief for SoS for Defence Committee, 13 January 1949, E733, FO to UN NY, 12 January 1949; CAB 21/1922 DO (49) I, 3 January 1949; and FO to Amman, 30 December 1948.
69. FO 371/75334, E360, MELF to War Office, 14 January 1949; Ben-Gurion, *War Diary*, 30 December 1948; and ISA 38/12, IDF Spokesman, 4 January 1949.
70. Kimche, *Both Sides*, p. 261; M. Bar-Zohar, *Ben-Gurion* (Tel Aviv, 1977), p. 858; H. Wilson, *Chariots of Israel* (London: Weidenfeld &

Nicolson, 1981), p. 232; Zasloff, 'Great Britain', p. 164; Ben-Gurion, *Medinat Israel Ha-Mechudeshet* (The Restored State of Israel) (Tel Aviv: Devir, 1969), p. 336.

71. Wilson, *Chariots of Israel*, p. 232 and accepted by Bar-Zohar, *Ben-Gurion*, p. 858.
72. ISA 36/12, Ministry of Foreign Affairs to US Government, 3 January 1949.
73. FO 816/142, Campbell to Kirkbride, 31 December 1948.
74. FO 141/1246, BMEO to FO, 30 December 1948.
75. FO 816/142, BMEO to Amman, 31 December 1948; Beirut to Amman, 2 January 1949, and FO 371/75334, E454, Campbell to FO, 10 January 1949.
76. FO 371/75334, E156, Troutbeck to Bevin, 4 January 1949; FO 371/75336, E1273, FO Minute, Sir Orme Sargent, 17 January 1949. Israeli sources: IDF, *Toldot*, pp. 349–55; Ben-Gurion, *Ha-Mechudeshet*, p. 335 and *War Diary*, editorial note in p. 815.
77. Ben-Gurion, *War Diary*, 31 December 1948, pp. 914–15 and Bar Zohar, *Ben-Gurion*, pp. 859–60.
78. Bullock, *Bevin*, p. 650.
79. FO 371/75041, E1967, FO Minute, 3 February 1949; CAB 128/15, CAB 3 (49), 17 January 1949.
80. FO 371/75380, E362, Middle East HQ to Air Ministry, 2 January 1949. In Rhodes the Israelis were told by the Egyptians that the flight was taken contrary to their wishes: *Israeli Documents*, Vol. 3, doc. 99, meeting of the delegations, 5 February 1949. See also *FRUS 48*, ASoS to US UN Paris (reporting a telegram from the British Embassy in Cairo to FO), p. 1689.
81. FO 371/75339, E154, Attlee to Bevin, 30 December 1948; E297, Alexander to Attlee, 1 January 1949.
82. Ibid.; and see also CAB 128/1, CAB 3 (49), 17 January 1949; and CAB 21/1922, DO (49) I, 3 January 1949.
83. FO 371/75334, E338, FO to Washington, 11 January 1949: this was a correct assumption.
84. E. Monroe, 'Mr. Bevin's Arab Policy', St Antony's Papers No 11 (London, 1961), p. 44, and Bullock, *Bevin*, p. 650.
85. FO 371/75339, E154, FO Minute, 31 December 1948; Bevin to Attlee, 28 December 1948, found by Lord Bullock in *Bevin*, p. 650.
86. CAB 128/1, CAB 3 (49), 17 January 1949. Israeli sources: Ben-Gurion, *War Diary*, 7 January 1949, p. 934; IDF, *Toldot*, p. 362; E. Weizmann, *Lecha Shamaim, Lecha Aretz* (Thou Own the Sky, Thou Own the Land) (Tel Aviv, 1975), pp. 69–73.
87. *FRUS 49*, McDonald to SoS, 9 January 1949, p. 633; and H. Sacher, *Europe*, interview with David Niles, 21 January 1949, on p. 527 reporting a conversation between Sir Oliver Franks and Truman on 13 January 1949.
88. FO 371/75334, E615, Washington to FO, 13 January 1949.
89. FO 371/75334, E614, Washington to FO, 13 January 1949.
90. Ibid.

91. *FRUS 49*, O. Franks–Lovett conversation, 13 January 1949, pp. 658–60, and Lovett to Douglas, 13 January 1949, p. 660.
92. FO 371/75334, E615, FO to Washington, 17 January 1949.
93. BGA, Ben-Gurion Diary, 9 January 1949.
94. Interview with M. Comay, 11 October 1982; and see A. Eban, *An Autobiography* (London: Weidenfeld & Nicolson, 1978), p. 137.
95. FO 371/68699, E15189, Bevin discussing the implication of *de jure* recognition on the privileges enjoyed by Britain during the Mandate. See also CAB 128/13 CM (48) 78, December 1948.
96. *FRUS 48*, conversation on Palestine, Bevin with army officers, in Douglas to SoS, 22 December 1948, p. 1683, and FO 371/75367, E999, BMEO (CiC opinion) to FO, 14 January 1949.
97. FO 371/75368, E1373, FO Minute, 17 January 1949.
98. *Spectator*, 'Whitehall, Washington and Palestine', 14 January 1949, pp. 88–90; *New Statesman and Nation*, 'British threat to peace'; *Economist*, 'Storm in the desert', 15 January 1949; and *Observer*, 15 January 1949.
99. CAB 129/31, Part I, CP (49) 10, 15 January 1949. Sharett supported the British offer: see Ben-Gurion, *War Diary*, 24 December 1948, p. 899. In fact, Bevin had already suggested it in June 1948, FO 371/68666, E6090, Burrows, 16 June 1948.
100. FO 371/75368, E1259, FO Minute, 24 January 1949.
101. CAB 128/13, CM (49) 3, 17 January 1949.
102. Brief for the SoS in FO 371/75369, E1510, 25 January 1949.
103. CAB 128/13, CM (49) 3, 17 January 1949.
104. Ibid.
105. Bullock, *Bevin*, p. 651; FO 371/75337, E1392, Franks to Bevin, January 1949 and FO 371/75334, E614, Washington to FO, 13 January 1949.
106. CAB 128/15, CAB 3 (49), 17 January 1949; and *Hansard*, Col. 934–45.
107. Bullock, *Bevin*, p. 651; and FO 371/75334, E614, Washington to FO, 13 January 1949.
108. Report by Bromley in the British Embassy in Washington to McLintock, in *FRUS 49*, 13 January 1949, p. 653. The debate itself is in *Hansard*, Vol. 460, 26 January 1949, col. 933–5, 943–5.
109. ISA 37/12, IFO Minute, undated.
110. Helm's interview with Bullock in Bullock, *Bevin*, p. 653, fn. 1.
111. At the end of October, Israeli forces attacked positions held by the ALA in Galilee. By that operation the Israelis completed the occupation of Galilee. The ALA was driven across the frontier into Lebanon: FO 371/68690, E13974, Beirut to FO, 29 October 1948.

5 The Creation of the Greater Transjordan

1. The term is first used towards the second half of 1949 by the Foreign Office and by the Jordanians.
2. H. A. Hassouna, *The League of Arab States and Regional Disputes: A Study of Middle East Conflicts* (New York: Oceana, 1975), p. 35.
3. FO 371/68365, E548, Amman to FO, 11 January 1948; *As-Shaa'b*, 7 January 1948, and *Chaiers de L'Orient Contemporain*, 13, p. 21, quoted

230

in W. Goldner, 'The Role of Abdullah Ibn Hussein in Arab Politics, 1941–1951' (D.Phil. submitted to Stanford University, 1954), p. 287.

4. *Ad-Difaa'*, 17 January 1948, and ISA 170/8, Military Intelligence Report to the Jewish Agency, March 1948.

5. K. Qasmiya, *Mudhokarat Fawzi Al-Qawqji, 1936–1948* (Fawzi Al-Qawqji's Memoirs) (PLO Publications, 1975), pp. 129–32 and ISA 170/8, Military Intelligence Report, March 1948.

6. They were not the national committees established in 1936–9 in the wake of the Arab revolt in most of the Arab towns and villages. There were new committees concerned mainly with defence matters which gradually replaced the old national committees; see A. Kayali, *Palestine: A Modern History* (London, 1979), pp. 189–92; and R. Gabbay, *A Political Study of the Arab–Jewish Conflict; The Arab Refugee Problem* (Geneva: Librairie Droz, 1959), p. 22.

7. Muhamad Al-Jaabri in Hebron and Rashid As-Shawa in Gaza, according to A. At-Tal, *Karithat Filastin* (The Palestine Disaster) (Cairo, 1959), pp. 31–2; Y. Nevo, *Abdullah ve-Ariviyei Eretz Israel* (Abdullah and the Arab Palestinians) (Tel Aviv, 1975), pp. 71–3 and J. B. Glubb, *A Soldier with the Arabs* (London, 1957), p. 66.

8. E. Wright, 'Abdullah's Jordan, 1947–1951', *MEJ*, 5 (1951), pp. 439–60 and FO 816/120, Kirkbride to Bevin, 18 May 1958.

9. FO 371/68373, E6493, Amman to FO, 18 May 1948; FO 371/68506, Amman to FO, 19 May 1948; H. Badri, *Al-Harb fi Ard As-Salam* (The War in the Land of Peace) (Beirut, 1975), p. 169.

10. Qasmiya, *Al-Qawqji*, p. 201; FO 816/120, Kirkbride to Bevin, 19 and 20 May 1948; FO 371/68641, E7589, Jerusalem to FO, 25 May 1948.

11. A. M. Al-Husseini, *Khaqaiq a'n Filastin* (The Truth about Palestine) (Cairo, 1957), p. 94; FO 371/68641, E7589, Jerusalem to FO, 25 May 1948.

12. FO 371/68374, E7209, Amman to FO, 30 May 1948.

13. Ibid.

14. FO 816/142, Bevin to Amman, 18 December 1948; FO 371/68374, E7209, Amman to FO, 30 May 1948. The quote is from S. Persson, *Mediation and Assassination: Count Bernadotte's Mission to Palestine, 1948* (London: Ithaca Press, 1979), p. 192, quoting *Till Jerusalem* (Suanstrom manuscript), p. 172.

15. FO 371/68861, E11809, Wright to Kirkbride, 19 September 1948.

16. FO 371/68375, E9618, Bevin to Kirkbride, 7 July 1948.

17. At-Tal, *Karithat*, p. 342; A. Dearden, *Jordan* (London: Robert Hale, 1958), p. 75.

18. FO 371/68641, E9552, Cairo to FO, 12 July 1948.

19. Hassouna, *Arab League*, p. 34: this writer based his information on the minutes of the 12th ordinary session of the League's Council (March 1950) when these resolutions were confirmed.

20. Ibid.

21. FO 371/68822, E10325, Amman to FO, 25 July 1948. The Political Committee consisted of the premiers and foreign ministers of the Arab states; W. Ad-Daly, *Asrar Al-Jamiaa Al-Arabiya Wa-Abd Al-Rahman*

Azzam (The Secrets of the Arab League and Abd Al-Rahman Azzam) (Cairo: Ruz Al-Yusuf, 1982), p. 233.

22. FO 371/68222, E10325, Amman to FO, 25 July 1948; and Nevo, *Abdullah*, p. 99.
23. FO 371/68376, E12392, Beirut to FO, 20 September 1948.
24. FO 371/68641, E12527, BMEO to FO, 24 September 1948.
25. FO 371/68861, E12277, Cairo to FO, 20 September 1948.
26. *New York Times*, 29 September 1948; Goldner, 'Abdullah', p. 292; *Al-Ahram*, 26 September 1948; and FO 816/142, Bevin to Amman, 18 December 1948.
27. FO 371/68376, E12392, Beirut to FO, 20 September 1948; Sir Alec Kirkbride, *From the Wings: Amman Memoirs 1947—1951* (London, Cass, 1976), pp. 57–8; Glubb, *A Soldier*, pp. 190, 192; and FO 816/142, Bevin to Kirkbride, 18 December 1948.
28. H. H. Abidi, *Jordan: A Political Study, 1948–1957* (London, 1965), pp. 52–53; A. Plascov, *The Palestinian Refugees in Jordan, 1948–57* (London, 1981), p. 7; Badri, *Harb*, p. 304.
29. Goldner, 'Abdullah', p. 292, quoting *Cahieres*, 16, p. 219; and Radio Ramallah, 21 September 1948, quoted in Nevo, *Abdullah*, p. 99.
30. At-Tal, *Karithat*, p. 343.
31. I. Abdullah, King of Jordan, *My Memoirs Completed* (London: Longman, 1978), pp. 12, 24.
32. FO 371/68376, E12392, Beirut to FO, 20 September 1948; *The Times*, 17 November 1948; Kirkbride, *From the Wings*, p. 58. The Copts represented Arabism and Christianity.
33. FO 816/129, Kirkbride to Bevin, 29 May 1948.
34 FO 816/130, Kirkbride to Bevin, 4 October 1948.
35. FO 816/130, Kirkbride to Bevin, 12 October 1948.
36. FO 371/68641, E12526, Jedda to FO, 26 September 1948 and FO 371/68861, E11809, Wright to Cairo, 19 September 1948. That is, implementing fully the Zionist aim of creating a Jewish state throughout Mandatory Palestine. The programme was accepted by the American Zionist Organisation in November 1942 after it had been presented to them by Ben-Gurion. This offer by Ben-Gurion made in the Biltmore Hotel in New York became the offical Zionist policy until the Jewish Agency accepted the partition plan in November 1947. See G. Lenczowski, *The Middle East in World Affairs* (Ithaca, New York: Cornell, 1980), p. 399.
37. *FRUS 48*, London to Washington, 29 September 1948.
38. Plascov, *Refugees*, p. 8; Goldner, 'Abdullah', p. 291; Kirkbride, *From the Wings*, p. 57; Glubb, *A Soldier*, p. 190; and in Al-Husseini, *Filastin*, p. 87.
39. Hilmi was the first military governor of Jerusalem and was replaced by At-Tal; Goldner, 'Abdullah', p. 291; Plascov, *Refugees*, pp. 7–9; and Nevo, *Abdullah*, p. 100.
40. Sheikh Husam Ad-Din Jarallah.
41. FO 816/130, Kirkbride to Bevin, 4 October 1948. After the government withdrew to Cairo, it became a department in the Arab League in 1952.

42. Plascov, *Refugees*, pp. 8–9; Nevo, *Abdullah*, p. 101; Badri, *Harb*, p. 306.
43. FO 371/68382, E12098, Amman to FO, 15 September 1948; FO 371/68641, E12502, FO to Amman, 28 September 1948.
44. *FRUS 48*, Vol. 5, Part 2, US Embassy in London to SoS, 7 October 1948, p. 1463.
45. FO 816/130, Kirkbride to Bevin, 2 October 1948; FO 816/129, Bevin to Kirkbride, 28 September 1948.
46. FO 816/129, Glubb memo in Kirkbride to Bevin, 30 September 1948.
47. FO 816/130, Kirkbride to Burrows, 6 October 1948.
48. FO 816/131, Kirkbride to Bevin, 19 October 1948.
49. FO 816/133, Kirkbride to Bevin, 13 November 1948.
50. FO 816/134, Kirkbride to Bevin, 6 December 1948.
51. Only 75 representatives attended the meeting in Gaza. Allegations about forced attendance can be found in Plascov, *Refugees*, an interview with Nimr Hawari, p. 11. The quotation is also taken from this source; however, unfortunately this observation is not based on any reference.
52. *Al-Ahram*, 2 October 1948.
53. Nevo, *Abdullah*, p. 109.
54. Abidi, *Jordan*, p. 53.
55. FO 816/134, Kirkbride to Bevin, 6 December 1948.
56. Ben-Gurion, *Medinat Israel Ha-Mechudeshet* (The Restored State of Israel) (Tel Aviv: Devir, 1969), p. 288; BGA, Diary, 8 September 1948.
57. ISA 2424/21, IFO memo, 27 July 1948.
58. ISA 63/4, Sharett to Shitrit, 18 August 1948; ISA 2444/19, Sharett's directive to the Israeli delegation in Lausanne, 25 July 1948.
59. Wright, *Abdullah's Jordan*, p. 446, fn. 99.
60. FO 141/1256, conversation between Chapman-Andrews and Nokrashi in Chapman-Andrews to Nokrashi, 11 October 1948.
61. Dearden, *Jordan*, p. 84; Kirkbride, *From the Wings*, p. 99.
62. Kirkbride, *From the Wings*, p. 66.
63. Plascov, *Refugees*, p. 12.
64. Abidi, *Jordan*, p. 53.
65. FO 816/142, Political Report – Palestine, 6 December 1948.
66. Ibid.; Nevo, *Abdullah*, p. 110.
67. At-Tal, *Karithat*, p. 375.
68. FO 816/142, Political Report.
69. This group was called the 'Munadilin'. Based in Ramallah, it succeeded in distributing leaflets in the Congress. FO 816/142, Political Report; Plascov, *Refugees*, p. 13.
70. At-Tal, *Karithat*, p. 376.
71. FO 816/142, Political Report.
72. The original draft was on the air, on Radio Ramallah, before the King had succeeded in preventing it. Hence the revised draft was broadcast by NER; Nevo, *Abdullah*, p. 113–14.
73. The original text in At-Tal, *Karithat*, p. 378; S. Musa and M. Al-Madhi, *Tarikh Al-Urdun Fi Al-Qarn Al-Ishinn* (The History of Jordan in the Twentieth Century) (Amman, 1959), p. 536 and Abidi, *Jordan*, pp. 54–5. The revised text in Nevo, *Abdullah*, p. 114 (dealt with also in Y. Nevo, 'Abdullah and the Arabs of Palestine', *Winer Library Bulletin*, 13, Nos

45/46 (1978), p. 60; and the detailed account in Plascov, *Refugees*, pp. 13–14.

74. FO 816/142, Kirkbride to Bevin, Political Report.
75. Ibid.
76. FO 371/75329, E2672, Dow to FO, 18 February 1949.
77. FO 816/142, Amman to FO, 13 December 1948. Yemen supported Abdullah since he had helped the Imman Ahmed after the assassination of his predecessor (Aden to Amman, 24 December 1948); the Iraqi stance: FO 141/1247, Baghdad to Amman (I/1642), 16 December 1948; FO 816/142, Baghdad to FO, 24 December 1948.
78. FO 816/142, Campbell to Kirkbride, 17 December 1948.
79. FO 816/134, Amman to FO, 14 December 1948; FO 816/142, Baghdad to Amman, 24 December 1948: a conversation between Mack and Abdullah.
80. FO 371/80398, Cairo to the Eastern Department, 17 March 1950: FO 816/142, Bevin to Kirkbride, 18 December 1948.
81. Ibid.
82. FO 371/75273, E407, Monthly Report, December 1948, 31 January 1949; FO 371/68832, E16137, CoS (48) 144, 20 December 1948; review of the size and shape of the Legion for 1949/1950.
83. FO 816/142, Amman to FO, 17 December 1948 – talk with Stabler and later (28 December 1948) with Bunche; *FRUS 48*, Stabler (Amman) to ASoS, 6 December 1948, p. 1648.
84. Plascov, *Refugees*, p. 28.
85. FO 371/75273, E407, Monthly Report, December 1948.
86. FO 816/142, Kirkbride to Bevin, 28 December 1948.
87. FO 816/142, Amman to FO, 17 December 1948. Farouk's adviser was Karim Thabet in FO 816/142, Campbell to Kirkbride, 17 December 1948.
88. FO 816/142, Bevin to Kirkbride, 15 December 1948; FO 816/134, Kirkbride to Burrows, 15 December 1948.
89. FO 371/75273, E407, Monthly Report, December 1948.
90. Ibid.; *New York Times*, 12 and 14 December 1948.
91. FO 371/75064, E3763, Dow to Wright, 15 March 1948.
92. FO 816/142, Troutbeck to Kirkbride, 22 December 1948; FO 371/75064, E3763, Dow to Wright, 15 March 1948.
93. FO 371/75064, FO Minute, Walker, 20 March 1949.
94. FO 816/142, Baghdad to Amman, 13 December 1948; Bevin to Kirkbride, 1 January 1949.
95. FO 816/142, Bevin to Kirkbride, 23 December 1948; Cairo to Amman, 20 December 1948.
96. FO 816/142, Campbell to Kirkbride, 22 December 1948; Cairo to Amman, 16 December 1948.
97. FO 816/142, Campbell to Kirkbride, 17 December 1948.
98. FO 371/68698, E13559, Jerusalem (Military Intelligence Officer) to FO (Department of Military Intelligence), 20 October 1948; FO 371/75332, E4626, Cairo to FO, 6 April 1949.
99. Ad-Daly, *Azzam*, pp. 399–423, a chapter entitled 'Negotiations with the Devil'.

100. Ibid.
101. *FRUS 48*, Memo by SoS to President, 30 August 1948, p. 1359.
102. *FRUS 48*, Memo by Satterthwaite, 1 October 1948, p. 1445.
103. *FRUS 48*, ASoS to US Embassy in London, 14 December 1948, p. 1669.
104. *FRUS 49*, Vol. 6, a meeting between Lovett and Samir Ar-Rifai, 12 January 1949, p. 648; *FRUS 48*, Jessup to Rusk, 1 June 1949, pp. 1081–2; SoS to Amman, 4 August 1948, p. 1284; Istanbul Conference (Agreed Conclusion) (26–9 November 1949), p. 171.
105. FO 371/75273, E4646, Monthly Report, March 1949, 4 April 1949; the decree was issued on 16 March 1949.
106. IDM, *Kovetz Mismachim Be-Toldot Ha-Medina* (A selection of documents of Israel's history), doc. 23.
107. FO 371/7386, E3848, Amman to FO, 24 March 1949; Kirkbride, *From the Wings*, p. 298, fn. 3; and W. Eytan, *Bein Israel La-Amim* (Between Israel and the Nations) (Tel Aviv, 1958), p. 41.
108. FO 371/75273, E5609, Monthly Report, April 1949, 2 May 1949.
109. This was reported by the American representative in Amman. A detailed analysis of both the Armistice and Shuneh agreements can be found in Chapter 8. The American source: *FRUS 49*, Vol. 6, Stabler to SoS, 8 April 1949, pp. 900–1.
110. The inhabitants of Wadi Fuq'in were driven out by the Israelis, as were 1200 villagers from Baqa Al-Gharbiya: FO 371/75279, E13468, Glubb memo to Kirkbride, 25 October 1949; FO 371/75329, E12432, Monthly Report from Jerusalem, September 1949. The circulation of rumours by the Israelis was done in order to prevent the return of some villagers to their villages: ISA 2431/6, Dayan to Ben-Gurion, 11 August 1949. Arab sources: H. Al-Majali, *Mudhakarti* (Memoirs) (Jerusalem, 1960), pp. 90–2.
111. FO 371/75278, E6817, Damascus to FO, 30 May 1949; the relevant paragraph was mentioned in a letter from Broadmead to the FO in FO 371/75278, E6817.
112. For instance, the various chambers of commerce formed a new legal Palestinian chamber of commerce. The paper *Filastin* which had appeared during the Mandate in Jaffa reappeared in February 1949, in Amman. FO 371/75273, E3399, Monthly Report February 1949, 2 March 1949.
113. They were Ruhi Al-Hadi (Foreign Affairs), Khulusi Al-Khairi (Trade and Agriculture) and Musa Nasir (Communication). In August Ragheb Nashashibi was added as Minister for the refugees: FO 371/75329, E12432, Jerusalem to FO, Monthly Report, September 1949; ISA 2431/6, Biran to IFO, 2 September 1949; Musa and Madi, *Urdun*, p. 538.
114. FO 371/75329, E12432, Jerusalem to FO, Monthly Report, September 1949; Musa Nasir was the founder of Bir Zeit College, so it was rather misleading of the Consul to conclude that he did nothing for the Palestinian cause.
115. FO 371/82703, E1013/1, Legation Report for December 1949, 2 January 1950.
116. FO 371/75273, E8261, Monthly Report, June 1949, 12 July 1949.

117. FO 371/75273, E4646, Monthly Report, March 1949, 4 April 1949; FO 371/75275, E5952, Damascus to FO, 27 April 1949.
118. FO 371/75275, E6034, Paris to FO, 12 May 1949; FO 371/75048, E8989, Amman to FO, 19 July 1948 and E9344, Jedda to FO, July 1949.
119. A letter from Hussein Saraj to Abdullah At-Tal, 26 February 1949, in At-Tal, *Karithat*, p. 542.
120. FO 371/75273, E8261, Report for June 1949, 12 July 1949; FO 371/75329, E13636, Monthly Report from Jerusalem, October 1949, 5 November 1949.
121. For instance, reduction on expenditure on health and education was expected to be of the order of 80 per cent, CAB 134/501 ME (0) (Working Paper) 6, 27 May 1949.
122. Ibid.
123. Ibid., Middle East Official Committee, 21 March 1949.
124. British annual assistance was £2 million and £3 million for 1949/50; the sum brought by refugees was £2 million: CAB 134/501, ME (0) (WP) 6, 27 May 1949. The ESM shared this estimation; see ESM report (Final), Appendix 2, p. 8.
125. FO 371/75273, E8261, Report for June, 12 July 1949; FO 371/81904, E1018/5, Glubb to FO, 20 April 1950.
126. FO 371/75329, E15042, Summary for Arab Palestine, November 1949. The Liberal Party merged with the Jordanian Nahda Party and adopted the Greater Syria plan.
127. FO 371/75329, E13636, Summary for Arab Palestine, October 1949, 5 November 1949.
128. Khulsi Al-Khairi and Musa Nasir. The *de facto* annexation was completed in March 1949. In April 1950 elections for a new Parliament and Government were held and they were followed by the formal declaration of the union.
129. FO 371/82704, ET 1081/61, Kirkbride to Furlonge, 28 April 1950.
130. FO 816/154, the situation in Jordan by Glubb, 15 October 1949.
131. FO 371/75206, E9789, FO Minute, Sherringham, 5 August 1949. Denouncing the plan meant giving up the West Bank. See also FO 371/75072, E9043, ME Conference, 21 July 1949.
132. *FRUS 49*, Vol. 6, ASoS to SoS, 12 June 1949, p. 1126.
133. ISA 36/12, Helm–Sharett conversation, 30 December 1949; ISA 38/8, note on extension of Anglo-Transjordan treaty to Western Palestine, 2 February 1950.
134. FO 371/75273, E10169, Monthly Report, July 1949; FO 371/82703, E1013/1, Legation Report for December 1949.
135. FO 371/75273, E11283, Monthly Report for August 1949.
136. FO 371/75279, E12317, Amman to FO (Tawfiq Al-Huda to Bevin), 10 October 1949.
137. FO 371/75279, E12317, Kirkbride to Bevin, 10 October 1949.
138. FO 371/75279, E12317, Bevin to Tawfiq Abu Al-Huda, 18 October 1949.
139. FO 371/82176, E1013/1, summary of events in Arab Palestine, December 1949; Musa and Madi, *Urdun*, pp. 532, 538.

140. FO 371/82176, E1013/1, summary of events in Arab Palestine, December 1949.
141. FO 371/75273, E13975, Monthly Report, October 1949. It was decided to assign only one-third of the import allocations to the Palestinian merchants: FO 371/82703, E1013/1, Legation Report for December 1949, 2 January 1950. See also FO 371/82176, E1013/1, summary of events in Arab Palestine, December 1949.
142. FO 371/82719, ET 1081/62, British ambassador in Ankara to FR, 3 May 1950.
143. The two ministers were Al-Khairi and Nasir: FO 371/82719, ET1081/16, Kirkbride to Furlonge, 28 April 1950, and FO 371/82703, E1013/1, Legation Report, December 1949.
144. FO 371/81908, bi-partite discussions, May 1950; A. Bullock, *Ernest Bevin, Foreign Secretary, 1945–1957* (London: Heinemann, 1983), p. 776; H. L. Roberts and P. A. Wilson, *Britain and the US: Problems in Cooperation* (Oxford: RIIA, 1953), p. 183.
145. Hassouna, *Arab League*, pp. 34–6; FO 371/82703, Legation Report, March 1950.
146. Hassouna, *Arab League*, 7th meeting of League's Council, 12 June 1950, p. 36.
147. *Le Progrès Egyptien* published Ahmad At-Tal's allegation of maltreatment of Palestinians in the West Bank (7 April 1950). *Al-Assas* (Cairo) reported that the Ulema of Al-Azhar demanded that the Arab League investigate At-Tal's allegations. *Al-Mukathem* (11 April 1950) published the story of Mohamad Fahmy Hashem (the Jordanian minister in Jedda) claiming that Abdullah wanted to invade Saudi Arabia and annex the Hejaz.
148. FO 371/82719, ET1081/59, Mack to Younger, 28 April 1950.
149. Hassouna, *Arab League*, p. 40; FO 371/82713, ET10398/2, Amman to FO, 27 May 1950.
150. FO 371/82719, E1081/57, BMEO to FO, 6 May 1950.
151. FO 371/82703, E1013/4, Legation Report for March 1950; FO 371/82704, E1016/4, HQ Arab Legion, 8 August 1950.
152. FO 371/82716, E1053/2, Kirkbride to Furlonge, 30 November 1950.
153. Ibid.
154. Ibid., Furlonge to Kirkbride, 23 November 1950.
155. FO 371/82706, ET1017/2, Kirkbride to Bevin, 2 August 1950.
156. FO 371/91788, E1011/1, Annual Report Jordan 1950.
157. Ibid.
158. Ibid.
159. FO 371/91796, E10389/1, Kirkbride to FO, 17 May 1951; E10389/2, Damascus to FO, 19 May 1951.
160. This fear of a Communist stronghold as part of a Russian grand design was common throughout the 1950s. See, for instance, W. Laquer, 'The Appeal of Communism in the Middle East', *MEJ* (Winter 1955).

6 British and United Nations' Conciliation Efforts

1. J. B. Schechtman, *The Arab Refugee Problem* (New York: Philosophical

Library, 1952), p. 21; *FRUS 49*, Vol. 6, Burdet (Amman) to SoS, 2 March 1949, p. 786.

2. ISA 2441/1, Sasson to Eytan, 9 March 1948. Sasson offered Geneva as the venue for a peace conference under the auspices of the PCC with the methods of Rhodes; then Ben-Gurion suggested Lausanne, meeting PCC with Ben-Gurion, 7 April 1948.

3. *FRUS 49*, Vol. 6, editorial note, p. 895, second progress report of PCC, 5–9 April 1949.

4. FO 371/82506, E1015/9, Annual Report 1949, Israel.

5. *FRUS 49*, Vol. 6, McGhee to SoS, 13 July 1949, p. 1219; Telegram Rockwell to SoS, 11 August 1949.

6. FO 371/75439, E12371, FO Minute, 12 September 1949; *FRUS 49*, SoS to US Embassy in London, 13 July 1949, p. 1223; and Porter to SoS, 5 August 1949, p. 1286. See also there Circular Telegram, SoS to Diplomatic offices, 16 August 1949, p. 1317.

7. *Yediot Achronot*, Sasson letters (March 1972), Sasson to Sharett, 14 August 1949 (most of the letters in this article can be found in ISA 2444/11).

8. ISA 2402/9, Report on the PCC by the IFO, 1951 (no specific date is given).

9. For information on the PCC's activities in 1950–2 see R. Gabbay, *A Political Study of the Arab–Jewish Conflict: The Arab Refugee Problem* (Geneva: Librairie Droz, 1959), pp. 314, 342, 449, 521–2.

10. *FRUS 49*, Ethridge to SoS, 12 May 1949, p. 988.

11. FO 371/82719, E1011/73, Helm to Furlonge, 8 December 1950.

12. D. Kaplan, *The Arab Refugees: An Abnormal Problem* (Jerusalem: Rubin Mass, 1959), p. 159.

13. The Israelis financed the Palestinian delegations which came from Ramallah in order to negotiate directly with the Israelis. However, the Jordanians resented this move and closed the offices of that delegation. Interview with Aziz Shadeh: FO 371/75329, E12442, Jerusalem to FO, September 1949.

14. ISA 2444/1, Sasson to Eytan, 3 September 1949.

15. FO 371/81911/1, FO Minute, Furlonge, 5 June 1950; Ben-Gurion, *War Diary*, 2 January 1949, p. 921.

16. Ibid.

17. ISA 2444/19, briefing by Sharett to the Israeli delegation in Lausanne, 25 July 1949; ISA 2444/1, Eban to Sharett, 30 April 1949. This is also mentioned in S. Hadawi, *Bitter Harvest* (New York, 1967), p. 165, and in A. Eban, *My Country* (London: Weidenfeld & Nicolson, 1972), p. 67.

18. *FRUS 49*, Ethridge to SoS, 9 April and 8 June 1949, p. 1096; Israeli sources: Ben-Gurion, War Diary, 16 June 1949, p. 922 and N. Lorch, *Korot Milchemet Ha-'Atzmaut* (The Independence War) (Ramat Gan, 1963), pp. 536–8.

19. Ben-Gurion, *War Diary*, 14 July 1949.

20. I. Pappé, 'Moshe Sharett, David Ben-Gurion and the "Palestinian Option", 1948–1956', *Zionism*, Vol. 7, No. 1, pp. 77–97.

21. *Yediot Achronot*, Sasson to Sharett, 1 August 1949.

22. CAB 129/1, Part 1, CP (49), 15 January 1949, Bevin on Palestine; FO 371/75334, E358, Bevin to Sir Oliver Franks (Washington), 11 January 1949.
23. The US, French and Belgian Consuls were members of the Council which supervised the truce in Palestine; *FRUS 48*, Vol. 5, Part 2, memo of conversation, Bevin–Marshall, 4 October 1948, p. 1450; FO 371/75346, E203, Dow to FO, 5 January 1949.
24. FO 371/75346, E32, Ankara to FO, 22 December 1948; Bullock, *Ernest Bevin, Foreign Secretary, 1945–1951* (London: Heinemann, 1983), pp. 643, 645.
25. FO 371/75346, E157, Washington to FO, 4 January 1949; see also E166 and E676.
26. Leader in *The Times*, 21 January 1949.
27. FO 371/81922, E10213, FO Minute by Wright, 22 September 1950: contrary to the American point of view which saw the GA as the best forum for solving the conflict.
28. CAB 129/31, Part 1, CP (49) 10, 15 January 1949.
29. FO 371/75351, E9, Ankara to FO, 11 May 1949; FO 371/75436, E582, FO to Ankara, 11 January 1949; FO 371/75354, E10201, Ankara to FO, 11 August 1949.
30. FO 371/75353, E12800, FO memo, 'The Palestinian Question', Sherringham, 14 October 1949.
31. FO 371/75067, E13727, FO Minute, November 1949.

7 British Policy towards the Refugee Problem

1. Bevin in the House of Commons, 26 January 1949 (Col. 931).
2. FO 371/82182, E1017/9, FO Minute, Thirkell, May 1950; ISA 36/15, Monitoring Service, 3 April 1948.
3. G. Kirk, *Survey of International Affairs: The Middle East 1945–50* (London: RIIA, 1954), p. 316.
4. *The Times*, 9 August 1949.
5. FO 371/75272, E768, Transjordan Annual Review, 1948; FO 371/68366, E1906, UK delegation UN to FO, 9 February 1948.
6. FO 371/75273, E407, Monthly Report, December 1948.
7. FO 371/68822, E11409, 'The Transjordan Situation', Glubb, 12 August 1948.
8. S. G. Thicknesse, *Arab Refugees, A Survey of Resettlement Possibilities* (RIIA, October 1949), p. 7: the group of rich refugees constituted 1 per cent of the total figure. Other statistics were provided by Gower of the American Red Cross, Sir Raphael Cliento (UN refugee expert) and UNICEF in ibid., p. 10.
9. FO 371/75332, E4510, Beith FO Minute, 31 March 1949.
10. A. Plascov, *Refugees in Jordan, 1948–1957* (London, 1981), pp. 34–5, and fn. 17 on p. 34, interview with Kirkbride.
11. ISA 2444/19, IFO Report, February 1949.
12. FO 371/82702, E1011/1, Annual Report for Jordan, 1949.
13. Thicknesse, *Refugees*, p. 8, fn. 4, p. 9, fn. 1.
14. FO 371/68371, E5684, Damascus to FO, 3 May 1948.

15. S. Persson, *Mediation and Assassination: Count Bernadotte's Mission to Palestine, 1948* (London: Ithaca Press, 1979), pp. 287, 308. In his first proposals the Count, for what Persson calls 'unknown reasons', inserted at the last moment a clause calling for the recognition of the right of the 'residents of Palestine' to return. In his second proposals he defined the right of 'Arab refugees' to return. In June, when the Count was not convinced of the Arab position, some AHC officials indicated to him that repatriation meant tacit recognition of Israel (letter from E. N. Koussa to Bernadotte, UN Archives, in ibid., p. 183, fn. 6).
16. UN Resolution, 194 (3), 11 December 1948.
17. Bernadotte suggested that Israel would facilitate a mass repatriation during the second truce or at least the return of the Haifa and Jaffa refugees. But Israel refused on security grounds: ISA 2427/9, reply of the PGI to CB, 1 August 1948; Comay to Sharett, 23 September 1948. Burrows' view in FO 371/68379, E1211, FO Minute, Burrows, 8 September 1948.
18. *Ha'aretz*, 3 May 1949.
19. Note from PCC Secretariat on the Israeli paper on refugees, 28 March 1949 in ISA 38/11; see also ISA 2444/19, IFO memo, 1 July 1949.
20. CAB 134/501, meeting McGhee–Wright, ME (0) 10, 13 April 1949.
21. ISA 38/11.
22. FO 371/82179, E1015/80, a meeting between the FO and the PCC, 18 July 1950.
23. This theme will be developed in the following pages.
24. FO 371/75436, E10285, FO Memo, 16 August 1949; FO 371/75454, E3302, Troutbeck to Bevin, 9 March 1949.
25. *The Times*, 7 July 1949.
26. ISA 36/10, Beith–Bentwich conversation, 4 July 1949.
27. FO 371/75067, E8752, W. Strang tour to the ME, 4 July 1949.
28. FO 371/75072, E9043, FO ME conference, 21 July 1949.
29. FO 371/75072, E9044, FO ME conference, 22 July 1949; CAB 134/501, ME (0) (49), 13 April 1949.
30. FO 371/75072, E9044, FO ME conference, 22 July 1949.
31. *FRUS 49*, Vol. 6, Telegram Keley to SoS, 14 July 1949, p. 1226.
32. FO 371/75072, E9044, FO ME conference, 22 July 1949.
33. Thicknesse, *Refugees*, p. 51.
34. FO 371/75438, E11150, FO to Baghdad, 15 September 1949 and 75051, E8512, FO Minute, Wright, 7 July 1949. The Iraqi Parliament consisted of rich landowners who objected to a land reform which resettlement would have necessitated. See M. Ionides, *Divide and Lose: The Arab Revolt, 1955–1958* (London, 1960), pp. 119–23.
35. FO 371/75136, E8537, brief for SoS talk with the Iraqi ambassador, 11 July 1949; CAB 134/501, ME900 (49) 10, meeting McGhee–Wright, 13 April 1949.
36. FO 371/75438, E11150, FO to Baghdad, 15 September 1949.
37. Ibid.
38. FO 371/75446, E13568, Baghdad to FO (Middle East Secretariat), 28 October 1949.
39. Ibid.

40. Thicknesse, *Refugees*, pp. 34–6.
41. FO 371/82706, ET1017/2, Kirkbride to Bevin, 2 August 1950; *FRUS 49*, Vol. 6, Telegram Stabler to SoS, 23 July 1949, p. 1247 and memo of conversation (Jones), 13 April 1949, p. 907.
42. *FRUS 49*, McGhee memo, 4 May 1949, pp. 984–7 and Bevin to American ASoS, 12 June 1949, p. 1123; CAB 134/501 (WP) (49) 6, 27 May 1949.
43. FO 371/75439, E11376, FO Minute, Morton, 16 September 1949.
44. ISA 2445/3, report on the possible settlement of refugees, undated.
45. FO 371/75333, E7648, 16 June 1949; ISA 2242/6, conversation of Young, Roosevelt and Eban, 22 June 1949 and ISA 2444/1, Eban–Ethridge meeting, 30 April 1949.
46. FO 371/75067, E13727, FO Minute, November 1949.
47. *FRUS 49*, Ethridge to Rusk, 15 June 1949, p. 1137.
48. FO 371/75333, E7648, 16 June 1949.
49. *FRUS 49*, Vol. 6, memo talk Elath–McGhee, 25 July 1949, p. 1248; FO 371/75438, E10383, BMEO to FO(MES), 31 August 1949. For the Egyptian position see *Al-Misri*, 24 April 1949 and FO 371/73460, J6065, WA, 21 July 1949.
50. FO 371/75071, E8512, FO Minute, Wright, 7 July 1949. This issue was raised in the Foreign Office's ME conference in London: see FO 371/75072, E9044, FO ME conference, 22 July 1949.
51. FO 371/75333, E7648, FO Minute, 16 June 1949.
52. FO 371/75072, E9044, FO ME conference, 22 July 1949.
53. FO 371/75332, E5533, Amman to FO, 20 April 1949.
54. *FRUS 49*, Vol. 6, telegram from US Embassy in UK to SD, 28 June 1949, p. 1180.
55. *FRUS 49*, SoS to US Embassy in UK, 30 June 1949, p. 1192; Cairo to SD, 7 July 1949, p. 1195.
56. FO 371/75067, E13727, FO Minute, November 1949; UN GA OR (4th session), *ad hoc* Committee, Annexe, Vol. 2, pp. 5–9.
57. *FRUS 49*, Vol. 6, Hildring to SoS, 25 July 1949, p. 1249.
58. ISA 2444/19, the Information Department, memo, 13 April 1949.
59. Ethridge influenced the State Department on this issue throughout 1949. See *FRUS 49*, Vol. 6, Ethridge to SoS, 12 June 1949, p. 1124; Porter to SoS, 28 July 1949; McGhee to SoS, 19 July 1949, p. 1237; Truman to Weizmann, 13 August 1949, p. 1300. The Israeli sources: ISA 36/10, Comay to Eliash, 29 April 1949.
60. D. Peretz, *Israel and the Palestine Arabs* (Washington, DC: The Middle East Institute, 1958), pp. 44–50 (*Ha'aretz, Hazofeh*); *Divrei Yemei Haknesset* (Knesset Diary), 1 August 1949, pp. 1195–6, 1216–36.
61. ISA 36/10, Comay to Eliash, 29 April 1949.
62. FO 371/75206, E9789, FO Minute, Sherringham, 5 August 1949; FO 371/75190, E9756, Tel Aviv to FO, 8 August 1949.
63. UN GA A3922, UNPC 4th progress report (9 June–15 September 1949); FO 371/75436, E10083, FO Minute, 16 August 1949.
64. *FRUS 49*, Vol. 6, memo by Rusk, 28 July 1949, p. 1262. On 15 May 1948 there were 655 000 Jews in Israel (Government of Israel, *Facts about Israel*, 1958).

65. *FRUS 49*, circular telegram SoS to Diplomatic Offices, 16 August 1949, p. 1317; Burdet to SoS, 16 August 1949, p. 1320.
66. FO 371/75436, E10083, FO to UK UN, 2 September 1949; FO 371/75437, E10474, W. Strang, FO Minute, 25 August 1949.
67. Hernes, *The Times*, 1 August 1949.
68. UN GA, Bunche Report (document A3689, 18 October 1949); E. Buehrig, *The UN and the Palestine Refugees* (London: Indiana University Press, 1971), p. 5.
69. *FRUS 49*, Vol. 6, memo to SoS (the decision was taken in March 1949), 4 August 1949, p. 1282; FO 371/75051, E8512, FO Minute, Wright, 7 July 1949; *The Times*, 30 August 1949.
70. It was Bernadotte's suggestion. The IRO replied that it had priorities (other refugee problems) and limited resources: Bernadotte's last report in ISA 2427/9, 16 September 1948.
71. FO 371/75072, E9044, FO ME conference, 22 July 1949.
72. Ibid.
73. FO 371/75051, E8512, FO Minute, Wright, 7 July 1949.
74. *FRUS 49*, Vol. 6, McGhee to SoS, 13 July 1949, p. 121.
75. FO 371/75436 (August 1949); 75437 (August 1949) and 75438 (September 1949).
76. FO 371/75046, E11420, McGhee before the Young Democratic Club, Chattanooga, Tennessee, 9 November 1949.
77. Ibid.
78. *FRUS 49*, Vol. 6, McGhee to SoS, 13 July 1949, p. 1219.
79. FO 816/153, and UN GA, doc. A/922, 4th progress report of ESM (9 June–15 September 1949).
80. This was supported by the Cabinet, CAB 134/501 (49) (0) 10, 13 April 1949.
81. CAB 134/501, FO to Washington, 13 April 1949.
82. FO 371/75471, E10651, FO Minute, Beith, 23 August 1949; interview with Sir John Beith.
83. CAB 134/501 (49) (0) 1, FO to Washington, 13 April 1949.
84. FO 371/75438, E11179, FO Minute, Thirkell, 16 September 1949; Washington to FO, 14 September 1949.
85. PCC (Palestine Conciliation Commission) final report of the UN ESM for the Middle East.
86. *Ha'aretz*, *Davar*, *Ha boker*, 26 August 1949; it was also approved by the Israeli government.
87. ISA 2444/1, Ethridge–Eban conversation, 30 April 1949; *The Times*, 30 August 1949; *New York Times*, 30 August 1949; FO 371/75441, E11922, Damascus to FO, 30 September 1949; FO 371/75442, Tel Aviv (Morton) to FO, 10 October 1949.
88. FO 371/75439, E11563, Washington to FO, 23 September 1949.
89. FO 371/75449, E14290, Beirut to FO, 26 December 1949.
90. FO 371/75439, E11297, FO (Strang) to Morton, 16 September 1949.
91. Ibid.
92. FO 371/75439, E11563, Washington to FO, 23 September 1949.
93. FO 371/75439, E11580, Beirut to FO, 23 September 1949.

94. FO 371/75440, E11830, FO Minute, Sherringham, 4 October 1949.
95. He added that Adam Smith's 'Economic Man' was not oriental: FO 371/75440, E11869, Dow to FO, 23 September1949.
96. FO 371/75441, E11917, Morton to FO, 1 October 1949; E11918, Morton to FO, 1 October 1949.
97. FO 371/75443, E12543, Morton to FO, 17 October 1949.
98. ISA 2444/1, resolution 302 (4) assistance to the Palestine refugees, 8 December 1949.
99. Ibid.
100. Ibid.
101. FO 371/75446, E13588, FO to Washington, 10 November 1949.
102. FO 371/75446, E13650, FO Minute, Burrows, 10 November 1949.
103. FO 371/75446, E13701, Troutbeck to FO, 12 November 1949.
104. *FRUS 49*, Vol. 6, Istanbul conference, 26–29 November 1949, agreed conclusions, p. 173.
105. Ibid.
106. FO 371/75055, E14210, Baghdad to FO, 11 November 1949; BGA, Diary, 26 October 1949.
107. FO 371/75056, E15031, FO Minute, 28 November 1949.
108. UN GA, Final Report of ESM, 28 December 1949, part 1, p. 2.
109. Buehrig, *The UN*, p. 34.
110. UN GA, Final Report of ESM, 28 December 1949, part I, p. 3.
111. Ibid., p. 12.
112. This was repeated from the interim report, UN GA, pp. 17–22.
113. FO 371/75329, E12423, Dow to FO, Palestine survey affairs September 1949.
114. FO 371/75449, E14428, FO to Cairo, 2 December 1949.
115. The Treasury hoped that a new IRO would commit the UK to a lesser contribution: FO 371/75449, E14332, FO to Beirut (Morton), 29 November 1949; FO 371/75448, E14139, FO Minute, 23 November 1949.
116. FO 371/75449, E14244, FO to New York, 5 December 1949. The Iraqis suggested Sir Edward Spears as a candidate in FO 371/75450, E14676, UN to FO, 7 December 1949.
117. FO 371/75449, E14459, FO to Beirut (Morton), 3 December 1949.
118. ESM final report.
119. FO 371/75447, E14033, Burrows to Wright, 23 November 1949; FO 371/75448, E14155, Wright to FO, 24 November 1949; FO 371/75452, E15406, FO Minute, 29 December 1949, and E15442, FO Minute, 8 December 1949.
120. The French were willing to give $3 million; see *FRUS 50*, Vol. 5, Geneva to SD, 18 April 1950, p. 860.
121. FO 371/82445, EE1825/39, FO Minute, 12 April 1950; SD asked for $13.5 million, otherwise Congress would not approve. Bevin pressed the Treasury for $9 million but the Chancellor agreed to only $7 million. See also *FRUS 50*, Vol. 5, editorial note, p. 921.
122. FO 371/82244, EE1825/62, Sir Henry Knight to Evans (MES), 10 March 1950.
123. FO 371/82445, EE1825/88, FO Minute, Evans, 14 March 1950.
124. Ibid.

125. FO 371/82719, E10110/60, Wright conversation with Aras (Turkish representative on PCC), 27 September 1950; FO 371/82719, E10110/64, Washington to FO, 11 January 1950.
126. FO 371/82247, E1825/141, Knight to Evans, 19 June 1950.
127. Israel was to receive $100 000; Syria $150 000; Iraq $200 000: see *FRUS 50*, ASoS to Diplomatic Offices, 12 September 1950, p. 280.
128. FO 371/91217, E11345/1, FO Minute, Evans, 17 January 1951.
129. CAB 134/501, FO to Washington, 15 April 1949; FO 371/75450, E14610, FO Minute, 3 December 1949.
130. FO 371/82195, E10010/2, Beith to UK, Geneva, 1 February 1950.
131. Press release PAL/COMM/18, 30 January 1950. Information Centre Geneva, UN Europe Office quoted in FO 371/82195, E10010/2, Beith to UK, Geneva, 1 February 1950.
132. FO 371/82178, E1015/23, FO Minute, 2 March 1950; FO 371/82196, E10110, Dow to FO, 20 July 1950.
133. FO 371/82196, E10110/40, FO Minute, Oliver, 17 August 1950; *FRUS 50*, Vol. 5, SoS to US representative in PCC, Geneva, 7 February 1950, p. 728.
134. FO 371/82199, E1821/3; E1821/7; E1821/8, January–February 1950.
135. *FRUS 50*, Vol. 5, Beirut to SD, 16 May 1950, p. 813.
136. FO 371/75329, E12423, Dow to FO, summary of events Palestine, September 1949.
137. FO 371/82196, E1052/15, Vogel memo, 4 September 1950.
138. UNRWA report (A/1905), OR of GA, 5th session, Supp. no. 19, pp. 56–9.
139. FO 371/81922, E1023/10, FO Minute, 22 September 1950.
140. ISA 2445/1, the head of the international organisation department to the Foreign Secretary, 30 August 1970; UNRWA report, pp. 12–13.
141. *FRUS 50*, Vol. 5, Austin to SoS, 2 November 1950, p. 1041–2.
142. UN OR of GA, 5th session, 7 November 1950; the US, as in previous times, agreed to contribute half the required sum, the British £10 million, Israel up to £1 million and the Arab states up to £6 million.
143. *New York Times*, 26 December 1950.
144. ISA 2445/1, research memo, 29 October 1949; *FRUS 50*, Vol. 5, memo Rockwell (in charge of Israel and Jordan affairs in the SD), 29 August 1950, p. 984.
145. *New York Times*, 9 March 1950; *FRUS 50*, Vol. 5, US Embassy in Israel to SD, 19 April 1950, p. 792.
146. FO 371/91185, E1024/24, FO to Washington, 25 October 1951.
147. FO 371/91182, E1022/9, Rapp to Bowker, 6 July 1951; FO 371/91185, E1024/23, Washington to FO, 22 May 1951; E1024/24, Franks to Bevin, 19 May 1951. The refugee office was formed on 22 May 1951: see FO 371/91367, E1071/69.
148. FO 371/91185, E1024/24, Kirkbride to Greenhill, 1 June 1951.
149. FO 371/91185, E1024/24, Burrows to Bowker, 22 May 1951.
150. FO 371/91788, E1011/1, Annual report for Jordan, 1950.
151. UNRWA annual report for 1951, A/905, supp. 16, September 1951, p. 67.
152. ISA 2445/1, Israeli Embassy to British FO, 25 March 1951.

153. ISA 2445/1, Weitz to Sharett, 10 July 1951.
154. ISA 2445/1, Biran to the General Director of IFO, 19 November 1951; D. Kaplan, *The Arab Refugees: An Abnormal Problem* (Jerusalem: Rubin Mass, 1959), pp. 9–10.
155. FO 371/75452, E15407, FO Minute, meeting with Clapp and Morton, 20 December 1949.
156. FO 371/91217, E11345/24, SD information bulletin no. 653, 20 July 1951.
157. See McGhee in FO 371/75054, E14782, 11 December 1949.
158. Kaplan, *Refugees*, p. 8; J. B. Schectman, *The Arab Refugee Problem* (New York: Philosophical Library, 1952), p. 43.

8 British Policy towards the Israeli–Transjordanian Negotiations

1. CZA, S/25 9390, L. Khon to Ben-Gurion, 19 May 1948.
2. ISA, 2083/6, Epstein to Shertok, 27 May 1948.
3. *FRUS 48*, Jerusalem to SoS, 8 June 1948, p. 1105.
4. ISA 2180/17, Eban to Shertok, 9 June 1948; ISA 2382/8, Goldman to Shertok, 9 June 1948; ISA 2180/21, Epstein to Shertok, 28 June 1948, reporting conversation with Harold Beeley and McNeil.
5. F. Bernadotte, *To Jerusalem* (London: Hodder & Stoughton, 1951), p. 196.
6. FO 371/68375, E9169, Kirkbride to Bevin, 7 July 1948.
7. Ibid., FO 371/68382, E8103, FO Minute, Cable, 16 March 1948; FO 371/68381, E3041, Kirkbride to Bevin, 27 February 1948; Abdullah warned that he would replace Abu Al-Huda with a loyal premier, Samir Ar-Rifai; see FO 371/68375, E9520, Kirkbride to Bevin, 27 February 1948.
8. ISA 3749/1, Sasson to Shimshoni, 30 June 1948; FO 371/68375, E10391, Beirut to FO, 2 August 1948.
9. ISA 2329/13, Sharett to Sasson, 17 August 1948.
10. *FRUS 48*, Douglas to SoS, 25 August 1948, p. 1342.
11. FO 371/68379, E10548, FO Minute, Burrows, 5 August 1948.
12. FO 371/68822, E11049, Kirkbride to FO, 6 August 1948.
13. CAB 128/113, CM 57 (48), 26 August 1948; Bevin; FO 371/68822, E11532, Amman to FO, 31 August 1948.
14. State of Israel, ISA, *Documents of the Foreign Policy of Israel* (Companion volume) (Jerusalem 1981), PGI minute, 26 September 1948 (note 557), p. 173. Ben-Gurion *Diary*, 24 May 1948; 8 September 1948. Ben-Gurion's change of mind is evident from the entries in his diary of 5 November 1948.
15. CAB 130/37, GEN 223/81st meeting, 7 November 1948, Bevin; the quotation is underlined by the writer and is from FO 371/68820, E3673, the Anglo-Transjordan Treaty, 16 March 1948.
16. A. Muhafaze, *Al-Alqat Al-Urduniya Al-Baritaniya, 1921–57* (Anglo-Jordanian relations) (Beirut, 1973), p. 168; J. G. Glubb, *A Soldier With the Arabs* (London, 1957), p. 301; and see also M. Faddah, *The Middle East in Transition, A Study of Jordan's Foreign Policy* (London: Asia Publishing House, 1974), p. 21.
17. *Hansard*, Vol. 451, col. 1011, 9 November 1948.

18. CAB 21/1922, MoD to GHQ MELF, 9 November 1948.
19. *FRUS 48*, ASoS to SoS (Paris), 22 November 1948, p. 1534.
20. FO 371/68822, E14531, Kirkbride to FO, 8 November 1948.
21. FO 371/68822, E14188, Amman to FO, 3 November 1948; E14813, FO Minute, Burrows, 22 November 1948.
22. Ibid.
23. Karami was a Palestinian in his origin and according to At-Tal worked in the past for the Jewish Agency, A. At-Tal, *Karithat Filastin* (The Palestine Disaster) (Cairo, 1959), p. 444; see also *FRUS 48*, Amman to SoS, 10 November 1948, p. 1564 and FO 371/68862, E14813, Amman to FO, 17 November 1948.
24. *FRUS 48*, Stabler to SoS, 10 November 1948, p. 1564.
25. Ben-Gurion, War Diary, 9 December 1948, p. 870: Ben-Gurion did not consider the talks in Paris substantial, 21 November 1948, p. 837; see also A. Murad, *Al-Dawr As-Siyasi Lil-Jaish Al-Urduni, 1921–1973* (The Political Role of the Jordanian Army) (Beirut: PLO, 1973), p. 60.
26. Murad, *Dawr*, p. 60; At-Tal, *Karithat*, pp. 420–1.
27. Abdullah's requests were explained by Tawfiq Abu Al-Huda to W. Strang in the latter's visit to the area: see FO 371/75067, E8572, 4 July 1948; see also ISA 2412/26, memo, British policy towards Israel, 12 May 1949.
28. FO 816/132, Kirkbride to Bevin, 3 November 1948; Glubb, *A Soldier*, p. 212.
29. FO 371/68862, E13635, Kirkbride to FO, 16 October 1948.
30. At-Tal, *Karithat*, pp. 443–5; Hott. Abidi, *Jordan: A Political Study, 1948–1957* (London, 1965), p. 32; M. Dayan, *The Story of My Life* (London: Weidenfeld & Nicolson, 1976), p. 104.
31. FO 816/134, Amman to FO, 14 December 1948; FO 816/142, Amman to FO, 14 December 1948; *FRUS 48*, Burdet to SoS, 23 December 1948, p. 1687, 1700; Ben-Gurion, War Diary, 30–1 December 1948, pp. 910–11; At-Tal, *Karithat*, pp. 447–8.
32. Ben-Gurion, War Diary, pp. 881–6 (several government meetings).
33. At-Tal's version is particularly reliable concerning the course of the negotiations from September 1948 to March 1949. However, his claim to have played a major role in obstructing them is rather misleading since he took an active part and objected only to decisions that hindered his own political career, and was less interested in preventing them out of patriotic zeal: see At-Tal, *Karithat*, pp. 437, 440, 441; and Vatikiotis remarks, P. Vatikiotis, *Politics and the Military in Jordan: A Study of the Arab Legion, 1921–1957* (London, 1967), pp. 102–5. See also FO 816/142, Amman to FO, 28 December 1948, and Ben-Gurion, *War Diary*, pp. 910–11.
34. FO 816/142, Amman to SoS, 29 December 1948; *FRUS 48*, Stabler to SoS, 29 December 1948, p. 1700; SD to American Embassy in Israel, 30 December 1948, pp. 1704–5.
35. FO 816/142, Amman to FO, 17 December 1948.
36. FO 371/68862, E15724, Amman to FO, 9 December 1948.
37. FO 816/142, SoS to Kirkbride, 16 December 1948.
38. Ibid.

39. This was dealt with in Chapter 1.
40. The King spoiled Al-Huda's plans by sending, a few days before the premier's scheduled visit, a message of support to the Mahdi of Sudan supporting the latter's claim for independence, FO 816/142, Amman to FO, 17 December 1948.
41. FO 816/142, Cairo to Amman, 16 December 1948.
42. FO 816/142, Cairo to Amman, 22 December 1948; BMEO to Amman, 22 December 1948.
43. FO 816/142, Kirkbride to FO, 22 December 1948; *FRUS 48*, Douglas (conversation with Burrows) to ASoS, 7 December 1948, p. 1650; FO 371/68822, E16002, McNeil to Bevin, 15 December 1948.
44. BGA, Diary, 6 January 1949; FO 816/142, Jerusalem to FO, 20 December 1948.
45. This was written in reply to Abul Al-Huda's question about the future of the Negev, FO 371/68862, E15023, Bevin to Kirkbride, 24 November 1948.
46. FO 371/68862, E15239, FO Minute, Burrows, 22 October 1948.
47. FO 371/68822, E15531, Wright to Kirkbride, 3 December 1948; ISA 2412/26, memo British policy towards Israel, 12 May 1949. See also FO 816/142, SoS to Kirkbride, 16 December 1948.
48. FO 816/142, SoS to Amman, 15 December 1948; SD 501BB. Palestine, Burdet to ASoS, 23 December 1948.
49. FO 371/68822, E15531, Wright to Kirkbride, 31 December 1948.
50. *FRUS 48*, Burdet (conversation with Dayan and Shiloah) to SoS, 22 December 1948, p. 1687.
51. Ben-Gurion, *War Diary*, 2 January 1949, p. 921; 6 January 1949, p. 936; 7 January 1949, p. 937.
52. FO 371/75376, E464, Amman to FO, 10 January 1949; Ben-Gurion, *War Diary*, 9 January 1949; At-Tal, *Karithat*, pp. 449–51; Abidi, *Jordan*, p. 35.
53. Ben-Gurion, *War Diary*, 13 January 1949, p. 949, conversation with At-Tal; FO 371/75045, E367, brief for the SoS for the Defence Committee meeting, 5 January 1949. The CiC ordered the transfer of units from Mafraq to Aqaba.
54. FO 371/75045, E733, FO to UN UK NY, 17 January 1949; FO 371/75051, E932, FO Minute, Wright, 10 January 1949.
55. FO 371/75054, E733, FO to UK UN NY, 12 January 1949; FO 816/142, SoS to Kirkbride, 31 December 1948.
56. Ben-Gurion, *War Diary*, 17 January 1949, p. 956. See also editorial note in this source on diary entries 11–12 January 1949; Ben-Gurion, *Hazon Va-Derech* (Myth and Reality), Vol. 1, pp. 88–90.
57. Ben-Gurion, *War Diary*, 17 January 1949, p. 956.
58. FO 371/75336, FO Minute, January 1949; *FRUS 49*, Stabler to SoS, 15 January 1949, p. 667.
59. Ibid.; FO 371/75336, E1191, Burrows, FO Minute, 24 January 1949.
60. FO 816/142, SoS to Kirkbride, 1 January 1949; *FRUS 49*, London to SoS, 4 January 1949, p. 607.
61. *FRUS 49*, ASoS to London, 13 January 1949, p. 658.
62. *FRUS 49*, Lovett to Sir Oliver Franks, 18 January 1949, pp. 672–3.

63. Ibid. The SD would have had to explain the failure of Bernadotte's plan.
64. *FRUS 49*, Lovett to Sir Oliver Franks, 18 January 1949, pp. 672–3; *Daily Telegraph*, 19 January 1949 and SD 867n. 01/1–1249, London, minute, 24 January 1949.
65. *FRUS 49*, Editorial Note, p. 692.
66. In the HC on 26 January 1949.
67. SD 861n. 01/1–2749, Amman to SD, 27 January 1949; FO 371/75330, E1105, Bevin to Adbullah, 19 January 1949.
68. *FRUS 49*, McDonald to SoS, 1 February 1949, p. 716; Dayan, *My Life*, p. 107; At-Tal, *Karithat*, p. 464.
69. Ben-Gurion, *War Diary*, 2 January 1949, p. 966; Ad-Daly, *Asar Al-Jamiaa Al-Arabiya Wa-Abd Al-Rahman Azzam* (The Secrets of the Arab League and Abd Al-Rahman Azzam) (Cairo: Ruz Al-Yusuf, 1982), p. 274.
70. FO 371/75330, E1105, Abdullah to Bevin, 19 January 1949.
71. FO 371/75331, E1281, Bevin to Abdullah, 27 January 1949; *FRUS 49*, Mcdonald to SoS, 1 February 1949, p. 716.
72. *FRUS 49*, Stabler to SoS, 7 February 1949, p. 773.
73. FO 371/75064, E4099, Cairo to FO, 26 February 1949; FO 371/75331, E2377, Amman to FO, 19 February 1949.
74. ISA 2425/7, Eytan to Vigier (Bunche's representative in Israel), 7 January 1949.
75. FO 816/170, Research Department memo, August 1950; *FRUS 49*, Stabler to SoS, 24 February 1949, p. 767.
76. N. Lorch, *Korot Milchemet Ha-'Atzmaut* (The Israeli Independence War) (Ramat Gan, 1963), pp. 533–4; Ben-Gurion, *War Diary*, 7 March 1949, p. 957.
77. For operation 'Uvda' see Y. Cohen, *L'Or Hayom u-ba-Macshach* (During Daylight and Darkness) (Tel Aviv: Yemcham, 1969), pp. 257–9. For the Arab side see, for instance, A. Muhafaza, *Alaqqat Al-Baritaniya Al-Urdaniya* (Anglo-Jordanian Relations) (Beirut, 1973), p. 186; and At-Tal, *Karithat*, pp. 475–6.
78. A battalion, a squadron of tanks and two destroyers were sent to Aqaba: see CAB 21/1922, GHQ MELF to MoD, 10 March 1949; see also ibid, Hollis to SoS for War, 11 March 1949 and Alexander to Bevin, 16 March 1949. Incidentally, no reconnaissance flights were ordered to prevent a clash similar to the one of January 1949.
79. *FRUS 49*, Acheson–Franks conversation, 16 March 1949, p. 812.
80. CAB 131/8, DO (49) 7, 7 March 1949; *FRUS 49*, Memo SoS to President, 10 March 1949, p. 810.
81. ISA 37/12, Linton–Wright conversation, 9 March 1949. See also ISA 38/1.
82. At-Tal brings this information which is confirmed by CAB 21/1922, FO to Haifa, 9 March 1949, on p. 476.
83. At-Tal, *Karithat*, p. 476; Murad, *Dawr*, pp. 58–9; S. Musa and M. Al-Madi, *Tan'kh Al Urdun Fi Al-Qam Al-Ishrin* (The History of Jordan in the Twentieth Century) (Amman, 1959), p. 529.
84. Ben-Gurion, *War Diary*, 11 March 1949, p. 974; CAB 21/1922, Campbell to FO, 12 March 1949.

85. Lorch, *War*, pp. 536–7; At-Tal, *Karithat*, p. 465. It includes the districts of Nablus, Tul Karem, Jenin and Kalkilya.
86. FO 371/75331, E1692, FO to Baghdad, 10 February 1949; FO 371/75386, E/510, Baghdad to FO, 16 March 1949.
87. Lorch, *War*, pp. 536–7; Ben-Gurion, *War Diary*, 14 March 1949, p. 976, 18 March 1949, p. 979. It should be noted that there were increased infiltrations from the Iraqi side: see FO 371/75386, E3562, Baghdad to FO, 17 March 1949.
88. J. and D. Kimchi, *Both Sides of the Hill: Britain and the Palestine War* (London, 1960), pp. 262–8.
89. FO 371/75386, E3460, Dow to FO, 15 March 1949.
90. At-Tal, *Karithat*, p. 493.
91. FO 371/75386, E3611, Amman to FO, 9 March 1949; Ben-Gurion, *War Diary*, 16 March 1949, p. 977.
92. FO 371/75386, E3510, Baghdad to FO, 16 March 1949, and Strang to Baghdad, 16 March 1949.
93. Ibid., E3679, Amman to FO, 21 March 1949.
94. *FRUS 49*, memo Satterthwaite, 18 March 1949, p. 845.
95. The British requests were reported by *The Times* and the *Daily Telegraph*, 16 March 1949. See also CAB 21/1922, NY to FO, 26 March 1949, and FO 371/68837, E16402, FO Minute, Walker, 14 December 1949.
96. Ben-Gurion, *War Diary*, 13 March 1949 and ISA 2431/2, Harkabi to Nevo, 16 March 1949.
97. Kirkbride's impression in FO 371/75386, E3790, Amman to FO, 21 March 1949. This impression was shared by the Americans: see *FRUS 49*, Stabler to SoS, 23 March 1949, pp. 854–61.
98. *FRUS 49*, Stabler to SoS, 23 March 1949, pp. 861–2.
99. FO 371/75386, E3844, Amman to FO, 24 March 1949.
100. CAB 21/1922, Bevin to Attlee, 24 March 1949.
101. FO 371/75386, E3790, Strang to Washington, 23 March 1949.
102. Ibid.
103. Ibid.
104. *FRUS 49*, Truman to Abdullah, 23 March 1949, p. 879. See also SoS Memo, Truman–Sharett conversation, 24 March 1949, p. 863.
105. Faddah, *Jordan*, p. 45; At-Tal, *Karithat*, p. 550; Musa and Madi, *Urdun*, p. 531; H. Al-Majali, *Hadha Bayan Lil-Nas Qisat Muhadathat Templer* (This is the Story of the Templer Affair), p. 92.
106. FO 371/75386, E3720, Amman to FO, 24 March 1949.
107. At-Tal, *Karithat*, p. 521; SD 867.01/4–249, Stabler to SoS, 4 March 1949.
108. FO 371/75386, E3848, Amman to FO, 24 March 1949; At-Tal, *Karithat*, pp. 415–16; Israel Defence Ministry, *Kovetz*, doc. 23. See also Sir Alec Kirkbride, *From the Wings: Amman Memoirs 1947–1951* (London: Cass, 1976), p. 298, fn. 3; W. Eytan, *The First Ten Years: A Diplomatic Story of Israel* (New York, 1958), p. 41.
109. CAB 21/1922, Price, Secretary of CoS Committee to Wright, 31 March 1949.

9 The Elusive Peace: Britain and Abdullah's Quest for Peace

1. Israel Defence Ministry, *Kovetz*, doc. 23.
2. FO 371/75338, E7024, Amman to FO, 8 June 1949; *FRUS 49*, Stabler to SoS, 16 April 1949, p. 919. The Jordanian representatives were At-Tal and Hamd Al-Farhan, the Cabinet's secretary: see FO 371/75273, E8187, Report on May 1949.
3. *FRUS 49*, SoS to ASoS, 3 June 1949; FO 371/75333, E6902, Paris (Bevin) to FO, 6 June 1949; FO 371/75338, E7023, Amman to FO, 7 June 1949.
4. FO 371/75338, E8347, Glubb to Amman Legation, 19 June 1949.
5. FO 371/75338, E8347, Amman to FO, 2 July 1949. Glubb was influenced very much by a conversation he had with General Riley.
6. ISA 36/16, Kidron to Comay, 17 August 1949; the conversation was on 19 July and the meeting in the FO (the conference was on 21 July); see also FO 371/75072, E9043, FO ME conference, 21 July 1949.
7. *FRUS 49*, Burdet to SoS, 6 July 1949, p. 1203; Truman expressed the same views in a letter to Weizmann, see ISA 2414/26, 13 June 1949.
8. *FRUS 49*, Acheson–Bevin conversation, 13 September 1949, p. 1377.
9. FO 371/75072, E9042, FO ME Conference, 21 July 1949.
10. *FRUS 49*, Burdet to SoS, 6 July 1949.
11. *FRUS 49*, Acheson–Bevin conversation, 13 September 1949.
12. It was made through General Riley in *FRUS 49*, Burdet to SoS, 18 October 1949, p. 1446; Fritzalan to SoS, conversation with Kirkbride, 4 November 1949, pp. 1468–9.
13. FO 371/75273, E10169, Monthly Report, July 1949; E12508, Monthly Report, September 1949.
14. *FRUS 49*, McDonald to SoS, conversation with Shiloah, 5 December 1949, p. 1521.
15. FO 371/75277, E14906, Amman to FO, 15 December 1949; SD 867n. 01/12–2049, Tel Aviv to SD, 20 December 1949.
16. A. Pollack and A. Sinai (eds), *The Hashemite Kingdom of Jordan and the West Bank* (New York, 1977), p. 325.
17. H. H. Abidi, *Jordan: A Political Study, 1948–1957* (London, 1965) p. 38; M. Dayan, *The Story of My Life* (London: Weidenfeld & Nicolson, 1976), pp. 114–15.
18. FO 371/75277, E14906, Amman to FO, 5 December 1949.
19. SD 867n. 01/12–2049, Tel Aviv to SD, 20 December 1949.
20. FO 371/75277, E14906, Amman to FO, 15 December 1949.
21. SD 867n. 01/12–2049, London to SD, 20 December 1949; ISA 36/14, Eliash–Strang, 19 December 1949.
22. *FRUS 50*, Fritzlan to SoS, 16 January 1950, p. 691.
23. This position was summarised by Furlonge, Head of the Eastern Department, in a conversation with the American Embassy in London, *FRUS 50*, Holms to SoS, 3 January 1950, p. 665.
24. *New York Times*, 23 January 1950.
25. Sinai and Pollack, *Jordan*, p. 326; FO 371/82715, E1517, Amman to FO, 30 January 1949.
26. FO 371/82715, E1051/2, Sir Eric Beckett and Mr H. Shawcross, 18 March 1950.

27. FO 371/82715, E1015/14, FO to Cairo and Amman, 27 January 1950.
28. Ibid.
29. FO 371/82187, Furlonge to Burrows, 2 February 1950. *FRUS 50*, Fitzalan to SoS, 9 January 1950, p. 677.
30. FO 371/82177, E1015/7, Amman to FO, 16 January 1950.
31. FO 371/75067, E13722, July 1949, FO Minute.
32. This plan was drafted as 'Instrument establishing a Permanent International Regime for the Jerusalem area', UN OR, 4th session, *ad hoc* political committee, Vol. 1, p. 10.
33. FO 371/75351, E11112, Jerusalem to FO, 13 September 1949; see the Israeli press reaction in *Ha'aretz*, 15 September 1949, and the Arab Palestinian in *Ad-Difaa*, 15 September 1949.
34. FO 371/75351, E11112, Jerusalem to FO, 13 September 1949; E11633, FO to NY UN, 27 September 1949 and *FRUS 49*, Greenhill (British embassy in Washington) conversation with Wilkins (NEA) 14 October 1949, p. 1426.
35. Ibid.
36. FO 371/75334, E14491, UN UK NY to FO, 2 December 1949; UN GA OR, plenary meeting of GA, pp. 35–7.
37. *The Times*, 30 January 1950.
38. *FRUS 50*, McDonald to SoS, 9 January 1950, p. 677.
39. FO 371/82177, E1015/7, Amman to FO, 16 January 1950. Dayan and Shiloah came to the meeting in February 1950: FO 371/82177, E1015/8, Amman to FO, 20 January 1950.
40. FO 371/82177, E1015/10, Amman to FO, 24 January 1950.
41. FO 371/82177, E1015/11, FO Minute, 2 February 1950.
42. FO 371/82177, E1015/17, Tel Aviv to FO, 3 February 1950; E1015/9, FO Minute, 27 January 1950.
43. Most of the financial problems between the two countries were solved by that time.
44. FO 371/82187, E1017/14, FO Minute, Wright, 3 February 1950; BGA, Diary, 31 January 1950. The British officers of the Legion submitted a memo stating that Jordan needed Mount Scopus owing to its strategic situation.
45. FO 371/82177, E1015/22, Amman to FO, 13 February 1950.
46. FO 371/82177, E1015/22, Amman to FO, 18 February 1950.
47. *FRUS 50*, Fitzalan to SoS, 20 February 1950, p. 753.
48. FO 371/82178, E1015/24, CRO (Commonwealth Relations Office) to Commonwealth Governments, 2 March 1950.
49. The Jordanian draft in FO 371/82178, E1015/33, Amman to FO, 22 February 1950, and the Israeli draft in ISA 2453/3, 24 February 1950.
50. The no man's land areas were those which had been defined in an Israeli–Transjordanian agreement of 7 July 1948 and included Mount Scopus, Augusta Victoria and Aissawiya village. See FO 371/82178, E1015/24, CRO to Commonwealth governments, 2 March 1950.
51. FO 371/82178, E1015/33, FO Minute, Thirkell, 2 March 1950.
52. FO 371/82715, E1015/18, Amman to FO, 6 March 1950.
53. FO 371/82178, E1015/40, Tel Aviv to FO, 8 March 1950; E1015/41, Furlonge memo, 9 March 1950.

54. FO 371/82178, E1015/41, Amman to FO, 9 March 1950; *FRUS 50*, McDonald to SoS, 6 March 1950, pp. 781–2; memo by Hare, 8 March 1950, p. 787; ISA 38/8, Comay to Eliash, 23 February 1950.
55. FO 371/82178, E1015/31, 1 March 1950; Abidi, *Jordan*, p. 77; Sir Alec Kirkbride, *From the Wings: Amman Memoirs 1947–1951* (London, Cass, 1976), p. 309, fn. 5.
56. *FRUS 50*, McDonald to SoS, 7 March 1950, p. 783.
57. FO 371/82178, E1015/33, Jedda to FO, 12 April 1950.
58. J. G. McDonald, *My Mission to Israel: 1948–51* (London: Victor Gollancz, 1951), pp. 194–6; *Observer*, 5 March 1950; *Borsque Egyptien*, 14 March 1950; *Le Monde*, 15 March 1950.
59. W. Ad-Daly, *Asrar Al-Jamiaa Al-Arabiya Wa-Abd Al-Rahman Azzam* (The Secrets of the Arab League and Abd Al-Rahman Azzam) (Cairo: Ruz Al-Yusuf, 1982), pp. 284–6, *Ad-Daba'a*, 16 March 1950.
60. FO 371/91705, Annual Report for 1950.
61. Ibid.
62. FO 371/82715, E1015/12, brief for the SoS for the Defence Committee, Furlonge, 14 March 1950.
63. FO 371/82715, E1015/14, Helm to Wright, 7 February 1950; ISA 36/12, Helm–Eytan, 27 April 1950.
64. Ibid.
65. ISA 36/12, Helm–Sharett, 2 May 1950.
66. Ibid.
67. FO 371/82715, E1051/19, FO Minute, 6 March 1950.
68. FO 371/82715, E1051/53, Tel Aviv to FO, 22 April 1950.
69. *FRUS 50*, McDonald to SoS, 27 April 1950, p. 877.
70. FO 371/82178, E1015/55, Amman to FO, 4 May 1950.
71. FO 371/82178, E10U5/55, FO Minute, 5 May 1950.
72. FO 371/82178, E1015/33, Amman to FO, 4 May 1950.
73. FO 371/91788, Annual Report for 1950.
74. FO 371/82178, E1015/57, Tel Aviv to FO, 10 May 1950.
75. ISA 37/1, London to Tel Aviv, 16 May 1950. Incidentally, Churchill at that time expressed strong support for a separate Israeli–Jordanian peace. See in *Hansard*, Vol. 474, col. 1137–9.
76. ISA 37/1, Sharett to London, 16 April 1950.
77. FO 371/82178, E1015/61, Amman to FO, 27 May 1950.
78. FO 371/81908, bi-partite discussions, May 1950, and A. Bullock, *Ernest Bevin, Foreign Secretary, 1945–1951* (Heinemann, 1983), p. 776.
79. Abidi, *Jordan*, p. 66.
80. FO 371/81907, E1023/10, FO Minute, Furlonge, 27 March 1950; B. C. Busch, 'Great Britain and Jordan, 1918–1956', in Sinai and Pollack, *Jordan*, p. 40.
81. FO 371/82192, E10213/11, FO Minute, Palestine Question, 22 September 1950.
82. FO 371/81908, E1023/6, bi-partite commission, Hare–Wright, 1 May 1950.
83. FO 371/81911, E1023/115, Kirkbride to Younger, 2 June 1950.
84. Ibid.
85. See also Chadwick's views in FO 371/82179, E1015/90, 22 August 1950.

86. FO 371/82179, E10U5/65, Tel Aviv to FO, 16 June 1950.
87. FO 371/98856, introduction to the annual report of Jordan of 1951.
88. FO 371/82912, E1023/154, Wadrope, FO minute, 16 November 1950.
89. FO 371/91370, E1081/1, Amman to FO, 3 January 1951. See also files 91364. Abdullah suggested a meeting with Weizmann: however the latter was too ill to attend. BGA Diary, 3 January 1951.
90. FO 371/91364, E1041/8, Kirkbride to Furlonge, 15 January 1951.
91. In February 1950 Azmi Nashishibi became deputy Foreign Minister and in August 1950 Muhsin Adib al-Umari became general director of the Office; S. Musa and M. Al-Madi, *Tarikh Al-Urdun Fi Al-Qarn Al-Ishrin* (The History of Jordan in the Twentieth Century) (Amman, 1959), pp. 548–9. It should be noted that not all the West Bank ministers opposed negotiations: for instance, Suleiman Nabulsi, Minister of Finance: ISA 2445/1, IFO research report, February 1950.
92. FO 371/91716, E1053/8, Furlonge, FO Minute, 20 January 1951.
93. FO 371/82179, E1015/117, Furlonge, FO Minute, 20 October 1950.
94. FO 371/91716, E1053/8, FO Minute, Furlonge, 8 February 1951.
95. FO 371/91364, E1041/9, FO Minute, 6 January 1951.
96. Ibid.
97. FO 371/98856, Jordan annual report 1951; FO 371/91383, E1942/10, Amman to FO, 20 July 1951; FO 371/91389, E1942/64, Amman to FO, 4 September 1951.
98. FO 371/98856, Jordan annual report 1951.
99. Ibid.
100. Ibid.
101. ISA 2431/9, IFO research department, 29 July 1951; ISA 36/15, Furlonge–Eliat, 27 July 1951.
102. See N. Nashashibi's version. He was a director of the Royal Broadcasting Company and Abdullah's secretary. N. Nashashibi, *Man Qatal Al-Maliq Abdullah* (Who Killed King Abdullah) (Kuwait, 1981). The Jordanian court had implicated the Americans for not warning the King about an impending assassination attempt of which they had previous information: Musa and Madi, *Urdun*, pp. 552–3.
103. ISA 36/15, Furlonge–Elath conversation, 27 May 1951.
104. The report was in fact prepared by the Joint Intelligence Committee Middle East, of which the head of the political division of the BMEO was *ex officio* chairman. It was prepared owing to the information of Abdullah's illness and old age; FO 371/91838, E11942/40, Rapp to Furlonge, 23 September 1951.
105. FO 371/91838, E11942/40, Kirkbride to Furlonge, 2 August 1951.
106. FO 371/91716, ER1053/16, Morrison–Elath, 7 August 1951; FO 371/91839, ET1042/40, FO Minute, 2 August 1951.
107. FO 371/91839, E1942/40, Amman to FO, 23 July 1951; Abidi, *Jordan*, pp. 81–2; *Jewish Observer Middle East Review*, 7 (25 July 1958).
108. Ben-Gurion's diary reveals that an Israeli operation for the occupation of the West Bank was prepared in case of an Iraqi–Jordanian merger: BGA, Diary, 21 July 1951. The American position in *FRUS 51*, Drew to SoS, 10 August 1951, p. 992.
109. The Iraqi state trials after the July 1958 revolution revealed that the Iraqi

delegation and their embassy in Amman had been extremely active in trying to persuade Jordanian politicians to accept the idea of a union. The Iraqis were apprehensive of Britain's ability to maintain the Hashemite rule in Jordan for much longer: *Makhkamt As-Shaab*, Vol. 4, pp. 1255–6; *FRUS 51*, Crocker to SoS, 8 August 1951, p. 992.

110. ISA 36/15, Elath's conversation with Strang, 7 July 1951.

Bibliography

ARCHIVAL SOURCES

Great Britain

Public Record Office
Foreign Office: FO 141 (Egypt)
                FO 371 (Political)
                FO 800 (Private Papers) Ernest Bevin
                FO 816 (Jordan)
Cabinet Papers: CAB 21, CAB 128, CAB 129, CAB 130, CAB 131, CAB 134.
Colonial Office: CO 537 (Miscellaneous).
Defence: DEFE 4.
Prime Minister's Office: PREM 8.
Hansard (1948–1951)

Private Papers
Middle East Centre, St Antony's College
Sir Alan Cunningham papers
Elizabeth Monroe papers
Sir Thomas Rapp papers

US

National Archives (Washington, DC)
867N; 501BB. Palestine.

The Truman Library (Independence, Missouri)
Acheson Papers
Clifford Papers
NSC Files
President Confidential Files
Private Secretary's Files
Oral Interviews with G. Clapp and C. Clifford

Israel
Israel Defence Ministry, *Kovetz Mismachim Be-Toldot Ha-Medina* (Collection of Documents from Israel's History), 1981
ISA, *Documents of the Foreign Policy of Israel*, Vols 1–3
ISA, *Minhelet Ha-A'm* (Protocols of the People's Assembly)
Sasson Letters from Lausanne (*Yediot Achronot*, 1972)
Chaim Weizmann, *The Letters and Papers of Chaim Weizmann* (Israel University Publication, 1980)

Iraq
Wizarat Ad-Difa (Iraq Ministry of Defence), *Makhkamat As-Shaab* (The Iraqi State Trial 1958)

NEWSPAPERS AND PERIODICALS

Ahar As-Saa' (Cairo)
Al-Ahram (Cairo)
Akhbar Al-Yom (Cairo)
Al-Assas (Cairo)
Al-Baath (Damascus)
Borsque Egyptien (Cairo)
Ad-Daab aa' (Beirut)
Daily Telegraph (London)
Davar (Tel Aviv)
Ad-Difaa' (Amman)
Economist (London)
Haaretz (Tel Aviv)
Haboker (Tel Aviv)
Al-Hamishmar (Tel Aviv)
Hazofeh (Jerusalem)
Journal d'Egypte (Cairo)
Jerusalem Post (Jerusalem)
Le Figaro (Paris)
Al-Misri (Cairo)
Le Monde (Paris)
Le Progrès Egyptien (Cairo)
Al-Mokathem (Cairo)
Manchester Guardian (Manchester)
New Statesman and Nation (London)
New York Herald Tribune (New York)
New York Times (New York)
Observer (London)
As-Shaalb (Beirut)
The Times (London
Al-Yom (Jaffa)
Zionist Review (London)

INTERVIEWS

Ronald Baily (June 1982)
Sir Roderick Barclay (April 1982)
Sir Harold Beeley (May 1981)
Sir John Beith (December 1981)
Sir Ronald Campbell (February 1981)
Michael Comay (October 1982)
Eliahu Elath (October 1982)
Elizabeth Monroe (May 1981)
Aziz Shadeh (March 1983)

SECONDARY SOURCES (BOOKS AND ARTICLES)

Abd Al-Hadi, Mahdi, *Al-Masala Al-Filastiniya Wa-Mashari' Al-Hulul Al-Siyasiya, 1934–74* (The Palestine Question and its Political Solution) (Beirut, 1975).
Abdullah Ibn Hussayn, King, *My Memoirs Completed* (London: Longman, 1978).
Abidi, Hayder Hassan, *Jordan: A Political Study, 1948–1957* (London, 1965).
Amizur, Ilan, *America Britanya Ve-Eretz Israel* (America, Britain and Palestine) (Yad Ben Zvi Jerusalem, 1979).
Al-Aref, Aref, *Al-Nakbah 1947–1952* (The Catastrophe) (Sidon: Manshurat Al-Maktaba Al-Misriya, n.d.).
Badri, Hassan, *Al-Harb fi Ard As-Salam* (The War in the Land of Peace) (Beirut 1975).
Bar-Zohar, Michael, *Ben-Gurion* (Hebrew) (Tel Aviv, 1977).
Ben-Gurion, David, *Bhilachem Israel* (When Israel Went to War) (Tel Aviv, 1951).
—— *Hazon Va-Derech* (Myth and Reality) (Tel Aviv, 1951).
—— *Medinat Israel Ha-Mechudeshet* (The Restored State of Israel) (Tel Aviv: Devir, 1969).
—— *Yoman Hamilchama* (War Diary), ed. Rivlin and Orren (Israel Defence Ministry 1983).
Beer, Israel, *Bitahon Israel* (Israel's Security) (Tel Aviv: Maarachot, 1965).
Bernadotte, Folke, *To Jerusalem* (London: Hodder & Stoughton, 1951).
Berque, Jacques, *Egypt: Imperialism and Revolution* (trans. Jean Stewart) (London: Faber & Faber, 1978).
Bolitho, Hector, *The Angry Neighbours* (London, 1957).
Breecher, Michael, *The Foreign Policy System of Israel* (Oxford University Press, 1972).
Buehrig, Edmond, *The UN and the Palestine Refugees* (London: Indiana University Press, 1971).
Bullard, Sir Reader, *Britain and the Middle East* (London: Hutchinson, 1951).
Bullock, Alan, *Ernest Bevin, Foreign Secretary, 1945–1951* (London: Heinemann, 1983).
Busch, Briton C. 'Great Britain and Jordan, 1918–1956', in A. Sinai and A. Pollack (eds), *The Hashemite Kingdom of Jordan and the West Bank* (American Academic Association for Peace in the Middle East, 1977).
Cohen, Michael, 'The Birth of Israel – Diplomatic Failure, Military Success', *Jerusalem Quarterly*, 17 (Autumn 1980).
—— *Palestine and the Great Powers, 1945–48* (Princeton New Jersey: Princeton University Press, 1982).
Cohen, Yerucham, *Le-Or Hayom u-Bamachshach* (During Daylight and Darkness) (Tel Aviv: Yerucham, 1969).
Coury, Ralph, 'Who Invented Egyptian Nationalism?', Part I, *International Journal of ME Studies*, 14 (1982), pp. 249–81.
Ad-Daly, Wahid, *Asrar Al-Jamiaa Al-Arabiya Wa-Abd Al-Rahman Azzam* (The Secrets of the Arab League and Abd Al-Rahman Azzam) (Cairo: Ruz Al-Yusuf, 1982).
Darby, P., *British Defence Policy East of the Suez, 1947–1968* (London, 1973).

Darwazah, Muhammad I., *Al-Qadiya Al-Filastiniya* (The Palestine Problem) (Beirut, n.d.).

Dayan, Moshe, *The Story of My Life* (London: Weidenfeld & Nicolson, 1976).

Dearden, Ann, *Jordan* (London: Robert Hale, 1958).

Dilks, David, *Retreat from Power*, Vol. 2 (London: Macmillan, 1981).

Eatwell Roger, *The 1945–1951 Labour Governments* (London: Batsford Academic, 1979).

Eban, Abba, *My Country* (London: Weidenfeld & Nicolson, 1972).

—— *An Autobiography* (London: Weidenfeld & Nicolson, 1978).

Elath, Eliahu, *Ha Ma'avah Al Hamedina* (The Struggle for Statehood) (Tel Aviv: Am Oved, 1982).

Eytan, Walter, *Bein Israel La'-amim* (Between Israel and the Nations) (Tel Aviv, 1958).

—— *The First Ten Years: A Diplomatic Story of Israel* (New York, 1958).

Faddah, Mohammad Ibrahim, *The Middle East in Transition, A Story of Jordan's Foreign Policy* (London: Asia Publishing House, 1974).

Farnie, O. A., *East and West of the Suez, The Suez Canal History, 1854–1956* (Oxford: Clarendon Press, 1969).

Frankel, Joseph, *British Foreign Policy, 1945–1973* (Oxford: RIIA, 1975).

Furlonge, Geoffrey, *Palestine is My Country: The Story of Musa Alami* (London, 1977).

Gabbay, Rony, *A Political Study of the Arab–Jewish Conflict: The Arab Refugee Problem* (Geneva: Librairie Droz, 1959).

Glubb, John Bagot, *A Soldier with the Arabs* (London, 1957).

Gomaa, A., *The Foundation of the League of the Arab States* (London, 1977).

Granados, Jorge Garcia, *The Birth of Israel* (New York, Knopf, 1948).

Hadawi, Sami, *Bitter Harvest* (New York, 1967).

Harris, Kenneth, *Attlee* (London: Weidenfeld & Nicolson, 1982).

Al-Hashimi, Taha, *Mudhakarot*, Vol. 2, Beirut 1978.

Hashvia, Ariah, *A'in Achat LaMars, Moshe Dayan, Korot Hayim* (One Eye to Mars, A Biography of Moshe Dayan) (Tel Aviv: Achiasaf, 1969).

Hassouna, Hussein, *The League of Arab States and Regional Disputes: A Study of Middle East Conflicts* (New York: Oceana, 1975).

Al-Hawari, Muhamd N., *Sirr Al-Nakbah* (The Secret of the Catastrophe) (Beirut, 1955).

Hollingworth, Clare, *The Arabs and the West* (London: Methuen, 1952).

Hourani, Cecil, 'Experimental Village in the Jordan Valley', *MEJ* (Autumn 1951).

Al-Husseini, Amin M., *Khaqaiq An Filastin* (The Truth about Palestine) (Cairo: Maktab Al-Haya Al-Arabiya Al-Ula Fi Falastine, 1957).

Ionides, M. *Divide and Lose: The Arab Revolt, 1955–1958* (London, 1960).

Israeli Defence Forces, *Toldot Milchemet Ha-Kommemiut* (The Israeli War of Independence) (Tel Aviv, 1959).

Al-Jaburi, Salih Saib, *Mikhnat Filastin Wa-Asraruha As-Siyasiya Wa-Askariya* (The Palestine Ordeal) (Beirut, 1970).

Kaplan, Deborah, *The Arab Refugees: An Abnormal Problem* (Jerusalem: Rubin Mass, 1959).

Kayali, A. W., *Palestine, A Modern History* (London, 1979).

Kennedy, Paul, *The Realities Behind Diplomacy* (London: Fontana, 1981).

Kimche, John and David, *Both Sides of Hill: Britain and the Palestine War* (London, 1960).

Kirk, George, *Survey of International Affairs: The Middle East, 1945–50* (London: RIIA, 1954).

Kirkbride, Sir Alec, *From the Wings: Amman Memoirs 1947–1951* (London: Cass, 1976).

Kurzman, Dan, *Genesis 1948: The First Arab–Israeli War* (World Publishing House, 1970).

Laqueur, Walter Z., 'The Appeal of Communism in the Middle East', *MEJ* (Winter 1955).

Lenczowski, George, *The Middle East in World Affairs* (Ithaca, New York: Cornell University Press, 1980).

Longrigg, Stephen H., *Oil in the Middle East* (Oxford University Press, 1961).

Lorch, N., *Korot Milchemet Ha-'Atzmaut* (The Independence War) (Ramat Gan, 1963).

Lorch, Netanel, *Israel's War of Indpendence, 1947–49* (Hartmore House, 1968).

Lunt, J., *Glubb Pasha* (London: Harwill Press, 1984).

McDonald, James G., *My Mission to Israel: 1948–51* (London: Victor Gollancz, 1951).

Al-Majali, Hazza, *Hada Bayan Lil-Nas, Qisat Muhadathat Templer* (This is the Story of the Templer Affair) (no date, Jerusalem).

Al-Majali, Hazza, *Mudhakarti* (Memoirs) (Jerusalem, 1960).

Marlow, J., *Anglo-Egyptian Relations, 1800–1953* (London: Cresset, 1954).

Meir, Golda, *My Life* (New York, 1975).

Mills, W. (ed.), *The Forrestal Diaries* (London, 1952).

Monroe, Elizabeth, 'Mr Bevin's Arab Policy', *St Antony's Papers No. II* (London, 1961).

—— *Britain's Moment in the Middle East, 1914–56* (London: Chatto & Windus, 1963).

—— *Britain's Moment in the Middle East, 1914–71* (London: Chatto & Windus, 1981).

Montgomery, B., *Memoirs* (London: Collins, 1958).

Muhafaza, Ali, *Al-Alaqat Al-Baritaniya Al-Urduniya* (Anglo-Jordanian Relations) (Beirut, 1973).

Murad, Abbas, *Ad-Dawr As-Siyasi Lil-Jaish Al-Urduni, 1921–1973* (The Political Role of the Jordanian Army) (Beirut: PLO, 1973).

Musa, Sulayman and Munib Al-Madi, *Tarikh Al-Urdun Fi Al-Qarn Al-Ishrin* (The History of Jordan in the Twentieth Century) (Amman, 1959).

Nashashibi, Nasib Al-Din, *Man Qatal Al-Malik Abdullah* (Who Killed King Abdullah?) (Kuwait, 1981).

Nevo, Yosef, *Adbullah ve-Araviyei Eretz Israel* (Abdullah and the Arab Palestinians) (Tel Aviv, 1975).

Nevo, Y., 'Abdullah and the Arabs of Palestine', *The Winer Library Bulletin*, 13 (1978), nos 45/46, p. 60.

O'Ballance, Edgar, *The Arab–Israeli War, 1948* (London, 1956).

Pappé, Ilan, 'Moshe Sharett, David Ben-Gurion and the "Palestine Option", 1948–1956', *Zionism*, Vol. 7, no. 1, pp. 77–97.

Penrose, E. B., *Iraq: International Relations and National Development* (London: Benn, 1978).

Peretz, Don, *Israel and the Palestine Arabs* (Washington, DC: The Middle East Institute, 1958).

Persson, Sune, *Mediation and Assassination: Count Bernadotte's Mission to Palestine, 1948* (London: Ithaca Press, 1979).

Plascov, Avi, *The Palestinian Refugees in Jordan, 1948–1957* (London 1981).

—— 'The Palestinians of Jordan's Border', in R. Owen (ed.), *Studies in the Economic and Social History of Palestine in the Nineteenth and Twentieth Centuries* (London: Macmillan, St Antony's Series, 1982).

Polk, William R. 'A Decade of Discovery, America in the Middle East, 1947–58', *St Antony Papers No. II* (London, 1961).

Porath, Yehoshua, 'Agada U Meziut Be-Tahalich Hakamat Ha-Liga Ha-Arvit' (Fact and Fiction in the Establishment of the Arab League), *Zemanim*, 2 (1981), pp. 34–43.

Porath, Y. *Bemirhan Ha-Maseh Ha-Politi* (In Confrontation with Reality in Politics) (Jerusalem: Yad Ben Zvi, 1985).

Qasmiya, Dr Kahairiya, 'Abd Al-Qader Al-Huseini Fi Zikrahu Al-Khamisa wa-Eshrin' (Abd Al-Qader Al-Husseini in his 25th Anniversary), *Shuun Filastiniya*, 20 (1973).

—— *Mudhakarat Fawzi Al-Qawqji, 1936–1948* (Fawzi Al-Qawqji's Memoirs) (PLO Publications, 1975).

Roberts, H. L. and P. A. Wilson, *Britain and the US: Problems in Cooperation* (Oxford: RIIA, 1953).

Robinson, M., *Israel and the Arabs* (New York: Pantheon Books, 1968).

Sacher, Harry, *Europe Leaves the Middle East, 1936–1954* (London: Allen Lane, 1972).

Sacher, H., *A History of Israel: From the Rise of Zionism to Our Time* (Oxford: Blackwell, 1977).

Schechtman, Joseph B., *The Arab Refugee Problem* (New York: Philosophical Library, 1952).

Shafiq, Munir, 'Al-Qadiya Al-Filastiniya Min 1948 iola 1950 Wa Drusuha' (The Palestine Problem from 1948 to 1950), *Shuun Filastiniya*, 21 (1973).

Sherf, Zeev, *Shloshet Hayamim* (The Three Days) (Tel Aviv, 1959).

Shwadran, Benjamin, *Jordan: A State of Tension* (New York: Council for Middle East Press, 1959).

Sinai, Anne and Allen Pollack (ed.), *The Hashemite Kingdom of Jordan and the West Bank* (American Academic Association for Peace in the Middle East, 1977).

Stout, Hiram Miller, *British Government* (New York: Oxford University Press, 1953).

Sykes, Christopher, *Crossroads to Israel, 1917–1948* (London: Indiana University Press, 1973).

At-Tal, Abdullah, *Karithat Filastin* (The Palestine Disaster) (Cairo, 1959).

Thicknesse, Sibylla G., *Arab Refugees, A Survey of Resettlement Possibilities* (London: RIIA, 1949).

Truman, Harry S., *Memoirs*, Vol. 2, *Years of Trial and Hope, 1946–53* (London and New York, 1956).

Truman, Margaret, *Harry S. Truman* (New York: William Morrow, 1973).

Vatikiotis, P. J., *Politics and the Military in Jordan, A Study of the Arab Legion, 1921–1957* (London, 1967).

Weizman, Ezer, *Lecha Shamiym, Lecha Eretz* (Thou Own the Sky, Thou Own the Land) (Tel Aviv, 1975).

Wilson, Evans, *Decision on Palestine: How the US Came to Recognize Israel* (New York, 1980).

Wilson, Harold, *Chariots of Israel* (London: Weidenfeld & Nicolson, 1981).

Woodhouse, C. M., *British Foreign Policy Since the Second World War* (London: Hutchinson, 1961).

Wright, Edmond, 'Abdullah's Jordan, 1947–1951', *MEJ*, 5 (1951), pp. 439–60.

Dissertations

Goldner, Werner, 'The Role of Abdullah Ibn Hussein in Arab Politics, 1941–1951' (thesis submitted to Stanford University, 1954).

Moskovits, Shalom, 'The US recognition of Israel in the Context of the Cold War 1948–1954' (thesis submitted to Kent State University, 1956).

Wilson, Mary C., 'King Abdullah of Jordan: A Political Biography' (thesis submitted to Oxford University, 1984).

Zasloff, Joseph J., 'Great Britain and Palestine: A Study of the Problem before the UN' (thesis submitted to L'Université de Genève, 1952).

Index